#150

DeeTours

To Leo and Edda,
Enjoy life's detours,
Dee
Stay healthy at the Y!

DEE TOURS

by Dee Gagnon

Pegasus Publishing
Brockton, Massachusetts

Cover by Gilda Musgrove.
Graphic Design by Gilda Musgrove.

We recognize that some words, model names and designations
mentioned herein are the property of the trademark holder. We
use them for identification only.

Women On Wheels is a registered trademark.

You may contact the author in writing at:
Dee Gagnon
P.O. Box 2141
Taunton, MA 02780-0974
or by e-mail at RedPony09@aol.com

ISBN 0-9702122-0-8

5 4 3 2 1

Printed in the United States of America

This book is dedicated to my parents who adopted me when I was six years old.

Winnifred Elizabeth (Washburn) Gagnon died when I was twenty-one. She raised me with loving discipline and expected the best out of me. She believed that we all have God-given talents, and that we must not let them go to waste. She always reminded me that I was a special child, because she chose to keep me as her own. I thank her for my self-esteem.

George Roland Gagnon died six months after my journey ended, after a long and healthy life. When I was growing up, Dad gave me lots of outside chores to do on the farm, which taught me responsibility. His quiet strength set an example for me.

CONTENTS

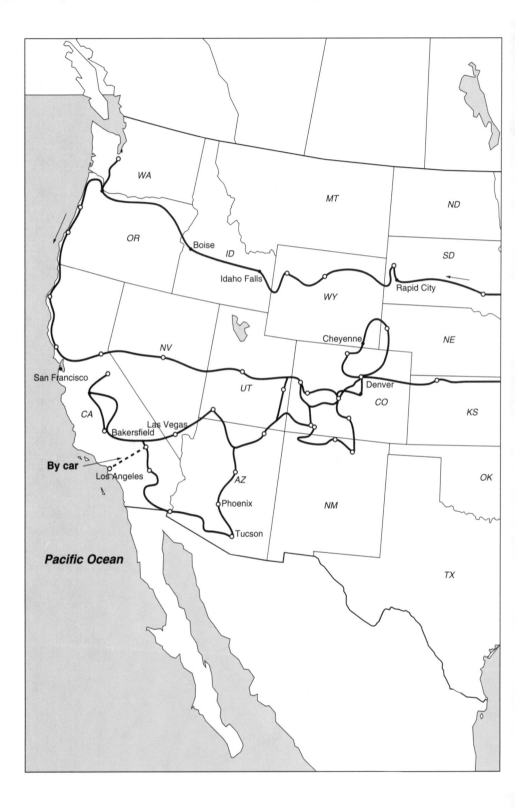

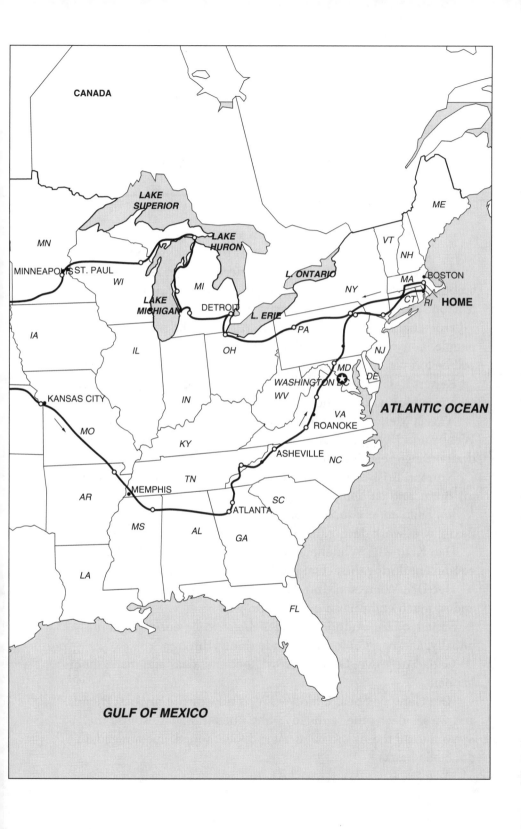

ACKNOWLEDGEMENTS

*W*riting this book was as much an adventure and learning experience as the one hundred day journey itself. It took self-discipline, determination, and a certain amount of faith. I went into the project the same way as I did my trip, one step at a time. When faced with doubts, I set them aside; I'd cross that bridge when I get to it. All along the way, there were people in my life that kept refilling my vessel with encouragement. I will be forever grateful.

Robert E. Cross allowed me to live under his roof, gave me my own room for writing, and never interfered with my independence.

Angela Melton, Art Sullivan, Tom Thibeau, Roberta and Ernie Webby and Fay Young all read or heard a great deal of my rough draft during their YMCA workouts, and kept asking for more.

Norman Briss constantly hounded me at the YMCA. He picked my brain, and pushed me whenever I needed it.

Jen Sullivan, my supervisor at the Y, willingly granted extensive flexiblity at work during the final stages of producing this book.

Dan Kennedy, Whitehorse Press, shared his expertise and equipment during the actual production process.

Dee Dee Winterson, InterCity Press, had an ever-present smile and so much enthusiasm over this project.

Susie Hollern, Author: *Women & Motorcycling,* encouraged me initially, and her 'Go for it!' attitude shined through.

Gilda Musgrove, Graphic Artist, took my ideas and made them happen.

Kim Gabriele Shea, Ohio WOW, is now one of my best friends, and we see each other annually. She's better than a sister to me.

And to all those who have nagged, questioned, encouraged, or doubted, thanks.

de-tour   A longer alternative route usually taken when the direct route is closed for repairs.

INTRODUCTION

A **traveler is granted much time to think.** As time and space pass on, new stimulation continuously imposes itself upon one's eyes, *what kind of tree is that?* And ears, *a midwestern accent.* And nose, *the smell of a peach orchard.* And skin, *the sun's intensity.* It is difficult to ignore.

Fifteen hundred indirect miles from my home in Brockton, Massachusetts, the landscape of the Michigan Upper Peninsula was marshy and pretty. With reeds, rushes and a Great Lake on my left, I saw more wetlands and forest on my right.

I fell in behind a Winnebago and left a comfortable space cushion between us. Over the next ninety miles, I followed, enjoying the day and looking for wildlife.

Suddenly a gull swooped down and got caught in the turbulent air draft over the R.V. It was sucked out of its flight pattern and tossed. As it fell, it slammed the top edge of the back of the camper and went tumbling, broken, to the side of the road. I turned my head as it fell, and saw it hit the asphalt, but couldn't tell if it was dead or not. Just a quick glimpse over my left shoulder, then eyes on the road ahead of me again. Dead or not, there was nothing I could do. I hoped it died spontaneously.

A great feeling of sadness overwhelmed me. Irrational, but very real. This unfortunate bird belongs somewhere, has flying pals, maybe a mate and young-uns, and now it is gone, and they have no explanation. A simple twist of fate.

Why do I feel so sad? I've seen dead animals on the side of the road every day. Maybe because I was there, this time, when this creature crossed the line, from being alive and flying free, to that fateful split second when *Bam!* Its life is changed, or gone, forever.

Life is that way with all of us. You never know when something will happen. I try to live each day to the fullest, so that when my time comes, I won't have any regrets, or feel as though my existence meant nothing.

That is why I took this trip. For sixteen years I've gotten up dutifully, and gone to the same job. For ten of those years I also worked part time, and during those ten years, I spent seven of them going to college and earned a Bachelor of Science degree, with honors. I was driven to succeed, to make something of myself.

Myself. My Self. It is time to be my Self. Society expects and fosters the "let your work define your Self." Well, not me. Not today. This summer I will be true to my Self.

So—who am I? What am I doing? What am I trying to prove?

The answer is not clear. Looking within, I saw pieces of a puzzle. How do I make it fit together?

I would describe myself differently than others would describe me. Think about it. I see myself as "determined." Another person might call me "stubborn." Still another would say I'm a go-getter. It's all in your perspective.

I consciously try to think well of myself. When I get hard knocks, instead of thinking, "Poor me, why do things always happen to me? Life sucks and then you die," I tend to think, "Here's a new problem to solve. How can I grow from this? How will it make me stronger? What have I got to learn?"

I want to experience freedom. I want to ride like never before. I want no time constraints, no compromises. Coastlines, mountains and forests beckon me to come explore. Sunsets await, and my tired eyes behold. Like a gloriously wrapped present, the gift of each day is tucked away, to be revealed again tomorrow.

When you're on the road, you can get caught up in memories you thought you'd forgotten, or create dreams and scenarios never before inspired. You have hours to problem solve. You have broken away from the tried and the true.

You feel the need to continuously evolve, adjust and accept yourself. Things take on new meaning. You learn to trust. You learn the depth of your faith.

Eleven days. For eleven days I have not gone to work, and I feel a different freedom, than one expects while on vacation. On vacation, I would be mentally counting ahead to how many days before I go back to work. Today, I am just getting used to the idea that I'm free. I've traveled so far, visited relatives, met strangers, made some friends, and I've only just begun.

Up until now I was following a plan, but now I am truly free. Only one tenth of my journey has passed. It seems hard to imagine, then I realize, I don't have to imagine. This is really *it*. I have done it! *I took the opportunity to break away.*

No words can explain the joy and self-satisfied rush that I am experiencing. Every American alive should do something like this, some time in their lives. Not ride a motorcycle across the country, but take a sabbatical from daily doldrums and follow a dream. Take a chance. Pay yourself off for all that responsibility.

*   *   *

It all started with a letter to the magazine published by Women On Wheels, a national organization of female motorcycle enthusiasts, of which I am a member.

Dear WOW:

This summer I will embark on an adventure many of you will envy. I am quitting my job, packing up my trusty steed, Red Pony, and hitting the roads for an extended solo trip around the U.S.A. I plan to camp at our National and State Parks mostly, but have a few friends and relatives here and there to visit as well.

I am writing to you with a special request. If you could put me up for a day or two, my wallet will really appreciate it, and you can bet I would enjoy a hot shower, meal and the hospitality that any one of you may offer, and I'd feel safe. Even though we're strangers, through WOW we're comrades. Strangers are often just friends you haven't met yet.

If you are willing and able to have a spur-of-the-moment guest (because I'm not sure where the roads will take me,) please send me directions to your home, on a 3 x 5 index card. Maybe I'll stop by between June and September. I am young and small and willing to sleep on the couch. Please respond ASAP and remember to include your phone number.

Part of my trail includes the WOW Ride-In in Washington State. I'm looking forward to meeting many of you there. Every now and then, say a prayer for me during the summer.

Thanks. Dee Gagnon WOW #4695

The response was terrific. In just a few weeks, twenty women from all over the country had invited me to their homes. *Psyched!* Excitement was building. Word was out. I had some people ready to take me in and I had a date for departure set.

I prepared for *one hundred days of ultimate freedom.*

My motorcycle is not one that you would typically expect to see ridden for long distances, but it was my bike, dependable, and owned by me since it was born, in 1986. I knew it inside and out, found great pleasure in doing my own maintenance and performing small repairs myself. In short, I trusted this nine year old machine, more than I would a brand new one.

The motorcycle I planned to ride all over the country was a Honda Interceptor 500, a racing styled, quick and nimble little number. I have crashed it before, and probably will again, but she just keeps getting up and going some more for me. After an accident last summer, I had it custom painted. No more red, white and blue here. This Interceptor sports a new red and black paint scheme, featuring three mustangs galloping along each side, behind me.

I call it my Red Pony.

It is June 17, 1995, just before packing up my Red Pony for one hundred days on the open road. The flowering bushes just behind my parking place were tinged with autumn gold when I returned at the end of September.

The question is whether you are going to be able
to say a hearty YES to your adventure.

—Joseph Campbell

CHAPTER 1

IN THE BEGINNING
June 17–25, 1995   Days 1–9

*I*t was the day before Father's Day. My friends and I had already said our good-byes, and this day has finally arrived. I lugged my stuff outside, and packed up my bike. My saddlebags contained raingear, tools, spare parts, chain lube and the like, on one side, and the other side was packed with camp related things, such as my burner, nestling pots, a little bit of food, and other things I wouldn't need every single day.

Then came the rest. A sleeping bag, ground pad, a duffel bag stuffed with clothes, then there was a bag with this and that, plus an empty knapsack, empty, to keep extra layers handy, my tent, and last but not least, my tankbag. There was a small mountain bungeed to my bike, saddlebags "out to there," and a slot where I would wedge my body, between my pack and my tankbag.

Funny, two weeks before, I had gone on a camping trip with a couple of my best friends on our bikes, and I thought it was a dry run. Packing for five days in one climate, is a far cry from packing for over three months, every climate.

One last look around my apartment, then with tears in my eyes I scooped up my cat and hugged her for the last time until my return. I went back outside wearing an outfit that was going to be a part of practically every day, all summer for me, my leather pants, fringed leather jacket and Timberland hiking boots.

Helmet on. Gloves on. Deep breath. Get on.

Oh-oh. Hm-m-m. I can't swing my leg over, due to my ninety pounds of luggage.

Start over. Lift leg. Slide foot through that space. Straddle saddle. Okay. Another deep breath. Grasp handgrips. Straighten handlebars. Push off with left foot to straighten the bike, ugh, wait! Try that again.

Grip handlebars and *yank* bike to upright position. Gosh, it's heavy . . . whew!

Okay, this is it. I turned the key and pressed START.

Varoom-mmm!" my Pony responded.

Cautiously, I drove across the lawn, then through the parking lot. At the red light I waited, and it began to sink in. I can't believe I am about to ride away and never come back until three full moons have passed. I'm going to ride my motorcycle as far and as long as I want, day in and day out, for the entire summer.

The light turned green, and I drove on down the road. "The journey of a thousand miles begins with but a single step." Or a twist of the throttle.

By six o'clock, I was registered at Tunkhannock KOA in Scranton, Pennsylvania. They were serving biscuits and gravy, for Father's Day. I piled some on a plate, and sat at a picnic table while some older ladies scurried around cleaning up.

At first I was too busy feeding my face to notice my surroundings, but as my hollowness gave way to being filled, I looked up from my vittles. Thirty feet away, my loaded up motorcycle was surrounded by a geriatric crowd. I could hear snippets of their conversation.

"That little pip-squeak rode in on this all by herself? How can she fit with all this baggage?"

"The license plate says Massachusetts. Do you think she rode it all the way here?"

"Say, back in '41 I used to . . . "

Listening, I chuckled. Boy, was I full. Not bad for fifteen bucks, a place to eat, shower, swim and sleep.

Miles: 340

My days of going to the Y for a workout on Stairmaster and Nautilus are no longer. The great outdoors will be my gym, cliffs and mountains will be my steppers, and a picnic table and sleeping pad make a dandy exercise mat.

This was going to be a back roads day, so I was pretty excited. My first order of the day would be breakfast. I traveled west on Rte. 6, and parked beside a Gold Wing at the Pink Apple. Inside, I found a couple in their forties seated at the counter. The Wing belonged to them.

The woman was quite impressed that I was the driver of my own bike. "Aren't you afraid? I'd be so scared. They're so big. I like the back seat," she admitted. When I told them I was on the verge of a cross country trek, she about flipped.

"You've got guts, that's all I can say."

The husband and I discussed some roads. Unfortunately they were departing in the direction I'd just come from, or I might have ridden in their company for a while.

I traveled Rte. 6 for some time. The road was scenic. Rolling hills and fertile farms dotted with red barns and tall silos dominated the landscape. After following a little old man in a compact car for an eternity, he finally turned off in a small town, then I got stuck behind a camper. It teetered and tottered in from of me, blocking my forward vision. Alas, there was a double yellow line, so I obediently and relatively calmly abided the law. After all, what's the hurry? I've got three months!

At last I came to a dotted line. I downshifted and cranked it, screamed past the camper, darted back in front of it and slowed to an amazing forty miles per hour. Ahead, I watched a police cruiser turn on its blue lights and roll down towards the road I was on. I passed his little hiding place and pulled over to let the nice cops go after whatever it was they were after, and it turned out to be me!

Son of a Bee! My second day and this already.

The two uniforms got out of their vehicle as I dismounted. I removed my helmet as they approached. "Can you ticket me for passing?" I said with a big smile.

"Oh, yes, when we have you clocked at 71 mph."

I kept smiling and explained how for the last half hour I was forced to drive 25 mph behind other vehicles. I pointed out how they *know* this is the first dotted line for ages, and I had to gun it to pass in time before oncoming traffic forced me back.

"License, registration, plus proof of insurance, please."

I sighed, "Okay." With a resigned pout I handed them the requested materials.

"Where're you headed?"

"Just passing through."

"Okay. You be careful. There are lots of deer around here, and we'd hate to be scraping you off the pavement. You're too young and pretty."

"But, if a deer ran out in front of that camper, how would I know? I'd be in even more danger. I waited all this time for it to be legal to pass, and then I get nabbed!"

"Listen, we're only giving you a Warning."

I restrained the urge to hug and kiss them. "Thank you! Thank you!"

"Yeah, well, don't be passing any more vehicles right in front of State Troopers, and do be careful," they admonished.

"Have a good day, Officers."

On the road again, I fretted. Two thirty PM on my second day and I've already had to deal with the police. The irony was that if I had scooted past those slow pokes in an illegal passing zone, I would've probably gotten away with it, but the police had their squad car parked purposely at the first broken line in umpteen miles so they can go after the law abiding citizens like me, when they quickly pass another vehicle, in a legal passing zone. Crazy.

*　　　　*　　　　*

A certain number gives me the creeps. I was going to shun my superstitions and travel on Rte. 666 through the Allegheny Forest. It was a narrow path in poor condition. Potholes, cracks and bumps were the norm, and I enjoyed the challenge.

The depths of the forest displayed centuries of growth, ancient trees, many fallen and broken. A rich, lush layer of ferns took advantage of the dark soil below. The place was seemingly untouched. I inhaled the earthy scent and continued through the untamed domain. I became pleased that I had dared to ride on the road named after the devil's number.

At the end of 666 I took a left, and that brought me into the town where I would be spending the night. I pulled into the driveway of a Women On Wheels member. Joanne and John Mlarkar wrapped their big selves around me in a warm welcome. Tonight their living room would be my bedroom.

They honored me with an outdoor dinner around a campfire, and a couple of friends came over to meet me. I heard about the bear and cubs, deer, raccoons, skunks and other critters that wander in and out of their back yard, regularly. We spoke of motorcycles, travel, work, responsibilities and home.

Joanne was known as the lady minister that wears leather a lot. She had these large, luminous, expressive eyes, framed by a fringe of long lashes, and wavy hair that fell to her shoulders. Everything about her exuded warmth and sincerity.

She told me she'd love to go far away sometime on her bike, but she was afraid to go alone. She said I inspired her to believe she could do it.

Later on, in the dark of night, I heard John. In hushed tones he told Joanne that a deer had been struck by a car, but it wasn't dead. He whispered, "Where's my knife?" then slipped outside after calling authorities.

Before he returned, I had drifted off.

Western Pennsylvania.

Miles: 262

John cooked a huge breakfast, then he and Joanne rode with me towards Ohio. Just before the on-ramp to I-80, we pulled off at a gas station. John insisted on paying for my tankful, and then they gave me snacks and hard candies. They would have given me a side of venison, if I had room for it. I stepped back and saw Joanne's large eyes fill with tears. Time for a group hug. We joined hands and asked the Lord to bless my journey. Joanne implored me to enjoy living her dream. I will.

It was a little saddening to leave these people, knowing I might never see them again, but it was too hot out to prolong the agony. We had to get back in the wind.

At the on on-ramps, they turned east and I continued westward. Alone again for a day's ride to my next destination.

*   *   *

Some time ago, I had read a story in the Women On Wheels magazine. Kim Gabriele Shea compared and contrasted horses with motorcycles.

"... the feeling you get from riding on those beautiful country roads, or galloping down trails. The wind brushing by you and flying through your hair. It feels great. *Freedom!* Just you and that wonderful sound of a strong engine going down a winding country road, or feeling so much a part of your horse as you gallop as fast as you can through a field, hearing the sound of hooves hitting the ground . . . "

I wrote to her, feeling a connection. Now I was on my way to meet her. I followed my directions into the rural outskirts of Toledo. I found the 'Pine Rock Ranch' after a bit of investigation and was greeted by Kim's husband, Dan, and their two daughters, Rachel, 5, and Nicki, 10. I got the grand tour of their home, barn and property. Dogs, cats, chickens and horses—these people had it goin' on!

Kim was at work until midnight. I heard her come home, and got up off the couch long enough to tell her I'd see her in the morning.

Miles: 293

Kim and I pulled on jeans and went outside to groom and saddle the horses before it got too hot out. Nicki wanted to come along with us, and generously offered to let me ride her black mare, Star. She would ride double behind her mom. Dawn, a tall and pretty chestnut seemed unconcerned as Kim and Nicki got situated two-up on her back. Her yearling colt, galloped around the paddock, whinnying shrilly, his tail held high like a banner.

We rode off on the side of the road. I gushed over Star's beauty, her thick mane and tail, and how when I was Nicki's age, this was my dream horse. She only smiled shyly. She was a girl of few words.

Kim's Toledo address was deceiving, not at all a big city as I'd imagined. She showed me some unusual things right in her neighborhood. A peacock strutted across a driveway at a nearby farmyard. Inside the fenceline, there were miniature horses, donkeys, and even miniature mules. In another pen, there were rheas, which are large birds related to the ostrich.

Kim and I are about the same age and we hit it off in person as well as we did through letter writing. We each had something the other could only dream about. Kim had the great husband, two beautiful children, a farm and horses . . .

I have my freedom.

Later on, we mounted our iron steeds. It was fun following her, a slim, pretty girl on her Magna, as she whizzed around town for a little cruise. Then Dan joined us and the two girls rode behind their mom and dad, to a restaurant where I tried Turtle Soup, which was spicy and delicious. By the time we finished dinner, it was 7:30 and the temperature had dropped to a tolerable 91 degrees.

The whole family rode into the night with me, leading me on back roads until I got to the highway that would take me into Detroit. Pulled over onto the breakdown lane, we said good-bye. Nicki handed me a wildflower, a silent, sweet gesture of friendship.

I arrived at my uncle's house in a Detroit suburb, shortly before midnight.

Miles: 159

For two full days I was generally spoiled by my aunt and uncle. We were always close, having written letters all of my life, along with a few visits. We talked about what I would like to do while there. My two top priorities were to get a new chain for my bike, and to visit my grandmother.

When Uncle Roger got home from work, he had me follow him to the bike shop where I was leaving it. Then, we headed for the nursing home where my grandmother resided.

Seeing her was a highlight of my trip. This is the second time I had traveled to Michigan by motorcycle to see her. The last time she was so ill, I thought I would never see her again.

My uncle mischievously told me to go in and surprise her. She was asleep with a novel on her chest. I gently nudged the bed and she opened her eyes. They widened and she exclaimed, "Diane! Oh my! Come here, what a surprise." Her son and daughter-in-law happily observed our reunion, looking smug and pleased. After much hugging and kissing, Uncle Roger said, "Mom, ya want to go for a ride?"

"On your motorcycle?" she directed at me, which made us all laugh.

I had to tell her I didn't bring my spare helmet.

"Well, why not?"

We took her outside in her wheelchair and sat under a shade tree. Grandma told me to be strong and to do the things important to me. She pressed me about my love life, but seemed to accept that marriage is not a major ambition for me. She stopped attendants and friends announcing, "This is my granddaughter. She rode her motorcycle all the way from Massachusetts to see me!" They'd react appropriately, while inside, my chest swelled with love for this little lady. My sweet grandmother, my friend.

*　　　*　　　*

Finally, it was time to go pick up my bike. Driving across the city, I worried about getting there on time. We barely made it before closing. I paid the bill and listened as the mechanic gave me some recommendations, something about a glider pin, whatever that is.

It felt good to be reunited with my bike, and I followed my uncle through a non-congested side-street maze, homeward bound. I noticed a scraping noise whenever I slowed before braking. I became perturbed, because I knew the shop was now closed.

We pulled into the driveway and I yanked off my helmet and squatted down by the rear tire and eyeballed the situation, my teeth clamped tightly. My uncle asked what was wrong, and I barked at him. "There's a noise that wasn't there before, and now I can't even bring it back, because they're closed. I wanted to leave early tomorrow, but now I'm going to be detained."

I pushed my cycle into the back yard and sulked.

Earlier that day, Uncle Roger had gone to Triple A and returned with a box loaded with maps, books and trip sheets. I couldn't take all this stuff with me. Where would I put it? Just the same, I sorted through it, selected some maps, and these little books called CampBooks. Those books turned out to be invaluable.

Miles: about 20

Over breakfast, Aunt Nancy wanted to help me plan my trip to Michigan's Upper Peninsula. We looked at some travel guides, and I selected a couple of options. Lots of campgrounds appeared to be in the Mackinac Bridge area, on either shore. I would have played it by ear, but she would not hear of it, so I made some phone calls to reserve a spot, three days in advance.

The campground at Straits in St. Ignace had openings, but required an extra five dollars to reserve. If I canceled the reservations I'd pay a fifteen dollar fee! Supposedly, this place was eleven dollars a night, but it would actually cost sixteen with a reservation, and fifteen dollars if I didn't camp there at all, after making a reservation. Go figure.

I told my aunt I was unwilling to pay sixteen dollars to camp out, and I'd rather take my chances. She left the room and returned with a twenty dollar bill. I couldn't argue.

My motorcycle got packed, and the hour was late morning. Uncle Roger had kissed my cheek and whispered "I love you" when he left for work at dawn. Now it was time to part with Aunt Nancy. We waved to each other as she watched me drive down Roseland Blvd., turn left and disappear from sight. I got going so late that I didn't want to go to the Honda dealer any more, and I didn't notice that troublesome noise so much either. Maybe it would work itself out.

Several hours later, I got registered to camp at Whispering Waters. The camp hostess was friendly and helpful. She asked about the pins on my leather vest, calling them badges. Instead of forming an opinion based on my leather and the machine I rode in on, Marge looked at my smile, and respected me.

"Aren't you afraid?"

"No. I am well prepared. This is something I want to do."

After a brief swim in the pool, I went to my site and set up camp. This was already my seventh night, but only the second time on this trip that I had camped. That trend would soon be changing. When I left home, I had the first week pretty much planned, but after this it would be different. I had a very open agenda.

From here, I would be on my way to Olympia, Washington, for the 9th Annual Women On Wheels Ride-In. I had given myself twenty days to get there from home, using this formula:

Boston to Seattle = 3,000 miles

My riding preference = 300 miles a day

3,000 divided by 300 = 10 days

Double that, for time to visit and explore = 20 days

End of formula

So, here I am in Michigan on Day Seven, relaxed in my own shady glen, contented and free. At my picnic table, I filed my nails and applied a coat of clear polish. For an entire summer my nails would lack their usual colored polish and length, but I still wanted to maintain a decent manicure. Girl stuff.

A young man driving a little tractor pulling firewood drove by a few times. There I was, tending my nails in a leopard print bikini, alone at my campsite, with a motorcycle parked beside my tent. He seemed to enjoy the contradictions, but was so shy he didn't even stop on the pretense of selling me firewood.

The sun got low, and I took a short walk before bed. My humble abode was comfortable, and I drifted off to sleep more content than I had been for a few days.

Miles: 183

Michigan's WOW State Ambassador, Donna Brown, had contacted me before I left home, and told me about a charity event sponsored by Chapter MIL-2 of Gold Wing riders. I hoped to meet some Women On Wheels members at a Big Boy restaurant where they were meeting up, before going to the Dawg Daze event.

There were no motorcycles in the parking lot, until I arrived. Just a few minutes later, another cycle pulled in and parked next to mine. A woman dismounted, checked out my ride and its load, then came inside. She introduced herself to me with an extended hand. Before long, two other lady riders joined us, with news of cancellations from other club members. We ate a hearty breakfast, then went to the rally. A map of a one hundred mile tour amongst lots of little lakes was handed out. I got to ride with several WOW members, before returning for the rest of the rally happenings.

As the afternoon wore on, Maggie invited me to ride home with her. She had time off from work the next day, and offered to ride with me on back roads to some of Michigan's scenic places. I followed her to Kalamazoo suburbs, and met her husband, Scott. He began making plans for supper.

What is it with Women On Wheels' husbands? They all cook! Interesting. It must have to do with accepting roles as they come, disregarding gender issues. A man who indulges in a knack for culinary delights, apparently has no problem putting up with a woman who rides her own motorcycle.

We sat outside at the picnic table and enjoyed corn on the cob, steaming baked potatoes, green salad and juicy grilled steaks. My laundry was in the wash, and I was looking forward to a good night's sleep on the couch.

Miles: 110

Morning light crept across my face, then the dog tried to reclaim "her" couch. Another day has begun. Scott was in the kitchen making a mess. Maggie packed a bag. Donna Brown arrived on her Gold Wing, to meet me.

While the coffee was brewing, Donna and I poured over some maps trying to figure out a way we could meet up with each other en route to the Ride-In. With the comfort of a full dresser, this woman has no problem riding six hundred miles a day. I do. No way could we ride together for any long distance, and judging from our opposing departure dates and riding styles, we resigned ourselves to Plan B. We'd meet in Washington at the Ride-In.

Another unhealthy, yet delicious breakfast. With tummies fully loaded, Maggie and I got our butts in gear and pulled our bikes out of the garage. We said good-bye to Donna, bye to Scott, and then we were gone with the wind.

This is great! Just about every time I get together with WOW folks, I get escort service. I don't have to worry about finding my way, I just follow the leader.

Maggie rides a Kawi streetbike with a windshield. She has a thick, brown ponytail that hangs down beneath her name painted on the back of her helmet. With large sunglasses, lipstick, leather vest and chaps, it is easy to see that this motorcycle rider is female.

I followed her easily, through metro Kalamazoo into more rural places. Maggie zig-zagged her way on roads that cut through farms, wheat and corn fields. Now and then, we'd encounter a slow moving tractor. I was amazed she knew where she was going, it all looked the same to me. All the roads were at right angles to each other, not like where I come from. Still, I was confident that she knew where she was leading me.

In about an hour, we reached the shoreline of Lake Michigan. We got on to the main road and stopped for red lights at every block. Now and then, Maggie would lead me off the main road, to cruise on a scenic circle loop that would take us by summer cottages, quaint tourist shops, past in-line skaters, sailboats and kite-flying competitions.

The lake looked like the ocean to me. It is hard to comprehend that this body of fresh water is larger than any of the states in New England.

Back on the main drag, a series of shopping centers, parking lots, fast food restaurants and Sunday drivers, I got the urge to cool off with some ice-cream. I pointed to a TCBY, Maggie nodded a confirmation, and we worked our way over to it. Both of us ordered some frozen yogurt in waffle cones. When we went outside after eating, the sky suddenly looked ominous. We had barely pulled our raingear out of our saddlebags when the sky literally opened, and drenched the area.

Raingear. There's no easy way to put on the stuff in a hurry. The two of us became spectacles as we huddled under the TCBY's building overhang, leaning against the glass, laughing and cussing as we attempted to change into our highly attractive and fashionable rain suits. *NOT!* With that finally accomplished, we waded into the three or four inches of rain on the pavement and got on the bikes, hoping to ride out of the rainstorm.

Maggie was obviously an experienced rider, and I felt confident being with her, even under these conditions. It wasn't very long before either the rain went away, or we rode out from under it. After the rain, it seemed to have the usual cooling off effect, and we continued on our way.

In the afternoon, we rode into Silver Lake State Park. This was a recreation spot for sure. Offshore there were huge dunes rising out of the water like overgrown sand bars. Everywhere we saw people in bathing suits and sandals. Four wheel drive was the vehicle of choice, and dune-buggy rides were a major attraction. There were para-sailors and jet-skis and small boats everywhere. Had I been on my own at the moment, I would have camped there, but on this day I had company, and a better offer . . . to sleep on a boat.

We worked our way to Ludington, taking little detours here and there, to see lighthouses and interesting buildings. Maggie is one heck of a tour guide.

In Ludington, we pulled up to a parking lot guard at a ritzy marina. He waved us on and I followed Maggie in. There was a boat, *BOOMER,* just pulling into the slip. The crew tied it off and the Captain waved to Maggie.

"Need a place to sleep? You're just in time!" It was her friend, Mike, just coming in from a fishing trip. Introductions all around. One woman on board was particularly interested. Her name was Wendy. She was pretty, with long dark hair and a deep suntan. She came over to my bike to check it out, and talk some more, and asked a million questions.

"How long have you been riding? What kind of bike is this? Doesn't your back get sore? Where are you going? All by yourself? Aren't you afraid? Where do you sleep? You're not scared camping by yourself?" The usual.

She said she would love to do something like this, but wouldn't have the guts. She was envious and happy for me. By the time the boat was docked and secure, we were still standing in the parking lot, and Wendy was offering me some kind of pre-paid calling card through the company she worked for, ninety-nine dollars worth.

Mike and Wendy and their friends departed, leaving Maggie and me to make ourselves at home. We took a walk on the beach. We sat down near a long pike that jutted into the wet expanse of Lake Michigan. There was a picturesque lighthouse even further out. A huge ferry left port, with lots of people waving towards the shore and gulls circling overhead. We watched until we could see it no more.

The sun began to sink towards the horizon, slowly, as Maggie and I talked about our lives. She shared with me her history, her tears and fears, and dreams. We talked about life, love and the pursuit of happiness. I felt privileged to see inside, because as open as I tend to be, Maggie struck me as a very private person. I felt honored that she allowed me to see some of that inner self, even if just a little.

A man with a telescope lens on a fancy camera sauntered along, shooting the sunset. I raised my automatic everything Nikon to my eye and took one perfect picture, the pastel colored sky, rippled waters, a small orange sun over the horizon, and a lighthouse silhouette. Sunset over Lake Michigan.

Darkness set in, we doused ourselves with bug spray and walked back to *BOOMER*. We had to move fifteen fishing rods off of the bunks in order to sleep.

"Good night, Mags. Thanks."

Miles: 187

Traveling and freedom are perfect partners
and offer an opportunity to grow in new dimensions.
—Donna Goldfein b. 1933

CHAPTER 2

LIFE'S LESSONS
June 26–27   Days 10–11

BLAAAAMP! BLAAAAMP! Being jolted awake by
the rude blast of an air horn at five AM isn't my idea
of a pleasant start on a day, but, BLAAAAMP! Again!

It was a great ferry boat nearby, announcing its intention to leave
the wharf to make its trip to the other side of Lake Michigan and
deliver human cargo to Manitowoc, Wisconsin.

From within the belly of the twenty-six foot fishing vessel
christened *BOOMER,* I listened as the nearby ship pulled its anchor
and made its way out of the marina and across the sea-like lake.
Having a couple of hours left to sleep, I snuggled back into my
borrowed blankets and closed my eyes.

Before long, we arose, and looked over a map of Michigan
together. Maggie told me where the best riding would be, and what
to skip over if I found time getting short. Straits State Park is just on
the other side of the Macinack Bridge, and that's where I had
reservations for, tonight.

"That bridge is five complete miles long, and is probably the
largest suspended bridge in the U.S. Because it is suspended, it
sways in the wind. Some people fear crossing, so there are drivers
there who, for a fee, will drive your vehicle across for you. Back in
the fifties," Maggie continued, "so the story goes, a woman driving a
compact car got blown right off of the bridge."

Earlier, my aunt and uncle had been incredulous that I was
planning that route, but how else would I get to the Upper
Peninsula?

Maggie shared some concerns also, but to me this was just
another bridge—or was it? In the back of my mind, I wondered. Am

looking back. He 'gives birth,' and cares for the miniature seahorses, until they are ready to strike out on their own.

The facts are strikingly familiar, but comical if compared with the human process, except, often in our society it is the female who is seduced, then left to raise her young all alone and forgotten.

Because of the folds in the shirt, and the girl's long hair, I couldn't read all of it, so I got her attention. This led to a conversation about where the tee shirt came from—a rock concert, then talk about Lalapalooza, depicted on the other girl's shirt. They noticed my riding gear and asked if that was really my motorcycle outside.

"Honest? That is so cool! And you're just riding around wherever you want? Where do you sleep? Aren't you a-scared? O'm'god, that is so awesome. Where are you from?"

"Massachusetts."

"No way! You rode it all the way from Massachusetts? How long did it take you?"

"This is my tenth day, but I stayed with relatives for a few days, in Detroit, and spent a couple more days with Women On Wheels."

"What's that?"

I explained the organization, and how I'd written to the magazine months prior to my departure, and how many women had responded, and had put me up, most of my nights so far, but now I was going to be camping, for the most part.

"Are you going to California?" The young ladies' eyes sparkled.

"Yup. First I'm going to Washington State, for a Women On Wheels rally, as a matter of fact. There I'll meet up with about three hundred ladies from all over the country, who ride bikes, too. We spend a weekend at a hotel, and have games, contests, awards, make friends—a typical, but not so typical motorcycle rally. From there I plan to ride the Pacific Coast Highway, the one right on the edge of the cliffs and surf, that you see on TV. I'll ride that as far as I can, until I have to go to another rally I have planned on, in Colorado."

"Wow! That is so cool. You are so lucky. I want to travel someday like that, but in a van, and maybe with some friends. Not alone. Aren't you lonesome?" She took another bite of her doughnut, and washed it down with milk.

"No. Just about everywhere I go, people come up and meet me, like you two right now. I figure, if I was traveling with a boyfriend, or something, people would just leave us be, and we'd soon tire of each other's company, besides. This way, I can do what I want, when I want. I can go to the bathroom five times in an hour, if I need to, and won't have anyone telling me I shouldn't drink so much coffee. That should be up to me." They laughed. "Being on the motorcycle, especially packed up the way it is, fills people with such curiosity they come over to meet me. It's really neat."

After a sip of coffee, I continued, "Nope. I'd be more alone together, than I am by myself, I think. Sounds like a country and western song, doesn't it? 'I'm more alone together, than I am by myself.' "

"Yeah."

We sat in quiet for a little while, me thinking about having to get a move on, and the two friends imagining themselves on an adventure.

"Are you girls students?" I asked.

"Yes, but we work at the hotel over there." She pointed. "We're on break now."

"How old are you?" I was curious.

"Sixteen. We're both sixteen."

"Well, it was really fun to meet you." We started to walk out together.

"O'm'god. It was great to meet you! You are so awesome."

"Listen, guys. Follow your dreams. Work hard now. Be responsible. Save some money, and in the future, if you want to do something wild, do it. Do it! Don't act impulsively. Plan well. Prepare. But, do it. Opportunities like this don't come along. You have to make them happen. I'm not 'lucky.' I quit my job and took a chance, but, I don't regret it, and I've barely begun. I still have three months to go. But, let me say—if there's something you want to do, and you believe you can do it, then *do it!* Never mind what anyone else says . . . the what-ifs? Be true to yourself."

One of them, the more talkative one, grabbed me in a quick hug. "Good luck, and have a great time. You are so cool."

"It was great meeting you guys, too. Take care, and remember, follow your dream." When I watched them walk away, with their backpacks slung across their shoulders, I felt like a fairy godmother.

Soon, I left the hustle and bustle of Traverse City behind. I continued on Rte. 31, through towns sporting names containing words depicting the waters they were settled by. Rapid City, Elk Rapids, Suttons Bay, Eastport.

I began to think about 'the time.' At first I thought that on vacation 'time' wouldn't be important, but now I realized I had no idea what time it is, or more importantly, how many hours of daylight I had left. This didn't make me feel very secure, so I decided that I'd best replace my watch, which broke this morning.

At a K-Mart, I shopped, made my selection, and left with my shiny new watch wrapped around my wrist. Ten bucks.

With that done, I got back to my route for the day, and enjoyed the rest of the ride as I followed the shoreline until the road veered away from the water's edge. I began to notice signs.

MACKINAC BRIDGE - 35 MILES

BRIDGE MAY BE CLOSED IN HIGH WINDS

The road I was on became relatively straight and as the afternoon wore on, the winds increased. Gusts would slap at me forcibly and I gripped the handlebars tightly, and concentrated on keeping my body relaxed, yet alert.

My mind became a whirlwind of doubts. What am I doing here? What am I trying to prove? I rode all this way to cross a bridge that may toss me off to my doom. Surely, I can ride across. If only I didn't have this bulk of luggage. I suppose I can get a pick-up truck driver to haul me over . . . Nah. I want to ride it. Am I chicken? Yes! And there are butterflies in my gut, and I can't make them quit.

MACKINAC BRIDGE - 5 MILES

What if they don't let me drive across? That'll settle it for me. No! That'll set me back for days. I could take a ferry, but I don't want to pay the fare. If I ride and something happens . . . Sh-sh-sh, don't think like that. But, what if something *does* happen? It would be my fault, for being so stubborn. Yeah, but what a way to go.

Female motorcyclist blown off the Mackinac Bridge. I can see the headlines now. At least I'd die doing what I love best, not suffering from some disease, in a hospital sickbed, with tubes attached to all orifices.

Man! It's windy here. This is scary. I've got to be crazy.

MACKINAC BRIDGE - 2 MILES

MACKINAC BRIDGE - 1 MILE

TOLL - $1

I get to pay for the privilege of suicide.

There it is! I can see it. Wow, it's pretty. I'm gonna do it. God, be with me. I'm scared, but I won't do it, if I don't try.

I pulled over just before the tolls, to get out one dollar. I waited for a delivery truck to get to the gate, and positioned myself behind it. I looked ahead, but couldn't see which lane was the metal grated one. The truck moved forward, then it was my turn. I handed my fare to the person in the booth, then flipped down my shield as the bar came up. Here I go.

My heart was pounding, and the wind came at me from the left, so forcefully I had to slant the bike into it. I wanted to get into the pocket of air behind that truck, and when I did, the wind dissipated somewhat. I was in the lane desired, too!

In a few seconds, I was actually on the bridge, and below me was the huge expanse of water. Cars on my left passed me, but I just kept my eyes ahead, my jaws clenched tight. I was holding my breath, I realized. Not good. I started to concentrate on breathing, and watched the other side approach. Hey, this isn't too bad.

KA-CHINK, KA-CHINK, KA-CHINK, in a steady rhythm, as I crossed over expansion bands in the construction beneath my tires. In my rear view mirror, the shore appeared farther away than the one I approached. I'm halfway across.

I began to feel exhilarated. In minutes, it was over. I was over! No harm done. I made it on my own two wheels. I did it! The thirty-five miles before the bridge, the anticipation, was way worse than the actual ride across the bridge itself. I was psyched.

Now I had to pay attention and find my campground. No problem. There was a sign right there, telling me where to go.

STRAITS STATE PARK - CAMPERS REGISTER HERE

My ten dollar a night budget for shelter, on this night has ballooned to twenty. Five to reserve, plus eleven for the campsite, and now four bucks to park! I had the money . . . that wasn't the point. I just wondered if this kind of thing would happen most of the time. If so, I'd be in trouble.

Only, I had extra money now, due to all the hospitality I'd had on my way here. Oh well, my average spent on shelter was well below ten dollars per night at this point, since I was a houseguest for most of my nights so far. I decided not to make too much of a stink over this.

I was instructed to choose a site in a certain area, then to report back to the office when I had settled. I circled the large open grassy loop a few times, and picked out a site with a tree. A young man was pitching a pup tent in the site next to mine.

"Hi. What's up?" He greeted me as soon as I pulled in.

I parked, and pulled off my helmet.

"Wow! You're a girl!" he exclaimed, scrambling to his feet.

I was a *hot* girl at the moment, and excused myself to go to the rest room, to change into shorts. No way was I gonna set up camp with hot leather pants on.

When I entered the bathroom, I went to the last stall, a handicapped stall, because it would be larger, allowing me room to change. However, the floor was all wet. I went to the front where the sinks were, and there was a girl, oh, about thirteen, doing her hair. I leaned against the counter and lowered my pants, and to my surprise, she fled out the door. I heard her squeal to someone, "She just took off her pants right in front of me!"

A man's voice replied, "Oh, really?" then the door opened and three teenyboppers, plus the same girl came back in. By now, my shorts were on and I was tying the laces on my hiking boots.

"Is there a problem here?" I inquired.

"Oh, no. She just forgot her barrette," one girl stammered, as she handed one to the uncoiffed young lady.

I pressed on, "I thought I heard something about me changing my clothes right in front of your friend here. This is a ladies room, and we all are girls, are we not?" Feeling as though I'd committed some kind of crime, I plucked my leathers off the counter and walked out, to leave them whispering behind my back. Strange.

My campsite was directly across the oval of green grass that comprised the loop, so I cut across and got busy unpacking my bike, and setting up my tent. The young guy next door sauntered over and introduced himself as James, and launched into twenty questions. I ended up telling him about the bathroom incident, because for some reason, it was really bugging me. He passed it off, "Dee, it's no big deal."

But, I couldn't agree.

I felt as though some kind of judgement had been passed. Like, here I am, riding in on a motorcycle, wearing leather. I must be some kind of dangerous lesbian, about to put the make on unsuspecting, young, female campers.

I got busy writing in my journal, and tracking my day's route on my map. As I sat writing, I heard a man say, "Is that the one?" and I turned in time to see him pointing my way. The girls seemed embarrassed to see me so close by, as if they'd been caught tattling on me.

Again, I found myself justifying my actions. I exclaimed, "That is the ladies room, is it not? Should I have just changed my clothes right here in the open?"

The man, father of at least one of them, I supposed, just shrugged and explained, "Girls will be girls."

Still, I felt jilted. I thought to myself, kids learn attitudes from their parents. I felt the sting of prejudice, sharp and biting. I turned back to my writing, but couldn't shake the uncomfortable feeling that I was being watched.

A grocery store was close by, and inside I purchased a few post cards depicting the foreboding Mackinac Bridge, plus a can of tuna, a cucumber and some hamburger buns. A couple of wine coolers rounded off the menu.

When I came back to my site, I used my Swiss Army knife to peel my cuke, and I put dry tuna into hamburger buns and enjoyed my meal. It was good to eat healthy like this, and reasonable, too. Some sea gulls arrived and I tossed them bits of bread, starting a chain reaction of squawks and screeches.

James came by and talked to me about his new job in sales, how he had the company van, and expenses paid to travel, but he preferred to camp and save money from his overnight allowance. He was talkative, and I had to ask him to go away so I could finish writing postcards and stuff, but he didn't get the message. Finally, I put it bluntly.

"James, it's getting dark. I need to write. Come back later, thank you."

He reminded me of an overgrown boy, not quite used to being an adult. He shuffled off. In moments, I heard the Family Group Conglomerate members call him over to their site to have dinner with them. I couldn't help but feel slighted. Hey! What about me?

The temperature cooled and I slipped into sweatpants. I tried to ignore the laughter, and the crackling fire over there at their site, and struggled with my own feelings of being dissed. Left out for no other reason, other than that I was riding a motorcycle, and "normal" women don't do that. It was not like me to care what other people think, but there I was, feeling self-conscious and indignant.

When the sun was setting and turned the sky to peach and orange, I took a walk. James ran to catch up with me. "Mind if I join you?"

"No. Feel free."

We walked in silence, amazingly, and out through a thicket of trees, arriving at the water's edge. There against the dramatic backdrop of the sky at sunset, was the Mackinac Bridge, lit up from shore to shore, with red and green lights. It was breathtakingly beautiful. We watched until the sky was deep blue/black. The day had ended, and quite a day it was. It was difficult to believe that this morning I was awakened on a boat on these same waters, two hundred and fifty shoreline miles away, but, that was the truth. It seemed so long ago.

Suddenly, I felt tired, and I turned away from the lights. James was bragging about the steak that the Family Group Conglomerate had forced on him, and I just swallowed my feelings of resentment. I was happy for him, only sorry for myself.

My night eyesight kicked in, and I led the way through the darkness and the trees, back to our campsites. "Good night, James. If I don't see you in the morning, good luck with your new job. Thanks for your company."

"Bye, Dee. Do you mind if I ask how old you are? I know some women don't like that." James looked down at his Nikes, as he pushed some dirt around with his toes.

"I'm thirty-five."

"Really? You don't look it. Too old for me."

"Yes, James. Good night."

Inside my tent, I smiled to myself. This was going to be a mighty interesting summer.

Miles: 245

There was a water spigot a short distance from my campsite, and I saw a white-haired man hobble to it, with a pot in his hand. He got to the faucet and as he filled his coffee pot he stared at me as I strapped my belongings onto my bike. I unzipped a saddlebag and withdrew my burner and pot. The old man was still at the faucet when I went to fill my pot.

I smiled at him, "Good morning, sir."

He tipped his hat and answered my greeting, all the while looking past me, at my motorcycle. "That yours?"

"Yes, it is."

"Where you from?"

"Massachusetts."

"You rode it all the way from Massachusetts?"

"Yes, I did."

Leaning on his cane, he set his pot on the spigot post and rubbed his beard stubble. "Hmmm. Nothin' wrong with that, I guess. Where're you headed?"

"I'm riding around the U.S.A., camping and seeing the country, just like you are."

"Hmmm. Nothin' wrong with that, I guess." He didn't look too convinced, though. "All by yourself?"

"Yes, but I have people here and there to meet, as well. For the most part, I expect to be alone. Then, I can do exactly what I want, and go where I please. No compromises, y'know?"

"Well—nothin' wrong with that, I guess. Never seen the likes of it before. All alone . . . Not safe for a woman these days, and on a motorcycle! Young lady, you be careful. Hmph." He then collected his water and shuffled his way across camp, sloshing water onto his shoes.

Nothing wrong with that, I guess.

I started my water to boil, and continued my task of rolling up my sleeping pad and stuffing my sleeping bag into its stuff sack. By the time I'd finished, my water was boiling, and I prepared my breakfast of instant oatmeal and tea. Between mouthfuls, I looked at my maps, CampBook and Hostel Guide.

With reservations, I could sleep at a hostel in Wisconsin. It was less than three hundred miles away. I used the campground pay phone, and made my reservation with Alex.

With that done, I felt focused, knowing exactly where I was going, and I was looking forward to my day's ride through the Upper Peninsula of Michigan. I expected it to look a lot like Canada, not that I know much of Canada, but I was anticipating a lot of wilderness.

James was waiting for me back at my site. He followed me as I packed. After I'd gotten most of my things on the bike, I decided I didn't like the arrangement. Starting over, off came the tent, the duffel of clothes and the sleeping bag. It was nerve wracking, because James kept hovering around, making me nervous. My morning chore of packing up, was still a trial and error sort of ordeal, and having more than my own shadow made it worse. I felt unorganized, and that's rare. Some people don't take a hint, either. For example, I said, "I still haven't got the hang of the best way to load up this bike, and you standing there watching me take off bags I just spent ten minutes arranging is not making it any better."

So the tall, lanky lad agreed, "I know. Don't you hate it when you can't do something and at the same time you've got an audience? You're never gonna get all that stuff on that bike, you know."

Aggravating! "AAARGH! James! Go! Please, you're making me nervous. I don't want my every move watched. Please. I can't take it any more. You'll know before I go, because you'll hear me start my bike. That will be a good time for you to say good-bye, okay? Thank you, now, please go."

Why can't I be the kind of person who just says "Get the hell off my site!?"

I selected Route 2, which runs along the shoreline of Lake Michigan. The sky was cloudy, the temperature cool enough for me to use my wool sweater and a scarf.

The landscape was marshy and pretty, with reeds, rushes and a Great Lake on my left, while on the other side I saw more wetlands and forest.

I fell in behind a Winnebago that had just gone by, leaving a comfortable space cushion between us. Over the next ninety miles, I followed, enjoying the day, and looking for wildlife.

A deer boing-boinged its nimble self out of sight. There were two long-legged, large bodied, long-necked creatures tearing across the road erratically. Reaching the other side, they zig-zagged their way up a bank, and disappeared. Wild turkeys.

The seagulls looked different here, than from where I live. Most had a black cap on their head, and wings tipped with black. But, they still had that same annoying squall.

The road itself was unchallenging, more or less straight, with slight bends following natural terrain, and kept a traveler on higher ground. I'd drift away from my intense scrutiny of the environment, to stare at that rectangle ahead of me, and try to make out the bumper stickers, wondering about the places it has been.

That is when I saw an unfortunate gull crash into the camper, causing me to search my soul and examine My Self.

My Red Pony began to lag, and I reached down for the dial by my left knee and switched over to reserve. I never rode more than twenty or so miles on reserve in the nine years I'd owned the bike. Hadn't seen much in the way of a town or gas pump since I left camp, hours ago. I made a mental note of my tripometer, delaying all thoughts of worry for the next twenty miles, at least.

I pulled into the first gas station I saw. The parking lot was packed gravel, and the pumps stood by themselves. Thirty paces away, there was a store. In the windows, signs depicted beer, chewing tobacco, knives, fishing licenses, souvenirs, smoked fish and pasties.

Pasties, pronounced 'pass-tees,' not 'paste-ies,' was the regional specialty I'd heard about and wanted to try. I was told that it was like a pastry dough, with a meat filling, served with gravy.

In the store, I wandered around looking at all kinds of neat things, especially for the sportsman, or for tourists. I looked at the food, too, the fish with their eyeballs, skin and tails, smoked to perfection, but mustered up no appetite for any of that. The cooler contained, among other cheap frozen foods, some pasties, but they didn't look very appealing, either. I inquired of the clerk where I might get a hot meal. He pointed across the street and down some. This town appeared to be all of six buildings.

A local guy pulled in and got out of his pickup truck. "Whatta ya got for a bike there? Can you fit any more gear on it?" he laughed. He glanced at my license plate, and choked, "Holy Toledo! You've got guts."

So I hear.

We talked for a spell, but I was hungry and had to get going. Across the street diagonally was the cafe. Inside, I ordered beef and barley soup, the famous Michigan pastie, with gravy. When my pastie arrived, I couldn't believe my eyes. Here, in front of me, taking up half the plate was a huge D-shaped pastie, smothered in gravy, and complimented by a heap of mixed veggies beside it. I'm not sure if all pasties are this good, but this one was fabulous. I came to the right place.

I ordered some coffee and a giant cookie, chatted with some locals as they included me in their conversation. One man was a transplant from Boston, and said he'd never go back east.

I was stuffed. This would last me for some time. I used the bathroom, brushed my teeth, and complimented the chef. I bungeed my sweater to my pack, then took to the road, ready to digest it all, my meal, the realization that I am a traveler, and that I am free. The road is my address. My cycle is my home.

After a meal and decent break, getting back on the road feels great. It's as if the miles go by quicker. All of a sudden, you'll glance down, and you've traveled fifty miles, but you didn't notice. So that's what happened. One minute I am entering Hiawatha National Forest, and the next, I'm leaving it. Where did thirty-five miles go? I began to notice towns coming more frequently, and much about Paul Bunyan, Iron Mountain, and mining attractions.

Wisconsin would soon become my stomping ground, where I would visit my first hostel. I would likely need a sleep-sheet, which is required by some of the hostels. I didn't have one, so when I spied a Thrift Store, I stopped to shop.

I parked on the end, next to the handicap spaces, and a car with appropriate tags pulled in beside me. As soon as I took off my helmet, the little old man who had just climbed out of his car approached me.

"Excuse me, but do you have a minute? I'd like to ask you some questions. You see, we've never seen a woman traveling like this before, and we'd like to meet you." He turned toward his wife in the passenger seat, and she unrolled her window and smiled at me.

"We couldn't tell that you were a girl. We just pulled in and said to each other, Goodness, look at that fellow's load! Then you took off your helmet, and My! We just want to meet you."

They asked me all the usual questions. What kind of bike? Where am I headed, where am I from? All by myself? Aren't I afraid?

After all their questions were answered, they told me they thought it was wonderful, and to "do it while you're young, while you can, before you get old like us, and wish you had." Then, he apologized for taking my time.

"Not at all. The pleasure was mine." It was.

In the thrift store I quickly found bed-sheets. I looked at all of the flat sheets for one to suit my taste. I was ready to settle for a plain white sheet, when I found it. Peanuts. There was Lucy, Charlie Brown, Snoopy and the gang.

Sold. Two dollars. Deal.

All right! I got what I needed, and the price couldn't be beat. I'll just stitch it up the sides later. I have a needle and thread with me.

At this point, I had to change routes, cross the Wisconsin border and make my way to Laonia. I picked some roads that would take me through Nicolet National Forest, then I saw the sign.

WISCONSIN WELCOMES YOU
RECREATION, INDUSTRY AND AGRICULTURE

It was with great elation that I pulled over for my ritualistic state sign photo. I parked in front of it, and stepped back for my photo. This would be the first time I'd ever been in this state, and the end of a whole week visiting and exploring the state I was born in, Michigan.

Nicolet Forest succeeded in charming me. The road that would take me to Laonia was full of sweepers, wide easy curves, a joy to ride. There was no traffic, and nothing but acres of pine trees with long, soft needles, protecting a layer of green undergrowth.

For an hour or two I continued on this enjoyable ride, and the sun got lower in the sky. I began to feel chilly, but rode on. I'd bundle up next time I make a pit stop. Eventually I realized, there was no place, as far as facilities are concerned. Still, I rode on.

Full bladder, breasts sore from their automatic reaction to my being cold, I ignored the symptoms, like a crazy woman. The need to pee became urgent, yet I thought, I've got to be close to Laonia. I can hold it.

At last, I could stand it no longer. I pulled over to the shoulder, frantically dug around in my tankbag for some napkins I swiped at the restaurant, and desperately tossed off my jacket as I stumbled into some bushes.

It wasn't cold out, but with wind chill factor of riding forty mph, I was. My fingers were having trouble with the zipper and snap on my pants. Meanwhile, my brain was sending the message, "Go," and I almost lost control. What pain, when I had to stifle that flow for two more seconds. I squatted and let-er-rip. Ah-h-h.

Unbelievable relief. I felt as though my abdomen was a balloon that had just let the air out.

I retrieved my jacket, got my sweater off the back of the bike, and got dressed. Warmth. Gosh, I felt like a reborn person when I got back on my Red Pony.

Why the heck did I do that to myself, anyway? Driving for hours in a thick forest, and not stopping to pee, when I had plenty of cover, and virtually no traffic. Crazy. This was the second time in one day. That can't be good for the human body. What if my bladder exploded? Hopefully, I'd learn from this.

Back on the road and dressed better, relieved physically, I was no longer anxious about each mile passing by. Laonia signs appeared very soon. I took a right onto Route 8. I checked my Hostel Guide once more, where there is a picture of each hostel.

About eight miles later, I arrived, and there on the right was the house I was looking for, easily recognized by the I.A.Y.H. sign outside. (International American Youth Hostel.)

A man in an apron answered the doorbell. He dried his hands on the dishtowel he'd been using and called for Bob. Excusing himself, he went back to washing dishes at the kitchen sink.

I was standing in the living room with several chairs, some bookshelves and a TV. The walls were lined with huge maps, of the United States and of the World. There was a brochure rack that contained pamphlets of A.Y.H. all over the country, and magazines such as National Geographic.

There was a guest book, and I felt I had traveled a great distance to be here, as I bent to sign my name with inner pride, *from Massachusetts*. Then I was really impressed, for the last few guests who had signed before me, weren't even U.S. citizens. Instead, Switzerland, Germany and Austria were their homelands.

Bob, in a suit and tie, entered the room and shook my hand, introducing himself. He asked for $9.50, some for him, and some for Uncle Sam. Then he showed me around.

"This is the kitchen, and here is the bathroom. There's no smoking indoors, but you can go out on the back porch. Follow me." He led the way upstairs. "We have three bedrooms, plus this common area, and a half bath up here. We can accommodate twelve guests. There are three bunk-beds in one room, two in another, and one private room, also a bunk-bed. You're our only guest tonight, so you can pick wherever you want to sleep. You can get a blanket and pillow out of any closet. Make yourself at home. Feel free to use the kitchen, but clean up after yourself. Any questions?"

"Yes. Can I pull my bike around to the back yard? Alex said on the phone that I could."

Bob reluctantly agreed.

"Great view here, Bob. What a nice place you have." I was looking at a large grassy yard, lined with tall hedges and trees, and beyond was a lake mottled with little islands. At the water's edge was a rickety dock, and in the yard was an overturned rowboat.

I moved my Pony to the back, and unloaded only what I would need overnight. There were birdfeeders and potted flowers strategically set up around the property. I liked this place. It was peaceful, quaint and pretty.

I went for a walk on a path between the trees out back, which ran behind many back yards. In the yards there were small garden plots, a tire hanging from a tree, a boy and his husky, with one blue eye, and one brown. A screen door slammed.

In a comedy of matters, a pot-bellied police officer tumbled down the steps and bolted for his cruiser. A woman in a typical housedress stepped onto the landing, her hands on her hips. He peeled out of the gravel driveway, sending loose stone a-flying. She shook her head from side to side and disappeared into the house, as the siren wailed away.

Next, a few houses down, there was a man with a rifle. He's cussing at a noisy bird in a tree, and fires a round of shots. Hmmm. Wisconsin.

I feel as if I've stepped back some forty-five years, and crossed into a TV sitcom from the 50's.

Later, I fixed some tea, and made a tuna sandwich, and ate outside. It was such a peaceful yard. When the sun sank low, I went for a walk down by the water. This was a nice stop. I have a bed to sleep in, I'm comfortable, and left on my own. No one is going out of their way to entertain me. That's cool.

The sky glowed, frogs chirped, bullfrogs grunted and insects filled the night with noise. I was covered with Skintastic, and nothing was biting. I fully enjoyed the environment and my solitude on this fine, warm evening.

In the dark, I walked back to the hostel, and found the sliding glass door between the deck and the kitchen was closed and locked. I tried some more. Definitely locked. I tapped on the glass. On the left, just inside, was another door marked "private." That door led to the basement, where Bob resides. He couldn't hear me knocking. I remembered a doorbell out front.

At first I rang patiently, with silent intervals in between. This gradually evolved to incessant ringing, for ten minutes. I banged and yelled, "Alex! Bob!" I began to think about setting up my tent in the back yard. I wondered, "Why won't they answer the door?" Eventually, I was ticked off. This really sucks.

I went around to the side of the house and banged on a cellar window. Bob's startled face appeared, and I yelled, "I'm locked out! Let me in."

He came upstairs and let me in, stammering, "I don't know how this happened. Alex must have locked the doors. We thought you went to bed. We didn't hear you."

I tried to be nice, but . . . "I've been banging and yelling and ringing the doorbell for fifteen minutes! I'm sorry if I disturbed you, but I'm a mite disturbed myself! I was locked out! This is where I'm supposed to have a room. Not fun."

Bob stood with his hand on the doorknob, waiting for an escape.

I continued venting my frustration. "I went down to watch the sunset over the lake, and I got locked out. That's understandable, but then when you wouldn't answer the door, and I know you're here . . . I'm sorry if I interrupted something, really, but what else could I do? G'night."

My room was stark and neat. Wooden bunkbeds, braided rugs, and walls covered with a collage of worldly places, maps, Native American lore, etc.

I got ready for bed, and settled into bed with my new Snoopy sheet. Except for getting locked out, I really enjoyed my stay. I hoped that the unfortunate experience wouldn't alter my hosts hospitality or their attitudes towards me in the morning.

Miles: 284

"Go West" said Horace Greeley, but my slogan is "Go Anyplace."
—Richard Bissell

CHAPTER 3

WESTWARD HO YOUNG WOMAN
June 28–30   Days 12–14

After my morning shower, I helped myself to some coffee. I chewed on a fudge flavored Power Bar while I got ready to go. Bob had already left for work, but Alex was up and about, despite last night's dilemma.

It was spitting outside when I left the hostel. Alex wished me well, Lemon Pledge in one hand and a dust rag in the other. I got onto Rte. 8 through Wisconsin.

Westward Ho Young Woman. Over and over these words repeated themselves in my mind.

Eventually I rode in and out of rain pockets. This was a road which gently meandered its way across the state. Occasionally, I'd come across a "wayside," which is their term for "rest area." Sometime after a couple hundred miles, I began to feel fatigued. I rode out of another rain burst, then stopped at a wayside to rest.

First I used the john, which consisted of a pit toilet and no sink. Then, still in my rain suit, I laid down on my back on top of a picnic table, covered my eyes with one arm and allowed myself to drift off.

I considered this action momentarily. Some people would tell me that I wouldn't be safe to take a rest here, in the middle of nowhere and all, but then I listened to my Self.

First of all, to look at me this second, one glance would give most people the impression that the person on the table was a man, given the fact that my shape was not evident with this rain garb on, plus there was a motorcycle parked there.

Secondly, taking a break to rest my eyes and body when I am this fatigued is much safer than being drowsy on the road. Falling asleep behind the wheel in a car is dangerous. Falling asleep on a motorcycle is stupid. Definite physical and financial costs would ensue.

Third, I just have to have faith. No one is going to hurt me. Notice me, maybe. Bother me, no. Then, in less than an hour, I'd be ready to hit the road again, rested and refreshed.

A gentle smattering of drizzle landing on my cheek and chin brought me out of my nap. I sat up and rubbed my eyes, stretched and yawned as I looked around me. There was a station wagon parked in front of the outhouse, and an old man winced his way to the men's side, while his wife stayed in the car. Also, there was a camper pulled into the wayside. The rain started to come down in earnest. It had caught up with me.

I put on my helmet and gloves, zipped up and climbed aboard. The Honda started right up, as usual, and I straightened the handlebars, then placing my left foot on the tar, I pulled the bike to straighten it from its slanted sidestand position.

Well, my foot slipped and my bike tipped over, slowly and noisily, as one hand inadvertently cranked the throttle, trying to keep from going down. Fortunately, my other hand squeezed the clutch, so the engine only screamed, but didn't engage. My wimpy horn squeaked, and then, silence, as I hit the engine cut-off switch. My motorcycle was over on its side, literally suspended, thanks to my ninety pounds of luggage.

During my struggle to stay upright, at a standstill, I saw the old lady exit the passenger seat of the station wagon and scurry to the john. What I saw next, however, made me cuss. She disappeared into the woman's side, as if she had no idea that I needed assistance. She had to know, but it was not in her nature to care. At first, I thought she was running to get her old man, but then I realized I was on my own.

I ran to the camper beyond, and banged on the door. A woman responded, and I frantically gestured towards my horizontal horsepower. She spoke in French to her companion, and he yanked his shirt off, and ran out into the downpour with me.

"Maybe motor-bike too beeg, no?" he asked in his French accent.

"My foot slipped." I motioned where to grab the frame, "One- Two- Three- Ugh." We lifted the bike and sagging luggage. I extended my hand, and he squeezed it so hard my bones hurt.

"Merci beaucoup, au revoir," I called after him as he ran for cover. Inside my helmet I reverently thanked God for providing this man to be right here, right now.

The bike while on its side, rested on a handgrip, but other than that, the entire motorcycle was untouched, due to my load of luggage. Everything was fine, no damage, no marks, no nothing. Only some mud on my saddlebag. I was quite relieved, but still when I climbed back on I felt my hands shaking, my heart pounding, and my chest moisten with nervous sweat.

I started her up again, and tested the ground where I placed my Totes-clad boot. Only minutes earlier, the tar had just enough rain to cause oily substances to rise to the surface, making it slippery. By now, this slick layer had been washed away. I left the wayside and rode on, in the rain, trying to look at the good side.

My raingear keeps my dry and is visible. My bike just got tipped over, but not scratched. Although my luggage makes it "too heavy" at times like that, it also serves as a protector. Instead of the run-and-hide lady being the only person available, with her rickety old man, I was aided by a man from Canada, who just happened to be there at my moment of need.

The rain continued off and on. The sun would fool me, at times, shining down forcefully, making me feel as though there's a layer of steam between my gore-tex and me, then a cloud would come along and douse the landscape with moisture. Despite the weather, I enjoyed the ride along Rte. 8 across the entire state of Wisconsin. Woodsy, pretty and rustic, I found it quite to my liking. After a day's ride, I'd be crossing over into Minnesota.

I had plans to sleep at a WOW's house, in a town on the far outskirts of Minneapolis. I had the address and telephone number, and could find her town on the map, but had no idea how to get to her house. I would have to drive into Jordan, take my chances and call her from there.

Just before I got to the Minnesota state line, the rain came down in such torrents, I had to get off the road and wait it out. I could barely see, and there was five inches of rain on the road. I was in an urban area, so I pulled into a mall parking lot and waited.

The rain let up, and I took off. I followed signs to Minneapolis. At the state line, I pulled over. I set my camera on my pack, with its timed release shutter activated, ran and stood below the sign for a photo. My expression read, "I'm not so sure if I'm having a good time today, or not."

Back on my home on wheels, I merged in with mega-traffic on mega-highways. What a horror show. I wasn't sure how to get to where I was going, and I did my best to circumnavigate the huge city of Minneapolis. I had to keep pulling off to check my bearings. After an hour of anxiety, I finally found the road that would take me to Jordan.

My hands relaxed their grip, and I began to breathe normally again. Entering Jordan, I pulled into a Texaco, and asked if I could make a local call. I dialed Karen's number.

"Hello?" a woman answered.

"Hello. Karen?"

"Dee? Dee? Is this you? I was hoping you'd call! Where are you?"

"I'm at Texaco, as soon as you get off the Big Highway 169."

"You sit right there!" She sounded so excited. "I will come and get you right away. Oh, I'm so happy you're here. I wasn't sure because . . . oh, I'll talk to you when I see you . . . two minutes."

In a few minutes a station wagon pulled up and a lady jumped out and ran over to me, arms outstretched. I was well aware that I must look like hell, but I didn't care. Until I was able to shower and change my clothes, I'd look like a drowned rat.

Karen hugged me and squealed. "Hello! Oh, hi," she bubbled, "Oh I'm such a mess! I'm sorry you have to see me this way."

Like I cared, like I even noticed.

She continued, "Let me hug you! This your bike? Oh look at all your stuff! How do you drive it? I'm so excited to meet you."

A mighty warm greeting indeed. Finding her house would be a piece of cake, after all. I just had to follow the leader.

I followed her away from the main part of town, then in between farms, and along country roads. We made a turn and passed a horse farm that raised Percherons. Powerful, gray draft horses dotted the pastures, while their foals frolicked nearby.

Karen turned onto a long, dirt driveway which led between still more fields. A man was out on a tractor, and a dead snake lay stretched across the driveway where it had been run over. Ahead, a picturesque barn loomed beside an old house of historic architecture. Roosters and chickens scratched in the dirt, and a dog came running. A golden horse and a black pony raised their heads and watched as I rolled by. What a fabulous place, all surrounded by cornfields and horse farms. I could imagine myself happy here, working hard, raising crops and animals, then riding along on country roads, on horseback or on my motorcycle. Dream away.

After I parked, Karen introduced me to a couple of her foster children and we all grabbed a bag and entered the house.

Whoa! What a place! It was like walking into a museum of Victorian decor. It smelled of fresh baked apple pies, and every wall, tabletop, nook and cranny displayed dolls, lacy things, dried flowers, angles and cherubs, country charm and old world Victorian memorabilia. Karen had an unbelievable collection, worthy of charging an admission fee, just to come and see. She led me upstairs to my bedroom, and it was like the rest of the house, all frills and flowers, lace and antiques. Not my style, but exquisite and delightful to visit.

The bathroom was set up with towels and soaps laid out especially for me, and I gratefully jumped at the offer to get cleaned up. We were going out for supper, I was informed. I said that really wouldn't be necessary.

Karen replied, "I insist. This will be so interesting. I have so many questions. In the meantime . . . you must have some laundry. We can get that done, too. After your shower, I'll show you to the laundry area. Okay, you take your time. Do you need anything?"

Whew—this lady was wound up, but it was good to be received so warmly by a lady I'd only met through an exchange of letters. She struck me as a high energy, motherly, slightly eccentric person, ready and willing to be an instant friend.

We both looked like different people when we met in the living room after our showers. With long brown hair hanging straight to her hips, and a shiny black outfit, she looked quite pretty. I felt pretty, too, with my long sundress on, and my hair hanging free, bangs pulled off my face with a pair of combs.

We rode in the car a few miles to a chain restaurant, Peabody's, which I'm unfamiliar with. Dinner was fine, and Karen and I never stopped talking. She was a new member of Women On Wheels, and did not ride her own bike, nor did her husband, but she loved motorcycles and the freedom they represent. She was proud of a vacation she'd taken to Sturgis, during Bike Week. It was the most independent thing she'd done in her life, and speaking of it made her glow. Then a glimmer of doubt cast a shadow across her face. This great feat was tainted by her husband's disapproval.

I could understand how she felt. I, too, was feeling my heart ache, as I had left a man behind who didn't want me to take this trip. But, I'm not married. It must be very difficult for Karen under these circumstances.

Here I was, a guest in their home. An independent, motorcycle riding, young woman, excited about my journey, sharing my adventure with them. He was polite enough when she introduced the two of us, but he was none too thrilled. He went back outside, got on his tractor and returned to the fields. He was still out there, when we came back from town.

I tossed my clothes into the dryer, and hung my raingear up to dry. It wasn't late, but I was wiped. I went to bed in my old-fashioned, fluffy, lacy, ruffly, sweet-smelling twin bed, and drifted off as cherubs played their harps, and motorcycles lined the streets of heaven, and Karen stood and watched all the bikers walking around.

Miles: 348

Karen had a morning appointment to keep. She was afraid to say good-bye, and depressed that my motorcycle wouldn't be in the driveway when she returned. She said she finds it hard to let go.

Throughout this trip, I will constantly be faced with saying good-bye, and people I have come to know will have to let go when it's time to. I realized that for a traveler, letting go is a requirement. I try to be thankful for the blessings I encounter, and accept the fact that life is full of changes.

Anyway, we did have to go. Karen to her appointment, and me, I wanted to make it to South Dakota by that evening. Before I left, I used her phone and called my answering service. I left a new outgoing message for my friends. Those who called my number, were able to keep tabs on me. Every few days or so, I would change it, and retrieve messages left for me.

Today I said, "Hi. So far I've traveled through Massachusetts, Connecticut, New York, Pennsylvania, Ohio, Michigan, Wisconsin, and now I'm in Minnesota. I hope to reach South Dakota by tonight, my thirteenth day away. I'm having a great time, my bike is running fine, and the weather has mostly been good. Leave a message after the beep."

The answering service indicated I had a couple of messages and I was able to hear my friends' voices. Next, I collected all of my belongings and packed them on my bike.

There was a campground in Mitchell, S.D. that I planned to check out as my destination that night. It was under ten dollars and I liked the name, "Mallard Cove."

The ride through Minnesota was kind of chilly, and fairly windy. The sky was dismal all day, but there was no rain. I rode on a main highway, to a small connecting road, to the major Interstate 90, about the only means to cross South Dakota.

On I-90, wind gusts were strong. Anyone who thinks riding a motorcycle is a passive activity has got the wrong idea. Those big bellies you see come from eating too much good food, not from the riding hobby, because riding long distances is hard, strenuous work. I'd be riding along, tense with anticipation for the next crosswind blast. Coming at me from the side, it felt as though it could knock my bike right over. I had to always be ready. I felt my neck and shoulder muscles tighten, partially from being chilly, and partially from being in a state of readiness.

It wasn't cold out, but on a motorcycle you have to figure in terms of wind chill factor. So, according to a chart in my MTS (Motorcycle Towing Services) handbook, at 55 mph, in fifty-five degree temperature, the wind chill factor is 32 degrees, ie. freezing. Believe it? If you ride, you do.

Taking into consideration my small frame, and lack of body fat, it makes sense that I really feel the cold, so appear overdressed out here during my stops, but actually, I am wise to have long johns, a sweater and lots of leather on.

Mitchell, was about sixty miles west of the state line where I'd stopped for my photo.

SOUTH DAKOTA—GREAT FACES, GREAT PLACES

The image of Mt. Rushmore graced the sign when I entered that state.

My CampBook gave me directions which led me right to Mallard Cove. I entered the office and a man who smelled of beer greeted me, and sold me a site. He was full of information about sightseeing in South Dakota, and gave me advise on what to see, and what to avoid.

The tent section was all mine. I selected a spot near a small pond surrounded by tall marsh grasses and bulrushes, and set up my tent so that the opening faced the prettiest view. The wind had not subsided, and challenged me as I struggled with my rain fly, as it flapped wildly before I could fasten it down. I changed into jeans, cleaned my bike superficially, and noted all that took only forty-five minutes.

There was time before sunset for me to do some reading. I had an imaginary list of required reading. *Blue Highways,* by William Least Heat Moon, *Travels with Charlie,* by John Steinback, but for now, I was into *Walk West 2,* a sequel to *Walk Across America,* by Peter Jenkins. These books were inspiration for me.

The sun sank low, and the sky turned apricot and orange, and reflected off my duck pond. There was practically nobody here, I was alone, and enjoyed the solitude. My tent was beginning to feel like home. I felt exceptionally content this evening. It is well with my soul. I crawled into my down sleeping bag, and searched the sky for stars until my eyes were heavy.

Miles: 281

Morning arrived chilly and gray. I pulled on jeans and a thermal shirt and trotted over to the shower house, but decided against taking one, because without a hair dryer, I would not be able to warm up. Instead, I washed the crucial areas with a wash cloth. While I was braiding my hair, I was surprised when the door opened and a woman entered. Ah, there were others camping here after all. It's just that the temperature had kept them inside their campers last night.

The lady and I discovered we had something in common. We were both women traveling alone. She was cruising America in her mobile home for an extensive period of time. She was an older lady, and came from Alaska. We shared our thoughts on the benefits of going it alone, and how the general populace reacted toward us with amazement and surprise. We agreed that we were both having the time of our lives. There is something so self-satisfying about being independent, and going wherever you want, without compromise. We wished each other well, and then I went back to my site to break camp.

Just as I was strapping the last of it onto my motorcycle, she came by to look at my home on wheels. I hoped that when I get to be her age I will still have the gumption to break away and take advantage of my abilities to take care of myself. She wistfully stated that she wished she had started earlier in life. Feeling refreshed by our meeting of happenstance, we bid farewell, and she walked away. I changed into my leather pants, with long johns underneath, and got going.

Down the road a bit, I stopped at a diner and ordered a huge breakfast and coffee. I checked my map, made my plans and wrote out some postcards. My waiter was stopping by my table to ask questions about me, my motorcycle, and journey whenever he had a spare second.

In Mitchell, there are a number of tourist traps, and I was in a tourist kind of mood, but rather than visiting Corn Palace, I opted to check out the Prehistoric Indian Museum. Admission was a dollar-fifty. It was rather small, and self-guided outdoors, but indoors I had my own interpreter, a guy about high school age. He was well informed, and answered my questions intelligently. Then it was my turn to answer his queries. He was eager to hear about my adventure, and I was more than happy to indulge him.

I purchased a small leather pouch which hung from a thong, to wear around my neck. I tucked a pewter medallion of St. Christopher, protection for travelers, into it, and a special touchstone that was etched with the rune for *Strength*. Now I had an amulet to protect me and keep me strong as I travel. Out by my bike, I reverently placed it over my head, and felt the slight weight of it resting between my breasts. I clutched it, closed my eyes and made believe that I breathed my spirit into the symbolic item.

I-90 through South Dakota is a long, straight and boring stretch of road. The wind was constant and strong. My bike was leaned into the wind, slanted to one side continuously. It was tiring, but kept me from drifting into a state of tedious monotony. Besides concentrating on the physical aspect of my ride, I searched the landscape for nuances that would separate it from familiar territory.

There was barbed wire, endless strings of it along the side of the road. Here and there signs clung to the fence-line.

HUNTING, TRAPPING AND THE FUR TRADE
SOUTH DAKOTA'S INDUSTRY
ENVIRONMENTALISTS ARE NOT WELCOME HERE

Or something to that effect. That gave me something to think about for a while. I consider myself an environmentalist, but out here, already I see a difference in the countryside, as I know it. It is wide open. I tried to imagine how I would feel about this topic if I grew up in these parts. The weird thing was, I was able to put myself in their shoes, and it seemed to make sense.

Sometimes you have to be in a situation before you can fully understand it. It is easy for me, being a yankee, to worry about our national wildlife, and to get worked up over needless slaughter, but out here in this wilderness, I realized it's a different world. Activists do their best to persuade us of an exaggerated viewpoint. My mind expanded, and part of me accepted and embraced the new growth.

By noon, it was not even sixty degrees yet, and on the bike at about 80 mph, I was getting cold. My trusty wind chill factor chart doesn't contain data for speeds over sixty-five miles per hour, but on this stretch of road, I'd get run over if I went that slow. At 60 degrees and 65 mph, however, I was supposedly exposed to a temperature of 39 degrees. I could believe it. I was using my cold weather gauntlet gloves, and grateful that I had invested in these babies before my trip.

Somewhere along the line, the billboard assault began in earnest. At first, reading them kept my mind occupied, and gave me a visual focus, besides the center line. After several hundred, I was getting annoyed. Wall Drug definitely over-indulged in its enthusiasm to let the world know, WHERE THE HECK IS WALL DRUG? There were hundreds of them. Big signs, small signs, modern signs and olde style signs.

What started out as a poor man's pharmacy a century ago, has turned into a profitable business, where tourists can purchase anything from western art, Indian jewelry, blankets, souvenirs and postcards, to buffalo burgers, but, not water. Their claim to fame is their FREE WATER.

It didn't look like I'd have much trouble finding a place to camp once I arrived in Rapid City. Many campgrounds were announced a hundred miles ahead of their location. It was a shame to see this barren landscape spoiled by these structures, but I guess Man's gotta do what Man's gotta do.

One billboard that caught my interest, was for another Indian Museum, and I exited the expressway to visit the Akta Lakota

Indian Museum. I needed a break from the saddle, and wanted to warm up.

The museum was located at a school for Native American children. It was full of sculptures and paintings done by the students there. I was impressed. Displays of Indian artifacts, a video, weapons, quill work and jewelry all artistically exhibited, occupied me for at least an hour.

I asked a curator how quill work is performed, and she dropped what she was doing to bring me "behind the scenes," to explain. I was led into a classroom. There she showed me actual samples of unfinished projects that young children were creating. It was fascinating. The woman didn't stop there, however, she also showed me books and a list of literature on the subject. The special attention was an unusual surprise, and much appreciated.

Back on the road, the miles flew by and my brain was busy processing the new sights and events I had most recently encountered. A highway sign indicated a scenic overlook ahead. Scenic? Well, that shouldn't be missed, because so far the landscape has been fairly dull.

I pulled into the parking area and dismounted. The rumble of a Harley approached, and pulled off the highway, too. A man and woman were on board, and got off to stretch their legs. He lit a smoke, and she strolled up a slight rise to the scenic overlook. I joined her. As we crested the top, off in the distance we could see the badlands. The landscape seemed to suddenly transform into a rippled crater-filled area. It was miles off, though still appearing wild and awesome.

"Hi, where ya from?" I spoke first.

"Alabama. How 'bout you?" she responded.

"I'm from Massachusetts. Wow—isn't that something? I thought I'd never get here. Can you believe all the billboards? What a sin."

"Yeah. So—what are you, all by yourself?" she asked in a strong southern accent.

"Mm-hm. I'm going to travel the U.S. for a hundred days. I've been taking back roads most of the way, except for crossing this state. I didn't have much alternative, here."

"A hundred days? That's more than three months! How long have you been on the road so far?" She looked incredulous.

"This is my fourteenth day, two weeks."

"That must be fantastic."

"It is. I still can't believe it." We stared off into the distant scene a moment. "When you get to the badlands, there's a motorcycle road not to be missed. I heard about it in touring magazines, and from other riders. It cuts right through the badlands like this . . . " indicating with my palm waving back and forth through the air, to show a set of curves. "It's Rte. 240, check it out."

We walked back to her husband and their Ultra Glide, and introduced ourselves. Janey told Al about my trip, and the road through the badlands. He said the two of them would be trying to secure a motel room, and wasn't sure if they'd have time today to cruise 240, but they would do so the next day.

"So what kind of BMW is that?" Al motioned towards my mount.

"It's a Honda Beemer," I jokingly replied. "No, really it's a Honda Interceptor 500, under all that luggage. It's no wonder you can't tell what it is, plus it's got a custom paint job, which is unusual for sportbikes. You've got a nice bike," I commented. "Sure looks a lot more comfortable than mine is for touring."

"Man, you've sure got an accent, where ya from?" Al drawled. I could barely understand him, either. After a couple minutes of small talk, I got back on my Red Pony and headed for Badlands National Park, considered to be 'the Gateway to the West.'

The scenic ride through the Badlands was well marked, and I was charged $3 to enter by motorcycle. As soon as I came to a pull off, I did. It was astounding. Before me was a panorama of rugged, canyon-type, striped craters and ridges stretching the reaches of my imagination. If I could visit the moon, this is what I might expect to see.

There were people and RVs all over the parking area, and short trails leading out onto ledges and precipices. I felt the sun shining down, replacing my goosebumps with welcomed warmth. Strangers were looking at me as if I was nuts, in all that leather, but they haven't been exposed to the elements at high speeds, as I had been all day.

I pulled out my Nikon camera, and asked a man in his fifties if he would take my photograph, with the Badlands in the background. "I have all these pictures with my bike in front of all kinds of places, but not me, too." I explained.

He took my automatic-everything, just aim and fire camera, and obliged me.

I strolled out onto a footpath, and wished I was wearing shorts under my leathers, instead of long johns, so that I could hike. Funny, all day I was grateful for the warm attire.

It wasn't long before I had to get back in the breeze, so I set off and followed the spectacular and curvaceous Route 240. I had to keep pulling over into the overlooks to gawk, and absorb the wondrous vistas surrounding me. This place is unreal. Some areas within appear to have come from a time when Earth was still a stellar embryo, and I could imagine dinosaurs stomping around seeking a place to hatch their eggs, or find a mate. The Badlands were so named because the earliest settlers learned the indian words for the region translated to "bad lands to cross."

For the first time since leaving home, I felt the tugging pull of an intense emotion. Loneliness. Until now, I luxuriated in my solitude, but now I missed having a comrade to share in this experience with me. There was no way I could adequately explain the terrain, or the elation of being here after riding two thousand miles on a motorcycle, to get here. I took more pictures and attempted to squelch this sad, yet significant mood.

At one pull-off, I heard a motorcycle passing by. It was Al and Janey on their Harley. They spotted me, and Janey waved broadly to me, and they continued on their way. Eventually, we found each other again. I whispered a thank you, to higher powers.

"Hey, girl! Isn't this something else?" they greeted me, and together we stood and gazed around in awe. "We got a room, no problem, and came back to ride through here, before it gets too late."

It's not like they're my best friends or anything, but at the moment I felt like I was at a reunion. Now I had someone to "ooh and ahh" with. Not only that, but they were riders that had indeed traveled a couple of thousand miles to arrive here, too. They could relate to the overwhelming emotion that this unworldly place evoked.

Al mentioned that he could sure go for a steak. We were nearing the end of the scenic tour, and it was past supper time. After a split second of hesitation, I blurted "Mind if I join you? I could sure use some company, if you wouldn't mind."

"Why, sure. What's at Wall Drug? Do you suppose they have steaks there?" Al inquired.

"I don't know, but I would guess they do. Let's go." We took one last look around, then left on our bikes together, a Harley and a rice rocket. I felt privileged to ride with them, glad I hadn't stereotyped them as 'typical Harley riders.' So many times I get dissed by H.O.G. riders, just because I don't have the 'right' kind of bike. But not these two.

We followed the signs to Wall Drug, and found a place along the congested street to park, side by side. The three of us entered the mall-like Wall Drug, and with the help of a directory, found the diner. Western art hung all over the walls, and pillars of wood were carved into famous cowboy figures. The perimeter of the room was decorated with dozens of cattle brands, such as Double D, Circle M, Bar T, etc. The dining room also contained beautiful stained glass lamps which hung from the ceiling, illuminating the place. There was a hustle and bustle, and overall noisiness about the cafeteria style restaurant. We picked a table, and looking like the bikers that we are, ordered our individual meals. I was brave, and ordered a buffalo burger, which looked and tasted suspiciously like a cheap, frozen hamburger, that was overpriced. The *free water* tasted sulphuric, no wonder it was free! So, for my unsolicited restaurant review, I'd say, atmosphere: good, and food:lousy.

The meal was devoured, nonetheless. We deposited our plastic utensils and baskets, and headed out to the numerous shops that comprise Wall Drug. It was indeed a place where you could locate any type of souvenir you wanted. Janey picked out fifteen postcards for a dollar. Out back was a courtyard with all kinds of things to take your picture with, a stuffed bison, a life-sized statue of a saddle bronc, and more. I climbed on the back of a giant jackalope, for a silly photo, and took a picture of my new southern friends.

We got a lot of laughs trying to understand each other's regional accents. Luckily Janey was able to translate much of what her husband and I said to each other. We had a hard time without her help.

"Huh?"

"I *said,* 'What?' "

"I can't understand," which to me sounded like, "Ah cay-ent unner-stay-en."

"Never mind."

But then Janey would come to our rescue. "He said . . . " translation. Talk about communication gap.

All of a sudden it was dark. I had to get a move on. I still had to find a place to sleep. Back at the bikes, we exchanged addresses and promised to be in touch once in a while. After a big hug between Janey and me, and a tight handshake from Al, I watched the two of them in their fancy chaps and jackets mount up and pull out.

Time to get situated for the night. It was late, but not to worry, there were tons of campgrounds, and billboards with directions to point me to them.

Rapid City is about forty miles west of Wall Drug, and I planned to set up camp at one of the many campgrounds on the outskirts. On the approaching highway where I anticipated making my selection based on all the billboards, I discovered that the vast array of signs were just dark silhouettes against a starless sky. That was a surprise. Back east, billboards are illuminated after dark. I hadn't figured on this. The structures were far enough off the road, that my headlight didn't touch them. Well, I had a CampBook inside my tankbag. When I got closer to the metro, I would take a look at it. I kept my eyes peeled, so that I wouldn't inadvertently drive by a place to spend the night.

In the distance, Rapid City sparkled with a zillion lights, so pretty and inviting. Still, no clue as to where I was going to camp. It was after nine when I left Wall Drug. Now it was approaching ten o'clock, and I was approaching the big city. As I got closer, some of the billboards were lit up, but they were useless to me. Hotels, fast foods, casinos and such, and a few RV parks, which are more like resorts, than places to lay down for the night.

I was getting cold and worried. How could I have been so careless and irresponsible? I drove into the city, pulled over to look at my CampBook, then drove out the way I'd come from, to check something out. This went on for at least an hour. I found a campground, and rejected it, because the price for a tent site was seventeen dollars. Too much money. I searched some more, and tried to fight the chill I was experiencing. Every muscle was clenched tight and I was beginning to shiver. In and out of the city I cruised, and eventually came upon a sign advertising a KOA. I'll take it!

Where the heck is Wall Drug? Leave the Badlands of South Dakota at Exit 10, and learn the history of the Hustead family business, which started during the Great Depression. In order to attract customers, they offered free water. Today Wall Drug Store is a huge tourist trap. Incidently, Jackalopes do not exist!

I found the Kampground Of America and entered wearily. It was late enough to warrant self-registration. There were a couple of tent sites available, and as I contemplated the price, eighteen dollars, I stood shivering, trying to get my fingers to work, so that I could fill out the papers. Then I heard it, loud and clear.

There was a racetrack beside the campground, and this was a race night. Cars were whizzing by, roaring and screaming, a race had just begun. *No way.* I wasn't staying here. I'd never sleep. There's no way I was paying eighteen bucks, being this tired, to be kept up half the night by race cars. I left.

In the city, I saw a series of signs that I followed until I was led to the National Forestry Department Headquarters. I thought, even if they weren't open, I could look at a map, or snag some handouts that would help me know where to go. Someplace natural, not all concrete and amenities. Plus, even if it was closed, maybe I could go into a lobby and get warm. Heck, I'd even sleep on a bench inside if I could. I was that desperate.

I pulled into the Headquarters to find the doors locked tight. There was no information that I could see. I paced around, then got back on my Pony. I tried to backtrack, but got tangled up in the metropolis. I couldn't find my way back to any place familiar. The more I tried, the more hopeless I became.

I began to have my doubts. What am I trying to prove? Here I am traipsing around the country, in worlds unknown, all by myself, with limited funds, on a motorcycle, in the elements. I *don't* want to ride all night. I'm cold, really cold, and tired. This is not a fun span of hours.

But, I had so much fun today. The museums . . . the day's ride across a state I'd never before been in . . . riding my cycle at a slant through a steady wind blowing across the terrain . . . Badlands . . . meeting new friends . . . What a way to wrap it all up.

Still not getting any closer to sleepytown, I began to fatigue, and my resolve to rough-it started to weaken. Under the circumstances, I began to look for a cheap motel. The cold was affecting my judgement, and so the first place I came upon, I stopped at.

A handsome, black man behind the desk in the lobby, looked up to see a young woman enter, clad in black leather, warm heavy gloves, and a red plaid scarf.

"How much for a room for one?" I stammered, removing my gloves to rub my hands together.

"Eighty-seven dollars."

"Oh, that's way too much. Man, I'm so cold. Would it be okay if I just sit here a minute until I warm up? Maybe use a ladies room?"

"Certainly. You do look a bit chilled. Would you like some coffee? Let me get you some. You can use the bathroom, through that door." The man was a dark angel.

When I came back into the lobby, he had a styrofoam cup of hot coffee, and a small carton of flavored cream. "Would you like cream?" he asked.

"Yes! Real cream! Not that powdered crap that ya get around here. Thanks so much." I cupped my hands around the beverage, and inhaled deeply. Never before had a hotel lobby felt like such a haven.

When I asked for a second cup, the host smiled. "Yes, but it will cost you some answers. I want to know, what's a young, pretty girl like you doing, riding a motorcycle in the middle of the night?

Where's your accent from? Where are you going? What's your story?" He disappeared to refill my cup.

I told him I didn't plan well today, and couldn't find a campground once it got dark. There was one campground, Berry Patch, that if I could just get back on the big highway, I would be able to find, but I was lost in the heart of the city. I didn't know how to get back on the big highway anymore.

The man pulled out a city map, spread it on the counter, and together we located the Berry Patch. He gave me directions to get back on the Interstate, bless his soul. Feeling ready to face the night, perked up from the caffeine and warm again, I bundled up and walked out of the Best Western.

"You're a brave girl. Have a great journey, and be safe," he called out from behind the counter. It's guys like him that make me unafraid, and reinforce my faith in humankind.

The directions were accurate, and with relief I saw the Berry Patch exit ahead. This was the same place I'd left hours ago because of the cost. Now I prayed for an available tent site, so I could gladly pay seventeen dollars. Had I known I would have had this much trouble, I would have stayed here when I got here originally.

I parked my bike on site T-4. It was ten past one in the morning. By now I was cold again, and hurriedly dismantled my pack as quietly as possible. By the light of my headlamp, I set up my tent. I dashed to the bathroom, brushed my teeth, changed my clothes and crawled into my down sleeping bag within fifteen minutes of my arrival. What a relief. I was exhausted, but wound up like a coiled spring. At long last, I slipped off into dreamland.

Miles: 350

es-ca-pade   A usually adventurous action that runs counter to approved or conventional conduct.

CHAPTER 4

POWDER RIVER PASS
July 1–2   Days 15–16

*B*efore the early morning light, a train rolled on by, and nearly shook my tent down. I sat up to watch it pass. The tracks were about a hundred feet away. It wasn't too much later when I heard the sound of my neighbors stirring. I took a deep breath then stuck my head outside the tent. "Hi. I'm sorry I set up so close to you all last night. I got in, in the middle of the night and couldn't see very well. If you want to help me, we can both grab two corners of the tent and drag it further back, it's not staked down."

The man laughed and said, "Oh no! No problem. Hope we weren't making too much noise over here."

As the sun got higher, my tent became warmer. Next door, I heard the man ask "Did you see the girl that rides that motorcycle, son?"

"No. But I wish I did." A young man's voice replied. I couldn't waste any more time trying to sleep. I gathered together everything I would need for a shower and headed for the shower house.

The bathroom was large, well lit, and clean. The shower stalls each had a dressing room, and the water was hot. At least the camping fee reflected its expenditure. This shower house could be mistaken for a woman's locker room in an upscale gym.

I braided my hair in two braids, indian style. I felt refreshed and excited to begin this day. As I approached my site, there was a guy squatted down inspecting my cycle.

He apologized, "I hope you don't mind. I'm just looking."

"Gosh, no. I don't mind. Hi. I'm Dee."

"Disc brakes . . . What's this—a five hundred?" He seemed to know. We talked bikes for a few minutes, then he was called back to his site, next door.

They were the perfect family. Father, Mother, Son and Daughter. Their boy was on leave from the service, so the whole family picked him up, and they would spend his time off camping and sightseeing. They were taking off to do some mountain biking. They told me to go ahead and use their picnic table, as my site lacked one.

I began my procedure of breaking camp, then fixed my breakfast of tea and instant oatmeal. I spread my paperwork before me on my neighbors table. First I marked yesterdays route on my maps, then wrote in my journal. I listed my expenditures, as I did every day. I overspent yesterday, almost doubled my day's budget, but, it had been a great day, except for the last part.

Still, last night taught me a lesson.

There were some responsibilities, I realized. My trip was not entirely care-free.

#1. Secure a place to sleep as early as possible, or know where I'm going to spend the night, before I get there.

#2. Track each day religiously, on maps, in journal, and record expenses. Too much happens in a day, to remember it all.

The sky was a gorgeous blue, and I anticipated a quick trot over to Bear Butte State Park, where I wanted to camp and hike. I finished packing, and departed.

According to Cheyenne religion, a prophet named Sweet Medicine received the tribe's four sacred arrows and four commandments on Bear Butte. (Rhymes with "cute") Also, the Souix revere Bear Butte as the place where the Great Spirit appeared before Chief Crazy Horse in the form of a bear.

Today the mountain is a place for ceremonies and worship by Native Americans. Visitors are asked to respect the privacy of groups and individuals who come to practice their religion and rituals.

I arrived in Sturgis, and cruised around, up and down, checking it out. I stopped at a motorcycle shop, surprised that it wasn't Harley-Davidson, and solicited some help to get my bike onto the center stand. My ninety pounds of luggage made that task difficult, but I needed to lube my chain. From there I got directions to Bear Butte.

When I got there, the first thing I did was scout out the campground. There were fifteen sites, on a loop, with the Bear Butte in plain view. I had to ride one mile on a gravel road to get there.

Carefully. I went to the registration area. The honor system was used here. A sign instructed would-be campers to select a site, set up, and return to register within one hour of arrival. Then, you'd put six dollars into an envelope provided, and fill out the form on the envelope, then drop it into a slot in a hollow post. Later a ranger would come along, and verify.

I didn't have the exact amount. I had to break a ten. There were only a couple of sites occupied, but the residents were out sightseeing. I could buy my pass at the Visitor's Center, and get change there.

I mounted my Red Pony, and drove back along the dirt road, towards Bear Butte. There was a long winding road leading uphill to the Visitor's Center. On it was a light layer of sand, again demanding caution while driving. When I rounded one bend, I came upon a tiny sign.

BUFFALO ARE DANGEROUS
STAY IN YOUR VEHICLE

"Nice touch" I thought.

The road curved back, and what I saw caused some concern. There at the edge of the road, was a buffalo! Not just any buffalo, either. She was a mama buffalo, and beside her was a tiny image of herself. She lowered her head, protectively. I worried. Ten feet beyond, there was another mother-baby pair, and she too, watched me suspiciously. There was no fence between us. I rolled off the throttle in an attempt to keep my engine as quiet as possible. They were so close, I could get a great picture, but, NO WAY! I was too vulnerable. I was on a road covered with sand, on a motorcycle, just beyond a sign warning people to stay in their vehicles! My vehicle did not seem too safe, at the moment. I tried to squelch the butterflies in my stomach, as I inched my way past that closest mama buffalo.

My heart was pounding. She appeared to be larger than my packed up Pony and me. She chewed a mouthful of tall grass, and turned her head as she followed me with her eyes. Whew. I made it.

At the Visitor's Center I bought my park pass, got change for my camping fee, and viewed the displays within. When I got back to my bike, I hung my camera around my neck for easy access, hoping I could quickly snap a picture of the buffalo when I backtracked.

She was farther away, and I was able to take a photo without alarming her.

My next mission was to buy some groceries and water at the grocery store in town. Inside the market, I was amused by all the people wearing Harley-Davidson tee shirts, while their pick-up trucks waited outside. These people were looking right through me and my leathers as if I didn't exist. It was obvious that I was the rider of the jap bike parked outside, but, I got the feeling that because it wasn't a Harley, it didn't count. I wanted to scream, "Hey, I'm more of a biker than all of you. How can you diss me like this?" But, I just went about my business and got the heck out of that Sturgis store.

Once I'd set up camp, I changed into hiking attire. Bear Butte was waiting for me to climb to its summit, and it was a gorgeous day.

The summit of Bear Butte arose from the surrounding plains at 1,400 feet. Native Americans still travel from far and wide to worship and participate in traditional ceremonies on the mountain. As I dismounted, and removed my leather pants I could hear the beat of drums and the haunting echo of sing-song chanting wafting up from a meadow in the distance. There below, I could see a huge wigwam, and four smaller ones, a central hearth with smoke curling upward, and a score of people milling around, some in tribal costume, and some in jeans and flannel shirts. I watched for a few minutes, to implant the scene as a memory. I would honor the "no picture-taking" ethic.

There was an information board which I perused. A couple of trails guided the way to the top, and hikers were warned to stay on the trails, and to offer Native Americans respect and privacy. I chose to hike the trail indicated to be the most strenuous. With my camera in one hand, and a small bottle of water, I set forth, at my usual ground-eating pace. With each stride, my amulet bounced gently against my sternum.

As I continued forward, I couldn't miss the presence of unusual ornaments hanging from branches of trees and bushes along the trail. There were weather-beaten bandanas,strips of cloth material, in various degrees of fray, tiny leather pouches such as the one I wore around my neck, beads, and feathers. Even without an explanation, one could feel the aura and spiritual significance of each individual offering, as if disturbing it may cause a prayer to go unanswered, somewhere.

I wondered, who put this one here, and why? Or that one, the light blue "rag" with tiny yellow flowers . . . did that represent the spirit of a little girl, and protect her in some way? Not knowing the traditions, I could only wonder.

After a while, even though the air got cooler as I climbed higher, I started to feel the warming effect of exercise. I took my flannel shirt off and tied it around my waist, then continued on my way, stopping now and then to take in the scenery. Occasionally I overtook small groups, or pairs of hikers, and sometimes on the narrow trail, somebody would have to step aside to let others get by.

The trees became more stout, twisted and rugged the higher I got. There were little flowers growing in clusters among the many rocks that lined the trail. Many were unfamiliar to me, but I learned that the ones most prevalent were Blue Bells, and it was easy to see how they got their name.

There were a couple of resting places, with benches and a porch-like platform, affording a rewarding panoramic view. As I approached one, a family was leaving it to head down. "You're almost there, ten more minutes to the top," they encouraged.

Spread out before me was a flat, green, fertile landscape. The Plains Indians once used this place as a lookout to scan for buffalo.

After a few minutes' contemplation, I continued up the trail. It didn't take me long to reach the summit where there were more people catching their breath, and taking in the scenery. I sipped at my water, and listened as different landmarks were pointed out. My skin was moist with perspiration, and in the moments following, goose-bumps covered my bare arms. Time for my flannel shirt again. Everybody left except me, and I used this time alone to sing a fitting song and allowed my voice to carry across the land.

I missed my friend Lorrin. She and I used to hike together often, and then we'd sing. She would've loved this place, with its Native American spirit, and the South Dakota view. She was one person I really enjoyed hiking with, because she, too, kept a quick pace, and did not tire easily. I realized that I probably missed her even more, because I knew that when I returned home, she wasn't going to be there. She moved to Maine right after I left home. I allowed myself some time to think about her, and to miss her. I held my amulet close to my chest, remembering how she carved a symbol for *Strength*, into a smooth yellow stone, for me. I could feel her spirit, and knew that every time I went hiking, and especially if I climbed, I would remember her.

Taking the trail down required caution. Much of the trail was preserved by the use of stone, and with downhill momentum, one could easily twist an ankle, if careless. Still, I was able to catch up and pass many people on my way down, as I had done on my way up. The exercise felt great. I hadn't had an aerobic workout since I set forth on this journey, and couldn't think of a better way than this.

As I neared the base of the trail, the paraphernalia in the trees became more concentrated, than it was at higher elevations. The vegetation changed again, became somewhat less harsh, and meadows of yucca and columbine skirted the last part of the path.

Glad to see that no one had helped themselves to my leather jacket or pants, I got dressed for my jaunt back to my campsite. There was a pay phone outside at the Visitor's Center, so I stopped to make a call. I had to make a reservation at a hostel in Wyoming, where I planned to spend the following night.

When I returned to my campsite, I saw a couple, and two kids that I recognized as some of the people I saw on the mountain. The gal spotted me, and waved. When they had finished setting up their camp, she took a walk over to meet me.

Her name was Sue, and she was just beautiful. For some reason we found ourselves talking about rough spots in life, and trials and how we have dealt with problems and overcome them. Her two kids were busy playing around with a length of rope, and had tons of energy leftover, even though they had just climbed that mountain.

Sue asked about my motorcycle, and I noticed she was wearing a black tank top, with lace around the edges. It read Harley-Davidson. She was amazed that I was here, on my own. I was pleased that she had come by to talk to me.

We both were wearing very short denim cut-offs, and I had a bikini-type top on, and her legs appeared strong and muscular, like mine. She had blue eyes and brown hair, and, with no make-up, was a knockout.

As we talked, a ranger came by repeatedly trying to take orders for firewood. I told him if he was giving it away I would take some. Sue sent him over to her site, to her boyfriend.

She asked me, "Aren't you ever scared, all by yourself?"

"No, not really. I mean, I won't let myself get scared. Why ruin a good thing by worrying?" It's so hard to explain.

We talked some more, but as the sun lowered, so did the temperature. Wanting to change clothes we split up, and Sue invited me to share her fire. I felt like it at first, but I sat down to write a long letter to my buddy at home, which I promised I'd do every week-end. By the time I finished his letter, I was tired.

Over at their site, about two hundred feet away, I could see the fire, but, didn't want to intrude on them, so I just went into my tent. I gazed out of the opening, which I deliberately set up so that the opening faced Bear Butte. Outside my back window, there was a cow pasture. This is the life. This is what I came here for.

Miles: 78

The morning sun greeted me warmly. There would be no shower for me this A.M. The only running water was found at an outside spigot, near the bathrooms with pit toilets. I stretched my bod, then began the ritual.

Down with the tent, roll up my sleeping roll and put everything away, load it all on the bike and look around one last time to see if I've forgotten anything. Sue and her clan were getting set to go, too, and we waved to each other as they drove off in their mini-van.

Today I looked forward to seeing Deadwood, and the town of Lead, pronounced "leed." Also, there were the Black Hills, Mount Rushmore and Crazy Horse Monument, in construction at the moment. Needle's Highway attracted me, and Custer was reputed to have herds of buffalo. After all this, I would enter Wyoming, and make my way to the hostel in Thermopolis, about four hundred miles away. It would be a long day's ride, but I was raring to go.

Today I would be able to forsake the Superslab in favor of secondary highways. In a short time, I was cruising through Deadwood, with its storefronts lining the main street, and houses stacked up the steep hillsides. Next, I entered Lead, and stopped at a local attraction, a train depot. I needed to use a restroom. Ignoring the strange looks I got from the tourists, I drank my fill of water, straight from the tap, located the toilets, then was back on the road, southbound for the next forty miles, through the Black Hills National Forest, before heading west again.

During this time, I would be able to view Mount Rushmore, or so I thought. I came to a three-way intersection, and wasn't sure which way to go. I rode a few thousand yards, then decided, nah, I've gotta go the other way. I went 'the other way,' and doubted my choice. At the intersection I pulled into a little store, to review my map and get my bearings. I did not have a detailed map of the state, and could not make a determination. I asked two men that were pouring water into their car radiator, and thought I understood their directions, but on the road became confused again.

I went up and down those three roads, gravitating back to that shop so many times, that all three roads began to look familiar, yet wrong. In frustration, I ultimately picked one road, and stayed on it, completely missing the famous Mount Rushmore. When I realized that I wouldn't lay eyes on the ultimate patriotic sculpture, I didn't let that trouble me. I knew what to expect once I got there. Truly, the purpose of my journey was to discover the hidden treasures of our country.

It did strike me as ironic, however, that I couldn't find the erection of rock, where a man's pupil is as big as me. Funny, I was "right under its nose" and absolutely, thoroughly unable to get there. Oh, well.

The time wasted as I searched in vain, I made up for by bypassing a stop at Custer State Park, and driving past Jewel Cave National Monument. It was under blue sky dotted with fluffy clouds, that I came to the state line. I pulled over to the side of the road, and shot a photo.

WYOMING—LIKE NO PLACE ON EARTH

There, with bluffs in the distance, hung the sign, with a bucking bronco and cowboy in front of a mountainous background. I have arrived.

I continued along my way, having decided to take a side trip a bit out of my way, in order to visit Devil's Tower. In this day and age, many people see this geological wonder and think of the movie "Close Encounters of the Third Kind." But, historically, this imposing monument had a far greater significance.

What science describes as a sixty million year old formation of molten magma, which forced its way, through the softer earth layers, later being exposed as a column of rock as the softer layers surrounding it eroded away, is explained by the indians in a legend, passed on from generation to generation, involving romance, loyalty, battle, magic, and a giant bruin. To make a long story short, the tower's vertical crevices and fissures are said to be the result of a jealous bear scratching madly as he tried to climb to the top, in vain.

In 1906, Devil's Tower was the first designated National Monument in our nation. Had I gone to Mount Rushmore and Chief Crazy Horse, I would not have made it to this place. Because I never watched the movie, featuring this natural skyscraper, I didn't know what to expect. I cruised on a road of ill-repair, in the direction of the place. Soon, it loomed into my field of vision, and then I was there.

The parking lot was busy, being a Sunday, and all. I spied another motorcycle, and parked beside it. Above me, the sky had turned gray, and thunder rumbled ever so quietly. The air was moist and cool.

Visitor's Centers are invaluable, and I went inside to use the facilities, then to

Usually, I ride with shorts on underneath my leathers, so that when I stop to eat, hike or sightsee, I can get comfortable easily. Another couple riding motorcycles took this picture in the parking lot at Devil's Tower in Wyoming, before they took off.

educate myself about the history, flora and fauna, legends and future of the Devil's Tower, to better appreciate what I have come to see. Apparently, the huge plug of igneous stone is an excellent harbor for approximately ninety species of birds, many of them, birds of prey, including bald and golden eagles. Expert climbers scale the walls for an unforgetable challenge, much to the delight of those of us below, lucky enough to see through binoculars.

When I crossed the parking lot, to take the path leading to the tower of stone, I met the couple that was riding on the Harley I had parked beside. They were from Florida, and we commented on each other's bikes, and our method of packing our luggage. We hiked the short trail to the base of Devil's Tower together.

Tiny specks floated near the top, hawks and prairie falcons. Spectators with field glasses pointed to dots of bright color, hardly noticeable to the naked eye, where rock climbers clung to the side, and laboriously calculated their every move. No words were spoken between me and my momentary companions. We only stood, with our heads cranked backwards, looking up at this visage of Mother Earth.

The low rumble of thunder and light sprinkle of rain, was said to be an almost continuous occurance here. No wonder Native Americans revered this place as one of great spiritual significance. There was something ominous and powerful about its existence.

Filled with awe, I turned to go. The day was half over, and I hadn't gotten very far yet. I backtracked along the road, until I came to the place where I'd turn westward once again. I had to traverse a stretch of the Interstate for about a hundred miles. It was not tough to take, though. Unlike the same I-90, back home, here, the traffic was spread out, there actually was scenery, and the air I breathed smelled fresh, not like fumes.

When I got hungry, I stopped at a restaurant named Cowboy Kitchen, and took my break. While I waited for my Burrito Supreme, I looked over the gift shop. I found a bandanna with a western print and splurged. This would be a useful souvenir. Lunch was fabulous. I poured on the hot sauce, and savored each mouthful, then enjoyed an ice cream dessert, with coffee. In the rest room, I brushed and flossed my teeth, and felt ready to face the day again.

Some motorcycles have radios. Most touring bikes do. Mine does not. What may seem like an extravagance, has begun to make more sense to me at this point. I am going to drive myself crazy, singing. Inside my helmet, I can belt it out, and I even sound pretty good, to myself. The problem is, I'm getting tired of the same old songs, over and over again.

Every touring motorcyclist has had the overwhelming urge to sing certain songs that come to mind. I bet, if you've been on the road for as much as a two or three day trek, that you've sung at least half of these tunes to yourself, in the privacy of your helmet.

America the Beautiful   God Bless America
Born to Be Wild   Country Roads
Ramblin' Man   Riders On the Storm

and any tune that features whatever State you're in.

Okay, you understand what I mean. These songs just creep into your consciousness, and leak out. No matter what you do to try to quit, you just can't help it.

So, it's been days and days I've been on the road, and I'm tired of these songs. I started singing all the songs I know, or thought I knew. Many times I had to make up my own words, because I can't recall. Most of the songs I was singing on this day entertained me, and the miles fell behind me, one after the other.

Here and there I came upon an eyesore. Out in this spacious land, it seemed like everybody would leave their dead and dying vehicles in these fields, to rust and rot. No recycling, no auto salvage, no crushing the metals to be used for something else. Only acres of junk cars and trucks, spoiling the way I expected "the wild west" to appear.

Just before darkness fell, I stopped in Buffalo to get a bite to eat, and use a restroom. I stopped at a country store, and asked for a thick slice of hard salami, and another of cheese. I had some rolls leftover, and would make myself a simple sandwich.

"We can only sell you a half a pound or more, Ma'am." The guy behind the counter told me.

I made a face. "You can't sell me a thick slice, but you can make a sandwich to order? C'mon, be real."

"I'm sorry, but I don't want to get in trouble, and I'm not allowed." He turned to a waiting customer. "What can I do for you?" he asked as they placed their items on the counter.

I growled under my breath, then went to the ladies room. It would be dark soon, meaning it would get colder. Moreover, I was going onto a mountain pass of 9,666 ft. elevation. I pulled a pair of sweat pants on, over my leather pants, then went out into the store again, to figure out what I would buy for supper.

I selected a pint of tequila, some beef jerky, some nuts, and a Coke. Not much, but it would do. Twilight was approaching when I went back outside. I bundled up well after sticking my supper into my pack. Now I was ready to cover Powder River Pass, through the Big Horn mountains.

Definitely a mountain road, it curved and climbed its way through thick pine forests. Practicing safety skills I learned in the Massachusetts Motorcycle Riders Education course, I looked through each turn, and pressed on the handlebars in the direction I wanted to go, keeping my speed reasonable and legal. Occasionally someone in a pick-up truck or a beat-up old car would sail past me crossing into the other lane. I kept imagining that around each blind curve another vehicle could come careening my way, in my lane. This kept me alert, and made me thankful for the hours I spent on that training range honing my skill as a rider, last spring.

As the elevation increased, the occasional traffic I encountered, decreased. After I'd traveled thirty miles, a car came up on my rear-end, and made it evident I was in his way and holding him up, but there was nowhere I could pull over to let him pass, and up here the road had narrowed enough that he didn't pass immediately. Instead he drove too close behind me. I tried to put some space between us, but my Interceptor wasn't responding.

Flicking my throttle didn't cause a boost of speed, like I was accustomed to. This caused me some concern. At some point he'd had enough, and crossed the double yellow line and stepped on it. I let him go, quite relieved, but still my motorcycle's performance bothered me. She seemed to be losing power, altogether now.

I have been questioned in the past about how my bike holds up during mountain riding, and the answers always the same. "This bike is great. Everything I ask of it, it does, no problem. Especially in the mountains, because it handles so well."

Given the situation I was in, I mulled this over, and the answer came to me. I've never ridden her in elevation greater than maybe 5,000 ft., except for the Blue Ridge Parkway, which enforces a strict speed limit. In other words, although I was in high elevation I didn't place a high demand on my machine, and she handled it just fine. Today, however, I was already up to more than 8,000 ft. and I realized I was going to have to adjust the idle.

Just about the same moment I had that all processed, my bike chugged out. Scary. I rolled over to the edge of the road, and parked, leaving the lights on. Before I left home, I'd learned how to adjust the idle, so I crouched down, stuck my hand in by the hot engine, and carefully turned a tiny knob a quarter turn, the way the guys at the shop taught me.

The engine cranked strongly, but didn't turn over. Fearful of flooding the engine, I waited ten seconds (as per my owners manual) and tried again. She wouldn't start. Time to take a break, I reasoned.

That's when I looked at my odometer, then looked at my gasoline log. Oh, no. How stupid can I be? I ran out of gas! Well, not entirely, because I hadn't switched over to reserve yet, but still . . .

My day's ride was so enjoyable that I didn't realize how far I had actually driven, before I got to this Pass. I could have gotten gas, where I stopped to change, but I just didn't think I'd already blown through a whole tankful already. Duh.

Okay, well, switch over to reserve, I thought. Then what? I don't want to go back, it's at least thirty miles, so far I am only certain that I can ride twenty miles on reserve. Hm-m-m-m what to do, what to do?

It's getting quite nippy out, and the sun is long gone. It's late, and I can tell by looking at my map, that there's a town called Ten Sleep somewhere up ahead. I'm gonna take my chances, and keep on going. Besides going back, what else could I do?

My Red Pony came to life without hesitation, and I looked to the stars and fervently asked for protection, then tucked my amulet back inside my jacket. It's now or never. The seat felt cold when I mounted up, and it was cold enough for my breath to fog up the shield with each exhalation.

Twenty miles since I'd switched over to reserve, then, twenty one. Each mile crept by, slowly and agonizingly. The stars started to disappear behind dark clouds, and sometimes I would encounter light sprinkles. There was actually snow up here, off the road in gullies that evaded the sun's rays for most of the year. At least it wasn't snowing now, but I wondered if it would when I got higher.

What will I do if I run out of gas? Actually, I figured it would be mostly a pain in the neck, but I really wouldn't be in much danger. I started to think of my options. Satisfied, I narrowed them down to one plan.

I will push my bike just off of the road, enough to be seen, but not in the way. I would set up my tent, on top of my tarp, and crawl into my sleeping bag, and try to sleep. I know that it's warm enough,

I would be well protected from the cold, within it. Hopefully, a ranger, or a trooper would come along to kick me out, and then I would be rescued. That's why it would be such a pain, because I'd have to go through all the trouble of setting up camp, and breaking it down again, with numb and trembling hands.

Still, I hoped that wouldn't happen.

Twenty-eight miles. How much further can I go on reserve? Where is Ten Sleep? Thirty-two miles. I saw a sign and when I got closer my heart sank.

TEN SLEEP - THIRTY MILES

Oh God. I'm not gonna make it. That will make sixty-two miles on reserve fuel. There's no way. I can't believe I didn't get gas before I came up here. Thirty more miles? I'm so cold I don't even want to drive another three miles, but, I've got to. Thirty will take an hour, at least.

Every time I crested a hill, I pulled in the clutch and coasted down as far as I could in an effort to conserve fuel. This certainly is a challenge in endurance, and determination, not to mention keeping a cool head. With every curve I have to remind myself to stay steady and calm.

TEN SLEEP - TWENTY-TWO MILES.

So close, and yet so far. I continued on, thankful for each mile gone by, yet dreading each new one. I kept talking to myself, or praying, whatever you'd call it. Every few minutes I'd reach down and pat the side of my gas tank.

"I'm sorry, Pony. I've never starved you before, and I'm so sorry about tonight. Please, *please* pull through for me. Take me to safety. Don't die on me out here. C'mon Pony. You can do it. Just a little bit further."

Straining into the darkness, I spied a tiny sign and slowed as I got closer. There was a symbol for food and, (I believe in miracles) another symbol, for GAS. Resort ahead, it said, next left.

Next left? Correction; it was the *only left,* and that was good enough for me! I slowed down even more, and turned onto a rough drive which took me into a gravel parking lot, and there, by the side, was an ancient gas pump, standing there, like a hero.

"Thank you, thank you, thank you."

Shivering from the cold, I shakily made my way over to it. What appeared to be a restaurant/bar, was apparently where I'd pay for the gas, so I turned to walk over there, but I heard the click as the gas pump was turned on, and a woman opened the door and waved. There was darkness and distance between us, but I perceived her signal as an invitation to fill-up before paying.

With somewhat numb fingers, I unfastened and flipped my tankbag out of the way to expose the gas cap, then reached for the gasoline nozzle.

Hm-m-m, this thing is *old,* I thought. I couldn't figure out how to make the gasoline come out. There was some kind of lever that looked like it should do the trick, but I stood, shaking, with the nozzle inserted, but no gas would run. I looked over my shoulder repeatedly at the building, feeling impatient. "Come *on,* turn the damned thing *on,* will you?" Then I started to realize, the business proprietor wasn't waving for me to start pumping, she was telling me to move on, it doesn't work. It probably hadn't been in service for ages.

Someone played a bad trick on me. My hopes came crashing down. My nose had already been running, but now my throat constricted, and I felt my eyes well up with tears. I was digging in my tankbag for a napkin to wipe my nose, and dry my eyes, when a hand on my shoulder startled me.

The woman from the lodge gripped that lever, and I'm not really sure what she did, but she got the gas flowing, and explained, "You just gotta be aggressive with it, is all."

I'll say, plus having a clue how the archaic thing works would help. Anyway, she disappeared into the warmth of the building, as I proceeded to feed my Pony.

Leaving my motorcycle where it was, I crossed the lot, and country music wafted my way as I approached. I entered the warm interior, which caused my helmet shield to fog up, as I hadn't removed it yet. Through one door on my right, I looked into a dim lounge, as a guy with a guitar strummed and crooned to a room half full of customers.

Ahead of me, to the left was the cashier's counter, in a large room with a loft. Rustic woodwork adorned the walls and various hunting trophies, and wildlife paintings created comfortable visual interest.

I removed my helmet, and watched as the gasoline attendant/waitress changed her facial expression from expectation to incredulity. She was obviously taken aback by the appearance of a female face emerging from within that shell. I had not spoken a word outside, and she had assumed I was a man. *NOT.* She quickly recovered, and when I handed her my money she recoiled at my icy touch.

"Heavens! Honey, you're freezing! Please, sit and stay for a while. Do you want something hot to drink? It's on me."

With relief I expressed how for the last hour all I kept imagining was how good a cup of mint tea would taste, when I wasn't torturing myself with the prospect of running out of fuel on this God-forsaken mountain. "You don't know *how* thankful I am to see you. I could just hug you, I'm so relieved."

She called to the young woman sweeping the floor, asking her to heat some water, then motioned for me to sit down at a table. As the room temperature enveloped me, I began to thaw, and gradually loosened my leathers, eventually removing my jacket and sweater.

Meanwhile, Mrs. Cox sat with me, anxious to hear my story, because my eastern accent gave me away. She encouraged me to describe my adventure, and to explain the reason I came to be where I was at, at that particular moment.

"So, you just quit your job, and set off on this journey all by yourself? I admire your courage. Aren't you afraid?" She smiled at me, as I cupped my hands around my steaming beverage.

"For the last couple of hours I was beginning to get nervous," I admitted, then continued, "but overall, no, I'm not afraid. This is something I've decided that I need to do. I figure, I'm *more* afraid of growing old, and looking back and *wishing* I had done this when I could. What's to be afraid of? I'm strong, confident and able. I have the desire, and I believe that God is watching out for me. Tonight was a real test, though, but here you are, right when I needed you most."

I looked around at my rugged surroundings. There was most notably a huge, mountain lion, poised overhead, as if ready to spring down upon an unsuspecting guest. Below it, a framed newspaper story outlined the fate of the giant cougar, and heralded the fame of the hunter. All around me were paintings, and the like, depicting life in the wilderness. The woodwork was homey, and although I was the sole customer on this side of the establishment, I felt welcomed, and at ease.

"Where are you going? You must stay on here with us!" Mrs. Cox invited. She turned to answer a young man's query, at the door.

"Mind if I use the telephone?"

"Excuse me a minute." She left me at my table as she explained to the guy that he would have to wait, as the line was shared with the other party on the mountain. Her resort was in agreement to use the phone only during one half of the hour, and the other place was allowed to use it during the other half.

Wow, are we out there—or what? Only one phone line on the whole mountain? Man! The things we take for granted.

When my hostess returned I explained that I already had reservations in Thermopolis. At this, she tried to convince me to settle in here, but I insisted I had to go.

I was finally feeling warmer, and made my way to the ladies room, where I tugged my sweatpants off, and removed my leather pants. My thighs were cold to touch, and very quickly I put the sweats on. One valuable lesson learned . . .

Sweat pants do not help at all, if worn on top of leathers. Underneath, provided there is room, they make a great layer of insulation. As a top layer, useless. So, now that I had remedied the situation, I felt much better. I was going to have to hit the road soon. The hour was getting late.

"How far to Thermopolis?" I asked.

"Oh dear, you really are going to move on aren't you?" Mrs. Cox was such a sweet lady. She sat with me some more, and expressed genuine interest and admiration for my endeavor. "You just be careful young lady. What a treat to meet you. You keep on living your life to the fullest. Don't let it pass you by. You are doing the right thing. Before you know it, it could be too late. So much gusto for a young woman. I couldn't do it, but I truly admire your spirit."

Time to go. I stood, and pulled my sweater over my head, wrapped my scarf around my neck and put on my leather jacket. I knew it wouldn't be long before the night air would get to me, but now I was warm and comfortable. I felt as if I was leaving an old friend as we bade each other farewell at the door. I knew I wouldn't be coming back during this journey.

My motorcycle started right up, and I clambered aboard the cold seat. The gravel beneath the tires crunched, as I slowly made my way up the ascent, and turned left, to continue my trek to

Thermopolis. Fog appeared and faded with each breath, but many miles rolled by before I felt the chill settling in again. What a relief to have a full tank of gas.

I rode on in the darkness, encountering bouts of drizzle, and keeping a wary eye out for deer or other large game. The demands of the night weighed heavily. I could feel the burden, from my clenched hands, through my tightened neck and shoulder muscles, and inside my mouth, where my lips and cheeks felt cold as I massaged the inside with my tongue.

Eventually, the road ahead of me descended. Although there were still patches of snow off to the side in hollows, I sensed that I was over the highest point and hoped that I would encounter the town of Ten Sleep soon. Still, my destination was beyond there another seventy miles. I was tired and cold, but I knew that I'd have a warm place to sleep once I got to the hostel. I really had no choice. I gave up Mrs. Cox's offer to stay at the Meadowlark Lake Resort, an hour ago, and driving past Ten Sleep at 11:30 I knew how that town got its name. The town is asleep after ten! Nothing looked awake or open. I didn't waste the time to veer off the mountain pass to detour into town, I doggedly moved on.

On and on I rode, thankful that the little bit of rain wasn't enough to soak me. Each mile was beginning to feel like an eternity, and the joy of riding had somehow escaped me. I'd already logged more than four hundred miles that day, and on a crotch rocket, that's more than enough. Still, what else could I do?

Following the curve of the road, I sunk into a dip, then arose to crest a hill, and reaching the top there it was! A spread of tiny lights in the distance. Such a beautiful sight. Thermopolis lie ahead. There in the expanse of darkness in the valley before me, somewhere I had a bed waiting for me.

As I neared the region, the pungent odor of sulphur assaulted my nostrils, rising up from the numerous natural hot springs that this city boasted. Hence, the name,

Thermopolis. A marriage of the words Therm: heat, and Metropolis: a city regarded as a center of a specified activity.

Perhaps in the morning I'd be able to drag my butt out of bed and treat myself to a cleansing bath in one of the hot springs. My Hostel Guide Book indicated that sulphur springs were a feature of the Inn, if I ever got there!

With any luck, I would be able to ease my tired, stiff, cold muscles and bones into a steaming hot pool, minutes after I arrive. I kind of doubted it, but, if dreaming made me feel better for the moment, then so be it. One thing I knew, my hostel reservation was made with an Inn, set in Hot Springs State Park, home of the world's largest mineral hot springs. Daily, more than eighteen million gallons of gush forth at a steady temperature of 135 degrees.

Thinking about the warm bath surrounded by steam, did help me summons up the stamina to go the last half hour. Upon reaching the outskirts of town, I pulled over to refer to the directions to the Inn. In moments I found myself driving right up to the great Plaza Inn the Park. There was a steady drizzle going on, and I parked my cycle, and approached the front door.

It was locked! Huh? I looked at my watch and it was nearly one A.M. I peered in through the glass, and could see the lobby, and the front desk, but no one was on duty. Now what do I do?

The Inn was a huge building with several wings, and I walked around the side, to the rear. I was looking for the triangular sign indicating the Youth Hostel entrance, but did not see what I was looking for. The drizzle was developing into rain, and I headed for the front again. I noticed a motorcycle parked in the back under the overhang, and remembered the desk clerk had told me over the phone that's where I, too, could park. In disbelief, I knocked on the front door again, but there was nobody there.

Above, on the second floor, there was a light on, and laughter. Beyond courtesy, at this point, I put my fingers to my lips and let out a shrill whistle, then yelled "Hey you up there!"

Momentarily, a young man came to the window, and without wasting any time I hollered, "How do I get in? There's no one to let me in!"

He shrugged and yelled down to me, "It's too late, they're closed." He turned away, but I yelled again.

"Wait! I have a reservation here. How can I get in? I'm supposed to stay in the hostel." I realize, he didn't really care about my predicament, but I needed some answers.

The guy already tired of my intrusion, seemed derogatory towards me when he sneered, "The Youth Hostel's around the back, back there." He jerked his head in the direction I had come from, then pulled the shade.

Still, at least I knew where to look. I had to get my bike and belongings out of the rain, so I wiped the rain as best as I could off of the saddle, then rode quietly into the back courtyard. I pulled in next to another motorcycle, and collected myself. I was so glad to see another bike, because at this point I wasn't sure about the welcoming committee.

Okay, now to find the hostel section of this hotel. I tried the door directly in front of my Pony, and it opened into a tiny hall, and a set of stairs. There were a couple of doors in the hall, and I tried the one immediately to my left, and it, too, was unlocked.

Slowly, I inched my way in, my eyes already acclimated to the dark, and I could see that I was in a two-bedroom unit, with twin beds in the room that I was standing in, and a TV and large bed in the other. The room seemed totally vacant. No luggage, or any indication that any one was staying inside, but somehow, it just seemed a bit too good to be true. I used the little bathroom, before exiting.

I strode across the courtyard, and noticed another window open, this time on the ground floor, and could hear a man and woman talking and giggling. I tapped on their door, and asked about the hostel. The man who answered pointed to another doorway, and told me that was where the hostel section was.

I asked him about the room I just looked into and he laughed and said, "A TV? I don't think so. The hostel rooms are quite stark. They're over there. Good luck."

The door he indicated, squeaked as it opened into a small hall similar to the one across the way. Aha! There on the six or so doors in the hallway, were the hostel logos I was looking for. A couple of the rooms were labeled Common Area, and these were the kitchen, and the bathroom. Oh yes, stark is hardly the word, yet, it was a heck of a lot better than the predicament I could have been in, if I had gotten stuck up on that mountain.

People were sleeping in the rooms. I could hear them. I needed to sleep, too, but didn't know where. I would take care of business with the Inn come morning, but right now I had to find a bed.

I tried one doorknob, cracked the door open. Into the darkness I whispered, "Is this the hostel? Can I come in?"

At once, a male form in the darkness sat upright. A woman's voice muttered a question, sleepily, but the man told me, "Yeah, but this is a private room. Go away."

"Um, I'm sorry . . . your door was open."

Taking a deep breath as my heart fluttered with embarrassment, I crossed the hall to try a different door. This time, when I asked if it was a hostel room, I was told "This is the guy's dorm. The girl's dorm is across the hall."

Okay, process of elimination. Reaching up to knock on this door, I became aware of how I would appear to any hostelers at this moment. Clad in leather head to toe, helmet in hand, hair all damp and stringy, clinging to my red, cold face. I hoped it was too dark for them to see. I didn't want to frighten any girls, and at this hour, there was a strong possibility of just that.

I tried this doorknob, and it turned, and I gently pushed the door open, and discovered it was bound by a chain lock. Smart girls . . . safe.

"Hey, can you let me in?" I whispered as loud as a whisper can get. After waiting several seconds I tried again. "Hey! Wake up and let me in!"

Somebody stirred, then the rhythmic breathing continued.

Right about then I'd had enough. I was afraid that if I awoke the woman, she'd be taken aback by the spectacle outside her door, and it was the middle of the night. I still had to unpack some things off the bike, and didn't want to cause an unpleasant scene. Somehow, I felt the encounter would be difficult.

I went outside, and sat down at a round table under the balcony overhang, near my bike. I was drained. I was disappointed, and unhappy. No, not unhappy, upset. Ticked off that I couldn't even get a decent night's sleep, after such a trying day. That bottle of tequila sounded pretty good to me now, and I dug it out of my knapsack, along with the jerky and nuts and had my "supper." A few shots of tequila later, I folded my arms on the table and rested my head on them, to sleep.

This really sucks. I'm sitting outside, barely escaping the rain, sleeping sitting up at a table, in two or three layers of clothing, including leather, in the middle of Wyoming, with the stinking sulphur smell all around me. Not exactly what I had planned, to say the least.

Finally, I drifted off to sleep.

A dream jolted me awake. Everything about me felt stiff. I rotated my shoulders, rolled my neck around and stretched my arms. When I started to twist at the waist, I turned and faced a window, a window that belonged to the empty room I'd discovered at first. I had to pee. I tried to ignore the urge, and settled down again, with my head facing that window.

On the other side of that window is a bed, a few beds. I'm out here, cold, and inside, that room has a door that isn't locked, beds that aren't occupied. The registration desk has my name, and my credit card number, and I am outcast, outside. I can't ignore the unlocked door any more.

Furtively I tip-toed into the waiting room. I used the toilet, then feeling exactly like Goldilocks, I stretched out, in all my gear on top of the twin bed near the window. If the rightful tenants of this room show up, I'll apologize and explain my situation, and leave. Maybe they'll feel sorry for me and let me stay. I worried about 'getting caught,' but barely. I'm only gonna stay 'till I've warmed up. Just for a minute . . . I just need to lay here for a minute . . . Only a min . . .

Miles: 471

Character cannot be developed in ease and quiet.
Only through experiences of trial and suffering
can the soul be strengthened . . . and success achieved.
—Helen Keller

CHAPTER 5

LOST IN WYOMING
July 3   Day 17

The sky was barely turning gray when I opened my eyes. I was in the exact same position I was in when I laid down. My watch said it was 6:30. I made it through the night in this borrowed room. I survived, and it serves them right! Still, I cautiously sat up, taking care to be quiet. Although I never heard anyone enter in the night, I couldn't be sure. Between my exhausted state, and the tequila, I probably slept like the dead, and wouldn't have heard anyone, supposing they never noticed me in the corner. Ha! Wouldn't that be something?

Prepared to sneak out silently, I peeked through the door adjoining the two rooms. It was still ajar, and much to my relief, I discovered the bed was unmussed, and empty. Thanking the Spirit that watches over me, I stepped out of the room that sheltered me.

The Common Area was across the courtyard, and I went to take advantage of the quarters made available to hostelers. I hadn't had a shower since Saturday morning. Since then, I'd climbed a mountain, ridden more than 550 miles, and slept in my clothes. A shower was definitely in order, and then breakfast.

Before long, two women joined me in the kitchen and I shared my story, how I was traveling the USA on my motorcycle.

"And you don't have any trouble?" The younger one asked.

"Well, last night I slept on a table outside." I told them. "I didn't arrive until after midnight, and when I finally found the ladies dorm, the door was locked and I couldn't get in. I tried to wake somebody up, but then I was afraid to scare you, or make enemies, at that hour."

The older woman said, "Oh. I thought I heard something or someone in the night, but, I didn't want to get the door. You know, worrying about our safety and all. I thought I heard the door, but, oh, I'm sorry. You poor thing. It was awful out last night, rainy and cold."

"You're telling me." I replied. "I did end up sneaking into a room, for a few hours before dawn, so I'm okay. I figure, I paid to be here, so this morning I used the shower, and the kitchen, and soon I'll be on my way."

"Wow. What you're doing must be something else! Aren't you afraid? What an adventure."

We wished each other well, good times and happy travels, then I went out to my bike.

Back in the saddle, I felt surprisingly giddy. Last night, every mile was beginning to feel like torture, but now, I was rested and ready. I felt like riding again.

Yellowstone was a day's ride away. I found my way out of town easily, and discovered that the road I was on was made for motorcycling.

Canyon walls rose steeply on either side. My road twisted and curved along, following the path of a river dotted with rafts, canoes and kayaks. I was in Wind River Indian Reservation, and I was in heaven. Beauty surrounded me. The scenery went on and on. How would I have guessed that this would be such a gorgeous place to ride?

One good thing came out of my visit to the hostel in Thermopolis after all. This is what I was looking for. A drive through a fantastic location, a road that demands my attention, blue skies and the thrill of novelty.

My thoughts turned inward, as I struggled with emotions brought about by the intensity of the moment. I had to blink my eyes once in a while to clear them from the threat of tears.

Seventeen days. Here I am. I just conquered two harrowing situations, and as drained and uncertain about my circumstances as I was yesterday, I am equally satisfied with my condition today. In fact, I'm in my element.

I began to sing. It started with one song.

Oh give me land, lots of land under starry skies above
Don't fence me in

Let me be by myself in the country that I love
Don't fence me in
Let me be by myself in the evening breeze
Listen to the murmur of the cottonwood trees
Send me off forever, but I ask you please
Don't fence me in.
Just turn me loose, let me straddle my ol' saddle
Underneath the western skies
On my cayuse let me wander over yonder
Till I see the mountains rise
I want to ride to the ridge where the west commences
Gaze at the moon until I lose my senses
Can't look at hobbles and I can't stand fences
Don't fence me in.

One song led to another, and as I sang one tune after the other, I found myself further and further from the banks of the river. Although the road more or less followed, it was not right next to it any more. The canyons fell behind, and my focus point became the mountain range ahead, in the distance.

Now the ride was just that. A mere act of sitting astride my machine, and holding on and looking at the road ahead, and dreaming about the mountains beyond, which I would explore during my long awaited visit to Yellowstone Park.

Running through my repertoire of travel tunes, I ran out. I began in on love songs. So many broken-hearted love songs. I started to think about Russell, the man I'd left behind.

Loneliness crept in. Despair. Realization that part of my journey was flight. He doesn't want me, doesn't love me, won't believe in me, or offer emotional support.

My last date with him played through my mind, like an old movie. Over and over I heard our last words to each other. We were at a restaurant, a casual, brick oven pizzeria. The vibes between us were strained. I was leaving, and even though we generally only saw each other twice a month for the last few years of our time "together," he didn't want me to go.

*   *   *

I reached across the table, and laid my hand over his. I looked deeply into his eyes of blue, and told him, "I'm going to miss you. Heck, I'm gonna miss sex."

To which he replied, "You'll have plenty of opportunities for that, I'm sure."

My heart skipped a beat and I recoiled. "What's that supposed to mean?" I wanted to know.

"Well, you will." He looked away, and pushed back his chair, finished.

"Wait a minute—what's that supposed to mean? I'm supposed to grab the opportunity?"

"Opportunities." He corrected.

"Why? Is that what you're gonna do?" I was wounded.

"I didn't say that."

"I know, but you're insinuating . . . "

"Diane, forget it. You're putting words in my mouth." Signaling for the check, he added, "You're going to do what you're going to do, anyway."

I sat there with an obvious pout.

"Christ. What do you want me to say?" he appealed.

"I expected you to at least tell me you'd miss me too. Or—hurry home, anything but, *that.*" Feeling like a fool, I stood up to put on my coat. "Let's go."

*   *   *

Tears streamed down my face and I began sobbing, no holds barred. I cried as if a dam crumbled, and years worth of harbored emotions spilled forth. It felt good, too. The tears just poured over my cheeks, and I could taste them when they ran down to the corners of my mouth. I rode on this way for about twenty minutes, before I finally felt like I'd had enough. I hadn't cried for this long in ages.

Maybe this trip will break the addiction. For a long time Russ and I enjoyed our convenient arrangement. But, we were about as opposite as two people could get. As open and friendly, optimistic and overall happy as I am, by nature, he is private, skeptical, pessimistic and cynical, like a Prince of Gloom. When friends would ask me why I stay with him, I would tell them how I thought my cheeriness would rub off on him, but instead over time I learned that being around him too much only brought me down.

We couldn't even talk about the weather without an argument. We began to spend less and less time together, but when we did get together, it was evident the reason was because we felt safe with each other. We would spend the night together, or just meet for a frantic and satisfying quickie.

Carrying on like this worked out well for both of us. Neither of us had to put energy into a relationship, so to speak, and we didn't have to get physically involved with someone new. We weren't driving each other crazy, and the sex was great.

Occasionally, I would feel shortchanged, and would ask for some kind of a commitment, but he would remain silent. Four months before my departure, I got up the nerve to break the news of my plans. I had put it off for a long time, anticipating a negative reaction. His reaction was more or less what I'd expected, and after that he had a very difficult time dealing with it. We usually avoided the topic altogether, because combined, our two perceptions of what would transpire during my travels were volatile.

I told him, "I'll be gone for about four months. I'll miss about, what? —eight dates with you? Fine. When I come home, either you'll be here, or you won't. I'm not going to sit and twiddle my thumbs waiting around for you. I have a life, and goals and ambitions to achieve. With, or without you."

*   *   *

Riding along, I tried to take my thoughts off of the man, but I couldn't shake the feeling that this was a good time to be soul searching. I wondered if I was beginning to feel the effects of loneliness.

Part of me knew—it was my heart breaking, a painful process that I could only endure alone. This is something new. Now I am on my own, totally self-reliant. My best friends aren't gonna be there to rescue me, encourage me, or distract me. It's just me, and my motorcycle.

I have to cry on the shoulder of the road.

By now I was traveling on highway 26 and 286. 286 would take me all the way to Yellowstone, but I was beginning to consider the scenario. Tomorrow is the Fourth of July. Yellowstone is gonna be packed. The campgrounds will be filled, and rooms too costly, *if* I could get one.

On the other hand, Grand Teton Nat'l Park seems less well known, and I'd arrive there first. I could camp there for two nights, and commute to Yellowstone to explore it on the day in between, the Fourth of July. Yeah, that'll work. That's my plan.

Before long, the sky turned into a discouraging shade, and I found myself on the side of the road, pulling on raingear. It was only a slight mist, but I realized I was climbing to higher elevation, and already could feel the temperature dropping. I didn't want to get wet, and as anyone knows, if you wait until the rain hits, you're gonna get soaked just trying to put on the stuff that keeps you dry. Besides, that extra layer can actually help keep you warm.

I tucked my riding gloves into my tankbag, and dug out my bulky Gore-Tex pair. These were thick and warm gauntlet gloves, which reached halfway to my elbow, over the sleeves of my jacket.

The mountains that earlier loomed in the distance, were now beneath my Metzelers. Unexpectedly, I crossed the Continental Divide. At the moment, I didn't even know what that was. I looked for something obvious, like a fissure, but not wanting to pull over, I made a mental note to find out . . . what exactly *is* the Continental Divide?

Webster's New Collegiate Dictionary defines it as a "noun: a divide separating streams that flow to opposite sides of a continent" . . . this I found out later.

Hard to believe it is July, and I'm cold! There is rain falling, off and on, but I'm keeping dry. It's just that my gloves are beginning to leak. At the fingertips, four seams come together, and the rain is trickling in. My hands curve around the grips, and the Interceptor's fairing does nothing to protect the rider from wind or rain. Eventually, I learned that these fifty dollar gloves could stand some improvement. For a commute to work and home, they'd be terrific, but to cruise on tour, in steady rain, forget about it. They'll hold up nicely for the first half hour, and then the leakage begins. Still, the insulation is warm, and I am aware they offer much better protection than my every day pair.

I am cold. I yearn for a fire, and pray that I'll be able to camp at the National Park. Signs appear, inviting me to stop at the Visitor's

Center. Alright! I can stop here, inquire about camping, use the bathroom, warm up and be on my way.

I pulled into the parking lot at the Hatchet Grill and Visitor Center. Inside, there was a young guy working behind the counter. The only customer was me.

"Do you know if I have to camp at an official campground in the Park, or can I just pull off-road there and set up?" I asked the salesclerk.

"You can camp at the Park," he answered.

"Yeah, but, can I camp *away* from the campground? You know, like I was told? Out west you can just pull off the road and set up, as long as you're so far away from the road, and I don't know all the rules, and I was hoping you could help me." I rambled on.

"Well, there are campgrounds in the Park. Why don't you just go there?"

"Tomorrow's the Fourth. What if they're full? I just want to know if I *can* do it, so that if I have to, I won't get in trouble. Have you got information I can look at?" This guy just didn't understand. "Look, I've been traveling all day, I'm cold and wet and tired. I was hoping I could simply find a nice spot to set up camp, without having to deal with a lot of people. Never mind. I'll ask the Forest Ranger when I get there." I hoped I didn't sound too crabby. "Where's the bathroom?"

He indicated that it was out the door, and around to the side. Inside the ladies room, I had to strip down about a million layers before I could use the toilet. I piled my raincoat, my leather, and sweater on top of the sink, and stuck my gloves into my helmet along with my wallet, like I always did. That had become so much of a habit, I no longer even thought about it. These gloves were so enormous, though, that they stuck out of the bottom of my helmet, and I couldn't just set it down, like usual, or it would roll over, and fall. I rested it precariously on top of my pile of clothing, in the sink, then used the toilet.

When I finished, I grabbed my armload of riding gear, and walked back outside, around the building, and reentered the gift shop.

"Thanks for letting me hang around and warm up without spending any of my money!" I said.

At last I was ready to ride my last few miles for the day. Grand Teton National Park, here I come! Helmet's on, gloves difficult to put on when hands are wet . . . grrr. Slip into my little space on the saddle and I'm off.

I rode in light drizzle passing horse fields, on a wide road, until I came to a place called Moran Junction, where I would enter the Nat'l Park. Up ahead was the little Ranger Station, which I pulled up to, placing my left foot on the wet pavement.

"Four dollars, please." The female ranger held out her palm. "That will get you a seven day pass."

Slipping my right hand out of the glove, I unzipped my tankbag and lifted the cover to retrieve my wallet. What???

"Oh, shoot! I don't have any money." My heart pounded wildly. My wallet was not in its usual place!

"That's okay, we'll getcha on the way out." She assured me.

"No—you don't understand. I don't have my wallet. I lost my wallet! I have to go find it. I'll be right back." Never before have I pulled a U-ey as easily as just then.

How could I have lost it? When did I have it last? I bought gas back at Dubois, an hour away, at least. No wait—I had it at the stop I just made—didn't I? Or did I? Yes! In the bathroom. It was in my helmet, with my heavy gloves. Thank God I could clearly remember having it there at the Hatchet Grill rest stop. I definitely didn't want to have to truck all the way back to Dubois.

All these thoughts in only four seconds. I slowed my bike to a crawl, and scanned the road. I figured out what happened.

Doing the raingear thing distracted me enough that when I took my wallet and gloves out of my helmet, I set them on top of my load. When I was dressed, I grabbed my helmet and gloves, put them on, and took off. I must have driven away with my wallet sitting on top of my luggage behind me. It has to be in the gravel parking lot! There's not a lot of tourists coming in and out, and it's only seven miles. It's got to be there. Oh, pleeeease.

Still, I rode slowly, hoping to see a dark lump in the road, that would turn out to be my wallet. Seven miles takes a long time, when you're driving about ten mph. My wallet did not appear. Still, I did not fret, too much. It probably fell off the bike as soon as I took if off the side stand, or bumped out of the lot. I remembered, I cranked on it leaving the rest stop, all pumped to get settled and camped. It's bound to be sitting there, probably in a puddle, back at the Hatchet. Fine, I'll take a soggy wallet any day, over a lost one.

At last I reached the little store and restaurant. The object I sought was not in sight. I parked and dismounted, and stepped into the gift shop. The worker was on the telephone, but when he didn't immediately reach under the counter with a grin, I knew I was out of luck. I waited for him to hang up, and asked him anyway, "Did somebody turn in a wallet?" I knew the answer, though.

He shook his head, "Sorry."

I ran out to the ladies room. Maybe I left it in there. Wrong. It wasn't there. Now, the reality began to hit home. What if it *is* gone? My license, membership cards to various travel services, calling card, some cash . . . all gone. I'm fifteen hundred miles from home. Terrific.

No! I've got to stop the negative train of thinking. It has to be in the road between here, and the park entrance. Or, more likely, on the side of the road. It had to have bounced when it fell off my speeding machine.

I began the long slow trek, back toward the Park. First gear, second, back to first. Wibble-wobble, I felt like a novice rider, with my legs hanging down, like a set of outriggers. I rode on the extreme edge of the road, and every minute or so a car would veer around me. I searched the tall grass on 'my side,' and did so as if my life depended on it. In a way, it did. My fate certainly did.

The money didn't concern me too much. I had Traveler's Checks packed elsewhere, like a good doobie should. As best as I could figure, my wallet contained right around one hundred dollars, give or take a few. It was my license that concerned me the most. Getting a replacement could pose a serious setback. I didn't even know if I *could* get one, in another state. But, I couldn't be without it. Not for the scope of this trip—I had three more months to go!

I have to find it. It has to be here on the road, or in the tall grass beside it. Once in a while I'd spot a dark patch in the hay, so I'd kick down the side stand, and get off the bike, trudge down into the soaking wet grass, only to discover a worn out, flattened shoe, or a beat up fanny pack, but not my purse.

Coasting along at a snail's pace, I felt conspicuous, and less than safe. A small pick-up truck passed me, then turned around. The driver rolled down his window and called out to me.

"Are you okay? Having trouble with your bike, are ya?"

I flipped up my shield and hollered, "No. I lost something. I'm okay."

Instead of driving off, he turned around again, so that he could pull up and park ahead of me. The cab door opened, and the driver, a man perhaps sixty years of age, approached me with a hand extended. "Hello. I ride too, so I couldn't just drive by a fellow motorcyclist in need. You looked like you were having trouble."

I shook his hand, and told him I'd lost my wallet along this stretch of road not too long ago.

"I live right close by here. Let me help you look," he offered. "You traveling all by your lonesome? You sure are a long way from home. What ya go and do losing your wallet?"

"I dunno. I guess things weren't exciting enough." I said glumly.

"Hey, it's raining out and all that. Why don't you follow me to my place, and you can hop in the truck, and look for your wallet from where it's warm and dry. Then, if we find it, you're all set, I'll bring you back, give you something to eat—."

"Listen, Mister. Thanks for your offer to help, but if it's here, I'll find it. If it's not, then some body else found it. In that case there's nothing you or I can do." Something about him made me feel a little uneasy. Maybe he was just a nice guy, offering to help, but I went with my instincts, and told him I'd be okay.

He shrugged his shoulders and tipped his hat. "Okay. Being a biker and all I just wanted to help ya, and a lady biker at that. Sure didn't mean any harm in my offer. You're okay now, are ya?"

"Yes, but thank you. You're the only person who stopped to see if I'm okay."

"Yeah, well, that's because we bikers take care of each other." He wished me luck, then got in his truck, and drove away, with a toot-toot, and a wave out the window.

Each mile took about ten minutes, but to no avail. I noticed a Post Office on the right, practically at the junction. There was a lady postal clerk who provided me with a magic marker and a piece of cardboard when I explained my plight. She said I was more than welcome to post a sign, and wished me luck.

I made a sign. REWARD. WALLET LOST ON ROAD BETWEEN MORAN JUNCTION AND HATCHET GRILL. IF FOUND, PLEASE DELIVER IT TO THIS POST OFFICE ASAP

I really didn't know how I'd work this one out. The next day was a National holiday and the Post Office wouldn't even be open, but I wasn't leaving the area until the day after that anyway. I had to take a chance that someone local might find it and hoped that they'd see my sign. I posted the sign on the outside of the building.

Then I was back on the turnoff to the Park, approaching the Ranger's booth. About two hours had passed since the first time I got here. I stopped at the window, and explained that I had lost my wallet.

"I have Traveler's Checks packed deep in my luggage, if you'll let me pull over up ahead there, I can dig them out without holding anyone else up."

The ranger gave me permission, and as I parked and dismounted, I noticed another motorcyclist in bright blue raingear arriving. Digging out my Traveler's Checks was no easy procedure, and with a nod the other rider acknowledged me, as he rode by on his dual-sport BMW.

Finally, after unhooking some bungees, jostling my bags around, and retrieving one particular bag, I unzipped a series of zippers and got to the plastic folder containing several one hundred dollar traveler's checks.

Lifting the lid of my tankbag, I slipped the funds inside, climbed aboard the wet motorcycle, and pulled around to the end of the line of tourists waiting to register. "Entrance to the Park will be four dollars. We still have some camping." She stuck her head out the window and surveyed my luggage skeptically. "That's your luggage? You don't have the hard kind that you can lock? Do you have any food with you?"

"This is it. I do have a couple of packages of oatmeal, some teabags, and some Power Bars. Why?"

"This is bear country. We have very strict rules which are enforced, concerning bears and camping here. I'm going to put you in a Hiker-Biker campsite. See? You get by cheap! It's only two dollars. At your site you will find a metal box, which you will share with a neighboring site, okay?" She handed me a map, and some other papers, and began giving me instructions. "First you should read this information, then if you have any questions, come back and see me, if you can't find a Ranger to help you out."

She explained how to get to my site, Hiker-Biker A, and I left, following her directions. After cruising through a loop once or twice, trying to get a feel of the place, I spied my little clearing, and pulled in. Once I found a solid place to settle the sidestand, I went about setting up camp. The ground was all wet, but it wasn't raining any more.

I stood in the center of my clearing and turned in a circle, trying to determine where I should set up my tent. Off to the rear and side of my site was the bear box. Since I had never seen one of those before, I went over to investigate. It was much larger than I expected. It was a sturdy, metal box as large as a cedar chest, probably two feet high, two feet deep, and four or five feet long. The front wall contained two hinged doors, one on each side, equipped with tight hook-and-eye closures. There would be enough room to put lots of my stuff inside.

Turning back to the work ahead of me, I began to unpack and pile everything on the picnic table. "Next door" to me, there was a pup tent, and I could hear muffled voices, interspersed with giggles. Outside the doorway, there were two pairs of shoes. Two bicycles were locked to a tree, and I could only imagine how crowded the two people must be, inside that pup tent. But, I bet they were warm. I wasn't. I was downright cold.

Not only was I cold, but I had to go to the bathroom, so I left my site, and headed over to the little bathhouse on a path through the woods. When I crossed the road in front of my site, the BMW I'd seen earlier came slowly my way, and stopped. The driver flipped up his shield and said, "Do you know where Hiker-Biker C is?"

"Well, I'm in A, so-" I looked around, and pointed to the tiny sign that said 'C,' "You must be here, right near me! I'm over there." Indicating toward my bike across the street, I smiled.

Upon my return from the bathroom, I rummaged through my duffle bag, and pulled out my woolen hat. As soon as I put it on my head, I could feel the warmth. I thought back to the days in Ohio when I was so hot . . . now, here I was, grateful that I had the wits about me, enough to pack this hat, just in case. Here I was, still in my leathers, and my raingear, but my hands were uncovered, the cuffs of my white jacket were wet, and I needed to get set up, and stay here, in the great outdoors. No use just thinking about it.

This time, I spread out my tarp, and set my tent on top of it. Until this day, I hadn't used my tarp at all. After my tent was set up, I sat on a wet bench. Time for a break.

Just then, a tall, slim, strikingly handsome man walked right onto my camp site.

"You must be the biker at site C." I deduced.

"Yes. That is me." He commented on the weather, and looked at my bike. He had an accent which I could not place. Foreign. It sounded somewhat familiar, but when I mentioned it, he replied, "Well, where do you think it comes from?"

"I don't know. It's not German, or Spanish, not British . . . Is it French?" I should know that, but, I wasn't sure.

"No. You won't get it. It is African. I spent much time there. I now live in Colorado, but everybody says I sound different." He had a great smile, white, even teeth, olive skin, the bone structure of a model and dark hair. On top of these good looks, he had a shy demeanor. If I wasn't riding a motorcycle, he would have never approached, but, we had some tales to tell.

"So you're camping here now, and are you going to Yellowstone Park?" he asked.

"Well, I was hoping to, but now I don't know. I had a stroke of bad luck just before I got here, and I lost my wallet. I need to look for it." Suddenly that problem leaped to the front of my mind again, making me feel discouraged.

"How are you going to do that? Do you know where you lost it?"

"Yes. On the road just on the way in to the Park," and my explanation followed.

He cocked an eyebrow, "Good luck. I don't think you'll find it, though, if you didn't already."

I stood up, and began moving things around, as I still wasn't done setting up camp. He took this as a cue to leave, and as he walked away he said, "I'll see you later."

"Yes. Come on back later, if you want. Maybe we can go halfsies for firewood, and share a fire. I'm freezing!"

"Okay. That's a good idea."

"Wait! What's your name?" I called.

"Ben," he answered. "And you?"

"I'm Diane." It's easier to understand that, rather than Dee, when I'm not face to face with someone.

As he walked away, I couldn't help but notice his back view, every bit as nice as his face. Oh, boy. Calm thyself down Woman, I had to remind myself.

It was beginning to get dark, so I had to get busy. I took my sleeping bag and pad and tossed them into my tent with my clothes and other bag. My saddlebags were coming off the bike at this camp, too. They were wet enough already, even with rain covers, but, I would be here for two nights, and I had a place to stash them, out of my way.

When I opened the door on 'my side' of the bear box, I was dismayed to find it already crammed with paraphernalia. I whirled to see the pup tent nearby, with the two people inside of it, unaware of my glare.

I cleared my throat, and tried to not sound grumpy when I spoke. "Excuse me—you guys? Excuse me, but there's not enough room for my stuff over here. You guys in the tent—I'm wicked sorry, but I can't get my things put away here. Are you awake? Do you hear me?"

Finally, a zipper sounded, and a sleepy head stuck through the opening. In two seconds a man realized what I had been saying, and with some wriggling and wiggling he managed to extricate himself from the close confines of his tent, bag, and girlfriend.

We both apologized at the same time, laughed and said "that's okay" simultaneously. I felt really bad, because I didn't know where he was going to put his things, but, I had to lock some of my things up, too. I didn't want any bears coming around me in my tent.

While he was rearranging his things, a woman emerged from the pup tent. We all introduced ourselves, and with mutual respect and admiration we learned of each other's adventures.

Michael and Amy, probably in their forties, were riding bicycles long distance, camping, hiking, and visiting several National Parks in the USA. They were from Europe. I was impressed. Both of them looked well suited for the trip, and when they'd finished clearing a portion of the bear box for me, they walked off.

When my work was all done, I sat down to write. I was marking my maps, when Ben returned. Together we shared our experiences, and I learned that Ben was undecided whether he was going to Yellowstone the next day, after all, on account of the weather prediction. Because of my lost wallet, I already knew, in the morning

I was going back to look for it again. Unless I found it right away, I would not be driving to Yellowstone. I had to search for it, and I didn't know what I was going to do if I didn't find it. I was extremely discouraged, there was no hiding it.

"Ben, you're welcome to set up on my site tomorrow if you decide to check out Yellowstone. That way you don't have to risk not getting a campsite, since it'll be the Fourth of July. You can just do your thing, and if you want, you can stay here. It's already reserved, and I trust you. Feel free. If you don't, no hard feelings. It's up to you. You decide what you want to do, come tomorrow."

He thanked me, and we looked at the map some more comparing our agendas, and I offered him some tequila. He took one shot and laughed. "You can have it!"

Amy and Mike strolled onto my site, and met Ben. They offered us what was left of their supper. It was black bean something or other, and it looked gross. It was this dark brown goop, in a thick layer on the bottom of a camp pot. Ben took one look and said "No thanks. I don't think so. That looks like—well, I won't say what."

On the other hand, my stomach was growling, and I took a taste. It was spicy, and despite its appearance, it tasted pretty good, at the moment. I finished it, but I wouldn't recommend it, unless you were camping out and riding from state to state on a bicycle. They said it was a package of dehydrated camp fare. One thing it has in its favor is that it makes more than enough, compared to what the package indicates.

Michael and Amy left after I ate and I hopped on my bike and rode over to the camp store and bought a bundle of firewood. I strapped it to the back of my Pony, and returned to my site. Being a somewhat expert fire maker, I was surprised that I couldn't get the darn thing lit. The wood was a bit wet from rain, and I didn't have kindling wood. I did have some fire starter blocks, but that's all that was burning.

Ben kept telling me "It's raining," or "It's too wet out," but I wouldn't listen. I was so cold, and so bummed out. *I wanted a fire!*

"It's not that—this wood is green! It's not even seasoned. Even if it was sunny out, it would take a lot of kindling to get it going." I crouched near a flame about as big as my thumb, trying to dry a small log over it, hopelessly. "I can't believe what a rip-off this is.

Four bucks for freaking *green wood!*" I growled. I was *not* a happy camper.

Finally, I excused myself to go use the bathroom, and brush my teeth and get ready for sleep.

When I returned, Ben was gone. No wonder. I was a total grouch. Losing my wallet was a devastating event, there was no denying it, and I was being a bitch. I'd had enough of this day.

I climbed into my tent, and hurriedly undressed. Leaving my socks and sweat pants on, I crawled into my sleeping bag before taking off my two coats. My nose was cold and wet, my hands were freezing, and I was miserable.

I went to sleep wearing my woolen hat, and hoped the rain that kept sprinkling, on and off all day, would just go away by morning.

Adventure? Challenges? That's what I wanted. That's what I got. There was no doubt about it.

Miles: 225

Real difficulties can be overcome;
it is only the imaginary ones that are unconquerable.
—Theodore Vail

CHAPTER 6

THE SEARCH

The Fourth of July, 1995   Day 18

*I*t was still dark when the sad, sweet sound of coyotes carried through the morning air and reached me, stirring me away from my dreams. I opened my eyes, and closed them again, straining to hear more. For the first time in my life, I listened to the yip of coyotes in the wild. A shudder ran up my spine, but it was not a fearful thing. I felt excited, thrilled and elated. I tried to imagine them, loping across the mountainside terrain, leaping to the top of a rock pile and tossing back their heads to yowl across the valley to neighboring packs, or skipping along in a meadow, joyously running side by side with another, grabbing at a jawful of neck and shoulder fur in an expression of affection and playfulness.

Yellowstone was in the process of reintroducing wolves to the wild, but these were not wolves that I heard. High pitched yip, yip, yips, was what I was listening to, and answering yaps from another area.

This is so cool. How can anybody be scared to camp out? The idea of coyotes nearby enough for me to hear them, only made me wish that they weren't so far off in the distance. I wished I could see them.

On the other hand, I was in bear country, and the information given to me by the Rangers, instilled a grave respect for this dangerous animal. Food, and even items used to prepare food were required to be locked away in a safe place. Shampoo, perfume, lotions, etc., anything with a strong scent, could tempt a bear, and cause harm to a person trying to stop one from getting into it. Their sense of smell is so incredible, even menstruating women have special precautions to take. That was a scary thought, and I was glad it wasn't that time of the month for me.

Still, the thought intrigued me. Realistically, I figured I could count myself fortunate if I even managed to catch a glimpse of one. For some reason, I figured a bear, or wolf, or coyote, for that matter, would try to stay away from humans, not seek us out. I thought, this campground is the last place in Grand Teton National Park that a wild animal of that caliber would want to be.

Oh yeah, I'm at Grand Teton National Park! The focus of the day dawned on me, and my thoughts turned from bears and coyotes, to the fact that I had to get up and find my wallet.

In a way, I felt confident that I was going to find it. Somehow. But, I had to get up and begin my quest. Being the optimistic person that I am, I tried to convince myself that it *had* to be laying on the side of the road somewhere, and if I combed the roadside on foot, I would find it. If I didn't find it, that would mean that somebody else did. Part of me warned, that means it's all over. The other part of me justified, what comes around, goes around. How many times in my life did I find something of value, and return it to the rightful owner? Always, if there was any way I could do so.

Deep in my heart, I prayed that if someone found my purse, it would be someone like me. Someone honest, who would try to make it available to me. But how? How in the world was a person gonna find me? I'm on the road, for crying out loud. What if they mailed it to my address? That wouldn't help me much now.

A zillion thoughts ran through my head as I got out of my sleeping bag and gathered the things I needed to bring to the bathhouse. I unzipped the tent, and put my hiking boots on, outside of the opening, then hauled my butt out. My breath came out in clouds, it was that cold here, at this hour.

In the bathhouse, I endured splashing cold water on my face, but there's no way I would take a shower now. Maybe later on, if the sun comes out. I changed into tights and jeans, warm raglan socks, a tank top, thermal jersey, flannel shirt, woolen sweater and hoped that the sun would shine bright when it came up. Realizing that it was the Fourth of July made me laugh. I've never been cold on this holiday before.

When I returned to my site, I started up the motorcycle about four times before she quit stalling, and began warming up. I grabbed my tankbag, jacket, helmet and gloves. The gloves were very wet, so I left them, and put on the lightweights instead. I wasn't riding far, anyway.

Instinctively, I clutched the small leather pouch, that hung from a thong around my neck, looked up into the sky laden with a thick, gray cloud cover, and prayed for guidance and patience during this mission. If I was not meant to find my pocketbook, I asked for the wisdom and strength to accept that this is all part of a Plan, greater than my own.

Then, with a big sigh, I swung my leg over the saddle, noticed the absence of all the luggage I'd grown accustomed to, and waited as my body heat warmed the seat. When I pulled the bike off the sidestand, it was noticeably lighter, I almost pulled it over too far! Making my way through the camping area, I saw that there wasn't much activity going on yet, at this hour, and I respectfully rolled through as quietly as possible. On the short road that led from the Park to the main road, I maintained a low speed, and kept my eyes open, hoping for a stroke of luck.

Once on the main road though, I cracked the throttle and wound it up. In seconds I was speeding at 70 mph, and it felt great! Without all that luggage, the streamlined aerodynamics of my Interceptor were once again evident. All too soon, the Hatchet Grill appeared, and I downshifted, and slowly pulled in.

My plan was to comb the roadside on foot, one section at a time. I would be so thorough, that if I had covered an area, I would be certain that the wallet was not there. The day before, when I pulled out of this parking lot, I did so without hesitation. While I was still mounted, I decided to reenact yesterdays maneuver, so I returned to the exact spot where I was parked yesterday. Then I replayed my actions, as far as I could remember.

I reproduced the path of travel, and tried to account for trajectory, speed, and a bounce factor . . . anything to try to help me guess where my wallet might be. I turned around again and parked the motorcycle. Before I began the hunt, I needed breakfast.

Inside the Grill, I asked hopefully of all the workers if anyone had turned in a wallet, and they regretfully said, "no." I got myself a table, and ordered a filling breakfast, and lots of coffee. In between running around and serving customers, my waitress asked me all kinds of questions, and wished me luck in finding my wallet.

Breakfast went by quite enjoyably, but I dilly-dallied, knowing the task ahead of me. Finally, I had to get up and out of there. The wait staff and the cook wished me luck, and I walked out the door.

I was already certain the purse wasn't in the parking lot anywhere. I headed to the road. On each side there was a fence about ten feet away from the edge of the tar. Between the fence and the road grew tall grass. With each step, I tried to stamp down the hay in a lame attempt to keep my pant legs dry. The grass was wet and heavy, and it wasn't long before my pants were soaked to the knees. Back and forth I trod, purposely looking at every piece of debris there was.

Lots of horse hoofprints marked the sand right beside the edge of the road, and I remembered a riding stable up ahead. When I get there, I thought, I'd tell a trail guide. I've done a lot of riding on horses by the side of the road, and it's easy to notice all the litter Americans toss out their windows. I could ask the guide to look out for my wallet and offer a reward.

I have to hang onto hope.

As I approached one field, a bay mare was grazing, and keeping a wary eye on her fuzzy brown foal. He appeared to be only one or two weeks old, and was quite taken with the world around him. Curiously he stretched his muzzle toward me, and when I tickled him with a piece of hay, he snorted and reared, then spun and ran off bucking and kicking. He tore up the grass, and skidded around corners so fast that he lost his footing and slid out several times, but then he'd come trotting back to me, shaking his head and looking at me with bright eyes, tail held high over his back. He sniffed at my hands, licking the salty flavor off, and then would seem overwhelmed with life, and would run off again, doing his long legged dance moves.

I was delighted. I spent about fifteen minutes playing with him, but when his dam decided enough was enough, she made a low sound, and her son obediently complied, but first he had to pull her tail, and show off for me some more. He lifted his tail high and galloped circles around her as she plodded gently away. He was so intent on watching me watching him, that he barged into her, and ended up in the mud.

As I watched, I laughed. In spite of the difficulties, I was still able to stop and smell the roses. It was good to be able to find something pleasant, despite my situation.

Literally zig-zagging a path back and forth between the road and the fenceline, I wasn't missing an inch. The sky remained gray, but eventually I was able to unzip my leather, which, with all the bulk underneath, made me feel infinitely more comfortable. My Timberlands had been treated with waterproofer, but moisture was bleeding down into them from my socks, which acted like wicks.

After over an hour, I saw that I was out of sight of the Hatchet Grill. I picked a tree as my landmark, and when I got to it, I crossed the street and began searching the other side of Rte. 26.

This is one discouraged girl, here. Such a simple twist of fate. The closer I got to my starting place, the more doubtful I became. Whatever made me think I would ever find my wallet? I know one thing—at least I tried. It isn't here. I don't know if I can examine every square foot for the remaining half of highway, either. My wallet had to have fallen off along the stretch that I just scoured. It's gone. I don't know what I'm going to do.

To drive home to Massachusetts in order to get a new license will take a week. I'll miss the Ride-In. I can't go without it though. What if I get stopped? No license, no ID . . . no nothing.

I made a mental list of all that my wallet contained.

All of my membership cards, two credit cards, about a hundred dollars cash, and the bank receipts for three thousand dollars worth of Traveler's Checks.

What if some lunatic decides he's really gonna make my life miserable? He can't cash them in, the actual Checks aren't in my wallet (thank God), but what if some loser calls the bank to cancel the Checks? I don't even want to think. What good would it do him? None. So why would it happen? Just to screw me up. Now I have two big things to worry about.

Don't do it, Dee. Wait and see. I forced myself to calm down, and pay attention to the ditch I was combing. Not in my wildest dreams, did I picture this as one of the most important activities of my adventure, or was it just a waste of time? I wasn't too sure anymore.

Although a good portion of the day had passed, it was still early afternoon when I pushed open the door of the restaurant, all bedraggled, with my head hung low.

"Did you find it?" A chorus of concerned workers within asked me.

"Do you think I would look like this? No. It's gone. Can I please have some hot chocolate?" I slumped down at a table, and removed my jacket.

In a few minutes a steaming mug was placed before me, and I used it as a handwarmer until it had cooled off enough to sip. Business was slow at the diner, but I hardly noticed. The only things on my mind were my cold wet feet, and my lost wallet. My boots were soaked, from the inside out. Riding tomorrow will be a shivering experience, no doubt.

Friends at home had told me to call if I ran into any problems, but what could anyone do to get me out of this jam? Absolutely nothing. I wanted to call Russell, but I already knew he would just give me an "I told you so." This was something I had to figure out on my own.

At any rate, I had to phone home to update my outgoing message, and hopefully, hearing some friends on my line would lift my spirits.

I left a dollar on the table, and went outside.

I dialed my answering service and followed the step by step directions so that I could record a new outgoing message.

The canned voice told me, "Your callers now hear," and then I listened to my own voice. "Hi. So far I've traveled through Massachusetts, Connecticut," blah, blah, blah, "Leave me a message after the beep."

Gosh, that seemed so long ago! I was at Karen's house in Minnesota when I recorded that. I flipped back a page or two in my journal, to see that it was on my thirteenth day when I last called home. Today was my eighteenth.

"To keep this greeting, Press One. To record a new greeting, Press Two." Technology speaks.

I pressed Two, and feigning an upbeat voice, began. "Hi! I am camped here at Grand Teton National Park, which is near Yellowstone. It's extremely beautiful here, and cold. Adventures! Challenges! I wanted them—I got 'em! The last couple of days have been, um, quite trying, but I'm surviving. Today is my eighteenth day, and I'm on my way to the Women On Wheels Ride-In in

Washington State, and should be there this weekend. Okay, that's all for now, g'bye."

Again. "To keep this greeting, Press One. To rec-"

I pressed One. I didn't want anyone at home to worry.

"The greeting will be kept. To hear your messages, Press One." Done. "Thank you. You have fourteen messages."

Fourteen? Ha! Gold mine! Pen in hand I sat, ready to jot down any notes, if needed.

One by one, the canned voice told me the date and time of each call, beginning with the oldest one first.

1. My good friend Betsy, who I left in charge of my mail, bills, and houseplants, which she brought home with her. "Hi Dee! So good to hear your voice! Everybody at work misses you, and says to tell you 'hi.' I bet you don't miss work, though. Well, just wanted to hear your voice, and now I can tell everybody that you're in Minnesota, and we'll have to look it up on the map. I like this answering service, because I'll always know where you are! Talk to ya later. By the way, your plants are doing wonderfully."

2. My buddy, Angelo. "Hi honey. I got your letter the other day. It sounds like you're having a good time so far. Especially visiting your relatives. I bet you handled yourself really well, even if you were a bit frustrated. So, now you're in Minnesota. You be careful, and keep those letters coming. I miss you a lot, but I'm glad you're doing what you wanted to do. See you in three months."

3. hung up.

4. "Hello, it's me, Russell. I'm glad to hear you're having fun and your motorcycle is running well. I'm always home, so call me collect when you can. Okay. Bye."

5. hung up.

6. "Yeah, it's Russell. I can't believe you've gone through all those states and you haven't f—-ing called me yet. I told you, call me collect." Sounding a bit irritated.

7. "Yeah, yeah, yeah, Diane. I'm tired of hearing about all the f—-in' states Miss World Traveler is hitting. You don't even call me. Well, screw you, Diane, alright? Eat —-t!" Click. That was Russell, my drunken, upset man back home.

8. (The next morning.) "Diane, it's me. I'm sorry about last night. It's just . . . I miss you. I wish you would call me. If you can't spare a dime, call me collect, alright? This really sucks."

9. "Happy Fourth of July! This is Bobby. Hi Darlin', we're over at my sister's having a party, and I thought, why not call and see how you're doing? So—it sounds like you're having a great time, and I'm glad your bike is running fine, but it always does, anyway. Of course, I miss you, but I'm jealous. You just Go Girl! I'm so happy for you. I knew you could do it. Miss you like crazy, and can't wait till you get back." One of my buddies.

10. "Hey! Wait a minute! Now I'm getting worried. This is the same message as the last time I called a few days ago. This is Betsy, and I'm just calling to say I miss you dreadfully. I hope everything is okay. *Change your message!!!* Luv ya."

11. "Yeah. Thanks for not calling me." Russ again.

12. hung up.

13. "Hi, Diane? This is Mike Milton from Dubois, Wyoming. I found your wallet outside Grand Teton Park. It seems to be intact, and if you could call me, or my girlfriend, we can try to work something out, and get it back to you . . . "

And the operator said, "To hear this message again, Press One." You bet!

I listened with disbelief and relief as Mike quoted two telephone numbers and I wrote them down. After a couple of reruns, just to be sure I heard right, I went on to my last and final message of the day.

14. "Hi. Well, Diane. You still haven't called me, and I guess you don't want to. Don't bother, I get the idea. I wouldn't want you to waste your precious time. It was nice knowing you."

Talk about a roller coaster ride. My emotions have certainly run the gamut. At the moment, the agony over Russ's telephone manner was swept aside easily.

My wallet has been found! "Thank You, God."

I hung up the telephone, and pushed open the door to the diner. As if in a dream, I made my way back to my booth. There were only a few patrons in the place, and the servers weren't too busy. As soon as one gal made eye contact with me, the spell I was under got broken.

Incredulously, I exclaimed, "You won't believe what just happened! I just phoned home, and there was a message for me. Some guy in Dubois *found my wallet!!!* Can you believe it? He left his phone number and wants me to call him so he can return it to me!"

Every person in the joint cheered and applauded. I was beeming. A huge burden was just lifted, and my spirit soared. I was too excited to call the good samaritan just yet, so I ordered more hot chocolate. After explaining to those who didn't know the story, I was ready to go back outside and use the phone again.

When I tried Mike's number, I didn't reach him, and the same thing when I called his girlfriend's house. I left a message, and realizing it was the Fourth of July, guessed I might end up having to wait until later, or even the next day. At least I knew, I was going to get it back, and my journey would continue, as planned.

Next, I had to call Russ. When I tried to call collect, the call didn't go through, because his answering machine picked up, so the operator intervened. I needed to speak to him though, so I dialed direct.

After the beep, I started. "Hi Russell. I can't believe you would call me on purpose and leave such nasty messages. I am on the road, staying in campgrounds where I'm lucky if there's a telephone. I'm traveling back roads, driving about three hundred miles a day. It's not like when you've gone on your trips, staying in hotels every night, and gassing up at service stations on the interstates. There are no pay phones on the trees out here. I miss you, and then, when I finally got to hear your voice, I heard you swearing at me. I can't believe you would do such a thing. I understand if you get mad at me, but keep it to yourself. *Don't* call my number and be so mean! There's no need for that. Anyway, I guess now you understand how I felt when you were away from me on your long trips. It's not easy, huh? And that's *not* why I haven't called. Not at all. I haven't called *anybody.* This is the first time I've checked in to my own machine since last week. God, I miss you, but I can't believe the way you talked to me. I'm gonna hang up now before I get cut off. I will try to call you again, when I'm in Washington this weekend, and I'll have a phone in my room, like luxury. I've got to go now, bye."

Whew. That was awful. But, it's done. Time to move on. I've got places to see, things to do, people to meet. I felt the energy seeping into my being, once again. The lost wallet ordeal had drained so much from me, but now my outlook was back to normal except for one dark, empty portion of my heart. Then again, even that, *for me,* felt pretty normal. I was used to that lonely, sinking feeling, when it came to me and 'my' man.

I hopped on the Pony, and cranked on it, enjoying the sound of my pipes. I hadn't noticed, but all packed up, that special sound was muffled by the mass of luggage when I was loaded. Now I could clearly hear my Supertrapps, and I felt like whooping.

"Yee-hah!" So free. So far away. *So lucky.*

Swooping in to the Post Office, I tore my REWARD sign off the wall, and stuck it in my tankbag. I would light my fire with that piece of cardboard tonight.

Entering the National Park, I slowed to a respectable rate before I was waved past the ranger station. I made a turn here, and another there, as I approached my camp site. What's this? Another tent? It's Ben's! Alright!

All of a sudden I had so much to do.

At Grand Teton National Park, you are allowed to collect deadwood to burn. Knowing that the immediate area surrounding the campground would be picked clean, I set out on my motorcycle, to find a better place to look. I cruised along some roads in the park, and parked in a pull-off across from a commanding view of the mountains.

There was a span of soft dirt and short grass acting as a buffer, between the road and the tree's edge. Beyond that, the undergrowth was fairly dense, and I could see a tree that had fallen. I'd be able to get plenty of dry wood right there. As I walked toward the forest edge, I looked carefully for tracks, as they were plentiful in the soft earth I was stepping upon. I was able to identify rabbit and raccoon, but I was looking for moose.

I pushed my way through the branches, and thrashed through undergrowth, on my way to the fallen pine. Just as I thought, no one had come here to gather wood, and there were lots of branches that had broken off when this old goddess crashed to earth, several years ago. Twigs and small dry branches snapped easily, as I collected them into a neat pile. This would make fine kindling.

For a moment I stopped what I was doing, and leaned against one erect tree trunk nearby. I peered through the brambles and trees towards my bike. The magnitude of what I was seeing, what I was doing, struck me just then.

Here I am. It's just me. There's my bike, my Red Pony, and behind her I can see a panoramic view of fabulous, snow encrusted mountains, so tall that the tops are encased in huge thick white clouds. I have traveled here, astride my nimble mount, all by myself in a quest for freedom, and I've only just begun. Against all odds, I have faced trials, and I have conquered helplessness. My motorcycle is an extension of myself, and although it is an inanimate object, the emotion which bonds me to it is increasingly stronger, with each day that I spend traveling to places unknown, territories I've only explored in my mind.

I begin to feel giddy with elation. So excited by Life, and this adventure. Any one who rides—do you ever feel like you're in love with your machine? I was falling in love again at this moment. No one thing, no person, has brought me to such a realization of my Self, and my own worth, as this ride has. And I've only just begun.

After I gave myself time to 'Just Be,' I stacked one outstretched arm with as much wood as I could handle, and fought my way back to open air. I arranged the firewood onto the back of my bike, and secured it using bungee cords, then delivered it to my campsite.

The Visitor Center's Orientation Program would start in just a few minutes in the Auditorium. A Park Ranger entered the room, with her uniform and badges, and began her well-rehearsed, yet interesting, informative and somewhat comical rendition of Park history.

"How did Grand Teton get its name?" She'd scan the room looking for an answer from the crowd, and if there was no one to try, she'd inform us herself. "Fact is, French explorers first came upon the mountain range that this park is named for. Legend has it, after months and months of expedition without female companionship, the leader took one look at the peaks, and said, 'Grand Tetons,' or, to translate, 'Big Ta-Ta's,' and that is how it came to be." Everybody laughed, especially the young boys.

The long haired woman went on to describe the different sights to see, what was special about each particular road within the park, and where to go for your best shot at seeing moose. "As a matter of fact, we have one old bull who fancies himself a movie star. He'll go to the water and pose, turning his head just so-" as she demonstrated a profile view for us, "so you can get wonderful photographs. The best time is early morning, or at dusk."

"It is the Fourth of July, and although we do not put on a fireworks display, they put on a fabulous display at Jackson Hole. You can either make the drive for the festivities in town, or you can go to these spots," using a pointer, she indicated a couple of places on the huge map. "And watch from a high vantage. Any questions?"

After a brief question and answer period, we were free to leave, all with a better understanding of the youngest mountains in the Rockies, which stand taller than a mile over Jackson Hole, and contain a dozen mountain glaciers.

I was totally impressed. I couldn't remember ever hearing of this place, due to Yellowstone's fame, yet, here I was now, and couldn't wait to get out and check it out some more.

Deciding on the road that would bring me to the lake where I'd most likely see some moose, I cruised along slowly, inhaling the fresh, crisp air. I stopped and parked and got off my bike, and stood gazing at the gray-blue snow-streaked visage. Here and there, tourists with binoculars and fancy cameras watched and waited. The lofty clouds draped themselves casually around the mountain peaks, and the lake below appeared as a mirror. This was a truly beautiful place. I hoped for moose, but it was not the recommended time of day, and none appeared.

Eventually, I realized I should try to call about my wallet, and not knowing where else to go for a phone, I drove out to the Hatchet Grill again. One number I got a machine, and the other number, I got Mike. After some deliberation, it was finally decided that he would ship my wallet to Washington State.

"Mike, I know there's about a hundred dollars in my wallet and I want you to keep it."

"No way. I can't do that."

"Sure you can, it's your reward, for being honest. Please, take it." I insisted.

"Nope," he answered. "This is how we do things out here in Wyoming. We take care of each other. I just want you to get it back. I hope you don't mind that I opened it and looked through your stuff, for a number or something."

"Mind? No—I could hug you. You did the right thing. Anyway, at least allow me to pay for you to ship it to me, insured, FedEx."

"Alright, that's fair." He complied.

So, I gave him the address of the hotel where the Ride-In would be, thanked him profusely, and he told me, "When you come upon someone else in trouble, or in need, help that person out. That is how you can repay me."

"Deal. Thank you, good bye." I hung up the phone. I stepped out of the booth and jumped up and down. I felt like the luckiest person alive.

It was time to start thinking about moving on. I ordered lunch, then opened my map book to the full spread of the U.S.A. The next few minutes found me skipping back and forth, between my journal, calendar, and maps of Wyoming, Idaho, Montana, Oregon and Washington. From here, there was no easy way to get to where I was going. I wanted to at least drive through Yellowstone, but the materials I received from the Park Ranger warned that many roads in Yellowstone are not motorcycle friendly, plus there were some roads closed off. It didn't look like the best way to go.

A problem slowly surfaced. I was facing about nine hundred miles to get to Olympia. Tomorrow would be Wednesday. I wanted to be at the Ride-In by early Thursday. I had three days of riding to do in two. I didn't realize I was so far away, and the time just kind of crept up on me. It's already Fourth of July. That I knew. I just hadn't stopped to figure out that the Ride-In begins the day after tomorrow.

Once my meal was finished, I headed straight 'home.' I sat down at the picnic table to write in my journal, and record expenditures. Then I studied my maps some more.

If I drove off tomorrow morning, I'd have to ride 450 miles each day, and arrive at the Ride-In Thursday night. Another choice I had would be to pack it up tonight, and drive . . . no way. I was overtired, and needed a good night's sleep.

My last option would be to head out in the morning, and drive straight through. Not an appealing idea, but, I had pulled an all-nighter before, I could do it again. What turned me off about riding two high-mileage days in a row, (for a crotch rocket) was the time and effort that stopping to spend the night camping would involve. If I didn't stop for the night, I could stop for twenty winks, then hit the road again as soon as I awakened.

The unique sound of Ben's dual-sport machine interupted my focus, and in a few minutes he appeared. He told me that Yellowstone was 'okay,' but, I didn't miss much, some of it was closed, the weather was lousy, and this park was probably better for bikers.

Excitedly I shared with him how a stranger found my wallet, and how seeing his tent set-up here had surprised me. I thought he didn't like me.

He motioned toward the pile of wood and commented in his accent, "You've been busy. Think we'll have fire tonight?"

"You better believe it. I haven't had a fire since I left home. It's just not the same without someone to share it with. If I'm cold, it's easier to just crawl into the bag, you know? But, I have got company tonight, and we already bought the wood. I'm not going to fireworks, are you?" I asked.

"Nah. I've had enough for one day." He replied.

Together we went over our plans, and discussed the different routes out of Grand Teton. Ben would be heading north, but he too, decided to go south out of the park, rather than ride through Yellowstone again. We discovered we could leave in the morning and ride together, for a bit, before we'd split off onto separate routes.

Darkness filtered in, and I squatted by the fire ring, and set up a tepee of twigs and dried leaves, around a base of paper. A small flame licked at the fodder, and caught on. Piece by piece, I added sticks, and twigs, until I could add a handful. Soon, I had a glowing bed of coals, and arranged the unseasoned logs in a manner that would allow them to dry somewhat, and catch fire eventually.

Ben and I sat on opposite sides of the fire, full of thought. I finished the last little bit of tequila, before standing up to go.

"I'm gonna go wash up now," I said. I washed my face, then stripped down to my waist. Using a bandanna for a washcloth, I sponged my arms, torso, shoulders and armpits. The air felt chilly, and individual hairs on my arms stood up to protest, but shoot, it felt good. After putting on my long-sleeved button-up shirt, I removed my jeans and leggings, and sticking one foot at a time into the sink, I washed my feet, and legs, and groin. Feeling fabulous, I put on my cozy sweat pants. Next, I unbraided my hair, and combed it out. This procedure had me feeling as good as any hot shower might. Maybe even better, because, I really needed it. I looked at the dull mirror, and I liked what I saw. Fresh faced, I wove my hair into a neat french braid, brushed my teeth, and enjoyed the renewed feeling.

As I approached my campsite, I could see the fire blazing brightly, but Ben was not in sight. He must've gone to get ready for bed, too. I sat and watched as the fire slowly ebbed out.

"Ben, are you here?" I called quietly, but got no answer. He was already asleep.

Well, it was that time for me, too. I thought it was weird, he didn't say good night, but then again, I was gone for quite a while. It was nice to have him around. I stayed up a while longer, gazing into the magical depths of the coals, thinking.

Leaving home, I didn't anticipate asking a virtual stranger, especially one as handsome and appealing as this tall, dark, mysterious male, to share my camp, and come ride with me, with no thought of romance, no threat of violence or evil doing. Yet, here I was, with this Ben, asleep soundly in his own tent, twenty feet away from me, his brand new motorcycle parked near mine.

The fire hissed as I dutifully poured water on it, and I crawled into my tent. I had quite a ride ahead of me, starting tomorrow. Today was full of surprises, and things were looking up. I closed my eyes, and sleep came easily.

Miles: 53

Onward! to that which is endless, as it was beginningless, to undergo much . . . to see nothing anywhere but what you may reach it and pass it. To look up or down no road but it stretches and waits for you—To know the universe as a road— as many roads—as roads for traveling souls.

—Walt Whitman

CHAPTER 7

MARATHON
July 5–6   Days 19–20

"**A**ren't your hands frozen?" I asked Ben, as I scraped the film of ice off of my tent using my bare hands. During the night, condensation on the tent froze, and now it was time to be breaking camp.

Ben answered with a grin, and continued working. He had already been up, and I awoke when I heard him say my name, and tell me "It's time to get up."

By 8 AM we headed out. I would be driving out a different way than I had come. We were right on schedule, but came to a line of traffic about half a mile long, leaving the park. Station wagons, trucks and RV's, big cars, little cars, all stopped, with drivers and passengers sitting on the hoods, with cameras, binoculars and children.

Up ahead, we could see the delay was caused by a cattle drive. Real cowboys on horseback! Wow! The herd stretched across the road from one side to the other, making their way to somewhere. Ben wasn't as thrilled as I, because he's seen this kind of thing in Colorado, and to him it was just a set-back in our departure time. I couldn't contain my excitement, however.

A couple of times a year the cattle have to be moved from one place to another. Although there are always some complaints, the overall feeling is that the reason for the hold-up is another genuine sample of Wyoming's way of life, and most folks on vacation welcome the interruption.

We had to wait about a half hour, and the performance was fabulous. The vehicle behind us was a large RV, and I asked the woman in the passenger captain's chair if she would take some pictures of Ben and me, and our packed up motorcycles. Seeing her step out in her slippers made me wonder just for a second—is that really camping? She's not roughing it—she's in bedroom slippers!

We watched the last of the bunch give the cowboys some trouble, as one stubborn cow kept whirling and making a dash for the direction she'd just come from, and causing another five or six to follow suit. Finally, with whoops and hollers, they made it across. A wave of applause and cheering worked its way along the stalled procession, and engines started up.

It didn't take long for the traffic to spread out, and we began to make time. The scenery continued to be breathtaking, as we snaked along on winding roads which wrapped themselves around the foothills of staggering mountains.

Ben rode at a pace which to me seemed best described as urgent. Each time we came upon another vehicle on the road, he would waste no time passing it, regardless of the zone. This would leave me hanging back, behind a car or camper, and as I watched Ben pull away, I'd force myself to downshift, then crank on it, passing the car, then driving fast enough to close the distance between him and me, only to repeat this feat over and over.

These maneuvers were wearing on my nerves, because I worried constantly about getting pulled over. We were speeding, we were passing cars in illegal zones, and I was now in the undesirable position of driving without a license. I cruised along just the same, because, with Ben as the pace maker, I was indeed making better time. With nine hundred miles ahead of me, eventually I would be glad for his lead. Besides, we'd be riding together for a maximum of a hundred and fifty miles, then I'd see Ben no more.

The Red Pony was capable, she's made for speed. The huge load strapped on made a difference, as did the engine size. My 500cc's had to work a little harder than the Beemer's one thousand. Ben was a good rider, too, accustomed to mountain roads, which curved left and right, as well as up and over. As usual, I felt like I was still learning to be a better rider, and this was one of those times where I felt I was pushing my limits. We tooled along, at speeds no less than 75 mph, and up to a hundred.

We got to the state sign, high on a mountain side, and pulled over.

COME CELEBRATE WITH US - IDAHO - CENTENNIAL

Here I, sat astride my race-replica-turned-tourer, beside a brand new Paris-Dakar BMW on its virgin voyage, ready to enter the state of Idaho.

I was enthralled by the vision that unfolded before me as we rolled through the Caribou National Forest, and then along Snake River as we approached Idaho Falls an hour or so further on. We had agreed to stop at the junction where our two roads would split. Arriving at a non-descript parking lot we stopped the bikes.

"I had no idea Idaho was like this!" sweeping an arm towards the ranches, and tall mountains in sight. "I really didn't know what to expect. Potatoes, I guess. This is a well-kept secret. No wonder . . . they must want to keep it all to themselves."

Ben looked around appreciatively, nodding his head, then we both were quiet. We had to go. I grabbed him by the shoulders, and leaned into him real quick, slapping him on his Hein Geriche armored back, then ducked away. I pulled my helmet on, and watched him mount his enduro, then held my arm high. He returned my wave, then blasted off.

Beep-beep. Bye-bye.

The next few hours found me more relaxed in the saddle. I could ride at my own pace, and eliminate the fear of getting stopped by police, and getting in lots of trouble for having no license, no identification, no luck.

The rustic beauty continued to amaze me, and I drove on, ever westward. Taking a day off from riding had worked wonders, yet at the same time, I knew there was a very serious stretch of road ahead of me.

I could have opted to eat up more miles, in less time by jumping onto the Superslab at the point where I left Ben, but I am drawn to the lesser roads. They speak to me more. The big highways seem so impersonal.

As if answering my thoughts, I came upon a sign indicating I was approaching *Craters of the Moon National Monument.* I found myself in a blackened, barren wasteland, like nothing I'd ever seen before. Curious, and due for a break, I pulled into a parking lot, and got off my bike to walk around and stretch my legs.

The dark gray earth crunched and crumbled under my thick, knobby soles, and yet, as bleak and gray-black as the surface for miles appeared, when I stopped to see, not just to look, down at my feet were tiny, perfect flowers. I squatted down, and touched the miniscule blossoms of red, and yellow, and marveled. They were barely visible at first glance, yet here they were.

What is this place?

The region was demolished when a certain mountain blew its top, and I was looking at the result, how many years later? Mother Earth vomited, erupted, and spewed molten lava which covered a hundred square miles. It looked to me as if a giant ashtray had water spilled into it, and then was dumped, and left to harden and dry out. Supposedly, the terrain looked much like the surface of the moon, thus, its name, "Craters of the Moon." Personally, I thought the South Dakota Badlands looked more like the moon, than this, but still, it was intriguing.

Having stretched my legs, and become aware of the sun's warmth, I drank the last of my water before getting back on my bike, but with hesitation I stopped, because I saw a puddle in its shadow. With concern, I stooped for a closer inspection, then laughed with relief.

From the corner of my rolled up tent-sack, water dripped. Melted ice from this morning was leaking out! No need to worry.

After riding for a time, hunger set in, so I stopped in the next town for lunch. When no one else was chatting with the man at the counter, I asked him questions about Craters of the Moon National Monument. He said that over the last couple of decades he had witnessed changes, himself, as evolution took its course. For example, the tiny flowers I noticed, were virtually non-existent thirty years earlier. We got into a discussion about preservation, ecology and nature, and in between customers I pondered his existence.

This large man in a blue work shirt, with his name spelled in an oval over one pocket, spent his entire life right here, in the town he was born and raised in. He'd never been out of his state, never traveled, never flown in a plane, and yet, he was able to brag about these facts, before I moved on.

The landscape continued to delight me, and I found myself sorting through a whirlwind of brand new memories. The words I had read somewhere long ago sprang to mind, and I repeated them to myself, with a clear understanding.

"If you want to be rich in pocket—*start working.* If you want to be rich in knowledge—*start studying.* If you want to be rich in spirit—*start traveling.*"

I have done these things. I have worked, ever since I got out of high school, I have supported myself, usually working a second job, as well as my full-time therapy.

Studying—I put myself through college, while working two jobs. Learning came easy to me when I put my mind to it, and I proudly accepted my Bachelor's Degree with a 3.3 grade point average.

Spirit—growing up with two remarkably beautiful sisters, I'd adopted an attitude when I was still a girl . . . my beauty would come from within. Now, as a grown woman, I've embarked on a journey I hoped would enhance and enrich my already willing spirit.

I was suddenly jolted out of my deep thoughts, by what I saw way ahead of me. There, in the middle of the road, a woman was frantically waving her arms, and jumping up and down. She would run towards an oncoming vehicle, obviously distraught, and I watched horrified, when these jerks swerved around her and sped on down the road, one after the other.

I downshifted, and when the lady heard the engine changing gears, and she realized I was actually stopping, she ran to me incoherently babbling, and flailing her arms. I surveyed the scene, half expecting to see a child crumbled on the roadside nearby, or some clue that would help me understand what was going on.

"Wait a minute! Stop right now! First of all, let's get out of the middle of the road," I ordered. She was standing beside me, right where I had put my feet down when I stopped. "No sense in both of us getting run over here."

We moved to the shoulder of the road, and I cut my engine down. "Okay, now calm down—take a couple of deep breaths, and try to speak slowly so I can understand you, and see if I can help."

She wrung her hands, and managed to get her panic somewhat under control. "Oh my God, you're an angel. My husband and I were on our way home from a camping trip, and-" her voice began to rise, and words flew past her lips so fast I could not decipher them.

"Hold it, you have to *calm down* so I can understand you. You're not making any sense to me." Quietly, yet firmly, I coached her to gain control.

After a few attempts, I got the gist of her position. Apparently, she and her husband were traveling home from a camping trip, when their trailer had a tire blow out. The outfit began to weave violently back and forth on the road, until the rear axle of the trailer broke, flinging the flattened tire up into the rear window of the pick-up's cab. The husband managed to keep the truck on the road, but discovered they were in a situation beyond repair.

"Somebody stopped and brought us to a telephone, and left me off there. My husband called his brother to come and help us. He told me to wait here," she turned and pointed out a roadside shelter across the street, "and he took off to try to get some parts in town, with the stranger." Tears leaped to her eyes, and began to spill down over her sunburned cheeks. "My brother-in-law went by, but he didn't see me. He's gonna find our truck, but we're not there, and I don't know what to do!" Again her voice rose to an uncomfortable wail, but at least now I knew the reason.

"All right. What's your name?" I asked.

"I'm Chris, and my husband's CJ." She sniffled, wiping her tears with her shirtsleeves. "Can you drive up ahead? It happened seven miles away. Will you go there, and tell my brother-in-law that I am stranded here, and to come and get me? I'm afraid he will find the truck, and think we're all set."

Here we go again, she's gonna start crying.

"Easy, Chris. Everything's going to be okay. I can do that. No problem." I assured her.

"Really? You're gonna help? No one else would even stop!"

"I know. I couldn't believe it when I watched cars actually swerving around you. How could they do that? I couldn't just drive by."

"Why did you? You're an angel."

"It's my job." I kidded. "I just drive around the countryside, looking for people in need."

"Well, I don't know about that, but *thank you* from the bottom of my heart . . . " said the petite woman. "The truck is brown, with a camping trailer, on the side of the road. My brother-in-law drives a blue truck, so you'll know it's the right person. He should be there now, wondering where we're at. Please tell him to come get me, first. Be careful, and thank-you."

All the while, I remained ready to ride off in an instant. Noticing her cheeks, flushed from emotion, and burned by the sun, I tossed her my bottle of sunscreen. I had more. She needed it right now, more than me. I touched my starter, and roared away, glancing at my odometer and making a mental note how far before I came upon said scene.

The area was somewhat remote, the road fairly narrow, and I drove fast, thinking about this circumstance. Yesterday, a man said, "When you come upon someone else in trouble, do what you can to help. This is how you can repay me."

Well, it certainly didn't take long for the chance, and truly, it didn't take much sacrifice on my part. Just a moment of my time. Time? What's the hurry? I've got three months! Point is, I might have driven by, like so many others, because they don't want to be bothered, but by stopping, I discovered, without even going out of my way, I would make a difference. To Chris, I was a hero.

There it is—there's the truck and camper. As I slowed, and parked in front of it, I became puzzled. There was no one else there, and I wasn't sure what to do at this point. I got off of my bike and checked out the situation. I circled the truck and trailer slowly, and whistled slowly as I saw the damage, and imagined the incident that Chris had described. The road sloped downhill, and rubber marks showed where things got out of control. The rear end of one side of the trailer lurched toward the ground, the axle clearly separated, the rear window of the cab was cracked, a side of the pick-up bed was badly dented, where, I guess the tire slammed into it. No wonder Chris was so upset. She had been through quite an ordeal.

When I found that the brother-in-law was not there, I didn't want them to think I had not stopped, after all, so I began to write a note. Before I'd finished, a truck pulled over and parked before me. Three adults spilled out, one being Chris.

She came straight to me, explaining that when her brother-in-law arrived at the truck, he realized he must've missed the rest area, so he turned around to go back.

The man who had been driving exclaimed, "Oh yeah, just before I got to where Chrissy was, I saw you on your motorcycle going like a bat out of hell. She told me about you, and I said, Yeah, I saw her alright. You can really ride that thing!"

Can a person feel proud and embarrassed at the same time?

"CJ, this is, gosh, I don't even know your name! This is our angel. This is my husband, CJ." Chris introduced us, and we shook hands, but in two seconds he was hunkering down inspecting the undercarriage, the damage, and together with his brother trying to figure out their course of action.

Meanwhile, Chris offered me a cold drink, and I accepted, plucking a peach flavored seltzer water from out of a cooler. She handed me my sunscreen, and began to ask me some questions. The usual.

"Where are you going? Where are you from? All by yourself? Aren't you afraid?"

Then some new ones. "What made you stop, when nobody else would?"

"I told you. It's my job. I'm like a super hero, ready to rescue." I was beginning to enjoy the fantasy.

"I'm starting to believe you," Chris admitted.

Feeling like the truth was even more astounding, I told her about my lost wallet. "The man that found it wouldn't accept a reward. At last, he told me to repay a kindness to someone else in need, and that would be his reward. Because of you, I have been redeemed. Chris, all I ask is that the next time you come across someone in need, Stop, and Do whatever it takes. That will be my reward. It is true. You wouldn't believe how *good* I feel right now . . . Imagine, if the whole world behaved this way. One at a time, I believe we can make a difference."

The small woman, with the brown legs, and short, sporty pony-tail sticking out of her cap, gazed at me with a smile, and agreed.

Tilting my bottle back, I drained the last of the liquid into my throat, and handed it back to her. She took it, and acknowledged that I had to be moving on. We embraced. The men stood, and shook my gloved hand when I got back on my bike and was all set to go.

Just before I pulled out, as I revved the engine and looked over my shoulder, I heard Chris call, "Bye—Angel. I'll never forget this. Thank-You."

Redemption is mine. Redemption is mine. These words repeated themselves like a mantra, within my mind. I rode away with a new awareness concerning human behavior, specifically, my own.

As the miles rolled by, I thought about all the drivers today who saw what I saw. A woman, obviously in a desperate frame of mind, trying to flag someone down, for help. The sense of indignation that I initially felt for all those who had gone before me, and ignored her plea, began to subside. I started to analyze the situation. What was it that caused me to stop, and how could those other drivers just pass her by? I'm no better of a person than they are, am I?

No, I answered myself. The truth is, there have been times in my life, as I've gone about my daily duties, that I have turned away when someone cried out in need. How about driving past a motorist on a darkened highway, with, maybe a flat tire? Or what about the old lady in my apartment complex with heavy grocery bags to carry? Perhaps these folks aren't running into traffic, and yelling "Please help me!" yet I kept my eyes ahead, because I couldn't be bothered.

We all have such busy lives, always on the run. How can you stop to help someone who has run out of gas, when it will make you late for work? Why should you take time out to visit a shut-in, when you know that their home will be uncomfortably hot, and they'll be so thrilled that they don't realize their endless chatter is boring you? Never mind that you have made their day, and sometime in your life, you should be so lucky, to have someone care enough to stop and check on you. Right now, you just can't find the time.

I realized, the major reason I stopped today, was because, *I could.* Granted, I have a lot of traveling to do in the next couple of days, but, the fact is, I'm not on a time clock. Heck, I've got three months! I'm not so special. I'm no angel. I just chose to seize the moment, and take advantage of the fact that I am free. Free to change my mind, free to stop and smell the roses, free to give someone a hand, and free to be me. I didn't have to drive by, and wonder if, or hope, that somebody else had the time to stop and help this person.

Whew. I feel as though my heart is swelling every day with a renewed outlook. There is so much time for me to delve deep within, and coax new growth, nurture ideas, squelch unnecessary fears, and encourage self discovery.

By afternoon, I had reached the big highway, and found that I had to concentrate more on my driving, as I became part of the frantic freeway transit. Huge rigs, commuters, and everything in between, sandwiched me on all sides as I continued on my northwestern trek.

Becoming parched, I got off an exit and pulled into a service station. I parked in some shade and dismounted. Two rows of gas pumps were filled with customer's cars, and I crossed the lot and entered the food mart. The chill of air conditioning enveloped me as I waited in line to pay for a bottle of Snapple.

When I pushed the door open to leave, I happened to catch a glimpse of a big, ugly man wearing nothing but a pair of shorts and sandals. His large, protruding belly stuck out, and he was digging in a side pocket of his shorts for money, pushing the waistband down and revealing a fleshy crease, where his abdomen hung over.

Gross, I thought to myself. Yuk, I don't want to see that! How can somebody let themselves be seen like that? I would be so embarrassed.

I headed straight for my bike, parked by the street, and the paunchy, hairy man walked towards me as he went to pay inside. We crossed paths.

"Whee . . . Bitch!" he muttered, his icy blue eyes darted right into mine.

Without missing a beat, I continued to walk to my bike, and I sat down on the curb behind it, his words echoing in my head. What is *that* supposed to mean? *Whee . . . bitch.* He doesn't even know me. What's he got against me? Jeez. Some people.

I popped open the top of my beverage, and sipped at it, enjoying the flavor. In a moment, a thirty foot camper came rolling in and parked between the store and me. The driver got out, to fill it up. While I watched him, the ugly man came out of the store and got into his van.

Casually, I sipped at my drink, stretching my legs out before me, as I sat and looked around. From inside the van, the driver just sat, and stared at me. I began to feel self-conscious, and then worried when I noticed my heart pounding, and my hands shaking. Trying to appear nonchalant, I forced myself to take my time. Clearly, I would wait for this guy to leave before I did.

Minutes went by, and the neanderthal just sat, staring at me, his lips moving furiously as he talked to himself. When I looked his way, he would turn away, and I was getting the heebie-jeebies. Cars and trucks poured in and out of the service station, but he just sat in front of his pump, and forced others to wait, or drive around him.

What is his problem? What does he want with me? Maybe he hates motorcycles. Maybe he hates bikes that aren't Harleys. Maybe he believes that women shouldn't drive motorcycles. Whee—yeah, that might refer to my crotch rocket, maybe I passed him on the highway and ticked him off. Maybe someone he loved was killed on a bike, and he hates them all. Bitch? Me? But why?

All these questions, and no answers.

Still sitting, and feeling conspicuous, the Interstate on-ramp was just outside the service station, and I watched tons of traffic, drive up onto the superslab, where I was going, but not just yet. I was afraid to leave, perceiving this red-haired, bearded person as a threat. Intuition kept me parked, fearing for my safety. I felt like he was going to follow me, and try to run me off the road.

Where's a cop when you need one? I kept hoping a police car would arrive on the scene. I would ask for assistance, but no such luck.

Minutes were ticking by, and I started to think this through. How was I gonna get out of here safely? Looking around, I saw a truck-stop to the right of this station. To my left was the on-ramp to the Interstate. Straight ahead were the gas pumps, lots of comings and goings, and still that long camper was getting fueled. Must be a huge tank.

Then, much to my surprise, before I could react, from the other side of the camper, a state cruiser drove away. No way! All this time there was a cop and I didn't know it! He was screened by the camper.

Great. I don't want to stay here much longer, but I can't jeopardize my safety. This man was scaring me, by his presence.

At last, a tired engine tried to start, and I sighed with relief when the faded blue van with the white top pulled away from the pumps. Then my heart pounded again because it stopped, right beside the station's exit.

I sat and waited, and so did my stalker. I need to keep a cool head, and figure out how I'm gonna get out of this jam. There has to be a way. Too bad I didn't see that cop, but he was hidden behind that RV.

Wow! That gave me an idea.

I got on my bike, and instead of heading towards the highway, I did the unexpected. I turned left, and left again, ending up in the truck stop parking lot. I circled around a few times, slowly, formulating my plan. When I found myself in a position where I was out of sight from that van, I parked my bike, and it just happened to be by the window of the building there, where lots of truck drivers were eating, drinking coffee, and making on the road purchases.

Purposely drawing attention to myself, I got off my bike, and circled it slowly, bending over to inspect tires, look for leaks, etc.

A group of guys came out eventually, and climbed up into their rigs. This interesting convoy consisted of amusement park rides. The trucks were already running, and one by one, they began to exit, in a chain.

Here's where I made my move. Knowing that these men were well aware I was a female on this motorcycle, I positioned myself on the outside of their convoy. As they passed the gas station I had come from, I rode on the opposite side, using sets of tires as a screen between me and my antagonist. We drove up the on-ramp, and from high above the gas station, I was able to look down and see the faded roof of the van, still sitting, waiting.

I foiled him. I was safe. I stayed with the circus for a little while, hoping that they would protect me if they saw something strange going on. Finally, I began passing the trucks one at a time, and the drivers would give me a thumbs up as I came alongside.

Little do they know, the part they played in my life that day.

On the big highway, I was able to make good time, as I sailed along with the flow of traffic. I had so much to think about and digest. It was only the day before yesterday that I lost my wallet. Hard to believe. And since then, I have discovered that my wallet would be returned to me by a good samaritan, scraped ice off my tent, camped and ridden with a tall, dark stranger, rescued a damsel in distress, and eluded a weirdo by using circus roadies to screen me from view. What next?

I hadn't realized I had left Idaho, until I saw the sign on the outside of a building at a rest stop.

STATE OF OREGON WELCOME CENTER

For a little while, I laid on my back in the lush grass and rested, then felt ready to tackle the demands of the road again.

The environment took on a different look with each passing stretch of hours. There was a span where the landscape appeared to me as if the face of Mother Earth suffered a bad case of acne. The ground swelled and dipped, pock marks marring the surface of endless hillocks. Gradually, this acne scarred turf gave way to grassy slopes, and mountain vistas in the distance.

Finally, I estimated I must be about halfway to Olympia. As I rode on, westward ho, young woman, a faint drizzle began to appear off and on, spattering onto my face shield and the low windshield of my Interceptor. Off in the distance I could see dark angry clouds assaulting the range to my left. There was a distinct gray shadow cast down from above, which I realized was a visible rainstorm.

Taking an opportunity to prepare for rain, I took a random exit, and circled around to stop under the overpass to put on raingear.

The sign said to return to the Interstate west bound, for me to follow this tiny country road. The byway ran alongside the Interstate for a few miles, and I began to doubt the directions, or my interpretation of them, so I turned around and rode all the way back to the bridge.

I had indeed, followed the directions correctly, so I set out again, in the rain, on this road less traveled, set in between a couple of agricultural fields of potatoes, or soy beans, or some sort of low lying vegetation. With the Interstate beside me, but way up high to my left, I cruised along, gradually increasing my speed to match the pace set by those above. For a moment, I noticed that indeed, I was keeping their pace, on this dowdy lane below. I shifted my attention ahead again, with alarm. In front of me, seemingly creeping along, there was a cruiser!

A police car, out here? Just when I'm driving about fifty miles above the speed limit! Well, I was going to use this to my advantage. I slowed down, but continued to catch up with him, and then I drove up alongside, and motioned for him to pull over.

Much to my relief, he seemed to be surprised to see me. "What can I do for you?" he asked, through a window rolled down partway.

"How do I get on that highway, westbound? Am I going the right way?" I waved towards the highway parallel to us.

"Oh, you've got to keep going, but this will take you there." He paused for a minute, looking at me and all my luggage. "Not looking like very good weather up ahead. How far are you going?"

"All the way. I just wasn't sure, one minute I got off of '84' to put on my raingear, only to discover, there's no on-ramp right there, and this road looks as though it could bring me to Ma and Pa Kettle's, or to the middle of no-where, except the highway is right there." I shrugged my shoulders, tucked my collar into my helmet a little better, and said, "Okay, thanks a lot. Have a good night. I'm glad you were here."

"Yep, you take care of yourself." Shaking his head, he rolled up his window, and I sped off, at a reasonable clip.

Twilight was approaching. The raingear was an added layer that would help keep me warm after the sun went down. It looked to me like I would be riding up into and through the mountains tonight, if I ever got back on the big highway.

Suddenly, the way to get back on the great road appeared, and I left my doubts behind.

From the high vantage point of the Interstate, I was blessed with the drama of a night sky unfolding before me. Ahead and to my left, the sky was dark, and the mountains were silhouetted against the ominous backdrop. Lightening bolts flashed incessantly, striking out towards the massive peaks. Ahead and to my right, the sky was clear of the storm brewing yonder. The horizon became orange, and red, brilliantly enhancing the mountainscape before it.

All at the same time, I could witness a major thunder and lightening display, ahead to my left, then, ahead to my right, on the other side of the road that stretched before me, was the most spectacular sunset I'd seen so far on this trip.

I had to try and capture it on film, so I pulled over for a shot. In two more minutes, the colors had magnified, and I had to stop again for another photo, but I knew there was no way a photograph could convey the magnificence of this scene.

Soon darkness fell, and the sunset disappeared, leaving the strobe-light show lingering. The rain fell softly upon my Red Pony and me, as we continued on our trek into the night, on an Oregon highway.

*   *   *

Twelve hours passed since I rode out of Wyoming. Surprisingly, I was doing alright. The terrible thunderstorm that occurred far off, kept its distance much to my relief. The night air chilled somewhat, and off and on I'd encounter showers, but nothing too serious. As the night wore on, I began to get bored with riding. I couldn't see my surroundings, and found myself merely following the taillights of automobiles way ahead of me.

Typically, I'd adopt a vehicle that is driving at a speed I am comfortable with, and settle in behind it, following for as long as it is going my way. As it got later, there got to be less passenger cars, and more big rigs. Often these trucks would travel together, and I found myself falling in with them, comforted by the trail of lights leading the way. Some places I could see for a mile ahead how the road was going to curve, because of them.

While riding with the convoys, I remembered other trips where I learned how to position myself, and stay out of their way, give them room to pass each other, pay attention to all their signals, and most importantly, *to stay out of their blind spot.* If I was, for some reason, going to pass a tractor trailer truck, I would do so, quickly and deliberately.

Weariness began to set in, somewhere around five hundred miles. White line fever started to play its tricks, and I had to do things to keep the little orange and red lights ahead of me, from blurring up my vision.

The temperature got noticeably cooler, as I rode into higher elevation. I sensed a mighty river to my right. Moisture saturated the air, and I was glad that I was wearing my rainsuit.

The highway curved and weaved, as it followed the course of the great Columbia River, and as I continued west, on my left, Mount Hood National Forest climbed up the steep incline, while to my right a guard rail skirted the side of my route, and down below I could sometimes catch a glimpse of the dark waters, or reflections of small towns that were planted on the other side.

Logging trucks abounded, and with unbelievable skill they led the way for me, around dangerous decreasing radius turns, and up and down steep grades, until sometimes they rode right out of sight, because I let them, they drove so fast. Obviously, these men know these roads intimately.

Not me. When I was on my own, with no guiding lights, I was uncertain, and extremely cautious. The skill of those crazy night riders impressed me. Eventually, another truck would come up behind me, and I'd allow him to pass, and then I would pick up my pace, in order to take advantage for as long as possible before losing him.

For quite some time, I fell in behind a hulky, shiny black rig, with all kinds of extra lights and gadgets. It was the kind of truck you'd see in a Trucker's Rag Mag. It looked like a show truck, and I let my imagination go wild as I drove in his wake.

I bet the driver of this truck fancies himself a real stud. I wonder what he's hauling. He's probably a hulking, burly man, with a handsome face, and longish hair, big, bulging biceps, and a chunky gold ring on one finger. He probably thinks he's all muscle, but if I looked at him, I would say, oh, yeah, he's strong, but he's fat. Look at that girth—that's not muscle. And he'd slap his belly, and say, "Solid, look at me. I'm a real man."

Oh boy—I'm getting tired.

The way the lights are set up on the back of his truck, and the lines of the rear doors, huge macho pipes sticking up and curving out from the cab, all together, gave me the illusion of a tiger snarling. I couldn't tell if this was intentional, or just my overtired imagination, but since I adore the big cats, I continued to "see" a tiger, or was it a black panther? I couldn't tell because it was night, but I was glad for the diversion. I was beginning to feel the effects of this demanding excursion.

The motorcycle began to chug out, and I reached down with fingers thick and fumbling from the cold night air. The insulated gloves I wore made it difficult for me to switch over to reserve, but as I did so, it was with relief. I'd be able to take a brief break, when I stopped for gas. Part of me needed to stop riding, just to alleviate the wind chill factor so I could warm up, and I could take a moment to close my eyes. They were beginning to burn.

With anticipation, I forged on, waiting for the next exit, wondering how long before I'd reach it. Once I began to think about stopping for a moment, I realized how badly I needed a break.

At last, I saw a sign indicating a gas station at the next exit, and I left the highway only to discover that it was closed. After several more miles on the highway, there was another exit to go and get gas, but again, it was closed for the night. I still had plenty of miles left, (at least now I knew I could easily ride on reserve for more than fifty miles) so I wasn't too concerned. What did concern me was . . . what if they're all closed overnight? I didn't want to have to stop anywhere for the night on account of needing a service station to open up.

There's got to be some stations open . . . with all these trucks on the road, obviously savoring the empty lanes as they careen along the snakelike route, but how far can they go between fill-ups? I realize their tanks are huge, but they must get such low mileage, with the massive loads they're hauling.

Okay, here comes another exit. Should I waste the time and check it out? What choice do I have?

The exit rolled me downhill, and curved around to deposit me at a humble gas station, where it was dark all around, but for the light within. I tried not to get my hopes up, but when I pulled up to the pumps, a heavy set guy opened the door and approached.

He was groggy and grumpy, and non-responsive when I babbled on about how glad I was to finally find a gas pump open at this hour. He looked at me as if to say, "What do you expect? It's three o'clock in the morning."

When I was finished, I rode away, not directly to the highway, but down the lane some, looking for a lonely place to park for a few minutes so that I could pee somewhere, and stretch my legs a bit. The service station didn't look like it would keep its rest rooms very clean.

There were some empty, dark buildings, that appeared to be warehouses, and beyond, the land sloped steeply upwards, to where I could hear the occasional "whirr" as a diesel made its way along the super highway, where I too would be after I rested.

I seemed to be in a block, where it was not a through way, but rather, a few streets that would only be occupied during business hours. I parked my bike in a parking lot near a streetlight, and dismounted, then bent over and stretched my poor cramped legs, knees and lower back. When I returned to a regular position, I arched my back, leaning backwards, stretching, this way and that, keeping my eyes closed, enjoying the soothing sensation of my eyelids, and natural moisture returning to my sore, tired eyeballs.

I continued to stretch various parts of my aching body, and it was while I was slowly doing head rolls to relieve the kinks in my neck, that I opened my eyes, and looked towards the heavens.

It took my breath away. I was so close to the stars that I felt I could reach out and touch them. Each star contrasted vividly, against a velvet sky, and the milky way appeared as a thick, sparkled veil, stretched across the firmament. For a long time, I simply stood, and breathed, and stared upward, thankful that the threat of rain no longer existed. Normally, I would have removed my raingear at once, but, I was afraid I'd be cold. I left it on, for its excellent wind breaking properties.

Ignoring the discomfort of a full bladder for long enough, I found a spot between a storehouse and the ribbon of highway at the ridge of a steep, grassy slope, and there I relieved myself, envious for the moment, of men's plumbing.

How easy it is for a male to take a leak, compared to a female. We have to expose so much of our anatomy, squat down, be careful not to urinate on our ankles, keep our balance, and hopefully, remember some tissue, regardless of what 'duty' we're taking care of. Plus, if we suspect a person approaching, we can't simply turn our back and walk off with a simple *z-z-zipp,* nope—instead, we get to be mortified that somebody caught us in a position that we consider far from desirable.

Such is life, for a woman indeed.

Feeling better, I noticed a pay phone on the outside of the building there. I called home to retrieve my messages.

The answering service indicated that I had a couple of messages. One message was from Russell. He responded to my last call to him, when I'd chastised him for leaving such mean messages. He said he didn't appreciate hearing me calling him and telling him how to behave. Hearing him turn things around like that only made me throw up my hands in despair.

Feeling a jolt of surprise, I listened to a message from my roommate at home. She mentioned receiving a post card from me, and assured me that my cat was fine, but seemed to miss me, pacing around and meowing all the time. She broke up with the guy she had been seeing, and now was dating another man, who loves cats and gives mine tons of affection.

After hanging up, I gazed at the stars a bit more, then tried to get comfortable on top of my motorcycle, in order to rest my eyes for a little while, but, I was too restless.

Russell's attitude bothered me, and I wanted to speak with him. Thinking of the time changes, I counted back, and figured if it is 3 AM here, on Pacific Time, then it would be midnight in Rhode Island. Surely, I can get a hold of him now, and we can smooth things over.

Once more, I went over to the telephone, and with a bit of trepidation, asked an operator to put a collect call through for me. I listened to his phone ring, then when his machine picked up, the operator cut us off, "Ma'am, we've got an answering machine. Would you like to dial direct?"

"Um—no thanks, I'll try again some other time, thanks." I set the receiver back into place. Oh well, at least I tried.

Slipping back into the saddle felt familiar and comforting, except for the extra bulk and constriction caused by wearing raingear. Although the stars were announcing a clear night, I realized that once I was back on that high road, winding its way over mountain passes and along the Columbia River, the extra layer would be a welcomed addition.

I was right. After a half hour or so, the temperature dropped, as I rode into higher elevation, and the river breathed moisture into the atmosphere, and still, I rode on into the night. I hated missing out on seeing the scenery. That's the only thing I don't like about night driving. You can't drink in your surroundings. Now here I was, on the opposite side of the continent, riding through a mountain range, that I don't know if I'll ever get to look at. Now I have an excuse to come back some day a decade from now. Just so I can see this river-side highway, by day.

My roommate Barbie's phone call caught me by surprise. Well, not so much the call itself, but my reaction to it. Hearing her voice on the line, I realized that I didn't miss her one single bit. Not one iota. Naturally, I often thought of my cat, and wondered if she was being treated okay. Now, I drove ahead, thinking it was really nice of her to let me know that somebody is giving the kitty some attention, but I was taken aback at how little I cared about the woman who lived in my pad. When I get home, we'll have to see what we can do about that. Life is too short to have to share it with people who don't want to share it with people.

Hours passed and the misty, chilly air started to get to me. I pulled into a rest area to use the head. I had to get out of the wind long enough to restore some warmth to my body, which desperately needed it. Using available resources, I took my beach towel out, and after getting situated in the saddle, I draped the towel over myself so that it covered my head and shoulders, and hung down each side, capturing some heat from my Honda's engine, and funneling it upward to envelope me, as I rested my head on my arms, folded upon the top of my tankbag. I was actually quite comfortable, and as soon as I let myself go, I fell asleep.

Suddenly, I awoke, and wiped a puddle of drool from my arm. Wow! I was zonked right out. Twenty minutes of shut eye did me a world of good, and after a jaunt to the toilet, I was ready to rock and roll.

The sense of renewal lasted for as long as I felt warm, which wasn't long. Eventually, I needed another break, and I found a State Park to stop at. I followed a road a short ways, before coming to the ranger station. I pulled over, before reaching it, and repeated my towel trick, using the engine's heat to warm me, allowing my tired eyes to rest.

When I came to, dawn was turning the sky a pale gray over the horizon. I ducked behind a weeping willow tree, and squatted near a lake. With the promise of daylight arriving, I thankfully removed my raingear, and packed it away.

After I hit the road again, my gut roiled, announcing my emptiness. Watching for signs, I decided I would force myself to go on for the fifty miles or so, until I arrived in Portland. There I would reward myself with breakfast.

No longer was I cold, and no longer did I own the road. Traffic came out of no where, as commuters began their daily pilgrimage to work. A glance at my odometer indicated I had traveled eight hundred miles since yesterday morning. Truth is, I felt like it, too.

The nap refreshed me, and the world around me began to come alive. The highway, so nearly empty in the dark of night, except for me and all the midnight cowboys, was now crawling with steel, fumes and impatience.

Once again, I have pulled an all-nighter astride my mighty steed. It's not something I like to do, though. Dire circumstances cause me to stretch my endurance to these limits. My arrival at the Ride-In, on the first day, was important enough to deem this marathon trek.

Each year I attend the Women On Wheels Ride-In, no matter where, it becomes my summer vacation's destination. In fact, when I heard the '95 Ride-In would be in Washington State, my plan to ride to it evolved into this major lifetime adventure. Attending the Ride-In is just a tiny segment.

There were so many friends I would get to see again, and new people to meet. With the morning sun, my excitement rose to brighten the day. When my ride ends later today, I will be surrounded by motorcycle riding women and men, I will have a roof over my head, a long, hot overdue bath, a real toilet, running water . . . ah, the thoughts of it.

Finally reaching Portland, I relied on instinct to get through the congestion of morning commuters. It was bad, but nothing compared to Boston, where the worst drivers in the world are reputed to reside. So, my Pony and me, we battled it out, and I looked for an exit that would promise me a feast to break my fast. I noticed a huge billboard sign, instructing me where to go for said meal, and managed to get off the Interstate, and after a sloping curve that took me under a network of bridges and highways, I found myself near the water, in the parking lot serving the desired restaurant, with the busy highway zooming by in plain view.

A quick glance in my rear view mirror verified my suspicions. I was a wreck. I took my travel kit into the establishment and waited a few minutes for the hostess to seat me. She attended to other matters, however, and so I disappeared into the ladies room.

Inside, it was immaculate, and smelled of cherries, and I dumped my leather jacket into an armchair, followed by my kit, and woolen sweater. After I used the toilet and washed my hands, I spent five minutes cleansing my face with clearasil, and splashing water on it. My hair was still mostly in a braid, but lots of strands had come loose, and were tangled and twisted, matted and knotted. I worked them all out, then combed it until it was tangle free. The new tight braid I fashioned disguised the oiliness that had developed from days without a shampoo.

How many days? Let's see, I drove all night, and camped out the two nights before that. My last real shower was at the hostel, three entire days ago. Wow. I've been in the saddle so much, I wouldn't know. When I get to the hotel, one of the first things I'll do is sink into a tub, filled up to my chin.

A little mascara, a touch of lip color, and I feel like I look a lot better than when I walked in. I was over-dressed at this point, and knowing the day was going to become warmer, I took off all my extra layers, and with an armful of clothes, and my travel kit, I returned to the lobby, and waited to be seated.

Again, the maitre-de bustled about, glancing my way, but ignoring me.

"Excuse me—may I please be seated?" I asked politely.

"Why, yes, of course. Two?" She looked past me, expectantly towards the entrance.

"No. It's just me."

With a look of surprise and embarrassment, she stammered, "Oh, I'm so sorry I made you wait. I was wondering where your husband was. I thought he was still outside. I saw you come in, and then you disappeared, so I thought you went back outside, and-"

I interrupted, "That's okay. I'm alone. And I'm starving."

As she led me to a table, I asked for one where I could keep an eye on my bike. She sat me at a booth, beside a plate glass window, and nearby two men sat at a bar.

"Where are you from, anyway? You talk funny."

"Massachusetts."

"Did you ride that all the way here?" said the maitre-de, looking out at my loaded up two wheeler.

"No—I pushed it," I teased. Being overtired made me think that was a pretty stupid question. "Of course I rode it." I corrected.

"All by yourself?" she had to ask.

I must explain, the young lady was blonde. "Well, there's not much room for anyone else now, is there?"

She shrugged her delicate shoulders, and announced that my waitress would be right along.

Thankfully, she was right. In a moment, a woman heavy with child, offered me coffee, and laid a menu on the table. I was in a fancy place, but I felt I deserved it. I wasn't about to go in search of someplace else.

The breakfast menu contained huge meals, and it was hard to decide, but taking a chance, I decided to try something new, the restaurant specialty, Oyster Omelet, described as a three egg omelet filled with bacon, green pepper, onion, tomatoes and fresh Pacific Coast oysters. In addition, potatoes and toast would complete the meal. Price—almost eight dollars!

While I waited for my food, I made some notes. When I looked up for a second, one of the men at the bar introduced himself, telling me he couldn't help but overhear as I spoke with "the help." He wore white slacks, a shirt and tie, and when he told me he owned a sail boat and lived nearby, I was not surprised. He looked like a yuppy, just a little older.

He seemed very interested in my trip, and asked all sorts of questions, revolving around my riding gear, which was taking up the whole seat across from me in my booth, why wasn't I on a Harley, where was I headed and how come?

"You must get lonesome. I'm in real estate, and have a condo overlooking the river. You're welcome to drop in and stay a few days while you're in the area." He stood up, and reached into his pocket, then handed me his calling card. "My name is Richard, just give me a call, I'd love to have you."

I bet you would, I thought, but out loud I said, "Thank-you, but I won't be needing this. I have somewhere to go, and then I won't be coming back this way." I tried to hand him back his business card, but he wouldn't take it.

"No, no. You keep that, and if you change your mind, you just let me know. I'm a nice guy. You don't have to worry." He laughed. "I'm the one who should worry. You've got more balls than me, honey."

The more he opened his mouth, the less I liked him. His friend shook his head and rolled his eyes, and Richard went on. "I have a jacuzzi, and could pop open some champagne. I know how to wine and dine a lady, and you would be something else. I'll bet you could use a royal treatment."

"Thanks, but I can take care of myself just fine."

"I can see that." The man with the attitude of someone going through middle age crises proceeded to run his eyes from my boot tips, up the length of my tights, to meet my eyes flashing rejection his way.

Just then, my waitress arrived with my platter of energy, and I forgot all about that fool.

With great gusto, I dove into the eggs, and detected a slight fishy flavor. There were eight huge lumps, which were the oysters. I cut one in half, and green slime oozed out, so I hurriedly covered one half with toast, and without looking, scooped the other half into my mouth.

I chewed it up, and swallowed, trying to figure out if I hated it, or would maybe get used to it. After all, it's got to be good if it's the house special. I ate some more eggs, then had the other half of the oyster. The potatoes tasted much better, and I cleared out the flavor with more potatoes, then continued with the omelet, and another attempt at an oyster.

This time I put the whole thing in my mouth and squashed it with my tongue, then gagged when it burst its slime into my throat. These things are totally gross. Seeing them drip black and green putrid leakage, I quit. Here I was, a fully grown adult, forcing myself to gag my way through this breakfast.

My waitress returned. "How is everything?" she asked.

"Great," I told her, "except, I don't like those oysters. I can't eat any more of them." I made a face, showing my disgust.

"Is there anything else I can get you?" she asked as she refilled my coffee cup.

"No thanks."

My 'friend' had to leave for work, and he came over to my table and tried to point out where his condo was, but I wasn't interested. He wished me luck, and I wished he'd leave already.

When I finished my potatoe home fries, I was full. On and off, the waitress had come to my table, where it was out of the way, and she could sit for a moment on a bar stool and rest her feet, and chat with me. I waited around until she had another free moment so that I could say good bye, and wish her a trouble free birth day, which was coming soon.

It was nine o'clock when I was ready to get moving again.

The coffee, food, rest, and wash job made me feel much better, and with renewed energy I was able to conquer the last leg of this marathon.

In moments, I was entangled in the maze of bumper to bumper traffic, on my way to Washington. After making my way through the labyrinth of roadways, I found myself on a steel bridge, and upon crossing it I discovered I had thus entered the north-westernmost state in our country.

A colorful flowerbed announced our arrival.

WELCOME TO WASHINGTON

The chaotic scramble of frantic motorists prevented me from getting my ritualistic photograph.

Already, I longed for the solitude of the open road, but, I recognized I was in a major metropolitan city. Because of the river, the bridge I had crossed was practically the only access between Vancouver and Portland. Eventually, traffic filtered down, and I was able to pick up the pace again.

The last few miles slipped away quickly, and I kept noticing motorcyles, many sporting riders wearing pink, or fancy leathers that women like to wear. I was in Women On Wheels territory!

The Host hotel was a little tricky to find, due to an error in the directions, but, with a little investigation, I reached my destination.

Nine-hundred and fifty-six miles, straight through. I made it!

Miles: 956

Women have always yearned for faraway places .
                                              —Roslyn Friedman, b. 1948

CHAPTER 8

RIDE-IN
July 6–8   Days 20–22

*W*hen I entered the hotel lobby, it was like a homecoming. After loads of welcoming hugs, I got settled into my room. Before leaving home, I had arranged to share lodging with a woman, Annis Cassells, from California. We found each other, and she helped me unload my bike. Within one hour of my arrival, I recieved two packages.

One package contained my wallet, with eighty-six dollars cash inside it. The other was a care package from my girlfriend, Betsy, at home. I was *supposed* to get a thousand dollars worth of Traveler's Checks, but that was Russell's job.

I sunk into a bubble bath, up to my chin, and looked at all the goodies Betsy had sent me. Sample size packets of bubble bath, a variety of tea bags, some rolls of film, and a slew of letters. She was responsible for getting my mail and paying my bills, and she let me know that all was well. I read and reread each letter, treasuring them all.

After a good long soak, I dressed and joined the welcoming committee in the front lobby for a little while, but exhaustion took over. I retired to my bed and slept from two until seven o'clock.

Refreshed, I went to the ice-breaker party, then went to bed for the night. I had a lot of sleep to catch up on.

*   *   *

In the morning, I reveled in the soft, warm, cushiony mattress, and ran my limbs over the smooth sheets, enjoying the luxury.

Soon, Annis came out of the bathroom fresh from her morning shower, and told me of her plans to ride with some friends. "You're invited, too." She added.

I couldn't go, due to a meeting for the WOW State and Chapter Directors, but I did accept her invitation to join them for breakfast, in their room.

Sharon and Linda were dressed in matching off-road racing jerseys, of brilliant colors, and leather pants. Both appeared to be in their late forties, and graciously welcomed me to their room, offering me instant coffee, cereal and milk, fresh fruit and cookies.

Instantly I liked them. "Are you sisters?" They shared similar features, short curly blondish hair, slim girlish figures, and eyes that sparkled when they spoke.

They laughed, no, they're not sisters, but they are best friends. Annis knew them through work, and they were buddies. Linda was usually a passenger on Sharon's bike, but planned to learn to ride and own her own machine some day.

Annis is a black woman, with graying hair, probably right around fifty years of age, and she cut a rather styling image, in her black leather pants and riding boots. Several other women met up with them in the parking lot, and the group set forth to go and visit the living volcano, Mt. St. Helens.

I went to the Director's Meeting, and was reunited with Donna Brown, the Gold Winger from Michigan.

Afterwards, I had a chance to speak with the Big Wigs of WOW, and was made to feel like such a special person, as each of them asked me questions regarding my trip, my immediate plans, future plans, etc. They knew of my freedom tour, and were very excited for me.

As leaders, the four National Directors, Kathy Heller, Linda Stone, Sue Konopka and Sue Frish, were real people, not at all high and mighty. Each of them had her own personality, and despite their "position" within our Organization, each treated me with genuine friendliness, respect, and encouragement.

Suddenly, it was noon. I had a million things to do, while I was here. The motorcycle's drive chain needed lubrication, and a grinding noise squeaked out as I turned the rear tire. That same sound I'd heard back at my uncle's! Since leaving Detroit I hadn't noticed it at all, but, there it goes again, most definitely, *a noise*. One that I don't like. It seemed to be coming from the brake calipers, or at least from where everything sort of comes together at the rear tire, but, I didn't know what it was.

I felt terribly foolish for letting it go for this long, thinking it had fixed itself, then actually, not even thinking about it any more. Two thousand miles, and my poor Pony had a problem that I ignored and forgot about. Shame on me. Tomorrow I would bring her in to the shop recommended at the Ride-In.

There was a bike wash area set up in the hotel parking lot, which I took advantage of, with others doing the same.

"Nice horses." A woman stopped to comment when she saw the bright red mustangs galloping on each side of the rear panels of my bike.

"Thanks. This is my Red Pony, and I had her customized after a crash last year. Except, now I can't see the horses anymore because my saddlebags cover them up. I'm thinking about having that artist who is here, do some more." I indicated the front fairing, "Right here."

She said, "That would be nice. I love horses." She explained that she was a WOW member, but wasn't registered at the rally. She lived really close by, and had taken a ride over to check things out. After some coversation we decided that if my traveler's checks hadn't arrived by Sunday, that I would sleep over her house, until they came.

Before she got on her Harley and roared off, Judy Steinmetz said, "Now I know there was a reason for me to come here. I'm so involved with our local chapter of Ladies of Harley, that I don't do anything with WOW, but, I'm glad I stopped by here today."

With the bike all washed, I went over to see the artist at work. He had a photo album of his work, and I settled on a design I liked. With great anticipation, I left my spotlessly clean motorcycle by his station.

My budget allowed me thirty dollars a day. Ten for food, ten for gas, and ten for shelter. Thanks to my overnight visits with my relatives, and the Women On Wheels who had put me up, I had saved money on food and shelter, thus was able to justify the extravagant expense of this paint job.

What better souvenir to have, than one that will become part of me and my Pony—one created during our journey? Especially, in the future when people ask about the horses they're admiring. I can say "I had it done in Washington, the state." You know, bragging rights.

At supper time, Annis and her pals were still out riding, so I had fruit for supper, rather than spend more money. Using the box Betsy had sent me, I packed it with things I wanted to mail home. Letters from friends that she sent to me, I needed to send back, lest they turn into fire starter on some desperate night. Used film cartridges, and some photos that I had developed, doubles, so I could send copies home, to prove I'm alive and well, went into the box that I would send to Betsy.

Another best friend of mine, Robin, is wild and carefree. She is typically late, and undependable, yet she is also spontaneous, loyal and honest. Despite our differences, we have maintained a close relationship for decade, and have seen each other through many of life's ups and downs.

She'd started a letter to me, before I left home, then added to it for a couple of weeks, before mailing it to my home address, knowing Responsible Betsy would forward it. I read her letter over and over.

Her friendship shined through, and even though we were three thousand miles apart, I knew we held each other in our hearts.

Some of what she wrote went like this:

> Hi Dee, There are so many things I want to say, that concerned mother thing, like, wear clean underwear (or none at all!) You're not a child so I won't baby you. I will say, have a great trip. I can't wait to have you back here and hear about your adventures. In many ways I guess you could say our lives are going to change. It's always good to have those special friends of which we can share the good and bad, the happy and sad. I don't say it as much as I should, but, I love you. If I had come up to see you off, I would have had a couple of sniffles about you being safe, and you would have told me you're a grown woman. Don't forget your mace for those pesky raccoons, and the 2-legged animals. Take care and have fun. Love ya, Boppin' Robin
>
> P.S. How are those legs of yours?

Feeling melancholy, I folded up her letter, studied the collage she'd drawn all over the envelope, of fields, and sunshine, horses and Me and my Red Pony. Finally, this too, I tucked into the box, and I wrapped it and hoped to find a parcel post the next day.

*   *   *

Sometime later on, Annis returned. The hour became late, and still we tried to stretch out the day, just a little bit longer. We tried to figure out when I would reach Southern California, but I didn't really have an itinerary, so she patiently mapped out the directions to her house. No matter from which direction I came, I had a different set to follow. She included dates that she knew she would not be home, and informed me that any other time I showed up I would be more than welcome.

Satisfied that we'd settled that matter, we finally said good night to each other.

Sharing space with Annis was exactly how I wanted it to be. She did her thing, I did mine, and yet we still cared about the other person. We became friends, despite the years between us. Her wisdom was good for me.

*   *   *

Saturday morning, where does the time go?

Outside, John, the custom artist, was mixing colors, seated on a stool next to my Baby 'Ceptor. A sample drawing was taped onto a place near where I wanted the artwork done. My heart was beating with anticipation, like a child about to open birthday presents, I was so excited.

With magical precision and skill, he worked.

"Are you the girl from Massachusetts that rode on back roads all the way to get here?" He asked, making conversation.

"Well, mostly back roads." I corrected. "Let's put it this way. From Boston to Seattle is three thousand miles. I took 4,875 since leaving home, traveling westward, the whole time. I did have a couple of stretches on the Interstates, but for the most part I tried to stay on state highways, through small town America."

"I wouldn't think this is the most comfortable bike to be riding cross country." He observed. "Most of these," he nodded toward the parking lot full of parked motorcycles, "are the big tourers, like Gold

Wings. Actually, I am quite impressed at the women I have met here. Some of you people really ride!"

"I know it. When I look around at a lot of these machines, I can't imagine riding them, and yet, they are owned and driven by ladies."

"Would you want a touring bike someday?"

"I don't know yet. Somehow, it's not 'Me,' but maybe when I'm older, and comfort becomes more of a factor in my riding enjoyment."

John began mixing pigments, occasionally swiping up a particular shade and comparing it to the blend of colors on my mustangs.

"Tell me about your trip. Are you going home after this?" He made his first stroke, and within a few minutes, a horse's face emerged, and then, a dreamy, long mane was suggested, and as he worked, I shared with him my plans.

I took a couple of pictures as the man performed his magic, then left him to finish the detail work while others came by to watch him bring those horses to life.

*   *   *

A small dog, with a bow in it's topknot caught my attention, and I stooped down to pat it, as its little tail wagged furiously, while I spoke with its mistress for a few moments. The little tyke belonged to the vendors, 'Creature Comforts,' and they traveled around with their huge RV, and sold accessories for the motorcycle rider. Sounds like a pretty cool lifestyle for a couple in their retired years. There are so many motorcycle rallies going on all over the country, every weekend. They had quite the schedule to keep.

A lady named Jana tapped me on the shoulder. Looking at the name tag on my vest, she asked for my address, as she scribbled into a small notebook. "Diane 'call me Dee' Gagnon, okay . . . " she noted, "I'm doing an article about this rally for *Thunder Press,* a newspaper serving West Coast bikers, and I wanted to interview a few of the more interesting women that I met here, and you happen to be one of them. Would that be okay with you?"

"Me? Really? Well, sure," I laughed. "Absolutely."

For a few minutes we played question and answers, then she put her pen and paper away. I was flattered.

With so many old friends, and beautiful motorcycles to look at, getting from Point A to Point B at a rally is a time consuming process. It seems that every time you turn a corner, there's somebody you want to meet, or someone who wants to talk to you, or a bike you've got to check out.

Finally, I managed to get to a Honda dealership. The guys there were great. I explained what was happening with my Interceptor, and once again observed incredulous expressions as the mechanics and salespeople discovered that I had ridden across country on this particular bike, all by myself.

"Come on you guys. This is a great little machine. It's almost ten years old, I had it since it was born, and I take really good care of it. Everything about the engine is original, I've performed regular maintainance, and except for accident related repairs, I haven't had to do anything to it." I praised its virtues shamelessly. "Of course it can go the distance. I've only just begun!"

Before long, someone rolled my bike out into the parking lot, and told me that the sound that bothered me was nothing serious. The brakes were not completely releasing, so they were causing the sound, but only when the bike wasn't weighted down. He explained that they had to replace the glider pins, and that I should be all set.

I hung around, and hung around some more, as another customer received and paid his bill. Finally, I questioned the mechanic as to how much I owe, and was stunned when he told me to "Get out of here, you're all set."

"But I don't owe anything?" I was confused. For labor alone, I expected to drop forty bucks.

"Nope. Just get out of here, before someone changes his mind." In a quieter voice he added, "Hey, kiddo, you're on the road—take it for what it's worth. Somehow you struck a soft chord in the dude, so get going, and good luck."

Taking no chances, I rolled on out of there. How come I'm so lucky?

*   *   *

Before the banquet, I put on my long dress and hiking boots, resulting in a lot of good-natured teasing about my shoes, but I didn't care. I thought the outfit looked outdoorsy and cute. My hair was plaited into two braids and fastened with indian style leather braid wraps, and I felt as dressed up as any of the other women who had managed to pack a nice outfit for the banquet.

When the Longest Distance Rider award was announced, I basked in the applause, as I went up to collect my plaque. Before we knew it, the evening was over, signaling the final stages of the 9th Annual Ride-In. The laughter seemed to give way to sadness, and good-byes. All around hugs and kisses were spreading, and 'just in case I don't see you again before I leave,' wishes for a safe ride home were given. Gradually the room cleared, but not before I met a couple who asked me where I would be headed from here.

I told them I would be riding the Pacific Coast Highway, until it was time to head towards Colorado for another rally in two weeks.

"We live a good day's ride away from here, and very close to the PCH, Route 101. We'd love for you to stop and stay overnight at our house." The husband spoke as he opened a map and began detailing the directions to their town.

I explained how I needed to stay here another day or two, because I had to wait for my money to come in the mail, as it had not arrived yet.

"That's all right. When you come into town, there will be a restaurant, and a pay phone. It should be evening by the time you get there, and we'll be home from work. You drop a dime, and we will come and get you." The wife assured me, then she wrote their name and telephone number on the map, near Sheridan, Oregon, and gave it to me.

"I'll be there," I said. "I'll call you from Judy's house to let you know when to expect me. Thanks!"

Before I left, they advised me which route was the more scenic and less hectic of all my choices. "We highly recommend that you come this way, unless you have bad weather, then you might as well stick to the boring way."

We shook hands and I left, noticing the banquet hall almost empty by now.

The foyer contained the spill-out from the banquet hall, and in the half hour that followed, many women introduced themselves to me. Some of them were those who had written to me prior to my departure, and people from many states said, "Oh, *you're* the one. I wanted to write, but, not having met you, I wasn't sure if I should. If you're in my area, don't hesitate. I'd love to have you visit."

I learned of a Bike Wash that would take place by the Colorado Gold Chapter in August, and jotted down that information. That would be something I would try to make. I had friends from that chapter, although they missed this rally, I hoped to see them at their chapter fund raiser.

During the day, my money orders never arrived, so I picked up the phone and called Judy Steinmetz, to tell her I would need to take her up on her offer. She immediately told me that she would ride over to the hotel in the morning to lead me back to her place. Good, that makes it easy for me.

The hour was approaching midnight, and I was tired. Annis arrived, and I proudly handed her the attractive plaque that I had received. *Longest Distance Rider!* How exciting it was, to be recognized for this accomplishment at an International rally.

"Congratulations!" Annis stated sincerely. "You deserve it."

"Most everybody here deserves it—I just happen to live the farthest away, that's all . . . But, I'm psyched. Thanks."

We looked around our room, and sized up all the packing that needed to be done.

"What do you think? Tomorrow?"

"Sounds good to me."

We were able to agree on a wake up time, and despite our best intentions, stayed up talking long into the night. At last we determined that we must shut up, and shut down, so we did.

For a few days I was surrounded by three hundred eighty six people that I liked. My motorcycle had some time to rest, and had minor repair work done. For a couple of days, I hardly rode at all, my social needs were met, and I was sleeping in a very comfortable bed. Plus the fact that I didn't have to pack everything up daily was a treat. The Ride-In had worked wonders to refresh me.

Miles: about 20

Sit loosely in the saddle of life.
—Robert Louis Stevenson

CHAPTER 9

WASHINGTON
July 9–10   Days 23–24

*H*eavy rains covered the parking lot pavement with inches of water. Brightly colored rainsuits livened up the dreary grayness out of doors, while riders moved their bikes to underneath the lobby carport to be loaded up under shelter. The hustle and bustle was somewhat chaotic in the lobby, where piles of luggage were scattered all over the place. The downpour was predicted to last all day. Preparations took a little longer, spirits were dampened, and the day's ride ahead appeared to most as a chore, rather than a joy, understandably so.

Looking through glass streaked by rain, we could watch others drive off, plowing across the lot, leaving a rooster tail in their wake. Small groups, couples and individuals one at a time made their exit after wet good-byes. After I saw some of my favorite people off, I returned to my room to finish packing.

Later, I shuttled my things out to the lobby, and knew the motorcycle arriving just had to be my new friend Judy's. Who else would be coming *to* this hotel? Everyone else on bikes were *leaving*.

Drenched, she came into the lobby laughing. "Are you ready for this?"

I was impressed she chose to ride over. It would have been so much easier for her to take a car, but no, she said. "That wouldn't be fair. I would feel terrible riding in a truck, knowing you're getting soaked to the bone. Nope—we're in this together."

Now it was my turn to pass around soggy hugs.

Judy set forth with me right behind her, slicing into the river of rain on the byways, leaving a wake behind us. Within moments my gloves began seeping wetness through the seams at my fingertips, but it was warm out and didn't bother me. I would be out of this assault relatively soon, nonetheless, it took us a long time to travel the thirty-two miles to her house. Visibility was poor, and caution was a mandatory guest of honor on this ride.

We were on some back road, cutting between farmlands and forest, when the rain let up somewhat. Suddenly, up ahead I saw a deer cross the road ahead of Judy, and was relieved to see how she handled the situation. Like me, she cut her speed dramatically as the doe ran along the fenceline beside the road. The animal seemed to be looking for a particular spot, as every couple of seconds she dropped to her knees and tried to crawl under the lowest wire, but when she couldn't squeeze through, she would leap away, and scamper a few more yards along the fence.

You never know what a deer is going to do around traffic. They are completely and absolutely unpredictable. To hit a deer in your car, you are going to do some damage, to both the unfortunate beast, and to your vehicle. Hit a deer with a motorcycle, and you are the one in grave danger.

I have developed the habit of slowing down as much as possible whenever I see a deer, until I know that it is out of harm's way. This deer was acting confused and slightly panicked. The hole in the fence that it sought wasn't evident, and the rumble of Judy's Harley was scaring it. At any moment I was well aware that it may leap back into the road, and put us all in danger.

By now, we were nearly upon it, and barely rolling. Our feet would have to go down any second, then, Voila! She found the dip below the fenceline, which allowed her to scramble under the wire and she bounded away with terror in her eyes.

Knowingly, us two women looked at each other, then rolled on the throttle and continued down the road a bit. The left blinker started winking, and I followed Judy onto a dirt driveway, where she stopped her bike and got off to unlock a large swinging cattle gate. She motioned for me to go on, then she locked it behind her after bringing her bike through. The drive went about a half mile into the woods, then opened into a pocket of land.

On my left was a barn, and a big garage. Ahead, a trailer sprawled across a lawn, and on my right was a field where two brown horses stood with their heads over the fence, watching our arrival. All around the edges were tall ponderosas, hundreds of years old. We have arrived.

The two dogs came a-running, and ran circles around their mistress, casting wary glances my way, but their tails were wagging, and their mouths hung open joyfully. No need to fear. After a quick inspection of my tires, a sniff at my hands, I was accepted with a wet swipe of the tongue.

I unpacked my bike and using their well equipped garage, took care of some basic motorcycle maintenance.

Judy helped me put the bike on its center stand, then, I had to remove the lower cowling. After this I placed a pan underneath the bike and loosened the oil plug, and drained out the lubricant, black as sin. Using my oil filter wrench and tools, I unscrewed the oil filter. Carefully, I dribbled some oil around the groove of my new filter, before putting the rubber ring into place. Next, I had to screw the new filter in, 'finger tight.' I cleaned the threads on the oil plug, before replacing and tightening it. Lastly, I funneled clean, golden oil into the oil reservoir, and replaced the cap.

Meanwhile, Judy did some tooling of her own on her machine. While I had mine up on the center stand, I lubed the chain. Since I planned to ride about three hundred miles a day, this is something I should be doing every three or four days. Normally, once a month used to do the trick, but things are different now.

"All done." I said as I wiped my hands with a rag. "There is something so satisfying about doing my own maintenance."

"Yeah, I agree." Judy responded.

We had some chicken noodle soup and got to know each other. The more I listened, the more I liked her. I envied the fact that she grew up with horses in her family, and often had vacations when they all would go camping on horseback, something I've always fantasized about. She told me about the variety of jobs she'd held over the years, school bus driver, which afforded her the freedom of time off in the summers, and construction, and truck driving.

The timing for my visit was good for her, because her husband had been called away on business. Ironically, he was on the East Coast, in Rhode Island, forty-five minutes from where I lived.

We stayed up for the eleven o'clock news, hoping to catch a glimpse of the Women On Wheels rally.

A TV camera man had been there while I was packing up my motorcycle in the AM, but he doubted he would get anything usable, because he said he had the wrong type of film for the horrendous weather. He was concentrating mostly on a wonderful woman who won our respect at the rally, for the unusual accomplishment of learning how to drive a motorcycle while in her seventies. Eileen McAfee had taken and passed the MSF course, and due to her age, and with the support of her son, she owned and rode in style on a Gold Wing Trike.

Out in the rainstorm, she zipped around the parking lot, showing off figure eights, tight circles, and enticing everyone to whoop and holler as she maneuvered that thing like a pro. She came splashing up beside us and ordered the camera man to "Get on!" and he did.

With his heavy camera, covered in plastic wrap and balanced on his shoulder, he crawled aboard, and went for a wild ride around the asphalt sea, hoping to get view from close to her perspective. What a riot!

So now, as the news droned on and on, Judy and I convinced each other that they were saving the best for last, but alas, the news ended, with nary a glimpse into the world of WOW.

By now Judy and I were really drowsy, but we poured another glass of wine, threw another log on, and poured out our hearts a little more. Mostly me. I found myself confiding in her, telling her about my trials and tribulations with Russ.

"Lose him, Dee. He doesn't sound good for you." She advised me.

"I know, but he does have his good points, too. You're just hearing about the things that give me doubts."

"I know, I have no business telling you what to do, and I know you're a strong and a smart woman. You'll figure it out. Maybe this trip is the best thing that could happen to you," she said.

"Who knows? Maybe Mister Right is out west somewhere, just holding out for a girl like me," I kidded somewhat hopefully. "Anyway, at least I'm not tying myself down, right? I'm free to do whatever I please. He said so, and even though I'm not looking, at least I know I can do whatever I see fit. He doesn't even seem to care. He'd probably be glad to finally be rid of me."

We both remained silent for a little while, then, figured it was time to hit the hay. The room offered to me was small and cozy, decorated with motorcycle memorabilia. My twin bed was warm underneath lots of quilts and blankets and I bade the night good-bye.

Wolf Haven is a refuge for wolves that have been exploited by man. Some of the beautiful animals that exist there have been retired from the moving picture business, and others are there for different reasons. At any rate, once the Canis Lupis has lived in captivity it is unsafe to ever be released into the wild. Some are destroyed. A few have gotten lucky, and were adopted by this agency to live out their remaining years. Their freedom has been sacrificed in order to teach Man the value of the wolves' niche in nature.

Judy and I were escorted by a guide in a small group of perhaps seven individuals. We listened and learned things we never knew, thrilled to observe the magnificent beasts.

Seeing the wolves up close like this was engaging. There was something about their eyes. They were yellow, and intensely deep. I wanted to lock eyes, and let my spirit absorb some of whatever it was that attracted me so completely, and compelled my being to stand in awe, and respect. After a spell so precious and solemn, the wolf would turn away, secure that he had done his duty. One more human has been touched, one more human has learned.

The Wolf is an endangered species.

The Wolf has a place on our continent, and in the realm of Nature, and within the ecosystem, here on Earth.

The Wolf is not a protected animal, yet its future is in danger.

We have been a menace to the Wolf. We have created the monster, through our fairy tales, and our encroachment on wild habitats, our ranching, hunting, and prejudices.

After a totally moving, fascinating, disturbing and enlightening monologue, interspersed with questions and answers, we were asked to visit the Gift Shop.

Before our time was up, however, John asked us to stop and listen to his imitation of a wolf's howl. Much to our surprise, from all directions around us, the wolves one by one began to raise their voices in response. An eerie sensation swept through me, as I watched, and as if on cue, different wolves would raise their muzzles to the air and wail. Some remained laying down, and some sat on their haunches and others stood, four feet square, head tilted back, singing the song of their ancestors.

During most of our visit Judy and I remained speechless, only jabbing each other to point out a favorite, or simply exclaiming, "Wow, they're so gorgeous."

Once we were back in her truck though we bubbled with new knowledge and excitement.

We compared wolves to bikers.

Both are misunderstood by society.

Both get a bad rap, based on stories of exaggerated evils.

Many wolves travel in packs. So do many of us.

The image of the lone wolf is one that many bikers identify with, particularly if traveling alone.

We idolize the symbol of freedom and wildness that the wolf portrays.

Often, that big, bad biker you shrink away from, is the kindest, most generous person you could know. Tenderness lies hidden beneath that tough exterior. Self protection.

We have an image that is hard to escape, harder to live with and accept. But, because some individuals, wolves or humans, have inherited hate, and do not control their rage, humanity remembers every injustice, and blames the Wolf, blames the Biker.

Still, I cannot get over the allure of either.

*   *   *

Earlier, Judy and I had awakened at an hour that would enable us to ride horseback before the heat of the day.

Having owned horses in earlier years, I knew how to prepare a horse for riding, and it's an activity I really enjoy, perhaps even more than the ride. I think that a horse enjoys the attention, and imagine that it must feel like a massage when done leisurely and thoroughly.

Porky came into this world as a wild horse, a mustang, on the ranges of Colorado. Judy had adopted him and raised him since he was a youngster. Now he was fifteen years old, and a fine, handsome, gentle animal. I held out my hands, and he snuffed at them, then standing to face him I spoke to him, and he brought his muzzle to my face. We traded breaths, and he gave me his approval. His horsey scent filled me with memories and happiness.

Judy let me ride Porky, while she rode her husband's bay gelding, Dandy. We rode off under bright blue skies with huge fluffy clouds. We got to a Christmas tree farm, and skirted the edges of it, acres and acres of little pine trees in various stages of growth, all perfectly trimmed in the traditional conical shape. The acreage was surrounded by tall old growth wild trees, and at times we crossed through grasses and meadows of wild flowers that were tall enough to tickle our steed's bellies.

The scenery was picturesque, the weather mild, and sitting astride this mustang to amble through the Washington landscape for ninety minutes was a relaxing experience.

All too soon, it was getting closer to high noon and the hottest time of the day. The horses took us home willingly, and after we removed the sweaty blankets and cumbersome western saddles we took turns treating them to a shower of cold water from a hose. We set them free inside their grassy acreage, all wet and shiny, and placed bets on which would be the first of the two to find the sandiest place of all to roll in.

"Let's go in and call the hotel to remind them that we'll be coming by to get your money, Dee," Judy suggested.

*   *   *

"Hello. This is Diane Dee Gagnon, and I was staying there at the Women On Wheels Ride-In last weekend. During my stay, I was supposed to receive a package, but it didn't arrive on time."

"Oh yes, Miss Gagnon? We got your package today, but the Women On Wheels have all gone, so I had it returned to the sender," said the young man on the phone.

"You did what? I left specific instructions on Saturday, and again on Sunday about that package. It was very important for me to have it! I said I would be staying in the area and coming by personally to pick it up on Monday. I can't believe this." I groaned, and rolled my eyes towards Judy, exasperated, as I listened to his whining excuses. "May I please speak to the manager?"

With great poise I repeated my complaint, and emphasized how I had left strict, implicit instructions to *"Hold onto that package! I will be back on Monday to get it.*

"Now, here I am, clear across the country, at my only address for a month. I'm on the road. That was supposed to be my money for the next six weeks. Now, I've got to wait for it to get all the way back to the East Coast before I can figure out how . . . "

"I'm sorry. I see we have a problem here," she deduced.

The woman put me on hold, then returned. "Miss Gagnon, I'm happy I can be of service, you see, your package was placed on my desk just a few hours ago." (And here my heart made a little leap.) "But, because it had WOW written on it, I personally had it sent back." (And here's where my heart sank.) "However, I know the courier. He's a friend of mine. I will ask him to bring it back to my desk personally, tomorrow."

During my conversation with the hotel manager, Judy was playing charades, indicating that I would sleep over another night. After I hung up, we grabbed each other in a schoolgirl hug and jumped up and down giggling like idiots. "I don't know why there has been so much confusion over this whole money thing, but, something good has come out of it," I confessed.

"Yup. We would have never have gotten to become such good friends. I'm really glad you're here, Dee."

"Me, too."

Funny how you can meet some people and feel like you need to keep your thoughts private. Then, one day you meet a person that you think you can trust, you sense a kinship, and you open up and share your hopes and dreams, mistakes and triumphs. What makes you feel skeptical in one situation, yet causes you to spill your guts in another? Is it intuition that guides me in my choices for fellowship?

These things I pondered as I fell to sleep in this twin bed, thankful for the people who have come into my life as the result of this journey. Some, I expect I shall see again. Others, like Judy, I may never see again, but will always remember. Such an intense friendship that was bonded during my unexpected visit can never be taken for granted. There had to be a reason that our paths crossed, and I am able to take a part of Judy's spirit with me when I move on.

Miles: 32

*We all live in suspense, from day to day, from hour to hour; in
other words, we are the hero of our own story.*

Mary McCarthy, b. 1912

CHAPTER 10

WEST COAST
July 11–13　Days 25–27

*I*t was early and cool when Judy and I put on our duds,
and headed out to the hotel together. My bike was all
packed, and after I collected my package, I would be leaving Judy's
hospitality.

As we rode along the back roads, I followed, listening to the
'potato-potato-potato' rhythm of her Harley, and inhaling the pine
fragrance on the wind. Judy's face was partially covered by a dark
pink wrap, and riding glasses. Her gloved hands controlled the
throttle and clutch smoothly, and black leather covered her entire
body. She appeared to be a different woman altogether, and yet I
knew, this was the real Judy, just like the Judy I spent the last couple
of days with.

When I get on my motorcycle and ride, I dress to protect myself,
and the outfit is second nature to me. But, looking over at my escort,
I see what the others see when they look at me. A biker. A tough
chick. Maybe.

But how wrong that perception is.

I am only a woman. I am sensitive, emotional to a fault, and I cry
sometimes.

My motorcycle brings me freedom. Takes me to places I have
never been. It teaches me balance, rewards me with thrill and
excitement. When I begin to dress for a day on the road, I leave
behind my worries and cares. Each part of my 'biker costume' serves
a purpose, and when I am ready, that's when I truly feel like 'me.'

It is sad that some folks will see all the leather, and shudder,
because, inside there is a female, strong, assured, confident and able.
Nature speaks to me, solitude calms me, and each day is a gift for
me to examine and enjoy. I love America. I believe in humanity.

Without this faith, I could not leave my home, my work, my loved ones, in this quest to see my country in this manner.

Side by side, we entered a busy part of town. Judy's Harley, and my sportbike loaded to the max. As we stopped at red lights, people stared when we'd make comments to each other. I wondered what they were thinking, after an entire weekend of seeing Women On Wheels from many states saturating the area.

My thoughts, however, were evident. Two dynamite ladies from opposite coasts, we came together in friendship and in the wind, (and in the rain.) As unlikely as it may seem, we have a created a bond stronger than a horsehair rope, and tighter than a bore and piston. But very soon we will be saying good-bye.

We pulled into the hotel, and the manager handed over the long awaited package, and I gratefully acknowledged her apology.

The postmark indicated that indeed, the parcel hadn't been mailed on time, but I'd already suspected that. At least I had it now. One thousand of my hard earned dollars, in the form of Traveler's Checks which should carry me through another month, after I ran out of the first grand. I still had plenty leftover from that, due to all the hospitality I had received when I was west-bound.

Mission accomplished, it was time for me to be on my way. Not caring what anybody thought, Judy and I hugged each other tightly and wished each other well. Saying good-bye was getting easier with practice. Instead of feeling sad, I tried to feel glad for the opportunity to have shared some time together.

At the end of the parking lot, Judy drove straight ahead at the lights, and I turned south.

*   *   *

It felt good to be on my own once again. My social needs had been met. The Women On Wheels Ride-In had given me the chance to tell, and listen to others' tales of their trips to Washington, to make new friendships, and strengthen old ones. Then, I spent two more days, jam-packed with activities and Judy's company. As much as I enjoyed every minute of the last five days, I realized, I was craving solitude.

My little Honda seemed happy to be on the road again, and we followed its course along the Columbia River. Soon we would be getting onto the famous Route 101. Anticipation was building.

The Pacific Coast Highway was one of the drives that I had planned as part of my limited itinerary. For so long I had heard about its attributes as a motorcycle road not to be missed. I was really looking forward to the element of danger, riding my Pony along the sea-cliff's edge and flicking her from side to side as we speed along the treacherous strip of asphalt.

Finally, I was on it. The first leg of my Journey was over. The miles ticked by, and I found myself passing one State Park after the next. I could sometimes smell the ocean air, but mostly I rode through little touristy towns, and then I entered the forest.

The trees towered overhead, and the road swung sharply to the left, then curled to the right as my Red Pony and I got settled into a pace that was exciting, yet comfortable. I had covered one hundred and fifty miles of joyous curvaceous lines, when I rounded an easy wide turn and snapped out of my revelling. A quick swerve to the left kept me from the rear bumper of the car that had suddenly slowed to a crawl before me.

On the right shoulder of the road a couple of cars were pulled over and as I inched my way past, I saw the reason why. A gold colored sportscar had gone off the road. It was completely turned around, its Corvette-type nose pointed in the wrong direction. Already a few motorists had gotten out of their vehicles to gawk, or offer assistance. I continued down the road, mindful of the scene that I just witnessed, and toyed with the notion that it could be me, if I wasn't careful. Except, my body and my heap of engine and luggage might go on unnoticed for hours, as I lay hurt and dying down in the ditch.

A shudder ran through me, and I did not try to push the thought aside just yet. Sometimes I need a wake up call to keep me from getting too extreme. I felt this could be one of those times. Not that I was driving crazy. I wasn't. Far from it. But, as the days wore on and my confidence and ability increased, I didn't want to lose my sense of respect. The incident served as a reminder for me.

Highway 101 burst out of the trees, and I could see that I was on high ground. The road coursed along yellow fields with spotted cows, in big, square pastures that sloped up steeply on my left. On my right, the hay fields dropped away dramatically and the sun felt warm after riding through the cool depths of forest.

I enjoyed the change in scenery, and began to notice little signs that predicted pull-offs coming up, around the next bend or two. Finally, I decided to make a quick stop so I began to watch for the next such sign.

I leaned into a curve, and suddenly, stretched beside me on the horizon was an expanse of blue, sparkling in the sun. The Pacific Ocean! In two seconds, it was gone, as I followed the road around a hillside, and through another bend.

A pull-off was indicated, and I down-shifted smoothly and drove into the small parking area, which overlooked the sea. Bordering the edge were huge logs that were set up on the ends, spaced apart as sentries standing guard at the cliff's edge.

The enormity of the moment suddenly struck me full force, and I leaped off my bike and grabbed my camera out of the tankbag. With one hand I unzipped my jacket, and the other freed my helmet chin strap. In one deft leap, I surmounted one of the two foot high posts, and raising my arms over my head, helmet in one hand, I twirled and whooped with sheer triumph.

My little Interceptor has taken me from coast to coast. This is my first glimpse of the Pacific Ocean, and I got here on the back of my Red Pony. I live forty minutes from the Atlantic Ocean. Across the continent! I did it! We did it! Me and my Red Pony. My heart wanted to burst.

When I drove in I hadn't noticed the van sitting there. A man got out of the driver's seat and spoke. "Would you like me to take a picture?" he asked.

"Oh yes! This is a big moment. This is the first time I've seen the Pacific Ocean. I live on the east coast. I drove my motorcycle from coast to coast! All along I had planned to ride on the Pacific Coast Highway, but it never occurred to me—the significance—how seeing this ocean would make me feel. Like, what an accomplishment."

With my Nikon camera, he captured me in elated emotion, standing up on that pillar, arms stretched upward in a symbol of victory. Then, as if he knew it was the right thing to do, he got into his van and drove away, leaving me to my moment, all by myself.

For the rest of the afternoon, my ride was straight out of my fantasies. My bike sounded smooth, the wind whistled in my ears inside my helmet. The familiar smell of salt air reminded me of beach days at Cape Cod. Ahead of me the road spilled out before me, aesthetically appealing and beckoning me onward, Come on. Look what else I have to show you, it seemed to call. The sun was warm on my right shoulder, but my scarf was snug around my neck keeping the sea side chill at bay.

The vast shoreline was edged by a silver-gold beach. Great rocks, big as buildings, jutted up out of the sand, casting shadows which grew more elongated by the hour. The emptiness amazed me. I had never seen a stretch of shoreline free of mobs, at least not in the summertime. Here, I rode for hours, looking out for someone to be walking the beach with their dog, or a couple of romantics on palomino horses cantering in the surf, but, the beach was bare.

Giant boulders thrust their shoulders out of the water, and stood stubbornly as centuries of salt water bashed itself unceasingly against these rock fortresses. The Oregon coastline reminded me somewhat of the rugged rocky shores of Maine, but here it was more dramatic, less inhabited, and much grander.

God is such an artist. To use the Earth as a palette, and create the visions that man attempts to copy, such imagination. I feel very fortunate indeed, to have eyes to see, and a heart that is willing, a mind that is open, and a soul that is free.

For today, I am glad to be alive. I am finding it hard to comprehend that I am out here, that I've left my job, took a chunk of my savings, to take off this way. There's no way anyone could change my mind about that decision now, either. Not ever. This action, leaving "life" as we know it, to cruise around the country aimlessly on my two-wheeler is probably the most outrageous, self-serving, and ultimately fantastic thing I have ever done.

It is well with my soul.

The hour came when I arrived in Otis, Oregon. There I was supposed to stop at a certain restaurant and drop a dime. A few minutes after I made my phone call, a four-wheel drive vehicle pulled into the parking lot, and Dale rolled down his window to yell, "Follow me."

So I did.

Here I am at another Women On Wheels home. Although I had met Nancy and Dale after the Ride-In banquet, we hadn't gotten to know each other at all.

Everywhere, all over, folks have been saying to me, "You've got guts. You don't know what kind of weirdos are inviting you to sleep over. Be careful. Blah, blah, blah."

Well, I have to say this, these people are inviting me, a total stranger into *their* home. That speaks of faith and trust, why shouldn't I feel safe?

Nancy and Dale Oakes greeted me warmly, and treated me to dinner at a Chinese restaurant. Conversation revolved around my day's ride, their family and work lives, and resulted in an invitation to go to the lumber yard where the two of them were employed, and have a tour, personally guided by Dale.

Sounded pretty interesting to me. I mean, when will I have the opportunity again to learn about the lumber making process? There are small companies all over New England, but did it ever occur to me to go visit one for educational purposes? No. Besides, I'm in Oregon, where timber is one of the leading resources. Not just timber. Redwoods.

Once again, I would have to set aside my personal feelings, in order to gain a better understanding of the big picture. "Save the trees. The redwood forests are declining. Save Mother Earth." Chants running around in my brain, but not spilling from my lips.

I told them that I would like to take them up on their offer very much. I thought I could learn a lot.

After we returned, I did my laundry and showered. The Oakes would be leaving for work at 5 AM. They gave me instructions to lock up the house in the morning. My tour was to be at 9 AM. I went to bed at last, thinking that a whirlpool bath first thing in the morning would be terrific.

Miles: 273

The first few moments of morning consciousness have started to seem like a memory game. I wait to see if I can guess where I am before I open my eyes.

When I awaken inside my tent, there is a curious quality of light that seems to surround me, and a humid stickiness in the air. Usually, I am immediately aware that I'm camping, but then I have to try to remember where I live, for that hour. Which state am I in?

What kind of place am I camped at? Are there shower facilities, or is there at least running water? Then typically, the need to empty my bladder becomes a barrier to any thoughts of catching a few more ZZZ's, so I need to get up and take care of that irritation.

When I awaken in a bed, my first perception has been that I am resting between sheets, and beneath my head there is a soft pillow instead of my leather jacket folded inside out and wrapped around my sweater. Again, I concentrate for a second, trying to get my bearings. Where am I now? What state? Whose home? Am I supposed to be gone by a particular time? What time is it? What day is it?

Each morning is its own mystery, during those lucid levels between deep sleep, and arousal.

On this fine morning in my grogginess, I became aware of the cushiony bed, and the darkness in this bedroom that used to be somebody's son's room. That's right. Oregon. Nancy and Dale Oakes. I have no idea what day it is, I'll have to check my journal, but, I know it's not a weekend. They told me they'd leave me locked in their house, so I could go when I want. I want to leave by 8:40, so I can see the lumber yard. Where's my watch?

Out loud, "Shoot! Eight o'clock! I can't believe it."

My hopes of a pamper-me session in the jacuzzi went down the drain in the shower.

Quickly I dressed, packed up the motorcycle and got on.

Fuel on. Ignition on. She's in neutral. Engine cutoff switch on Run. Choke open. Press Start.

Nothing.

Huh? Press Start.

A dull click.

Press Start five times in disbelief.

Five times a "Click" mocked my efforts.

This girl groaned. "It's my battery." I just knew it. I never have bike trouble. It had to be the battery. They can just go on you, with no warning or symptoms. They just quit.

Now what do I do? I wondered. First, I've got to tell Dale or Nancy, so they won't think I stood them up. Part of me hoped that one of them could leave work to help me, and the other part felt terrible for it.

I found Fort Hill Lumber Company in the phone book. A secretary took my call and delivered a message, "Call Dee."

Dale called, "Hey. What's up?"

I told him.

"Listen, I'll use my break to go home and get your battery charged. I have a charger."

I protested. "No. You don't need to give up your break on my account." The idea of a charger hadn't even occured to me. I was thinking I'd have to go out and buy a new battery, but where, and how would I get there? But now I didn't have to worry.

He considered for a second, then said, "Why? Do you know how to use a battery charger?"

"Well, yeah. That's easy."

He told me where to find theirs, and when I was through to come to the lumber yard. He would postpone his break.

How can I be so consistently lucky? My battery, (please let it be my battery) dies when I'm staying at someone's home, and they own a battery charger!

Five out of twelve cells had no more than an inch of water. The rest of them were somewhere around half full. I was so glad no one was here to see, this blackened, bubbly mess. I would have died of embarrassment.

Neglect was the main contributor. I chided myself for not bothering to check it at the Ride-In. The squeaky wheel got the grease. I forgot all about inspecting my battery.

With the battery all hooked up, I waited and used the telephone to call my answering service. Four friends had left messages, and I updated my outgoing announcement. "Hi. I'm in Oregon, now. Had a dead battery this morning, but luckily, I was at a WOW's house, and they had a charger. I'm headed down the Pacific Coast Highway for at least the next few days. Today is the twelfth of July, my twenty-sixth day since I left home. I'm really happy, and things seem to be working out just fine, so don't anybody worry. Bye."

I slipped a dollar bill under the phone after I hung up.

In about an hour's time, the battery finished charging. For lack of a better idea, I used a chewed stick of gum to plug up the opening where there used to be a broken cap. Then I slipped the Die Hard into its snug compartment, fastened all wires, nuts, bolts and attached the breather hose confidently. Then, I turned the key and pressed the starter button.

Varoo-oo-oom!

Good. I shut her down.

My Red Pony pulled through her open heart surgery, without complications. I replaced the side panel, the seat, saddlebags, and the rest of the baggage followed. Then I neatly returned the things I'd borrowed, and got dressed to go.

The lumber company was crawling with activity, as I rode in and headed for the trailer where Dale had directed me to go. I parked the bike by the door and climbed the steps and rapped on the door.

"Hello. Dale and Nancy Oakes are expecting me," I said.

"Oh yes," said the receptionist, as she picked up a phone and spoke to someone on the other end, motioning for me to be seated.

The inside of the trailer was cluttered, but clean. Somehow they had managed to squeeze a few offices into this small space, and I was seated across from the receptionist's desk. She shuffled papers around attempting to look busy, when suddenly she simply stopped, and placed her plump, middle-aged hands palms down on top of her work and looked me over, quite directly.

"Dale and Nancy said you're quite the adventurer," she stated frankly. "To look at you, I wouldn't guess. You're on a cross-country motorcycle trip?"

"Well, I've made it from coast to coast, yes—and this is just the beginning," I answered.

She sat in her cushioned office chair, with her crisp white blouse, and her no-nonsense skirt, opaque hosiery, and low slung pumps crossed daintily under her desk, looking across at me, with open, astounded admiration. She was perhaps fifty, ordinary and likable.

Across from her, I sat with my leather pants on, a long sleeved shirt, bandanna wrapped round my neck, and by my feet, my jacket, gloves and helmet lay heaped in a pile. I couldn't help but notice the contrast that we two women represented.

"What do you mean, 'this is just the beginning?' Where are you going now? You're not going home?" she asked.

"I'm planning to be on the road for one hundred days."

"A hundred days? Why a hundred?"

"It seemed like a nice round number." Simple enough. "This is Day 26." I figured I'd tell her before she asked.

"You have a lot of guts. What happens if you run into trouble?"

"Like what?"

"Well, like, this morning. Your bike wouldn't start."

"Yeah, well, that was *my* fault, not my bike's. I'm not worried about the bike. I know it inside and out, I have tools and a manual with me, and have the confidence to at least *try* to do my own maintenance and repairs," I said. "But, really, I like to say, the only trouble I have with this bike is the big nut on top of it."

She laughed.

I continued. "No. I'm not afraid. I am having the time of my life."

My new friend Susan continued to ply me with questions, and expressed her intrigue over my bravery, which I don't seem to think is all that spectacular. I tried to explain that I am just like anyone else, but she shook her head. "No, you have something special. God bless you."

At last, Dale came and formally introduced me to Susan.

"You have one heck of a little niece," she said, approvingly.

We both laughed, and told her there is no relation.

"Maybe Dale can explain what I'm doing here, some other time," I said, then, to Dale, "Come on. Let's go. We're burning daylight."

The air was permeated with sawdust. It assaulted my nostrils, and stuck in my throat. Immediately I sought protection for my eyes, thankful for the ugly goggles they lent me.

Dale led me from one point to the next, in the logical order of steps in the lumber making process, introducing me to different workers. Some times they would explain what their job was, or how things worked, and sometimes he would take over the narration. The jobs were rotated several times a year, so that individuals would stay fresh, not get burned out and careless. I noticed more than one hand with less than five fingers.

The noise level was high. Things squeaked, chains clanged, saws squealed, voices shouted, radios blared, engines roared, boards slapped, belts chattered and ears rang.

The mechanics and engineering here amazed me. My past life work involved people, so all this machinery and equipment was new to me.

As I went from one stage of the procedure to the next, I was impressed by the resources used and steps taken to avoid waste. I learned that nearly all the product from this company was destined for shipment to Japan, where redwood is in great demand. I tried to imagine the sultry steamrooms and garden decks that would be the ultimate destination and final outcome of the work I had witnessed on this day.

The lunch whistle blew, and as it turned out, the company was having a 'Safety Picnic' that day, and I was invited.

After I finished eating, I thanked everyone who'd insisted I stay and enjoy the picnic, and bade farewell to Dale and Nancy Oakes. They were granted a few extra minutes to see me off. We walked back to the trailer where my bike was parked, and I popped my head inside to say good-bye to Susan, the secretary.

"Bye, Sweetie. It was sure nice talking with you. Be really careful now," she said.

I trotted down the few steps and saw that Dale had a concerned look on his face.

"You're leaking oil," he said as he sniffed at his fingertips knowingly.

"What? I don't usually." Funny how we talk about our bikes as if it is ourselves we are talking about. "*I* don't usually leak oil." I should hope not!

I squatted down to inspect, and sure enough, there was a drip coming right off the end of my oil plug. Apparently, I didn't screw it in tight enough when I changed my oil the other day. Luckily, Dale had noticed the minor leak. It would be hard to detect when I was camped out. Dale produced a wrench and tightened the oil plug, and then I was ready to go.

With a big hug from the both of them, I was on my way. It was much later than I would have liked, but, the events so far made it all worth getting started five hours later than normal. My tummy was full, my intellect had been stimulated, and now I was ready for some solitude and adventure.

*   *   *

In a short time I returned to the coastline. Route 101 follows the coastline roughly, and along the way there are lots of tiny roads that take you right to the beach. These are the lanes where seasonal cottages sit, and hardly anyone travels on. Every so often there were signs indicating a scenic loop, which takes you right to the edge of the sea, and then brings you back to the Pacific Coast Highway.

Otter Crest Loop made me curious. Would I be likely to observe otters there? I turned off, and found myself on a twisty, narrow, pathlike little street which took me to a place where I could park among several other vehicles, and have a look-see.

I spotted a marmot on the grassy slope, eating plants and sunbathing, but wondered where the otters were.

Instead, I saw a whale. *A whale!* It didn't show off, it simply surfaced a few times, spouted some spray into the atmosphere, then disappeared.

Awesome. Time to move on.

*   *   *

After riding for some time, my craving for some coffee developed into a full-fledged need. (Am I addicted or what?)

Ah-hah! The Harbour Espresso Trailer. Yippee.

I was the sole customer, and the girl working in the tiny trailer welcomed the opportunity for some animated chit-chat. My Interceptor was a great conversation piece. So many people seemed to live vicariously through me during the short span of time that our circumstances threw us together.

Almost always the questions were the same. For me, the whole routine almost became rote. Sad to say, for many others the same conversation was the most exciting thing that happened to them for many days. It seems so weird to feel that others see me as some kind of hero, when all I am is Me.

The only thing that sets me apart is that I am living the dream that many people take with them to their graves. I am experiencing total freedom from career, family, and external expectations. How many people can make that claim?

Even I, too, will someday be stuck in a rut again, but I will always know that I did this thing once. I could do it again. Life is short. Play hard.

The girl at the coffee stand banged her hand on the counter when I told her that I had just encountered my first whale in the wild.

"No way! I've been living here for seven years, and still haven't seen one," she yelped.

Maybe I was just lucky.

Or maybe she stopped looking.

The coffee lady invited me to stay overnight at her house. "It's just a little place that my husband and I rent. We have a futon that you can sleep on. I'd love for him to meet you. You have such an exciting life," she said, adding, "It wouldn't hurt to save a little money, right?"

I pondered her offer for a few minutes. I felt perfectly good about her, personally, but I felt I hadn't traveled far enough yet today, and there was something else, but I couldn't quite put my finger on it. Then it came to me.

I hadn't camped for a week, and I missed it. Counting backwards I figured it out. Last night I was at the Oakes, the two nights before that I was at Judy's, for three nights before that I was at the hotel, and the night before that I drove all night. It had been a whole week since I'd slept in my tent, in the great outdoors, and today was a beauty. I couldn't give it up.

When I told her why I was declining, she looked over at my bike, then seemed to understand, as if she too could feel the pull of the open road.

Now I know I'm a vagabond, I thought. Instead of longing for a bed, I'm at the point where I miss the ground. Hard to imagine, harder to believe.

*   *   *

The next strange event was the sight of the sun sinking into the horizon over the ocean. During the times in my life when I was privileged to sleep on a sailboat in the bay, I had witnessed the sun rise many a morning, reflecting onto the sparkling ocean surface.

Now, I was cruising along and the huge orb in the western sky was suspended over the ocean, signalling the *end* of a day, rather than a beginning. It filled me with a subtle emotion, something I cannot explain.

Knowledge. We all know the sun rises in the East and sets in the West, but to *feel* the difference with the human senses, and in my soul, that was the emotion I was experiencing. It was so tangible I could almost taste it, similar to my first glimpse of the Pacific, when the realization hit me regarding what I had done. Seeing the sun set over the ocean for the first time was like a religious experience for me.

Then it was dark. I set up camp at Ballard's Beach State Park, in Oregon.

Miles: 192

*   *   *

How can I describe the Oregon coastline? Huge rocks like centennials jut up out of the blue ocean Pacific. Waves lap onto gradual beaches. Huge driftwood logs lie scattered on white or tan beaches. I rode on a road that is a biker's dream, except for slow moving traffic, (traveling at the speed limit, ugh.) Twisties, switchbacks, cool forest envelopes, sometimes. The ocean air makes leather, a sweater and scarf welcome. I could be in heaven.

The road swept along the land's end, and I leaned into the curves, feeling one with my machine. A dot appeared in my rear view mirror, and came closer. For a long time, another rider shadowed me as we carved our way along the famous road. Eventually he passed me, but settled in at my pace, and I realized I had acquired a riding partner. He rode a Ninja, and from time to time we switched off, first one taking the lead, then the other. When I stopped to refuel, so did he.

"I was wondering what you looked like under there," he said when I took off my helmet.

"Hope you're not too disappointed."

"Nah, not at all."

We were both going to be on the same road for the next couple of days, why not travel together? I asked him about sharing a campsite later on.

After we were back on the road, I found myself wondering about my decision. I felt as though anyone else in my life would lecture me for trusting a total stranger. Then, I came to the conclusion that I don't care. I am out here on my own, and I can do what I want. I know what feels right, and I know what makes me want to steer clear. This guy, I felt, was no threat. I trusted my women's intuition.

For hours we rode, each deep in our own thoughts. I felt free as a bird, wonderfully liberated, and innocent as a child. I fantasized a little. Not about Ninja Mike, but that I was on a road trip with a man with a matching bike, like the one in my mirror, and we were happy, trusting and in love. Just a dream, but it was fun to look ahead at a perfect road, to listen to the sound of my Interceptor, to smell the ocean breeze, and to see the reflection of another person enjoying the same things as I.

We came to the California border, and stopped for my obligatory photograph. A family on bicycles was already there.

The father asked casually, "Married?"

Mike and I looked so surprised when we blurted out "NO!" that the children chortled.

Making small talk, "Girlfriend and boyfriend?"

Again we had to say no.

"Gee, I'm not doing so good here, am I? What are you? Total strangers?" he joked.

Mike raised an eyebrow, I shrugged, and we agreed, "Yeah, that's about right."

"Sounds like fun."

Moments later, we were stopped by a barrier. While peering into our helmet openings intently, a guard asked a few questions, sternly. I didn't expect this, at all.

"Any fruit?"

I admitted I had a mango, and was told I had to relinquish it.

"My mango?" I whined. "Can I pull over and eat it instead?"

Mike waited patiently while I made lunch out of my mango. He told me that bugs and plant diseases could be introduced to the state by imported produce, and because California is such a major supplier of fruit, they control the state borders in this manner.

We continued our drive south. Again, a satisfying sense of accomplishment began to leach through my being. With each new experience, I feel the canvas of my soul being worked upon by a divine artist. Sometimes the strokes are bold and unmistakable, and other times there are subtle nuances that at first go unheeded, until a texture has somehow emerged, or a shadow lies, where once it did not.

Riding many miles is not my goal. Hitting every state is not on my agenda. There are travelers, and many I know are motorcyclists, who will clip across the corner of a state that hasn't been colored in yet. That cheating side trip is their measure of success.

My ideals are different. Indeed, I too, will color in the United States, but for every state I fill in, there will be a multitude of memories. Faces will come to mind, and bits of conversation will be recalled. I am tasting the flavor of America.

California tastes like mango.

*   *   *

One of the pleasures of riding is that one can sort through emotions, dream intricate scenarios, or make up glorious plans. You can delve deep inside, leave the world behind and become one with your machine and the narrow strip of pavement beneath your tires. You can share an excursion with a friend without saying a word. You can ride with a stranger and silently bond, then ride off on two separate paths without ever having seen the other's face. That's what it's all about.

In grammar school, I remember reading about the Redwood forest, and Douglas fir trees. I felt awed at the possibility of such enormousness. When my parents took their only cross country trip in the family station wagon, I was jealous to hear that they had seen the Redwood trees. When I announced, with my ten year old wisdom, that I would take a trip there some day, my mom told me it's awfully far away. Then she hugged me close to ease my disappointment, and asked me lightly, "Do you plan to ride your bicycle?"

I thought of her now, up in heaven. "Ma? Do you see me? I have made it to the Redwoods, and yes, I *am* riding my bike!"

The forest was magical, and the drive enchanting. Mike and I stopped, and wandered, apart from each other, each lost in our own thoughts. I caressed the raspy chunks of bark which encased the trees like callouses. Now that we were off the bikes, we found there were no words. The dryads and wood nymphs had cast their spell, and we were jinxed. Wordlessly, we mounted up, and respectfully continued our sojourn through the heart of the forest, back to the coast.

Hours passed and we rode through Eureka. We made it to Fortuna. We were tired. We were hungry. The KOA was situated just off the noisy highway exit. What a joke. We paid eighteen dollars for a patch of grass. Together we found pleasure in mocking the place we paid top dollar for. Like all KOAs, it catered to big RVs.

I knew I had made the right decision, to have Mike sharing this situation with me. We picked up food at a supermarket, and built a fire. The evening passed as we shared tales of riding and camping. After washing up, I told him I'd be turning in. He stood to stretch. I thanked him for riding with me, and splitting this awful campsite with me, and being a good sport. "Thanks. I had a really nice day," I said, and gave him a quick hug.

Mike placed his arms around me gently, and I rested my cheek against his chest. Shock waves rippled through me, surprising me, and I moved away shyly. I *was* giving him a buddy hug, but something happened.

Mike's bearded face gazed down at me, and I heard him breathe, once, twice. "There's room in my tent for two," he invited.

"Thanks, but I've got plenty of room, too," I replied, simply.

His hands rested softly on my shoulders. Ever so quietly he inquired, "Are you sure?" all the while, looking at my face.

For a second I couldn't return his gaze, confused by this temptation, but, he was on his way to visit a lady friend in L.A. The thought restored my honor, and gave me the words I needed.

"Mike, I don't want us to do anything that we'll regret later on down the road, understand?"

He pulled me closer, and in a brotherly way, placed his lips against my forehead. "You're right. I'll see you in the morning," then he turned away, a gentleman.

Miles:299

We all live in suspense, from day to day, from hour to hour;
in other words, we are the hero of our own story.

Mary McCarthy, b. 1912

CHAPTER 11

SEASIDE TO DESERT
July 14–16   Days 28–30

The 'moment' of the night before was never mentioned, and Mike and I went about the business of breaking camp, without a lot of conversation. Before taking off, we sat at the picnic table and talked over our agendas.

While it was still early, we took to the road and headed south, on the Avenue of Giants. This was more wonderous riding through the earthy magnificence of Redwood Forests.

We had a lot of riding ahead of us, but we would be separating at Leggett, when I would deviate from Route 101 in favor of the more intimate Route 1.

After a couple hours of more inland riding, we entered Leggett and encountered lots of major road construction. We decided to say good-bye right there, so with uncomplicated means, we each reached out a gloved hand, with motors running and shouted farewell wishes, and then he pulled away, leaving me on the shoulder of the road.

By one o'clock in the afternoon I turned onto Branscomb Rd. and shortly it turned to dirt. 'No big deal,' I thought as I slowed a bit, keeping things under control. The road was covered by a very light layer of loose pebbles, and with a shimmy here and there, I was reminded me to keep the pace down around ten mph.

After just a couple of miles, I rolled along, white-knuckled. A big old car driven by some wild-eyed teen sped along, leaving me in its wake of dust. He was on my side of the road, careering towards me at a speed that caused my heart to skip a beat, fearing that he may not see me in time, and that his monstrous machine would collide with me, as he skidded along just for the fun of it.

This kept me riding to the far right side of the road where the gravel is looser, for fear that I might get run off the road. I was well aware that a tap on my brakes, or a swerve, would put me in the danger zone, as if I weren't already. But, I had come a few miles, and frankly, I was afraid to try to turn around. The surface was too shaky, the road too narrow and curvy, and what if that maniac or some other California surfer boy came screaming around the next bend?

Cautiously, I continued on my course, concentrating on riding ten yards at a time. Somewhere along the line, I grew accustomed to the demands placed on me as pilot of this sportbike, on this type of road surface, all loaded up with ninety pounds of luggage, and I realized I'd feel better if I at least *pretended* to relax.

That's when I noticed my surroundings.

On each side of me, the giant trees rose towards the sky. The road wiggled before me, and cut through a world of grayness. Every tree, each pine needle, all the brush, bushes and saplings were shrouded by dust and dirt raised up from each vehicle passing on this road. All the flora appeared to be white, gray, tan or silver dusted. The only color I could see, literally, was the shocking blue of the sky, or the orange numbers on my motorcycle dash.

I felt as though I was in some misbegotten forest, that got left in somebody's attic.

A great feeling of awe fell over me, as if I was really being transported into a magical fantasy forest, laden with fairy dust. Imagine, trees larger than life, all color erased, and me, a tiny speck rolling along, tires crunching over the gravel. This is an unexpected treat, defying description. Maybe I could compare this monotone vision to a soft snowfall on a splendid winter day, but the temperature was just right, and the silvery shades were muted and yellowed, not sparkling. I was captured, and filled with great joy.

This motorcycle is carrying me along a road that attaches two of California's most famous motorcycle roads. Where the hell are the bikers? They're not here!

Who else would be crazy enough to be riding on this road? How many of my friends would have voted to turn back in favor of the road more traveled upon? Heck, I wouldn't have taken it myself, if I knew how tenuous the driving would be! But, here I am, about as far from home as I can get. I'm all by my lonesome, but I have hardly felt lonely. Again I have laid eyes upon a sublime sight that evokes magic, and sorcery, enigma and mystery, in the labyrinth of my mind. This is way better than church! Funny how a 'wrong turn' can end up so right.

These are the things I seek, this is the reason I have set forth on this open voyage. These are the visions I would never encounter in a 'normal' life. This is the time in my life that I can let my spirit soar freely on the wings of my unrestrained imagination.

I was so caught up in this make-believe world, that unawares, I crested the hill I had been climbing, and realized I was now on a downhill grade, which somehow always seems more scary than going up. I had to divert all of my attention back to riding on this demanding surface, and with great relief finally found myself at the end of the road, where I turned left.

Riding on asphalt again was so easy I felt transported, rather than challenged. I floated along the narrow band of tarmac, which chased the foamy skirts of the Ocean. On my right, lovely beaches were caressed by the gentle surf, while the sun shone down upon my shoulders once again.

The changing scenery wraps itself around a rider. It sucks you in, and you become part of the world around you. Every breath I take carries a scent, or a mixture of them. Back in the wood, I detected the dustiness that invaded Branscomb's misbegotten forest, and the aroma of redwood and pine, intermingled with the scent of my own fear. Thirty minutes later, I am rocketing through a mist of salt air, newly mown grass, and the occasional cow field.

How I love to ride. Every time out on the motorcycle is a separate and memorable event, it seems. Always a mini adventure. I still can't get over that I am riding out here, on the opposite coast, and that the majority of my experiences have been positive. I have succeeded, and continue on my trek confident that I am accomplishing probably the most significant event in my entire life.

As I cruised along Route 1, I thought back to the years, and individual days when I would be at work and daydream about one day just hopping on this iron horse and riding until I cannot go any farther. I have arrived. Better yet, I do not have to turn around and go back. I'm nowhere near finished. My spirit soars.

It doesn't get any better than this. How much contentment can I possibly stand?

As I rode along the seascape, I recalled a term I had heard from a friend in my past. When beauty is so astounding that you can barely contain yourself, you are experiencing an Eye-gasm.

So far, Route 101 and Rte. 1 made me weak with the sights that make me scream for more, and have forever burned their visions in my mind's eye.

*　　　*　　　*

In Guerneville, I stopped at a couple of private campgrounds and still, no luck. Then I came upon Schoolhouse Canyon Campground, and while I parked, was greeted by the host.

After a few minutes of small talk, I asked "How much for a tent site?"

"Twenty dollars."

"That's too much. Forget it, I can't stay here," I sighed. "Can you direct me to someplace cheaper?"

"Well, there are a couple of places, but they're more expensive than we are, and it's the weekend. I don't know what to tell you," he sympathized.

I could tell I had already won him over, so feeling I had nothing to lose, I bargained. "Come on, I'm just one person, I only need a place to set up my tent, so I can lay my body down. I'll take only one shower. Surely three or four people camping on a spot can justify that cost, but can't I get a discount 'cuz it's only me? Please?" I begged. "I don't even need-"

"Stop." He put up his hand. "I like you, I would say yes, you've made a good point. Let me go ask the Boss, my wife," he said with a wink, and in spite of his gray hair, he spryly climbed the stairs two at a time, and went into the office, motioning for me to wait outside.

In a moment he came back and told me to speak to the Boss. She looked me over, and stated that her husband said, "You seem like a very nice young lady, but you're asking for a break. How much are you willing to spend?"

"My budget allows me ten dollars per night," I said, looking directly into her eyes.

She sat forward and pushed the registration papers my way. "For twelve dollars you may stay, but don't tell anybody."

"Deal. I won't tell anybody here, but you have given me such a kindness that I know I will not keep it to myself after I leave. Thank you so much!" I exclaimed.

*   *   *

Living on thirty dollars a day was a challenge, for sure, but one I was sort of enjoying. Ten for food, ten for gas, and ten for shelter. Any dollars saved within these categories paid for beverages, admission fees, or any extras that I needed or desired.

I had to eat, and found myself at a restaurant, where the only thing I could afford was the small, garden salad. It was nothing special, but it was fresh and it would do. Meanwhile two older couples got seated at the table next to me. Before long they included me in their conversation. They were openly impressed. They couldn't fathom what it would be like to travel alone, to drive a motorcycle, to quit working in favor of a dream, to have an open agenda . . . all of this excited them, and I was urged to "hang onto this enthusiasm. It is very becoming."

The waitress came and took their orders, and then the ladies turned to ask me what I was getting. "This is it," I told them, adding, "I knew I couldn't finish a whole meal, I saw the plates on my way in, and I can't afford to throw food away."

The waitress came back with a tray of ice water, and proceeded to dump it on two of my new friends' laps. They howled with laughter, pushing back their chairs to jump out of their seats.

The waitress apologized profusely, and the party of four simply laughed it off, "Poor Charlie's been complaining about the heat all day. That'll fix him."

Because I was talking so much, I still had salad on my plate by the time The Ice Cube Quartet got served. Immediately, the two dear women cut off one half of their oversized burritos, and insisted that I eat.

They explained, "We come here enough to know that we can't eat the whole thing. We've had salad, and bread, and now we've got rice and beans . . . It's too much. Please, help us out and eat. We'll feel so much better."

"This I can't believe. Thank you," I beamed. "I will not forget this."

"Well, it's been so lovely to meet you, darling. What a wonderful, interesting life you are leading."

"It's people like you who make it wonderful and interesting," I returned.

Miles: 280

*   *   *

On Route 1, I was flanked by a motorcyclist.

Again, the unexpected thread of connectedness wove itself into my effort to remain independent. Still, the image in my rear view mirror offered me a sense of anticipation and comfort. I flicked the Pony to the left, then over to the right, aware that as I set up my corners, the rider on my tail was following in my tracks.

After a couple of hours I stopped for coffee. He darted ahead leading me to a corner where we parked.

Respectfully we shook hands and introduced ourselves. His name was Mark, and he was riding a Katana. He asked me about my journey. I told him that I would go as far as San Francisco, so that I could see the bridge, and then I would be making my way towards Colorado.

"Unless you know your way around, you could get all mixed up. Follow me, Dee. I will be your guide. It'll be fun."

"You're on! Let's do it," I agreed.

I stuck out my hand, and Mark shook it firmly.

The Suzuki led me away from Stinson Beach, and my Interceptor gracefully pursued, as Mark escorted me to the place most suited for viewing the Golden Gate Bridge.

He took me to Marin Headlands, stopped momentarily, but remained in the saddle, then motioned for me to follow him further. We continued up the winding road, to an overlook known as Hawk Hill, and dismounted.

With the voice of authority, Mark began to present historical facts, cultural anthropology and interesting points regarding the geographics of San Francisco. He was a wealth of information.

In the autumn, more hawks are observed here, than anywhere else in the country, because the migrating raptors prefer to stay overland, and this very place is the tip of the funnel on their route down the coast, thus the name, Hawk Hill.

"The Bridge," Mark continued, "is 2.5 miles across, was built in 1937, and is a suspension bridge, spanning the water 365 feet overhead, with about an equal distance below the surface. Most of the bay is *very* shallow, compared to the strait."

Thanks to his dialog, I had a greater appreciation for the bridge, and the city of San Francisco. For one thing, who would guess that the city now reputed to be so 'wild' and on the cutting edge, artsy and accepting of alternative lifestyles, was once a huge monastery of sorts, habitated by monks. How ironic.

Under different circumstances, I would have taken for granted the clear, sunny scene, not realizing that it is almost *always* foggy, obstructing the clear view that I observed that afternoon.

The impromptu history lesson was fascinating, and as I prepared to depart, and leave the coastline for good, I thanked Mark. "You could be a tour guide. Thanks a lot for your time."

He looked at me sincerely and answered, "Hey, the pleasure was mine. I didn't really have a destination today, I was just out for a ride, but meeting up with you was an unexpected surprise. I'm glad I could help."

At this point, I had to head east, and we said so long.

*　　　*　　　*

After the bridge, I had a series of interchanges and knots of four lane highways to unscramble, but Mark's instructions were exact and I made no mistakes, and I finally got myself onto Route 50, and the craziness of the overpopulated San Francisco region ebbed away gradually.

On this day I had the notion that I wanted to camp off road. I didn't want to pay for a campsite. I didn't want to deal with any people. I just wanted to be by myself, and find a place where I could pull off the road and sleep somewhere in the wild. I was excited to do the unthinkable, free style camping.

I hopped off a highway exit, in search of a suitable place to wrap up my day. A certain Silver Fork Rd. in the El Dorado National Forest caught my attention, and I found that it banked steeply up and around the sides of a mountain. I followed the snakelike road through modest dwellings, and tall thin pine trees.

I left the tar, and rode into the edge of the woods, and began to climb a rocky sort of trail which took me to a high, flat clearing, where I knew I would spend the night.

Satisfied with the location, I put my side stand down, but then found myself in a predicament. The ground was too soft to park on, but with my bike all loaded up I was required to put my side stand down in order to get on and off, because I couldn't just swing my leg over. Those days were long gone. Using the throttle's friction zone, I tried to inch the bike forward, aiming for some rocks or roots to set my side stand on.

Finally I managed to get that far, so I dismounted,but I didn't like the new position. My motorcycle was visible from the road, if someone was looking. As I stood there, a pick-up truck with some dirt bikes in the back went tooling by, and seeing that made me feel like I needed to get myself and my bike out of sight. I didn't feel up for unwanted company.

Not wanting to ride on this soft, root-entangled, rock strewn surface, I had to try to push my bike to a better location. It was so heavy, now that it wasn't on tar. Each bump felt like I was attempting to cross a log. Every ounce of my body weight, and all of my strength went into heaving the heavy beast just a few inches at a time.

You never know what you are capable of until you try. That is an understatement. As I tugged and balanced and pushed my motorcycle over the soft, hazardous ground, I was fully aware that if it tipped over, I was a goner. I was miles from the last house I'd seen, very little traffic was out here, and I felt as though I was in red-neck country.

"Come on, just a little further, ugh," I talked to the bike. I can't believe how heavy this thing is. I need to keep it leaning against me, because whenever I get it straight up and down, I feel like it might get away from me and tip over to the other side. "Argh—whew." I'd wipe the sweat off of my forehead, and tell myself, you can do it, you can do it. You have to do it, because there is *no one here* to help. You're on your own, kiddo. Now prove to yourself that you can do whatever you set out to do. You're the one who wanted to camp off road, scott free. Well, let's see what you're made of.

"Okay. This is good," I said to myself, and I stepped back to take a look around.

I stood in a clearing, edged by pine trees and a few oaks and other broadleaf trees. The road was out of sight, and well below my level. On the other side of the clearing, the mountain side sloped down, and I had a beautiful view of a valley, and the thickly forested mountain on the other side of that valley. Tall pines etched a design into the landscape over there, like needlework, under a clear blue sky.

Beneath my feet, pebbles crackled and twigs snapped. The air smelled pure, and I could hear the sound of water running, or falling nearby. I walked to the edge of my clearing and saw that a blanket of boulders had been flung down the steep slope of the mountain I had conquered. Down below was a small village, and all around me the stillness was punctuated by songbirds telling of my presence in their forest.

I took a little walk into the pinegrove behind my bike, looking for the source of the liquid musical, and found a stream running in between two mossy banks. At the head of the stream there was a waterfall sending cascades of crystal mountain nectar into a small pool below.

Feeling as though this little place was a direct reward for my tenacity of the last hour, I sat on a rock covered with rich green moist carpet. "It is time to just *Be,*" I told myself.

Then, the mosquitoes found me and chased me back to my world, where I found my Skintastik and applied it liberally. It was time for dinner.

I sat on a boulder, as the sun sank along an afternoon sky towards evening. I had soda, beef jerky, fresh fruit, a chunk of cheese, and a hard roll, followed by two wine coolers.

After my dinner, I had the need to eliminate. I crawled among some boulders, still modestly seeking cover before baring my butt. I squatted between two boulders, keeping my balance by resting my arms upon the rocks, and looking at the slant of the earth between my sturdy hiking boots as I tried to avoid getting anything undesirable on them.

Imagine my surprise when a *snake* slithered beneath my *butt* when I was in that position! Wonder who got the worst scare! The serpant disappeared in between the rocks and I finished my duties, buried the evidence and clambored back to higher ground.

The sun set, but I did not have a view of it. I simply saw the sky turn from blue, to gray to darkness, then a banner of stars spread itself overhead, with a moon so bright I was able to see.

The idea of sleeping in the open air without my tent intrigued me, and the work saved encouraged me to go ahead. Out here, I did not need the privacy, or protection. With a fleeting thought or two about that snake, I decided he lives over there in those rocks, I'll be fine up here.

I spread my tarp out on the ground beside my motorcycle, and fluffed my sack out on top of it. I noticed guitar music and voices wafting up to me from the valley below. Somewhere down there, there was an outdoor party with live music, and here I was, a vagabond in the forest, miles away and free as can be, with special entertainment provided to me for my personal enjoyment.

I leaned against my bike and instinctively curled my fingers around my soft leather amulet, feeling spritual and once again blessed. "Thank you for giving me Life, and showing me how to really Live."

Part of my God surrounds me, in the form of Mother Earth. Another part of my God is my own Spirit, which I have learned to pay attention to and nurture. When my Spirit honors Mother Earth, She in turn blesses my Spirit. I recognize the relationship, and am able to find peace in the simplest symbols, gifts from nature, and traits of my own which are gifts of my Spirit. Strength, kindness, energy and a positive outlook. These are things I cannot take for granted, but often I forget.

A simple off road respite in a California forest enhances my sense of balance, in a topsy turvy world.

I undressed, then shook my sleeping bag before crawling in. I want to share my life with Mother Nature, but don't want a snake in my bed.

Miles:264

*   *   *

It's the little things that bring the most pleasure, sometimes. The first half hour in the morning was spent stepping stones and balancing on a log fallen across the stream in order to fill my bottle at the waterfall. Later on I would toss back a swig and trigger a memory of the challenge I gave myself in the cool depths of this El Dorado National Forest.

As I dressed for the road, I mentally got psyched for what I perceived would be a difficult departure, after how hard it was to get here in the first place.

Obviously, it's not that I have "no fear," it's just that I don't let fear stop me. Sometimes fear is a messenger, and I obey. Other times fear seems to be an escape that keeps a person from doing the things that they think they want to do. More often than not, if there is something I want to do, really want to do, fear is not what will stop me. I don't want to hear that it cannot be done, or that I cannot do it, until I have tried. Maybe even tried again and again.

My bumpy trip away from my encampment was not too bad at all, which surprised me, because given a choice, I prefer going uphill on horrible surfaces. Going down hill scares me. Being fresh in the saddle, and not weary from a day of riding made a difference.

Soon, I was driving around Lake Tahoe, and enjoying the sights and scenery so much that it was an hour before it occurred to me that the lake was on my right. It was supposed to be on my left! How'd that happen?

I turned around to go back, and although I had wasted plenty of time, I didn't mind, for the sight of the mountains doubled by the mirror of a lake brought me pleasure.

Outside of South Tahoe, the road eventually became a jumble of on and off-ramps, and traffic was relentless. In the midst of a city, the highway disappeared into a tunnel which sucked me in and spit me out on the other side. Multi-lanes finally dwindled as I followed Rte. 50 out of Carson City, and the realization struck me that I had entered Nevada.

I had missed the state border sign, but the terrain changed dramatically, as if I had just walked from one room into another.

The air was saturated with the essence of sage, growing in clusters spaced evenly over the steep slopes of otherwise barren mountain sides. The sun beat down on my Red Pony and me as we began to earnestly cover some ground. My destination was at least two hundred miles further.

I delighted in how things looked. The low clumps of sage, the rugged pinyon pine, the sandy, dry earth, all this captivated my attention. The land swelled and dipped, but every growing thing seemed to stop at three feet tall. There were small mountains, expanses of range, pinyon pine, juniper and scrub grass no bigger than bushes.

Well aware that the desert is teaming with life, I looked for foxes and hares, but never caught a glimpse as I sped along the seemingly empty road. Barbed wire fences sometimes ran along for miles. What for? Are they keeping something in, or are they keeping me out?

Once or twice I noticed a long dirt road which led to a ranch somewhere out of sight. On the fence posts, cowboy boots were hung upside down, reassuring me of human presence, even in this remote land. Later on I was to learn that they served as a form of communication amongst the ranchers.

A ranch road was frequently several miles long. To save visitors the trouble of making an unnecessary trip, the people of the homestead would turn the boot on the fence post so that it faced away from the ranch while they were away. When they returned, they would reposition it so that the toe pointed toward the ranch. Sometimes everyone on the ranch had their own boot, Mr. and Mrs. Rancher, sons, daughters and hired hands.

After hours of driving, I grew increasingly aware of the lack of traffic. I had become accustomed to my new surroundings, and boredom set in. The road was relatively straight, towns were far and few, with a whole lot of emptiness in between. For the first time, I read the road sign that had marked the road at generous intervals.

RTE. 50—THE LONELIEST ROAD IN AMERICA

Ha! That's an understatement. I'd been driving along for the last fifty miles playing a mind game with myself trying to keep monotony at bay.

Hm—if I ride 75 mph, no, that's too hard to multiply—eighty—if I ride eighty mph, like so, for fifteen minutes, and count cars that I see during that time, how many vehicles do I predict I'll see in that time, and how many miles will I have covered?

By the time I'd figured out the math, not my specialty, I'd have covered another ten miles. Most of the time, there were zero cars, and I realized this Rte. 50 was aptly named.

So, when I noticed that sign, I wanted a photograph of it. I made a U-turn, and then and there my motorcycle stalled.

This bike never stalls! Now that I am driving on *The Loneliest Road in America* she stalled, for no apparent reason. I had to laugh, but my laughter caught in my throat when she wouldn't start.

With mounting concern, I climbed off and pushed the motorcycle off the road and took a deep breath. I tried pushing the start button again, but only heard *Ne-ne-ne-ne,* and nothing more.

I knew I had gas. I'd topped it off in the last town. What else could it be? I wracked my brain, and looked for oncoming vehicles, hoping that if I wished hard enough, help would come my way. Yup, on the loneliest road in America. There I was, standing next to an over-packed sportbike, with half a bottle of tepid waterfall nectar, in the middle of Nevada.

It would do no good to panic. Walking away was out of the question. Sitting down to wait seemed fruitless. What to do? What to do?

Think. Really think. Like a mechanic. Or with my imagination. If I were the Red Pony, what would make me stop working? It's not the battery. I hope it's not electrical . . . what else could it be? Already ruled out the gas. What else? What is different today?

The altitude! That's it! With fingers trembling with excitement, I reached in for the small knob and twisted it a quarter turn, adjusting the idle. I hadn't touched it since that day in Wyoming when I'd almost run out of gas. Maybe the combination of hot, dry air, and riding pretty fast, relentlessly for hours on end was effecting the Honda's performance.

When the motorcycle sputtered for a second, then started up powerfully, the pride and relief that surged through me could not be matched.

Once again I have conquered a challenge. I felt bigger than life, and couldn't resist whooping for the sheer joy of accomplishment. I grabbed my camera, and ran over to the sign and snapped a photo. I have passed another test.

"What will you do if you break down?" How many times I had heard that question.

Now I had the answer. "I have broken down on the Loneliest Road in America, and I solved the problem all by myself."

For a while, the miles flew by and I reveled in my glory. Gaining recognition for achievements is a wonderful experience, and worthy of humble pride. But this, this solo triumph cannot be compared to having an award or trophy thrust at me. When I rode away from that tense episode, I was a little bit stronger, a little more confident, and very thankful for my self control. As these traits are used, they multiply.

My soul could be a pearl. Layer by layer it is formed, more valuable with each new layer applied. Some people only see the shell, ugly, ridges and scars. Those who have wisdom can recognize the possibilities inside. I may be an oyster, but I must remember the pearl I carry inside. I may meet an oyster, but have to be aware of the hidden pearl.

The act of riding a motorcycle cross country wouldn't seem to be a spiritual journey, but for me it has become a great tool in the shaping of my spirit. The things I suspected I had inside of me are now emerging, one day at a time. I did not leave home to "find myself," but I am discovering all the traits that made me "Me," have been mere shadows of what they could be. Much of this I believe comes from being alone, too.

Being alone forces one to think entirely for one's self. All decisions are yours to make. You are responsible for much of what happens to you. You can change your mind when you want, and don't have to explain yourself, or let anyone down. There is something about feeling proud, when no one else is around to witness the reason, no one is around to boast to, but you feel proud just the same.

Exactly one month ago, four weeks ago yesterday, I set forth. I have spent less than eight hundred dollars, and traveled nearly seven thousand miles. I knew I could do it, and like every other day so far, I have no regrets. What a rush.

*   *   *

Austin, Nevada is practically a ghost town. With a wide Main St. and old-styled storefronts, it looked like someplace from an Old West movie. I rode in between stores with false fronts, and a huge bank where I imagined robbers on horseback getting away with murder. Small homely, unkempt houses dotted the scene, clustered closely nearby the main part of town, became more dilapadated the further away they were. Here and there however, a spotless homestead would stand out amongst the squalor, and I wondered, what kind of people live here?

One gas station with an unrecognizable name was closed for business. Shoot! It's Sunday. What if I can't buy gas on a Sunday in this forlorn town? I cruised the length of town and found the other one.

A whiskered man in overalls came out and turned on the fuel tank, then sauntered back into his store, leaving a stream of pipe smoke lingering in the hot, dusty air.

I thought I might spend five dollars instead of the usual four, because I was quite low, but the actual total registered with disbelief.

"Seven twenty-five?" It's never taken that much! Did I just pay for the last persons' gas, too?"

The sardonic gent drawled, "No ma'am, that's seven twenty-five," and held out his calloused palm.

I paid him, and muttered my way back to my bike. The old-styled pump stood like a big lump, and the numbers declared $1.85 per gallon. In a place like this! The going rate was $1.35 at the time, but here was a perfect example of supply and demand, price-setting, etc.

With no place else for hundreds of miles, travelers who pass this way must get gasoline. When there's no choice, cost doesn't matter. I clambered back onto my bike and made my exit, looking down the side streets, knowing full well that the locals knew the place to get gas. Wouldn't be surprised if it was around the back of this same station.

I pictured the locals, peering at me from behind dirty, tobacco stained windows, laughing at the sucker on the motorcycle who they hoped would never return. They want us all to stay away. All the curious travelers, tourists, and others who might come in and steal their lifestyle, their property and their history. Austin was one of those places that you just pass through. Outsiders are not especially welcomed with wide grins and hospitality, but, a part of me could understand.

No such thing as McDonalds, Jiffy Lube, or Super Stop & Shop. This was small town America, left over from one hundred years ago. If it was my home, I'd want it to stay the same, too.

I rode on, up, over and through some mountains. Childhood afternoons were sometimes spent watching a good ol' western on

TV, and I had memorized the way the land looks, and visualized riding horses for days on end crossing the great expanses, just like the cowboys. Actually being in this scene, seeing it three dimensionally, as I rode my iron horse, turned me inside out.

The promise of ancient Native American writings on rock brought me to Bureau of Land Management Hickison Petroglyph Recreation Area. The camp was free, but there was no water, and only pit toilets. My kind of place. The sign marking the turn-off was so unobtrusive, anyone would have to know what they were looking for. How did I get so lucky to learn of it?

I followed a dirt road for several miles into the wilderness, then arrived. Each of the twenty or thirty sites consisted of a small area cleared of the low lying scrub brush, a raised grill, and a picnic table set on a cement slab. A wooden shelter curved up and over each table, providing shade from the sun. Thick, lush, squat pine trees grew here and there.

A grizzled old man and handsome German shepherd strolled my way. I dropped to one knee to meet the dog, but he lunged toward me. The old fellow had a tight grip on the rope, restraining his canine.

"Just leave him be, he's ornery as hell," he warned. After a stern hand signal, the dog dropped to his belly, and growled at me, menacingly.

The tall, old man stood expectantly, eyeing my motorcycle. We chatted for a few minutes and he told me how he'd stayed here for "nigh two weeks." He sets up his trailer for two week intervals all over the place and gets back to nature the way the good Lord intended. "Ain't you afraid travelin' all by yurself? That's why I have this dog. You just can't trust no one these days, you know."

"But aren't campers some of the most down to earth, friendly, generous people you could meet?" I countered.

He rubbed his bristly chin and thought for a minute, then said, "I guess so, but ya never can tell."

I changed the subject and asked him about the hiking trail mentioned in the BLM pamphlet. He recommended I take a look for myself, "but if ya really want to go for a hike, you want to get up before dawn and go down to the water hole. I've seen a wild band of horses there, myself."

"Wild horses? I'd love to see them!" I cried, upsetting the dog who jumped up snarling, and received a sharp reprimand for its action.

"OK. What ya gotta do is," and he turned and stretched his arm, pointing. "See that fence? Walk along, oh about a mile or two, and look for a large rock placed atop a fence post. You'll have some canyons on your left. Leave the fence, and walk in between the canyon walls until you see a small watering hole. I seen the horses there a few times this week, at dawn. In fact, the stallion just stole a black mare from a ranch around here, and she kept trying to run away home, but he won't let her go. The lead mare and the stallion won't let her be for a minute."

He continued, "It's time for me to be moving on. I'll be busy getting packed to go. You go by yurself tomorra." He tipped his hat and shuffled off.

The prospect of seeing wild horses in their true environment had me elated. I could barely wait for the next day. For now, I took the BLM Petroglyph trail and viewed spirals, orbs, hand-prints, chevrons and animal shapes, all carved by indians hundreds of years ago.

As I made my way back to my camp spot, I thought of the despicable Fortuna Kampground of America, where I had stayed only three nights ago. For eighteen bucks, I had camped there and hated everything about it. Now, I was here, so far off the beaten path I'm surprised there are other people here, even, and it's free. I got a lesson in history, in recognizing certain plants, and have an opportunity to scout out some wild horses.

Again, I didn't set up my tent. Dinner was a Power Bar and a few sips of water. The daylight leaked away, replaced by bands of color which reflected off a thin cloud cover rising up from the horizon, almost undetected.

Miles: 312

Day 4
WOW member Kim Gabriele Shea and her daughter Nicki share their passion for horses and motorcycles with me at Pine Rock Ranch in Toledo, Ohio.

Day 11
I have a tradition of collecting photographs of state signs during my motorcycle travels. Check out the bag of hamburger buns tied onto my load of luggage.

Day 14
The Badlands—indescribable shadow lands, South Dakota.

Day 24
WOW member Judy Steinmetz and I went horseback riding. She is riding her husband's horse, Dandy, while I borrowed her horse, shown on the back cover. Roy, Washington.

Day 25
Judy and I in our duds. Same gals, different day.

Day 25
My little Interceptor has taken me from coast to coast. This is my first glimpse of the Pacific Ocean, and I got here on the back of my Red Pony. I live forty minutes from the Atlantic Ocean, across the continent! I did it! We did it—me and my Red Pony. My heart wanted to burst.

Route 50 is aptly named "The Loneliest Road in America" – Nevada.

Day 30

Day 32
Often I asked strangers to take my photo. My load of luggage is almost as tall as I am! This was taken at a scenic overlook in Utah.

Day 32
Soon I was carving my way along the road I had seen from above. Canyons rose up steeply on either side, offering a continuously changing view as each minute passed.

Day 37
Read all about Pat Washer and a man called Road, while I'm in Colorado.
Here we are together at the Top-o-the-Rockies Rally, in Paonia.

Day 53
My tent, a Coleman 3-man, offered plenty of space for my gear, myself and room to spare, yet still packed down to a manageable size for the motorcycle. Here it is at sunset, before the "huff-huff-huff" night at Riverside Campground in Nebraska. Notice the horse head painted on my fairing, and the missing V-Four scoop.

Day 52
The horse farm where my Pony turned 50,000 miles, near Buena Vista, Colorado.

Day 70
It was a lovely day to ride in the Arizona desert, not a monsoon in sight!

Day 87
All across America, barns are a source of rustic
beauty. This one is along Route 36 in Kansas.

THUNDER STRUCK RIDGE
100 FEET BELOW
ELEV HERE 4780

Day 94
The sky is gloomy and gray—matches my mood with less than one
week before my ultimate freedom comes to an end. I am taking my
time along the Blue Ridge Parkway, Virginia.

A travel adventure has no substitute. It is the ultimate experience,
your one big opportunity for flair.

—Rosilind Massaw, b. 1948

CHAPTER 12

WILD WEST
July 17–20   Days 31–34

*A*s a child, I had been taught to mark my trail in
unknown places, and to turn frequently and study
the appearance of landmarks behind me. Often they could be
unrecognizable when viewed from the other side. Such was the case
out here, and once in a while I dragged two branches of deadwood,
and laid them down together in such a manner that would point me
in the right direction. Had I only used one dry stick, then I would
have doubts; did I put this here, or was it already here? Having pairs
took away most uncertainty.

The watering hole appeared, and I sat down between some large
rocks about a quarter of a mile away and waited quietly. The sky
lightened to muted pink and yellow, and I canvassed the region,
wondering where the band would first appear. Time slipped by, and
behind me the sun came up, hidden from me as I crouched deep
within the ravine, and still no sign of the horses I yearned to see. I
laid back and yawned, studied the twisted clusters of scrub, the
hardy grasses, and the abundant, tiny yellow flowers, and red tufted
flowers I thought were called Indian Paintbrush. They were so
stunted, I wasn't sure. Dots of color rebelliously stood out against the
drab background.

Finally, it was well beyond sunrise and I faced the fact that there
would be no wild horses for this girl today. Sad and a little
disappointed, I started to retrace my steps. It was a good thing I had
marked my trail, because otherwise I might still be wandering today.

Even though I didn't catch a glimpse of America's symbol of wild
freedom, the act of hiking in their territory with the expectation of
seeing mustangs was intrinsically rewarding.

Instead of oatmeal and tea, I backtracked and returned to Austin for breakfast. It had been days since my last substantial meal. "Excuse me, sir," I said to the man holed up at the gas station on this day. "Where is the best place to get breakfast around here?"

Slowly he sized me up, as if debating whether or not to tell me, then he pointed diagonally across the road and answered, "Al-lownch. Best breakfast in town."

I noted neon beer lights in the small dark windows.

"Also the worst. It's the only place,"he stated dryly, then turned away.

Folks stopped and stared when I entered the dimly lit interior. As my eyes adjusted, I saw that the place was divided into two rooms. To gain access to the rest room I had to cross through both of them. A handful of people were standing along one wall of the second room. At first, I thought they were playing old fashioned pin ball machines or video games, but then I realized—the clunky, noisy games were slot machines!

This is Austin, Nevada. Breakfast and slot machines at the local bar, on Main St. in what is practically a ghost town. Definitely different than what I'm used to. In the ladies room, I washed up thoroughly, brushed my teeth and braided my hair tightly, feeling much better afterwards.

During breakfast, I made my plans. Today is Monday, and this Thursday is the first day of the Top-o-the-Rockies motorcycle rally, about eight-hundred miles away. There were only three towns between here and the Utah border.

*   *   *

Highway 50 continued, fast, pretty, lifeless and boring. I stopped for gas in Ely, where I learned the correct pronunciation is 'Eelee.' The gas price was normal, I was relieved to find out. A biker had warned me to 'top it off' in every town out here, to lower the chance of being stranded.

While touring, I knew my mileage capacity was between a hundred and fifty to one seventy-five miles before hitting reserve. Until I experienced the emptiness of the western region, I never thought too much about it. Now, numbers took on a lot more importance.

The camp I wanted to look for was near Oak City, Utah. I stopped at a grocery store, needing food and water, because once again I was resigned to a rustic camp. I spent four dollars.

As I rode further into Oak City, I kept my eyes peeled for the "Forest Road" indicated in my guide book. Within just a few seconds, I was driving out of town.

Oak City—if you blink your eyes, you'll miss it. I turned around and tried again. I looked both ways, up and down the manicured little main street, lined by tall oaks planted at equal intervals, a long time ago.

A short distance from me a pick up truck was pulled over to the side of the road. Four people stood outside talking to two more seated inside the cab. I pulled up, and stopped near them, waiting expectantly for them to acknowledge me.

Of the four outside, two appeared to be in their forties, and the other two were elderly. Inside the truck was another middle aged couple, with their heads turned, staring through the rear glass towards me.

They all shut up, and I sat motionless, waiting.

Then, springing to action, I hopped off the motorcycle, removed my helmet, and smiled politely.

Six mouths in a row gaped open, and stayed open. Their chins nearly rested on their chests, men's and women's alike.

"What's the matter?" I asked. "Am I the strangest thing you've seen in the last decade, or what?"

Still, they could catch flies. They just stood shock still and stared. Finally, the gray-haired lady's jaw flapped several times before she stammered, "We're just sayin', we ain't never seen a woman riding a motorcycle before."

Her partner clarified, "Exceptin' on TV movies."

I had all I could do to keep a straight face. The dark haired man standing next to his wife pulled her closer, and through the back window I could still see the wide eyes and maws hanging open in disbelief.

Trying to gain credibility, I held out my CampBook and implored them to help me find the Oak Creek Campground, help explain the directions, because there seemed to be a misprint here. I handed it to the protective husband.

"You're going campin' up the canyon?" The younger woman asked, looking a bit frightened.

"I don't know, is there a canyon? It's the Oak Creek Campground. It's not a fancy place, but it's supposed to be off of some Deptartment Forest Road."

The husband said, "Yeah, they mean the one right over there." He pointed to where I had just come from.

"I didn't find it there," I replied.

"Oh, it's up there, it ain't much of a place, y'know," the old timer explained.

All the while, the others stayed transfixed. The same lady again exclaimed, "Up the canyon? All by yourself?"

I motioned towards my bike and sassed, "See anybody else? Yes. By myself. Maybe not—maybe there will be some campers already there. After all, it *is* a campground."

"I can't believe it. My! Are you brave!" she blurted.

The old lady was fascinated by the motorcycle. "You're not from around here. Where you from?"

"Massachusetts, on the east coast," I answered.

"And you rode that all the way here?" The guy in the truck asked.

"All the way. Actually I'm coming in from San Francisco. I'm headed for Colorado, now. But, I need a place to sleep, and I was hoping I could stop here, at Oak Creek, if I can ever find it."

"How long have you been doing this?" they asked.

"It's been a month so far," I answered, but inched backwards towards my waiting machine.

Tossing a few last words of encouragement my way, they finally turned to each other and chattered like magpies.

My directions weren't accurate, and I already tried this road once, and it seemed to be headed no where. But, the folks from some other century sent me back this way, full of disbelief and concern. What kind of misfortune was in store for me? What am I doing 'up the canyon' where even the towns people are afraid to tread? What am I trying to prove?

*   *   *

The campground was a box canyon, with a flat grassy floor. Steep slopes surrounded it, and oaks, maples and cottonwood trees grew thickly from the edge of the road, to partway up the rocky ledges of the mountains. Elevation: 5,900 feet at this point. I cruised around the circumference, surveyed the scene, and in an instant saw a deer raise her head, startled. She bounded across one of the campsites and disappeared into the thick forest cover. I chose that site, using the doe as an omen.

For the camp fee, I slipped five dollars into the envelope provided and dropped it into the slot. There were still a couple of daylight hours left, so I scrambled up the canyon walls that started in my back yard. For a little while I sat and looked down at my world, thinking.

On my way down, I picked up kindling wood, then I made the rounds of all the empty campsites. At the second one, I scored big. Instead of charred chunks, I found a whole pile of wood. It appeared to have been dumped from a truck a year ago, as it was covered with a layer of dead leaves. I carried armloads to my camp.

There was one exceptionally large hunk that insisted I wrestle with it, and I landed on my butt when it dislodged from the rest of the pile. Something white caught my attention among the dark, rotting logs.

Incredible. It was a skull. An animal skull. With my bare hands I lifted the skull and inspected it, half curious, half horrified.

The lower jaw was missing, but the upper jaw contained molars. My fingers spanned the flat forehead. Large round empty eye sockets were situated on each side, blind. There was not an iota of decay. The bone was smooth and chalky, ominous.

What animal did this come from? How did it get here, under all those logs? Was that a coincidence or hidden evidence? What if it had been a sacrifice? A dog, or a colt, perhaps? A million foreboding questions arose. Discomfort grew out of my uncertainty about this faceless head.

Thoughts of my favorite outdoor companion crept around the edges of my trepidation. She would take this object from me, hold it high and begin singing. Lorrin would be fascinated, and make up a story to explain its existence. She would place grave importance on the find.

"I'm not going to let it give me the creeps," I talked to myself. I held it before me and ceremoniously hung it on a tree trunk at the edge of my campsite, high overhead. It looked a little spooky, but knowing that I'd placed it there, made it seem okay. The next people who set up here are in for a surprise, however.

Only two other campsites were occupied. Nearby, a young man and woman were unloading an old Volvo station wagon, and on the opposite side of the acreage, two grandparents camped with their grandson.

When we met, they couldn't believe I was on a solo adventure, except for the child. He stopped playing long enough to run up to me, swinging action figures through the air, and in his four year old innocence asked me, "Are you a Power Ranger?"

I answered truthfully, and he tilted his head and asked wistfully, "Do you *know* any of them?"

He thinks I could be one of the Power Rangers! Children have less trouble accepting me and my motorcycle than many adults do.

In the evening, I lit my fire easily. It cast a glow onto the skull, a totem to protect my camp, and shadows danced on the backdrop of leafy branches all around. Most of the time, on this trip I had no fire. This one was a treat. It roared. I sat and meditated.

This day had been full of mysteries. When I uncovered that skull, I had felt uneasy, but when I treated it like a gift of protection, I felt empowered.

An occasional owl, and a variety of nocturnal insects produced a symphony in the otherwise silent eve. The tent over yonder was dimly lit on the inside, and I could hear the rhythmic murmur of a male voice. With sweet envy I realized, the guy next door was reading poetry out loud. How utterly romantic.

As I fell asleep, I counted backwards. Tomorrow I'll be sleeping in Colorado. Tonight, it's Utah. Last night it was Nevada. The night before, California. Wake me up! This has to be a dream. It's too good to be true.

Miles: 313

*   *   *

At dawn I got up to hike with Courtney and Carter, two college students taking some time off in the summer to travel. We pooled our breakfast resources and the feast amounted to herbal tea, bread with peanut butter and banana, plus yogurt. As the sky lightened, we clambered up the boulder strewn mountain.

Courtney mentioned her 'last boyfriend' several times, telling Carter how he had measured up in some aspects, and fallen short in others. He listened but didn't react. Her openness surprised me, as did his nonchalant acceptance. 'Old boyfriends' were not a typical subject for me when I was with a new guy.

"Look at this—I hate this!" she exclaimed as she bent down and picked up a discarded candy wrapper and jammed it into a pocket. "How can people contradict themselves like that?" she looked perturbed, and continued. "They'll hike all the way up here to get closer to nature, and then destroy it in the same visit. It makes me sick," she said with conviction.

Carter stayed relatively quiet, maybe a little winded.

When Courtney started to speak of 'next time around' in regards to a boyfriend, right in front of Carter, she nearly blew my mind. No wonder he was being quiet. He doesn't know what to make of her, either.

We reached the summit, and looked around. There were mountains taller than ours blocking much of the distant view, but in the V we could see so far that I wasn't sure where the blue sky stopped and the blue tinted mountains started. Down below the campground looked like a big green velvet oval. The large rocks that edged the loop looked like a necklace of pearls.

Our conversation covered the four points, north, south, east and west. We discussed the environment and the role humans have played in its destruction. We talked about over-population, and about things we learned in college about pollution, global warming, and waste.

Natural beauty radiated from Courtney's face, with her sunburned lips, and tousled brown pony-tail, bright eyes that flashed when she spoke of people's ignorance. I liked her, and wondered what the story was with her and her handsome companion. Why was she seeming to take him for granted?

We hiked down, and separated to pack up and get ready to go. We were headed in different directions, so we wouldn't be traveling together at all. Courtney and I went to the water spigot near the bathroom and washed the dishes.

"I haven't seen my brother for six months," she was saying.

I interrupted, "Why, where is he?"

"Well, I meant before this vacation," she said, but stopped when she saw my confused expression. "Carter is my brother," she explained.

"He's your *brother?*" I exclaimed. "I didn't know that! I thought he was your *boyfriend.*"

She looked horrified. "My boyfriend—no way!"

"Well, the two of you on vacation together, I heard him reading poetry last night, you seemed to know each other pretty well, and get along good . . . I just assumed-," I stammered, and laughed. "You know what? He's so cute. Yesterday when I asked him to help me with my bike, he wanted to hang around but I sent him back to you! I didn't want you to get jealous. I wanted to go hiking, and you looked like the types who would. I wanted to make friends, not enemies. Your brother? I wish I knew that yesterday!"

I asked her not to say a word to him about any of this, until we were well under way, and she agreed.

The car was all packed by the time we'd returned and in a few minutes I waved as the two of them drove off.

*   *   *

I had to wash up. It was imperative. First I was just going to wash my stinky feet. But, the foot bone leads to the shin bone. The shin bone leads to the thigh bone, etc., etc. The private parts get washed at least daily, even if it's a 'sponge bath' in a rest room, but my limbs have suffered. It's been days and days since my last shower. Layers of dirt, sunscreen, bug spray and dry skin have accumulated. Now that I cleaned up, I feel much better than before.

Except, I need a shampoo. I tipped over, dunked my head and shampooed my hair until it squeaked. The cold water was invigorating, and my scalp tingled. I towel dried my hair, sprayed it with detangler and combed it. After my french braid, I was ready for the leathers, and ready for the road.

Route 50 continued through Utah, but no longer was it nicknamed 'the Loneliest road in America.' After leaving Oak City, it dipped south a bit, before joining I-70 for a lope through the canyonlands, red sandstone and mesa glory, stretching due east for the Colorado border. The part of Utah I had already seen did not prepare me for what I was about to witness as I traveled eastbound.

An older couple were sharing the view at a scenic overlook, but seemed taken aback upon my arrival. After the stunning scenery gave me back my breath, I turned to them. "Would you please take a photo for me?" I implored.

The wife took my camera, and followed my instructions, a trifle nervously, but she mustered up the nerve to talk to me. "You drove that all by yourself up that twisty road?" she asked.

"Why, yes. I drove that thing all the way here from California." She gasped.

"Wait—there's more, see?" I pointed to my plate. "I've come from coast to coast, and I'm not through yet!"

She was speechless.

Sometimes, I really enjoyed the effect I had on people.

*   *   *

Soon I was carving my way along the road I had seen from above. Canyons rose up steeply on either side, offering a continuous changing view as each minute passed, unlike the day I rode through Nevada.

The ride itself was fun. Tilt left, lean right, press hard, now gentle. Roll on, then ease off of the throttle. It was so breathtakingly beautiful I could hardly contain myself.

For the fourth time since I left home I saw a coyote dead on the side of the road. The first time, I had wondered what a German shepherd was doing all by itself out here, but now I realized, I was seeing coyotes that had been hit by cars.

In the worst way, I wanted to see some real coyotes, alive. I wanted to be able to watch some, see how big they are, observe their gait, or learn something—just be in awe, so I kept my eyes peeled. If they're getting killed by cars, they must be everywhere.

For three or four hours I was spellbound. Miles of nothingness, except raw beauty. A sign on the highway said EAGLES ON ROAD. As if on cue, a bird of prey dropped from the sky ahead and to my right, like a dive bomb. It struck, then shot upward with a hare twisting and writhing in its talons, fighting for its life. The hunter cut across the road in front of me, and as our paths intersected I saw a movement in my peripheral vision. The rabbit crashed to the tarmack behind me, and the rest of the story was left to my imagination.

Did the rabbit escape its assailants grip only to break its own bones in a desperate fall? Did the bunny survive crashing into the road? Did that eagle deliberately drop its prey to injure it? Who benefited from this drama? Who lost?

The circle of life. Another reminder, and something to think about for the next hour or so.

*   *   *

In the afternoon I arrived at the Colorado state border and a half hour later I arrived in Grand Junction, and made my way directly to a Honda Shop, where I made an appointment at the service desk. The next day my Interceptor would be taken care of.

There was a hostel in this city, and after a brief search I found it. It had been an old hotel, and it was located within walking distance of museums, shops, groceries, coffee houses, lots of eateries, and it was big compared to the other two hostels I'd visited.

None of my roommates were in our room. It was a rather small room, with two bunk beds on either side. One little sink, and one chair and one nightstand completed the furnishings, plus a modest closet, with one shelf overhead. Around the remaining edges of wall space, back packs, sweatshirts, hiking gear, and duffel bags were piled. I dumped all my things onto my bunk until I could figure out where to stuff it all.

To heck with the shower, when I saw that I could take a bath. Considering it was a family style bathroom, I asked all around and got the go ahead. I poured a warm soapy tub, and for the first time in four days got righteously clean. I even shaved my legs!

Much to my chagrin, as I got dressed in the last of my still-clean clothes, I realized my amulet was missing. Although I searched, and methodically went through all of my stuff, I couldn't find it. A sinking feeling came over me when I mentally backtracked, and realized that it must have slipped over my head when I was tipped over washing my hair in the canyon, under the spigot. I hadn't noticed, and now I had ridden more than three hundred miles. There was no going back.

Saddened, I accepted the loss. The small leather pouch that I had worn around my neck and called my amulet, was gone. It was lying at the base of a water spigot 'up the canyon,' at Oak City, Utah. A shadow of uneasiness hovered around, taunting me. How much did I believe in that thing, anyway? Was it truly a Power Object, or did I enjoy playing make-believe? Would my luck change now? Would I lose some confidence?

Nah, I had to admit, I wore it as a symbol. The amulet had become a tangible symbol of my inner fortitude. That was all, a symbol. Still, I had grown to find comfort in the knowledge that it was nestled between my breasts, and when I rode I could feel it floating in the updraft, banging gently against my breastbone. The sentimental value of the pouch itself, actually a souvenir from an Indian museum in South Dakota, and Lorrin's rune of *Strength*, could never be restored by other objects.

I clutched an empty fist to my breast, and closed my eyes, breathing deep and slow. "Time to let go," I sighed, and then it was over. I was on my own.

There was a pay phone on the premises, and I used it to call my pal Betsy, collect. She was overjoyed to hear from me, and then I called Russ. He wasn't too thrilled. I tried to explain why I wasn't calling him more frequently. I tried to tell him if he would be a bit nicer when we spoke, I might want to call him more often. I tried to convey the enrichment I was experiencing. All of it fell on stubborn ears and a rotten attitude. Dejected, I ended the conversation, then went outdoors.

Most of the hostelers were young people, like myself, but I was mesmerized by their banter. Nearly everyone had a foreign accent. At times they broke into German, or other languages. The hostel housed guests from Europe, Asia, and sitting around the courtyard there was a mixture of many different nationalities.

Most of the guests were there for more than a simple overnight. They were touring America by Greyhound bus. They were hiking and mountain biking in our National Parks. They seemed to have stopped here at Grand Junction, then stayed for undetermined amounts of time. It was that kind of place.

The staff were young men from Germany, or other European countries. They were here for summer work, and some kind of school credits. Many were getting educated in the field of travel and/

or hospitality. They were trim, nice looking, with dreamy accents, and they smoked cigarettes like they were going out of style.

The beer runners returned. A tall, tanned girl plunked a paper bag before me, and I peered inside, then pulled out two four-packs of wine coolers.

"Which one's are for me? What flavor?" I inquired.

"Which one? You said two, no?" The German girl asked.

I laughed. "Yes. Two bottles, not two packs! I can't drink all this in one night. I'll be wasted!" I admitted.

Her driver came to the rescue and said, "I'll buy one pack from you."

By then, I had already decided I was going to stay there another night. "Okay, and I'll drink the other two bottles tomorrow night."

The summer night was warm, and the interesting group of travelers kept me up later than usual. I knew I had a bed nearby, and I sat at the edge of the shadows, taking it all in. This was a drastic change from my last few nights, but I felt pleased and satisfied. The next day I'd get all my motorcycle maintenance done, and the following day I would drive less than a hundred miles to get to the Top-o-the-Rockies BMW Rally.

Miles: 329

*   *   *

During the planning stages of this trip, I had taken into account the fact that I would be doing much of my own motorcycle maintenance. There would be times, however, when I would have to bring it in for service. I entered All Sports Honda/BMW of Grand Junction, Colorado. Together, Scott from the service department and I reviewed my work order, and then I handed over my key.

One hour later, the job was done.

My Interceptor was now equipped with a new rear tire, a new headlight, oil change, filter, one of the tail light bulbs, a set of spark plugs, a new valve stem on rear wheel, and a new drain plug washer, which may explain the slight oil leak that I'd had in Oregon. Perhaps it was leaking since then, undiscerned at my campground parking spots. The mechanic also checked and synchronized my carbs, and said everything else looked all right.

Scott handed me the invoice and I glanced at it reluctantly. The total astonished me. All of that work cost only two hundred eighteen dollars and change. The shop gave me a *twenty percent discount on parts,* don't ask me why, because I don't know. Normally, at home, I would spend about two hundred dollars on a tune-up, another two hundred for a new tire and installation.

During my wait, I had gone over my record of finances, and confirmed that I had spent less than two hundred dollars per week since I'd left home. Using a Traveler's Check I paid the entire bill, thinking I could afford it.

*   *   *

The hustle and bustle of activity was happening as hostel guests arrived at the end of their day's activities. A bunch of us decided to walk to the grocery store and buy food for dinner. We could each have a much better meal if we shopped and cooked together, for less money or waste.

The German girl who had made the beer run the night before was one of my roommates. Her name was Gabi. She was tall and well proportioned. Her face was pretty, her hair endearingly messy and long, her smile as bright as a string of pearls. As we strode along the sidewalk, I noticed her camp shorts, baggy and long, they came to just above her knees. Her countenance suggested earthy naturalism, right down to the long blond hairs that glinted upon her unshaved legs.

The lanky long-haired male who had given her a ride reminded me of the greyhound he owned, so lean and lithe. The way the two of them interacted, I suspected they were smitten with each other, but because he was "Staff," they had to keep it a secret. They were hardly succeeding.

Most everyone at the hostel was in their twenties, and they were leftover from the night before. We were so relaxed with each other, it was hard to believe that we came from all over the world, and yet, on this sultry evening we could hang around, eat and drink together like close friends. As they made their plans for their hike the following day, I listened, and hoped that the coming BMW rally would be as comfortable and friendly as this place turned out to be.

After my first wine cooler, I went into the building to use the bathroom, and when I walked past the office door, I noticed a slim, leather clad leg. I backed up to see the person attached to those pants, and blurted, "Hello, Stranger! Fancy meeting you here!"

It was Ben, my tall, dark and handsome companion that I met at Grand Tetons. A totally unexpected surprise. Ben had said he lived in Colorado, but I sure as heck didn't expect to find him here, at 'my' hostel.

He gave me that slow easy smile, then turned back to finish the registration process, gesturing that he'd only be a minute.

The crew out back undoubtedly never noticed my disappearance, and Ben and I walked to a pub. We told each other tales of our travels. It was hard to believe that two weeks had gone by since we rode away from Wyoming together. So much had happened in that two weeks, it felt like months.

I expected that he must be on his way to Paonia, for the BMW rally, but he said he'd had enough, and had to go home. We walked back to the hostel, and said good night. The party out back was still going on, so I joined them for my last wine cooler, then I too, went to bed.

Miles: about 20

*　　　　*　　　　*

In the morning, Ben asked if I'd join him for some espresso, before hitting the road.

"Sure," I said. "Just give me ten minutes. I'm almost done packing up."

I collected my things, flattered. Ben was shy, but through our common interests we had become friends. When I finished packing, I pulled my bike around to the front of the building.

Dammit! Ben's BMW was gone! He did it again. He left without saying good-bye. What is it with that guy anyway? What a mysterious creature. I was glad to have enjoyed his quiet company, but relieved that I didn't get close, or let him know how my heart pounded if I thought about getting amorous with him. Better left well alone, something inside me would warn.

Later on, I was to learn that he had been waiting for me at the cafe, and wondered why I didn't show up.

*A travel adventure has no substitute. It is the ultimate experience,
your one big opportunity for flair.*
—Rosilind Massaw, b. 1948

CHAPTER 13

TOP-O-THE-ROCKIES RALLY
July 20–23   Days 34–37

*M*y ride to the rally site was uneventful. One last turn and I came into Paonia, and followed the small blue and white signs, the BMW emblem, until I was deposited into the town park.

I had pre-registered long ago, and in moments I was done. There were a few tents set up already, and motorcycles were parked strategically around.

At an honorary cookie sale, I stuck a buck into a jar and grabbed a couple of brownies. A young man joined me. I couldn't help but notice his slim and solid physique, and his cleft chin. I joked about the cookies being my lunch.

"Where are you from? You've got an accent," he asked.

"Massachusetts."

"Did you ride here? All the way? We saw you drive in, what are you riding anyway?" Lots of questions from someone my age. That's a change.

A man with a blond beezer cut strolled over, and asked for an introduction.

"We haven't gotten that far, but look where she came from." He turned back to me, and introduced his friend. "This is Pat, and I go by the name of 'Road.' "

We shook hands. "My name is Diane, but I prefer to be called Dee. This is my Red Pony."

We stood around chatting for a few minutes, then I said, "I'll see you guys later. I want to get unpacked and set up now."

They walked off together, and I crossed the baseball field to set up camp by the fence on the far side, where there were very few people. The majority appeared to be setting up in an area set aside exclusively for camping, but I wanted to be away from all the testosterone. Although there were women here, practically every female was associated with a male, and most were passengers. I was anticipating getting a lot of attention, and felt it would be easier to keep the animals at bay, if I parked away from the majority. I settled near a couple of couples, on purpose.

I had to. It was in my best interest. How long has it been since I have been really close to a man? I wondered what has gotten into me? I never used to think about men so much, or take notice in extra good looks. I guess it's because I had the 'physical department' all set. But now, I was lonesome. In a physical way. Lonesome for an embrace, for affection, and kisses. Everytime I turn around lately, I notice the opposite sex. Then, if I meet a 'nice guy,' it seems I'm controlling the urge to come on to him. Cripe, even highway construction workers are making me hot when I'm forced to ease on down the road, lusting after their brown backs, and tight muscular bods.

Later on, the day cooled off and I got hungry, so I went into the headquarters where there were some meals available for a reasonable price. For three dollars I was given a paper plate laden with cheesy scalloped potatoes strewn with chunks of ham. Home made and thoroughly satisfying.

Out of curiosity, I perused the message board and was shocked to see a message for me.

WOW DEE. I am here. Hope to meet you and go riding.
Love, Cindy Earle.

Cindy is a friend of mine, from Women On Wheels. She is a Southern beauty, with brunette hair cascading to her shoulders, and most noticable about her is her brilliant smile. She rides a red BMW K75, and consistantly wins high mileage awards, through both Women On Wheels and BMW contests. She has the sweetest sugar pie personality of anyone I know, and defies the 'biker chick' image with style and grace. She hails from Louisiana, and is a school teacher, which contributes to her freedom to ride tremendous amounts of miles, but that is no excuse. She still is the one in charge, the one who must get in that saddle and ride.

I couldn't wait to bop into her. The experience I was having was something new to me. It would be so much fun to share it with another woman who has traveled extensively on her own, who won't be trying to talk me out of it.

Granted, Cindy tended to have destinations all set in place, and she could afford to sleep in, and preferred motels, but still . . . I admired her so much. She is infinitely more beautiful than I, which I supposed might put her *more* at risk. She is softer and sweeter than me. I'm strong and sleek looking, and have an assertive no-nonsense air about me, but she's so, so—well, peachy. We had a connection right from the start, and I was glad that she wanted to meet up with me for a little while here, at the Top-o-the-Rockies Rally in Colorado.

Pat, Road and I engaged in a game of frisbee, and hung around together well into the evening. After a few hours of story telling, and laughter, I asked the two guys to leave me so I could get ready for bed. This rally is going to be something to remember, for sure.

Miles: about 75

"If you can't keep up with the Big Dogs—Stay on the porch!"

Pat and Road invited me to go riding with them. Cindy and I hadn't found each other yet, so I accepted. The guys were going to show me a picturesque old mill, someplace off the beaten path. The two of them drove dual-sport bikes, which they could take off road easily. We made a plan that I would ride my bike until we got to a certain place where I could safely leave it, and then I would hop on the back of Road's Beemer, and let him take me through the woods to our destination.

What the Top-o-the-Rockies Rally hadn't planned on that year, was the untimely maintenance from the Highway Department. As it turned out, just a week or two prior to the rally, the area roads had been oiled and sanded. The ultra-twisty roads, normally a biker's heaven, had become temptingly treacherous. They looked okay, but if you weren't on an aggressive lookout, the slippery, gravelly surface could sneak up on you.

The prospect of an enjoyable cruise with my two new buddies, quickly became a game of cat and mouse for me. The Paris-Dakar and Road's 'Bumble-Bee' were equipped with practical knobby tires, and front fenders that arched a good eight inches over the wheels. The motorcycles were each a thousand cc's, and the guys driving them turned into maniacs when they strapped on their helmets and slipped into their body armor.

They moved out, expertly hugging the curves, and the roads we took were so awesome that as I watched one guy ahead disappear around one curve, beyond him I could see the leader snaking back into my sight, only to disappear again. Their speed was uncomfortable for me. Within ten minutes, I felt like I was playing 'catch up,' and when a vehicle on the road slowed them, I'd close the gap, with sighs of relief, only to watch them pass the car, despite the double yellow lines.

Soon, I learned that posted speed limits meant nothing, that oil covered by a layer of sand presented not even an inkling of trepidation, and the sprinkles that were misting our face shields were merely a nuisance. As soon as I would catch up to the boys, they would jet off again, leaving me to glance at my speedo with horror as I approached 70 mph on these roads. My grip was steel, my heart was racing, and my teeth were clenched. It began to rain.

For a few minutes, we slowed to a realistic pace because we were trapped behind a woman in a red Volvo. She claimed the road, and drove so slowly that even I would have been annoyed, except I felt it was the lesser of two evils. Then, acting together as one, Pat and Road shot past her, dangerously taking a foolhardy risk, and I watched them fly off into the distance, amazingly still in control.

The act startled the car driver, and she drove a little faster, probably anticipating that I would follow their lead, but I didn't have the guts. I followed her, and bided my time when I could possibly make a safer pass.

The moment came, and I down-shifted, zipped by her, pulled back into my lane and felt my rear tire shimmy, back and forth, and back again. With the Volvo as my witness, I managed to keep things under control, but at that point decided to listen to my thoughts.

"What am I doing? This isn't fun. Riding should be fun.

"Those guys drive like nuts, their bikes are better suited for these lousy conditions, and their engines are twice the size of mine. Listen to the sound of my engine—it's not in its Happy Zone.

"Why am I trying to keep up? Aren't they being rude to leave me in the dust like this?

"Is this little trip worth an accident? No.

"Am I riding within my limits? No. Even if they are well within theirs, I'm not. I don't have to keep up. I have nothing to prove.

"Besides, after this, I'm supposed to get on the back of Road's bike? I don't think so! I'll be scared to death, *and* helpless.

"Nope. I can't do this. I'm gonna pull over."

Cautiously, I downshifted, and pulled into a convenient pull-off, which offered me a beautiful view of the snow-banked Mount Sopras. Somewhere way ahead, I could see the colorful specks that had been my riding companions, and I watched as they zig-zagged their way along McClure Pass, oblivious to my absence. Figuring they'd notice that I was missing, one or both of them would return to find me.

I'll just tell them I can't keep up with the Big Dogs, I'm going back to the porch. And, if they argue or make fun, I don't care. I'm not a macho guy, I don't have to be stronger, or faster, or stupider. I'll tell them I will see them, 'back on the porch.'

I waited around some, then gave up. Where I come from, friends would never keep on going if they lost a rider from the group. We'd at least stop to find out why. That's why I stayed there, just to let them know what happened to me, not let them imagine the worst. But, it had been twenty minutes, at least.

"I'm outta here," I growled, and then had a very enjoyable ride back to Paonia, at my own pace.

Once in town, I stopped at a tiny cafe, and got myself a muffin and fancy cup of coffee. Before I'd finished, the door burst open and Pat stepped inside, with a wild look on his face.

"What happened to you, Girl? We were worried sick! Road's out looking for you," scolded Pat, surprising me with his attack.

"Me? What happened to me?" I shot back. "I pulled over, then watched you guys just keep on going, and going, and going . . . Real nice of you to turn around to see what happened," I said sarcastically.

Pat countered, "Wait a minute—we stopped. We stopped and waited. We thought you must be putting on your raingear. Then you never showed up."

"Duh," I argued. "That's because I was waiting for *you*, probably twenty miles back."

Pat told me that the driver of the Volvo had come upon them, and she had rolled down her window and announced in a nasty tone of voice, "Your friend pulled over a long time ago."

"Oh yeah, that's the one who saw me sliding out, right after I passed her trying to keep up with you guys. That's when I'd had enough. Maybe you two were having fun, but I wasn't." He could tell that I wasn't a happy camper.

The two of us spat back and forth for a few minutes, but neither of us stayed angry. Pat seemed like a very concerned big brother who had been truly worried about me, and when he saw my bike outside on the street, couldn't hide how upset he had been. We worked out the problem, then sat together drinking our hot coffee.

Afterwards, I rode back to the rally site by myself. Moments after I parked near my tent Road came running. I cut him off, telling him Pat and I already settled the mess, and I didn't want to get into it all over again.

Road put his hands on my shoulders, and looked right into my eyes, and with dead seriousness admitted how worried he was that something had happened to me, and it would have been his fault.

"Well, I couldn't keep up with the Big Dogs," I admitted. "I didn't mean to scare you guys, but, I wasn't having fun, so I changed direction. First I waited, then I got mad at both of you for not coming back to me, but I'm over it now."

Eyes downcast, he looked so sad, I put my arms around him soothingly.

"Really, it's okay," I insisted, "but, you didn't have go to such extremes to get me to hug you. All you had to do was ask." Suddenly embarrassed about my brashness, I stepped away. Jeez, what has gotten into me?

Before long, we had a rousing game of frisbee started, then we got kicked off the field for the annual Bikers versus Firemen Softball game. I used the time to write some letters and postcards, and to look around for Cindy, but she must have been out riding.

I was trying to sort things out in my head. I kept thinking about Russ, and about my screwed up attachment to him. Until now, his flippant attitude towards our relationship disturbed me, but now I wondered, how little do I mean to him? Am I really free to do as I wish? Do I really love the man, or has it gotten so bad that it's only the sex that I love? When is the last time I let a guy get close to me?

Really close, emotionally as well as physically? A long time. I always kept apart from the men I really liked, out of respect for a man who I hoped would some day love me, unconditionally. A man I knew was so private, that even *I* couldn't see inside his heart.

Lost in my thoughts, I sat on the grass at the outskirts of the third base line.

"Can I sit with you?" a male voice jolted me back to the moment. It was Road.

"Sure."

We sat together, quietly looking at the game. Another inning went by. The Firemen were ahead. I was sitting with my arms wrapped around my knees, when Road moved to sit in front of me. He leaned back against my legs, getting comfortable.

Instantly, a million sensations coursed through me like wavelengths. I could feel his body heat radiating through his back, to my shins. His casual invasion of my "space" jolted me. I wanted to push him off. I wanted to pull him down on top of me. What's going on?

Morals sprang forward. "I need to ask you something, and want you to tell the truth, because I haven't asked you yet." I leaned forward and whispered quietly.

"Go on," he invited.

"You don't have a wife or a girlfriend at home, do you? Someone who loves you and trusts you?" I asked.

"No, not now." He twisted his head around to look at me. "What about you?"

"No. Actually, I'm free as a bird," I realized the truth as I stated it.

"Good. That makes two of us," Road answered, and settled back into his comfortable position, leaning against my legs.

The Firemen from town won the game, and darkness had set in.

Road invited me to share some wine with him, and I asked him to bring it to my tent. An hour later, we were inside my tent, talking and drinking.

I felt a need to explain my heartache. I had to validate my feelings that I had been let go, so many years ago. But it was I who had to do the letting go, still . . .

"You," I admitted, "I am attracted to. You and I have a lot in common, and I like you. I just wonder what it would be like if—"

Road stopped me in mid-sentence by placing a wine dipped fingertip onto that tiny dent above my top lip, then he drew it down, over the top lip, and came to rest on my lower lip.

I froze. My heart pounded.

Slowly, Road inched closer to me, and with a gentle mouth, he tenderly kissed me. I returned his kiss, like a whisper at first, and then fervently. It was like magic. My body responded wildly. Instantaneously. I melted, from the inside out. I could feel everything swell, tingle and ooze.

Forgetting that there was only a wall of fabric between us and the rest of the world, we focused on each other with shyness and abandonment.

When the sun came up, Road unzipped my tent and left me, dazed and amazed at my uncharacteristic behavior. I smiled at him before he winked, pulled the zipper closed and walked off.

*   *   *

At a booth called 'Creature Comforts' I paused to scan the variety of gadgets, and a smiling older woman came to show me her 'Roadwear' gloves. She spouted to me all the desirable attributes, encouraged me to try on several pairs, pointing out how the gloves are made in women's sizes. Within minutes I was convinced, and I bought a pair.

By the time I walked away from Creature Comforts, I had made two new friends, who pressed a business card into the palm of my hand with an open invitation to come and see them if I made it to Phoenix, Arizona.

Throughout my visit to their 'store,' I was catered to and teased by Jan and Earl. They were professional rally-goers, and earned much of their living traveling to numerous rallies all over the country. In fact, back in Washington, at the Women On Wheels rally I had taken a moment to pat a little dog with a bow in its hair. That dog was theirs. I remembered the little tyke. They had been at the WOW rally, but I hadn't actually met them, there. Small world.

The motorcycle games began. Suddenly I noticed another 500 Interceptor. It was being ridden by a girl named Nancy. She was sitting on the bleachers when I rode mine over to get registered for some of the games.

We played some of the motorcycle games, teamed up for some, with her driving sometimes, and me driving sometimes. In between we got to know each other. Eventually, I was reunited with Cindy Earle briefly, and then I coasted through the rest of the afternoon with Nancy.

We had a fabulous barbecue as part of the rally, and then they had the awards ceremony. Numerous awards were announced, but it was most exciting for me to hear them call my name.

"Long Distance Female Solo Rider, Dee Gagnon," the announcer heralded, "from Massachusetts."

Again! I had gotten one in Washington, too. I crossed the grass and collected my plaque, smiling broadly.

During the ceremony, I noticed a rainbow over the Sleeping Lamb Mountain. I watched until it faded, and then the sky grew dark.

Miles: about 75

The next morning BMW motors rattled all around, and after the first few folks made their early departures, everyone else took it for granted that we all had to get up and get going.

Already, the makeshift campground was half disassembled. Soon, my tent was down, and everything was packed. I rode over to where my friends were, and joined them for a huge buffet breakfast, served out on a picnic table.

Pat and Road were all packed up, ready to leave as soon as breakfast was over. Everyone sat around jabbering about their plans. We were all going to attend the National BMW Rally in Durango the next weekend, and most had the week off, in between. Pat was headed for Arches National Park with friends, but they were no where near ready to go. Road was headed home to change gears, and take care of some business, before our proposed camping trip on horseback. I was headed north, to stay at the hostel again, and take a day trip or two to Arches. Maybe I'd hook up with those guys, maybe not. We left the plans open. Less stressful that way.

Road was leaving. We took some photos, hugged, and then he was off. "Call me in a few days," he shouted.

Pat was pacing around noticeably irritated because his friends had hardly begun to pack. It turned out, he asked me if I would like some company, because, ultimately, we were going the same way.

"You sure you want to ride with me? If so, I'd love to have you," I said.

"Did you ever go to Grand Mesa?" he asked.

"I don't think so."

"How'd you get here from Grand Junction?"

"I took 50 to 92."

He said, "If ya want, I'll show you the scenic route. It'll be a bit further, but it's worth it."

"Fine. Grand Junction is only seventy-five miles away, anyhow. If you promise to drive sanely, I'll go."

"Okay, Dee. You lead. I'll come forward when it's time to change roads," he promised.

"Sounds good to me."

All of the guys planned to find each other at Arches, then Pat and I set forth together.

We took Local 92 towards Delta, then turned right and headed north on another paved road, 65, to Mesa, where we banged another right onto 330.

This road took us out onto Grand Mesa, the largest flat-topped mountain in the world. It was known as a recreational area, used mainly for hunting and fishing, hiking, and four-wheel drive off highway vehicles.

We rode along, and I drank in the cool, misty air. Somewhere along the way, we had stopped to put on the raingear, but it had only been a momentary shower. Tall, thin pines towered in stands that surrounded meadows of flowers, and I searched both sides of the road for wildlife. Ahead, there was a sign.

LAND'S END—12 MILES

Pat shouted, "Take this left!"

"Okay," I replied, taking notice of another sign.

4-WHEEL DRIVE ONLY

Four wheel drive? Well, between Pat and me we have four wheels, I thought cockily. I'll just take my time. Land's End! That must be some view. It's a little rough going, but, it's 'only' twelve miles.

The road was somewhat rutted, and on top of that, there was a fresh layer of new stone, about two inches deep. Where vehicles had driven, they left deep grooves, and I had to drive in the grooves, because the stone wasn't as deep, there.

I'd slowed right down to about eight miles per hour, after realizing I was on scary terrain. I've got all day, I thought. Obviously, Pat has been here before, and if he can do it, so can I. Besides, he's letting me lead, so we can take it at *my* pace. Slowly.

Every time my tire hit the edge of the tire tracks, my handlebars would yank at me, and keeping cool, I'd merge back into my track again. If my speed graduated to eleven mph, the bike would start to shimmy.

After a few miles, I began to doubt my decision to take this road, but, I continued forward, figuring, *it's only twelve miles.*

Pat shouted, "Look—I just saw a Mountain Lion!" pointing with an outstretched arm.

Awesome! If I could lay eyes on that, it would make this fearsome jaunt all worthwhile. While keeping my skittish Pony moving forward, I kept my eyes looking ahead, but cast furtive glances over the meadows on either side of us. The road ahead curved gradually to the left, but my tire skimmed the ridge of the groove I was riding in, and again the front end started vibrating wildly in my grips. I felt the motorcycle wring itself out, as the shaking transferred from the front end to the back end.

Get it back! Get it back! I fought for control. C'mon Pony. Don't do this! The rear end was violently wrenched from one side to the other, and I knew I wasn't in control any more. I watched as the edge of the road came closer to me, and prayed for my momentum to decrease, because I couldn't use any brakes, or that would definitely send me over the edge.

Over the edge, is what it *was,* too. As the road curved around to the left, the earth dropped away, forming a cliff on my right, still a hundred yards ahead.

Thirty seconds in slow motion seemed like an eternity. The motorcycle had a mind of its own, and I was on top fervently praying for a stroke of luck. My ninety pounds of luggage was just too much for me, and it exhilarated the thrust that fishtailed the machine uncontrollably.

Suddenly, I was at the shoulder of the road, then I was airborn! One, two, three seconds! *Air time!* I was still holding on, and watched horrified as my motorcycle tipped sideways in the air with me on top of it. We slammed horizontally onto a four foot boulder. **CRASH!**

We do not take a trip; a trip takes us.
　　　　　　　　　　　　—John Steinbeck, b. 1902

CHAPTER 14

THE AFTERMATH
July 23–27　Days 37–41

*C*RASH! In an instant, all the terror vanished, because my struggle had ended. For a second, I fell limp against the boulders, where I had landed. My motorcycle covered my left leg, and the front tire spun freely in the air, even though the engine had cut off, independently. I let go of the handlebars, and laid back against the side of the cliff, forcing myself to stay calm.

Shoot, I've got a riding companion today! I've got to move or he'll think I'm dead! So, I pushed myself up with one elbow, wincing in pain.

"Are you okay?" A shower of pebbles bounced down towards me, from the edge of the road, some eight feet overhead, as Pat scrambled down the cliff towards me.

Weirdly enough, I thought to myself, *This is the chapter I didn't want to have to write.*

"I think I'm okay," I yelled bravely. Amazed that I wasn't *really* hurt, I waited for Pat so I could extricate myself out from under my four hundred pound machine. Although my leg was jammed underneath, my luggage stuck out far enough to prevent most of the motorcycle's weight from crushing me. From where I was trapped, I could only imagine the damage that my Interceptor sustained. Mentally, I was performing a survey regarding my own damages.

Nothing broken. My lower left leg hurts a lot, my left hip, too. Come to think of it, just about everything along my left side hurts, except for my head. Thank goodness I love to wear my helmet. This is why.

Pat reached me, and grasping the handlebars, raised my bike enough for me to wrangle my leg free. "Are you sure you're okay?"

"Yes, just bumps and bruises, but, what am I gonna do?" I started to realize the gravity of the situation.

"My bike, my bike," I wailed sorrowfully, the defeated biker's lament.

Pat was helping me to my feet, holding me up, when my leg gave way. He reminded me, "It's just a bike. That's not important. As long as you're okay, the rest can be fixed."

"How are we gonna get it out of here?" I cried, looking up the side of the mountain, hopelessly. I tested my leg, lightly, and found that I could bear weight, now that my circulation had returned.

"Can you walk?" He was stripping some of the luggage off of the bike, preparing to stand it up.

"Yes," I limped among the stones and boulders strewn over the steep slope, retrieving items that had been flung from my tankbag when I crashed. Apparently, I didn't have the zipper closed, and my camera, water bottle and other sundries were scattered about. "My journal—where's my journal? I've got to find it!"

"Is this it?" Pat held up my small brown notebook.

"Yes. Thank you."

"Listen. If you think you can, crawl up to the road. We've got to get some help, and you're more likely to be able to flag down a car, than me," Pat instructed.

Yeah, I thought, if there is anyone up here.

"Do me a favor and take a picture first," I appealed. Pat's look registered disbelief.

"C'mon now, don't you see? This is a Kodak moment! How often do you think my Red Pony is lying crashed in a ditch, two thousand miles away from the place I call home?"

Pat tossed off his rain jacket, shrugged his shoulders and agreed. "Now off with ye, lass," he dismissed me, with a false foreign accent.

Because it was a lazy Sunday afternoon, fate would have it that in only a few minutes a man and woman in a small, red pick-up truck approached and pulled over. Within ten minutes I had a crew of beefy, outdoorsmen, ready to haul my crashed bike up out of the ditch.

As I stood at the lip of the road supervising, my gaze continued on, fifty yards further. The realization struck me that had I managed to ride out the fishtailing that much longer, I would have dropped off a *serious* cliff.

Instinctively, I reached for my amulet, breathing silent words of thanks, but my little leather pouch was missing. That's right, too. I'd lost my totem for protection at Oak Creek Campground 'up the canyon' in Utah, and now, less than a week later, I'd crashed.

My word, I just drove off the largest flat-topped mountain in the world!

And I survived. Maybe I'm still a pretty lucky girl.

In a detached sort of way, I watched the scene below, as the group of men organized, established an impromptu pecking order, and gathered their testosterone together, to collectively aid this damsel in distress. Clustered around the wreck, they grasped it, and heaved it forward, and taking care to place their feet, struggled up the treacherous grade. As if looking at a movie, I watched helplessly, not knowing the outcome.

A shout erupted when they got to the top under Pat's general command. The huffing and blowing guys shook their arms, and arched their backs, trying to dislodge the kinks that they'd suddenly incurred.

Still, I had not inspected the motorcycle. It was relatively intact. In a haze, I approached, and the men parted, falling silent. Calmly, I turned the key, and pressed START. My Red Pony protested for a few seconds, then started right up.

The biggest, burliest guy, the one with the Harley-Davidson tee shirt blurted, "Holy Sh—! Just like that."

"Of course—it's a Honda," I taunted, which brought a few snickers, but he accepted them tolerantly.

Changing the tone, I graciously thanked each of the men for taking a moment to stop and help me. The way they acted made their actions appear that this was the most natural thing in the world for them to have done. Without getting mushy, I slapped 'em on the shoulders, or grasped their meaty palms and shook heartily.

Lastly, I came to my friend and riding partner, Pat. His blue eyes looked directly into me. "How ya doin'? Are you all right?"

I straightened, and pushed some straggles of hair off my face. "Yup. Not too bad, considering." My eyes met his, and seeing his sincere concern, tears welled up suddenly, threatening to destroy my composure. "I have to leave," I choked, and twirled on my heel, and walked away from the scene.

Reality struck full force, finally. Now that my bike was back up on the road, and I was limping around. Now that I could see my helmet, all busted, and my luggage scattered on the scarp below.

Now that I noticed my rain jacket was torn, and my rain pants were marred by mud, and scraped up. Now it all sunk in. Aimlessly, I put one foot in front of the other, and sobbed, still proudly trying to keep my head erect, and my back straight so that the guys wouldn't know.

One by one I heard the various vehicles driving away, and Pat jogged to catch up to me, after a few minutes. When I heard him coming, and felt that the audience had diminished, I fell against his broad chest and cried hard for a couple of minutes, then stopped abruptly.

"Okay. I'm okay now," I stepped away, wiping away the tears.

He nonchalantly put a hand on my shoulder and steered me back towards our parked bikes. Standing near their red pick-up were Vicki and Dan, waiting. Pat explained that they had offered to transport my bike away for me.

After a great deal of discussion, and reassurance, I accepted the kind offer. The thirty-something couple insisted they had come to the plateau "looking for something to do," as Vicki put it. Ironically, they were from Grand Junction, and when I told them I had hoped to go to Hotel Melrose (my hostel), they knew exactly where it was, and told me they would bring me directly there.

Some people are fortunate to be called upon to be angels, if only for a few hours out of their life. Some people are able to *recognize* this paradox. I have been doubly blessed in my life.

Dan's truck featured a HD bar-and-shield, and he just happened to have tie-downs, and whatever was needed to secure my Interceptor in the back of his truck, surrounded by my luggage.

Dan and Vicki talked with me during our ride to Grand Junction. He rides a Harley, and couldn't let another biker down. He thought I was crazy trying to ride on that road. Looking back, I agree. When I was doing it, I didn't feel crazy.

"Why would you keep on going then, if you were scared?" Vicki asked.

"I don't know. I thought I could handle it. I wanted to see the fantastic view that Land's End promised. Pat has ridden out there before . . . A lot of reasons, I suppose." I said.

"That bike he's got is set up for that kind of riding," Dan pointed out.

"I know. I know. We thought if I led, we'd take it slow, and at my pace, but what we didn't count on was that freshly laid pebblestone. It's like, four inches deep in places! They're not just kidding when they said 4-wheel drive only," I continued. "I've come so far, and through so many circumstances, I think I got a little too cocky. A little too much, 'Never say die,' " I admitted.

Dan could relate. "I know what you mean. I couldn't drive a bike like yours. I'd kill myself, always pushing the limits, y'know? I know you do. But, you're a girl! Don't see too many out doing what you're doing."

Had the bike shops been open on Sunday, I am certain those two would have dropped the bike off and then brought me to the hostel. They were just those kind of folks.

"We're here," Dan announced, and I directed him to the back of the hostel.

My body rebelled when I moved to get out of the truck. All kinds of aches and pains made themselves known, as I gingerly stepped down to the ground.

A few hostel guests seated in the garden observed curiously, and I looked for a familiar face. I saw Jesse, the lithe, black-haired staff person that my roomie Gabi had liked.

"Hey! I'm back! Can you give these guys a hand?"

Jesse, when he recognized me, dropped his dog's frisbee and ran over, "What happened to you?"

"Had a little accident. I'll explain later. I don't want to hold up these fine people."

Another motorcycle was parked where mine had been the week before. In the garden, a big-bellied man rested, and at another table, a schoolmarm lady sat looking up from her book. A small wisp of a guy got up, and joined Dan, Pat, and Jesse, and together they hoisted the broken motorcycle to ground level, while the big guy, I'll call him, Mr. Otten, sat, with a sour expression on his face, claiming to have a bad back.

Jesse exclaimed, "It's good to see you again. There is room at the Inn!"

Thankful to hear that, I relaxed a little. After thanking the Chevrolet driver and his girl, I waved as they drove off.

Satisfied that I was in good hands, Pat and I said good-bye, and that we'd hopefully meet again at the BMW Nationals in Durango.

Returning to the hostel was like coming home again. Of all the situations I could have been in, this was the best. For ten dollars a night, I could stay here, shower, and eat breakfast. A rather nice city was outside my doorstep, and I'd have access to a kitchen, and a grill. There were plenty of intellectual pursuits within walking distance, and All Sports Honda itself was a mere two or three miles away. Besides that, I could do what I want, and not impose on anyone else. I considered what could have been my plight, as I returned to the back courtyard.

There was a hose handy, used to water the numerous potted plants and flower beds. I helped myself to it, and washed the mud and dirt off my bike, and inspected it critically.

The lady out there stopped reading, looked over at me sympathetically and asked, "Did you have an accident?"

"Yes," I replied, shortly.

Not feeling like explaining the ordeal to someone who wouldn't understand, I simply said, "I made a mistake in judgement." I couldn't talk now. I was finally seeing, what I had anxiously waited to look at.

My luggage had protected the sides towards the rear of the bike. The left front side was cosmetically destroyed. The fairing was gauged, broken and scraped severely. My windshield, broken. The radiator hose, split wide apart. The radiator itself, cracked open. One of my brand new horse paintings became history, and the prognosis of my entire front end, I could only guess. It was way out of whack. Visually, structurally, my Pony was doomed. I straddled the seat, and positioned my front tire to face forward. The handlebars were cocked seriously to the right.

While I was airborn, the bike had shifted, and smashed down on its side. The luggage buffeted much of the impact in the rear, however, the front wheel and forks slammed into a huge boulder, sideways. Things weren't looking too good. The more I looked, the more I felt that I had probably totaled my beloved motorcycle.

As I lingered over it, drying it, and polishing, the woman came over to speak with me. When she revealed that the cruiser I was parked near was her motorcycle, I was amazed.

"You don't look like a biker!" For a second, I sounded like one who first meets me. "I'll bet you hear that a lot, huh?"

Once I realized that she would understand my accident after all, I launched into a blow by blow account.

"Ooh, deep gravel! Enough said! Go on-" she urged. She could have been my mother, somewhere in her sixties. She heard the unfortunate tale, but when I was finished with the story, she sent me off to take a bath and go to bed.

"Honey, you're in shock. I can see it. Your bike is fine. It's not going to get any worse or any better for now. You just have to go take care of yourself now," she scolded.

"Yes, but-"

"No buts. Go, get yourself into the tub, take some aspirin, and get some rest. You've had a big trauma. You don't realize how hurt you are. You're in shock." She was sweet, but firm.

She was right.

There was aspirin in my pharmaceutical zip-lock bag. I poured myself a hot bubble bath, and swallowed an aspirin, then eased my aching body into the tub.

Outside, I had been trying to keep busy, so that I could avoid the big questions looming up before me.

What am I going to do now? What if my Pony is totaled? What'll I do? Where do I go from here?

Who can I call? Why call anyone—what can they do? If I call anyone from home, they'll probably expect that I would end my journey and come home. When I explain my bumps and bruises, they'll imagine that I am holed up in traction somewhere. "Now you'll give up that crazy motorcycle ride, right?" I could hear it already.

By the time my bath was half over, I was sure of one thing. My journey was *not* over, and I was *not* coming home yet. I didn't know what kind of twist this incident was throwing into my plan, but I was willing to go with it.

Gosh, that would be something if I end up backpacking and Greyhound bussing it for the rest of my one hundred days. Certainly not in my plans, but what an adventure that would be!

The bubbles were disappearing, and very gently I soaped and inspected my aches and pains. At this hour, I still lacked proof of injury in the form of bruises, except for an egg on my left knee, but I felt battered.

What if my bike *is* totaled, I wondered. Will I have to bury my Red Pony out here in Colorado, two thousand miles from home? I never dreamed I would have to do that. But, with limited funds, what else could I do? I couldn't ship it.

So, if she's dead, I wonder if I could find some kind of cruiser, like a Shadow, for say, fifteen hundred bucks. Could I really finish my journey as confidently on a strange, inexpensive motorcycle that I purchased in a hurry?

If my forks are bent, how much would it cost to straighten them? Will I trust that kind of work, or would I be better off to *replace* the forks? Right, on a nine-year-old model. How long would that take? How much would that cost? Could I trust them?

What about the rally? I wonder if I could get Pat to pick me up and bring me to Durango. Road would bring me back here afterwards.

I have a headache! So much changed during one little drive in the country today.

Things changed, but *I* didn't.

I shaved my legs, luxuriously, then carefully stood up in the tub, and looked at my upper body in the steamy mirror across from me. Certainly, there must be a bruise on my ribs just below my left breast—but, no, it didn't show. Yet. Despite the soreness in my left shoulder, my hip, and entire left leg, I was overjoyed that my right wrist, which I had broken badly the year before, was fine. I could still twist a throttle!

Going through this crisis alone was a difficult accomplishment. A huge part of me needed to call somebody to rejoice that I had come out of this test alive, and I was not going to be defeated. But who? Who could I call?

I plopped down on my bunk, feeling restless and incomplete. Taking a chance, I dialed the number Road had given me, and he was home!

Briefly I described my misfortune, and explained my plan of action. Rest; the bike shop won't open until Tuesday, anyway. Then I'd get the bike to Honda somehow, and wait and see what the verdict is. The camping trip on horseback was out of the question.

"I know I couldn't ride a horse now, because the whole inside of my calf is bruised. It'll be a few days of recovery. I'm going to try my best to make it to Durango."

Road, who seemed a little distracted, admitted I'd woken him up. He had a business trip ahead of him. "You remember, when you get here, you can take it easy and stay with me at my humble home. Be my guest. I'm glad you're okay. Everything will work out all right. I know. You're a real trooper."

After sharing my demise with a friend, I felt a little better. It was still fairly early, but I wanted to go to sleep, and forget about this semi-nightmare. Maybe I'd wake up, and find out all this was only a dream.

As long as I didn't move, as long as I stayed flat on my back, and didn't roll over onto my side, so long as I didn't inhale deeply or sigh, I was okay.

When I prayed, I asked God to show me the reason I had to endure this lesson, and with all my heart I thanked him for not allowing my bones to break, and that I was sleeping in a familiar bed, and not in a hospital somewhere.

For fourteen hours, my body produced new cells and regenerated wounded tissue. As I fell to sleep, the real Me fought my weakened Ego, and I realized, I was going to come out on top of this challenge. This would serve to make or break me, and I realized, the worst was over. Everything that comes from this, just like any other day, would be the result of my decisions, and my ultimate success would depend upon my attitude about the other things that must be decided for me.

Miles: 66

All human wisdom is summed up in these three words:
wait and hope.
—Alexander Dumas

The next four days seemed to blend into one long, anxious waiting game, as I recovered from my accident, and figured out what had to be done with my wrecked motorcycle. The hostel life here in Grand Junction proved to be a saving grace, when I considered that I could have been stranded alone at a campground somewhere, dependent on asking other people, strangers, for rides in to town. Even if I imposed upon a Women On Wheels members' hospitality, I would have fretted, for lack of freedom. Instead, I had a perfect situation, under the circumstances.

At a youth hostel, you are considerably on your own. You have freedom to come and go, and can escape the company of others without being rude. Alternatively, the atmosphere encourages socialism, and comradery, as well as affording opportunities to go off and explore the region.

This particular hostel excelled in these areas compared to the few I had already frequented. During the day, we were expected to leave Hotel Melrose, and in the evenings, it seemed general practice to gather in the common room to watch foreign flicks on TV, play board games, cards or whatever, or else to migrate to the garden court out back for conversation, libations, and chain-smoking. I was drawn to the more colorful, lively outdoor crowd.

One day, many of the guests had piled into the van for a hiking excursion in Arches National Park, and I watched enviously as they pulled away. My lower leg was in no condition for a strenuous hike in the hot, rocky canyons. Although the entire inside of my calf was black and blue, the rest of my body hurt a heck of a lot more than it appeared to. I rested and slept a lot, healing. I took care of some mending, and read my paperback book.

The need to tell someone who knew me, an old friend, was strong, but I resisted the urge to call anyone at home, still. I didn't want anyone there to know about this, until I knew the problem was solved. I didn't want anyone worrying.

The hardest part was waiting thirty-six hours for the shop to open, so I could get over there. The more I examined the bike, the more I was prepared to learn that the frame was bent, meaning, my bike would be totaled. Still, I knew, the adventure continues. I was not going to relinquish my expedition.

Gabi returned from her camping trip with another German girl named Leona, who would be my roommate for the next few days as well. Leona was nineteen years old, and had come to America to tour the hostels and National Parks, via Greyhound, like so many of the others who stayed here. This place was such a retreat, however, many, many of the foreign hostelers got sidetracked, seduced by the available recreational van trips, the lure of the pleasant city, and melting pot of cultures represented by the majority of guests, and ended up staying longer than they'd planned.

The robust crew, in the evenings, tongues loosened by brewed beverages, poked fun at grouchy old Mr. Otten, for he had gone to bed with the sun, and we wondered why such a disapproving, narrow-minded man would stay here at this hostel, at all.

The American lady on the motorcycle, I never saw again after that first night when she sent me to bed. Funny how I thought of her as 'the American lady,' but, we *were* in the minority here, indeed.

Conversation once turned to the motorcycles, or, more specifically, the women who ride them. The general expectation seemed to be that we would all be big-boned, tough, tattooed, ugly broads, either lesbian, or undesirable.

The other lady had been a door-mouse, like someone you would picture working in a library. I wished I had gotten to know her story, but, alas, it wasn't meant to be that way. The guys found it amazing that she had come and gone on a motorcycle.

They turned their attention my way. "Okay, look at this one, this 'Dee,' " they said. "To look at her now, you wouldn't guess it either."

Then Jesse reached down to pat Bones, his greyhound, snatched the dog's frisbee, and flung it across the lot. He noted, "Yeah, but I've seen this girl dressed for the road, and she looks serious in all that leather." He winked, and I felt a flush creep over my face.

Leone informed us all that she rode a "motorbike" a little bit in her country, and Stephan a striking young man on staff, also from Germany caused a lot of laughter by saying, "Leone, doesn't look like a motorbike girl, she looks like a puppet carrier!"

With her round, dimpled cheeks, and sparkling eyes, we were able to agree, but I couldn't forget that phrase. How often in this country do we compare a friend to a *puppet carrier?* I had to stop and think for a second, what *is* a puppet carrier, anyway?

This sort of banter continued throughout the week, expanding my views of other cultures from the other side of the world.

*   *   *

On Tuesday, I faced the dilemma of how to get the bike to Honda. The shop was two and a half miles away, and although I could push the machine, I wasn't big enough to push it up any more than the slightest grade. I set forth early in the morning, just in case I would *have* to push it, thinking that anyone one else might say I was crazy, but, I had to do what I had to do. I figured, I could possibly run the engine and walk the bike, holding onto the handlebars, using the friction zone. Because I could only touch my toes to the ground, I would not be able to straddle the bike the easy way, and "walk" it. My bumps and bruises hurt like the dickens, but, my bike had to get to the shop, and I was the one who had to get it there.

Out in the back, I assessed the damages one more time, then gingerly mounted it. After starting her up, I rode her slowly around to the front of the hostel, then sat for a minute, weighing my chances. Could I actually ride it there, if I stayed real slow, and stuck to the side of the road? I decided to go for it.

Somehow, I was able to ride the crooked, little wrecked machine to All Sports. It took an hour or so. The owner of the shop was out front when my Red Pony came limping in, and he recognized me, and brightened, "Hey Dee, you're back!" Then, his look changed, as the sight he saw registered. In a lower tone, more seriously, he repeated, "Oh Dee, you're back! What *happened?*"

As I yanked off my helmet, I asked him, "Would you believe I went off a cliff at Grand Mesa?"

He circled the bike, and whistled low.

"Listen, I rode two miles to get here, but *barely*. It's all out of whack. My forks or the frame might be bent. I don't know. I just need you guys to take a look at it, and see what we can do."

He ushered me inside to the cool air-conditioned store, and sent someone to take care of me.

Returning to the shop, where I was recognized as one of their customers and was respected as a serious rider, felt really good. All day I stayed around, reading motorcycle magazines, and haunting the mechanics.

The shop was booming with business as it was a Honda/BMW shop. The two BMW rallies had caused an influx of long distance riders, wishing service on their machines, leaving me on a waiting list.

After a couple of patient hours, I inquired of the mechanics. "Have you looked at it yet?"

"No. We're still working on that old BMW transmission."

"Can't you stop that for fifteen minutes, and tell me? Either the Pony is totaled, or it's not. I need to know now. Not tomorrow. I'm stuck here. C'mon, please?"

They told me to get lost, they'll get to it when they get to it. I went back to the store and waited.

In walked a familiar figure. A tall, weathered man in his fifties perhaps, strolled through the store, his most remarkable feature being the time tested riding leathers that he wore. They were entirely made of patches. Mostly brown, but some faded black, there were so many leather patches, I wondered, are the original chaps and jacket still there? Or has the jacket, etc, evolved into a retread sort of fashion statement?

The man had been at the Top-o-the-Rockies Rally the week before. Rarely had I seen him without this one-of-a-kind outfit of his on. While I was having breakfast with my friends on the last morning, I'd noticed him stretched out on the grass, with a Colorado map spread out before him. He had a highlighter in one hand, and was tracing some of the routes in the state.

I stopped to look over his shoulder for a second, and commented, "Looks like practically every road."

He swiveled around to face me momentarily, then continued coloring over the lines. "Yeah, I think I've finally ridden on every single numbered highway in this state," he said it in an almost bored tone.

I left him there, and when I mentioned it to Pat and Road, they didn't hide their distaste for the man.

"He's a pompous fool."

Now, here was that man, in his unpompous attire, asking the service desk for information regarding his transmission!

Aha! *His* transmission was holding me up!

From where I sat I tried to eavesdrop, but wasn't very successful. Apparently, they told him to have a seat, and the mechanic would come out to speak with him.

So, it came to pass, that he, too, recognized me, and we struck up a conversation, and I learned that, like his clothing, his motorcycle was also some sort of patched up replacement of its original self. He joked about getting his money's worth, because BMW, he claimed, had replaced most everything about the bike, at their expense, due to their illustrious warranty. He had hundreds of thousands of miles on the tranny in the garage there, and expected them (BMW) to take care of it.

His thick, kinky black hair was pulled back tightly into a pony-tail, and his freckled skin was sun beaten, and I didn't find him snobby at all. Haltingly, I admitted my reason for being at the shop, and expressed my aggravation at being made to wait.

Shortly, a mechanic came around to speak with the rider, Jeff, and after respectfully listening to the assessment and diagnostic plan, Jeff politely demanded, much to my surprise, that the mechanics halt the work on his engine, long enough to check out the status of my Honda.

"Why make the lady wait, up to her ears in suspense? Please, check out her forks, and whatever else it is that she wants."

After that exchange, Jeff Brody nodded to me, and swaggered out of the store.

When the garage door opened next, I got the news.

The frame and forks are not bent! The motorcycle could be fixed! The front end was out of line, mainly because the fairing bracket had gotten bent, and my slip-ons (handlebars) had also absorbed much of the impact and needed straightening and alignment. Hallelujah! I would ride the Red Pony once again.

Elated, I went to the service desk, and waited for the itemized list to come over the computer to him. I spent half a day waiting for what took them a half hour to discover.

Scott, the parts guy behind the service desk, went over the list of parts with me, and answered all my questions. He used his entire lunch break, to help me locate used parts at his brother's auto salvage store, and gave me his dealer's discount to boot.

A turn signal assembly ordered new from Honda would have cost me upwards of fifty dollars, but I ended up paying twenty-five. Besides that, I would be able to put scuffed up replacement parts on my bike, which would blend in much better than shiny new parts would.

Some of the more expensive things, I was unable to locate, such as the radiator, nearly three bills, or replacement windshield. Still, together with Scott's help, I was able to get the parts I needed on order, or in hand, for the least amount of money possible, for such a rush order.

It was imperative that I have the bike back by Thursday. Meanwhile, about a dozen Beemerheads rolled in and said the same thing. Everyone was going to Durango. The mechanics laughed at all of us. What could they do? They were swamped. It was either laugh or cry.

Late in the afternoon, Jeff returned to the shop, and seeing I was still there came to me straightaway. After my good news, he introduced me to another man, then the two of them offered me a lift back to the hostel. I accepted.

*　　　*　　　*

On the following day, I had decided I would hop in the van, and go with the gang to Colorado National Monument. I doubted I could hike the eleven canyons they planned on, but knew I could amuse myself, and read after I did as much as I could, considering I still felt battered.

The van was nearly full, and the driver informed me that I hadn't signed up. When I asked him if I could, he told me to go inside and pay the fee.

"What fee?" I hadn't realized there was a cost. It was a great value, but over my head. Downcast, I had to wave good-bye as once again, everyone left to have fun in fantastic natural surroundings, while I was left to amuse myself in the city.

Immediately, I decided to take a walk to Honda. There was an undercowling on my Baby 'Ceptor, that had gotten busted in the crash. Also known as a scoop, it's main job was to funnel wind over the engine to help air-cool it. Its second order of business was aesthetics. Unlike the larger displacement sportbikes with full-fairings, my motorcycle's V-Four engine was exposed; the bike had a smaller fairing.

Although the scoop was not an integral part of the bike by any means, I didn't want to go without it if I didn't have to, and a replacement was priced at one-hundred-eighteen dollars! Way too much money, plus, originally being white, it would no longer match my black and red paint scheme. I had hopes that mine could be repaired. Why not? If an auto body person could do what I've seen done to cars, then why couldn't they mend a simple cracked up piece of plastic such as this?

Leone was in our room, writing post cards. When she found out what my plans were she wanted to come along. The two of us donned pretty sundresses that came to our ankles, and slung our backpacks into place, and trekked on over to Honda, causing motorists all along the way to toot their horns at us. We ignored it all, and had fun getting to know each other, talking about the places we had traveled, and those where we wanted to travel to.

The motorcycle was not nearly ready, but I extracted my scoop, and convinced them to repair it for me, the best they could.

During the short time we were there, Jeff arrived on the scene along with the man who gave me the ride in his Sidekick jeep. Naturally, they offered us two young ladies a lift, but Leone hesitated.

"Don't be afraid of us. You must be dying in those long dresses." How will a man ever understand that a long dresses is *cooler* than it appears?

I had to explain, "Well, we appreciate the offer, but we were going to go the City Pool." I found myself saying it like Leone would, "Sit-Tee Pull."

The driver, a Grand Junction resident responded, "So we'll drop you off there."

"Yes, but we don't have our bathing suits. We need to get them first, and really don't want to trouble you," I continued.

"Nonsense. By the time you get to the pool, you'll die from the heat," the Beemerheads insisted.

The two of us girls looked at each other, and Leone, deciding to trust me, giggled and said, "Okay, we ride with them."

True to their word, the men escorted us to the hostel, waited while we ran inside to grab our suits and towels, then insisted on taking us for a frothy cappuccino, at a little outdoor bistro, in an artsy little corner courtyard someplace neat.

While Jeff and I shared tales of our travels, Leone gleefully carried on a conversation in German with the other man. After our refreshments, the two of them dropped us off at the public pool, and offered to come back for us later on.

Laughing, we told them, "No, you've done enough already!"

But, they insisted that they had to go back to the shop for five-o'clock, so why not swing by and give us a lift. We caved in.

Leone turned to me, and said, "You American motor-bike riders are very friendly and nice, yah."

I had to agree.

Again and again in the course of these few days I paid attention to my good fortune. During this setback, I don't think I could be at a better place. For ten dollars a day, I have above average accommodations, a complete and unlimited breakfast, plus a diverse group of young travelers who offer their unique experiences, personalities and cultures. Besides that, they are as adventurous as me. They aren't amazed that I am traveling all by myself, and they are much further from home than I've ever been! To them, the fact that I chose to ride a motorcycle for transportation was a most remarkable thing, not the fact that I traveled alone. I fit right in, and loved the atmosphere.

In addition to those things, outside my door, is a city which is pleasant and interesting, by my standards, and considerably safer than Boston. The Honda shop is also a BMW shop, and the thread of motorcycle experiences has given me friends, where only strangers may have been.

Seeking relief from the heat of the day, Leone and I traipsed around town, visiting museums in order to: #1 learn something, and #2 enjoy the air conditioning.

The Western Colorado History museum kept us occupied, and as I gawked in awe at history one to two hundred years past, Leone really brought things into perspective when she pointed out that in her country, two hundred years was *young!*

Together we made our daily pilgrimage to "Sit-Tee Market," for a thirty-five cent waffle cone with fresh ice cream, then we shopped for food. One day we saw a poster for a little lost dog, and realized it was the same little pooch we'd heard whimpering outside our window, where it had just spent the night.

"Poor thing!" we cried, and using my trusty calling card, I phoned the lady, and she was happily reunited with her little, lost, fluffy, white friend, before we'd even returned to the hostel on foot, the others informed us.

My motorcycle, I estimated, would be about a thousand dollars, to have fixed. With all the exercise I was getting, I felt better, and my aches and pains had subsided, although my leg was a nasty shade of greenish-purple and yellow. I took the forty-five minute walk to the shop, and found that their work was done.

Altogether, I had a new windshield, new radiator, replaced radiator hose, and headlight. Both turn signals on the left had been replaced, my fairing had been plastic welded. It was a rough job, but it would do, I had no complaints. They had also rebuilt the broken lower scoop to my satisfaction. The worst part of the job was forcing the front end into line again, but they had straightened it out, to my naked eye, and declared that it was structurally sound.

Cosmetically, the motorcycle was no longer a beauty, when viewed from the left side. The whole fairing on the left side was still scraped, and would remain so, for the duration of my journey. Fortunately, my brand new tire had survived the crash.

All Sports Honda/BMW of Grand Junction Colorado made one of the best business deals I would ever imagine. When I approached Scott at the parts counter for my bill, I found out that the shop *extended their 20% discount to me, again!*

I ended up spending $750, half of which I put on my credit card, the other half I pulled out of my account at home, using my ATM card for the singular transaction of the whole one hundred days of this journey.

After they brought my Red Pony around to the front of the shop, I accepted my key with nervous excitement. Climbing aboard, secure in the knowledge that she was supposedly safe, my heart pounded and the strange emotion of love for an inanimate object consumed me. Now I knew what it would be like to lose this thing, but what was lost, now was found. Once again, I was complete, and my journey would continue.

Like a homing pigeon I returned directly to the hostel. My first ride was not going to be around town. The Million Dollar Highway beckoned me, stretching between where I was, and where I would be. That was going to be my first real ride. Tomorrow.

The weight of the world came off of my shoulders. Like a young romantic reunited with a long lost love, a soldier returning from war, I was calm and contented once again, certain that all my doubts had only made me stronger, because I'd refused to let them bring me down. I never gave up.

Miles: all but 5 on foot!

vi-tal-i-ty   The quality or state of being strong, healthy, vibrant. The power to endure, to meet life's challenges. Highly developed physical or mental vigor. That which separates the living from the non-living.

CHAPTER 15

BMW-MOA

July 28–29, 1995   Days 42–43

*I*t was mid-morning when I hit the road. The first few minutes were shaky. My confidence was at an all time low, but at the same time, I knew the feeling would pass. I had to deal with a lot of traffic, and lights, and each time I had to stop and put my foot down to support the bike, I was reminded that my leg was still injured.

Once out of the city, however, the situation improved. The road was vaguely familiar, as I followed Rte. 50 for the first forty miles or so, because I had taken the same way to get to Paonia. After I passed Delta, though, things got mighty interesting.

Until then, I rode away experiencing a kaleidoscope of feelings and emotions. First, I had to get to know my motorcycle again. After such an accident, one doesn't know what to expect. The handling could be all messed up. So, I critically appraised its performance, gently and nervously, half expecting it to fall apart, right out from under me.

Then, I thought about all the different people I had met and made friends with during the week, and of my pending reunion with my friends from last week, at Paonia.

There was a junction in Montrose, where I continued my trek, headed south now, passing through Ridgway. Mountains surrounded me. Big, beautiful giants. The road took me out of my thoughts, and claimed my attention. S-curves abounded, and as I went along, I felt my confidence wax and wane. I was doing alright, taking things a little slower than my normal pace, then I'd become afflicted with flashbacks of my motorcycle fishtailing wickedly, then would suffer with cold sweats, heart pounding, fists clenched tight.

Continuing forward, up, around, and over the undulating ribbon of road, I would force myself to remember that I *am* a skilled rider, I trained extensively in the spring in order to become a motorcycle safety instructor. My error was one of judgement, not skill.

Important rule: Ride within your limits.

So, I struggled with myself, and reasoned with my doubts. After a couple of hours, I was feeling more relaxed, and began to let my mind wander a little bit once again. All that worrying was exhausting.

Thinking of the evening before, I remembered Pierre, and his off the wall ideas. As a whole bunch of us were hanging around in the courtyard, I inquired of everyone in general if someone would be willing to share a bottle of red wine with me.

Pierre, an average looking, frizzy-haired garçon, who seemed to constantly be staring at me, sighed, "Ah, oui, red wine ees for lovairs, no? You and me, we share for love, mm-m-h?"

I tossed my head back and laughed out loud. "For love? I don't think so."

"Oui. Yes. Red wine ees for love. In France, we have wine with every meal, but red wine and beautiful woman make romance. I weel show you, you weel see." He had a stupid grin, as he sat forward expectantly.

"No, Pierre. I want to share the cost of the bottle, not romance. Not love." I rolled my eyes, and laughed as if he were joking.

He continued his foreplay, "You laugh! Why do you laugh? I can see in your eyes . . . you say 'no,' but you mean 'yes.' "

"No I don't!" I retorted. "Now you're really starting to bug me." The screen door slammed, and Jesse arrived on the scene, his chest naked, as usual. "Hey, Jess!" I called, "You want to go to the store with me and get some wine?"

"Sure," he said, "Just let me tie up my dog. Come here Bones," he called, and his grayhound unwillingly complied.

So, I left poor Pierre sitting there sulking enviously. What a jerk, I thought. Gabi was away with Leone on a camping trip, and we had said our good-byes already. I knew Jesse missed Gabi, and so did I. We walked to the store, and back, then sat around with everybody, drinking red wine out of kitchen mugs, much to Pierre's horror. He pouted and became a little more sullen, with each passing hour. In the morning he'd avoided me altogether.

So, after replaying that incident in my mind, I realized I was feeling relaxed in the saddle, though ready, vibrant and alive.

The stretch of road I was on was known as the Million Dollar Highway. It is a most spectacular road, as far as scenery goes. It is fantastic to ride on, full of switchbacks, curves, decreasing radius turns, and exciting cliff edges. Not an easy road, this is a favorite among bikers, and as I traversed the tight corners and dangerous angles, all the joy of the sport returned to me, filling me with a new surge of power, and exuberance.

The best portion of the Million Dollar Highway stretched from Ouray to Silverton, etching its way through alpine vistas, leading me over the 11,000 foot Red Mountain Pass. Down below I could see the cross hatch of neat streets, and an old western town, and resisted the desire to drive down in order to see what hidden treasures might be there. It was probably just another expensive tourist town, I figured. Mother Nature was giving me the main attraction, around every corner.

The Million Dollar Highway, had a few legends regarding its name. Some speculated that the estimated value of its construction resulted in the title. Others said that a million bucks worth of silver ore was mixed in with the makings of the road surface. Whatever the case may be, I say it's because of the view. The Million Dollar view.

This U.S. 550, now one of my favorite all-time roads in America, clung precariously to the steep mountain sides, decending quickly enough to cause my ears to begin popping. Brightly colored riders in Darien road gear started coming and going, overtaking me, or waving broadly, welcoming me, aware that this motorcyclist has just arrived, evidenced by the giant pack strapped to my bike. Large numbers of BMW riders were taking to the road, for sheer joy. I knew I was getting close.

Durango. The streets were lined by motorcycles, parked at a slant, one right after the next, side by side, tight as matchsticks. Fantastic!

There were more motorcycles than cars creeping along the road, and leather clad people walking everywhere, talking with others dressed in typical BMW fashions. Most would appear to locals ridiculously overdressed, but not so. These people were riders first, pedestrians and tourists only for the moment. Signs directed me to the place where registration for the BMW-MOA 1995 International Rally, otherwise called the Rocky Mountain Rendezvous, was taking place.

The closer I got to registration, the more congested the motorcycle traffic was. The 23rd BMW Motorcycle Owners Association International Rally would be a huge success, I could see that already! As I parked my black and red Honda at the nearest edge of the parking area, I felt overwhelmed by all the people. How am I *ever* going to find my friends?

Still in my saddle, I hadn't even gotten off my bike, when I felt a hand on my shoulder. Standing there beside me, was Lee, one of the breakfast boys from Sunday morning, my last morning at the Top-o-the-Rockies.

He said he was talking to my friend Nancy, (with the 500 Interceptor like mine) and wondering if I'd be making it to Durango, when she saw me ride by.

Within thirty minutes I found Pat and Road, too. Hugs and happiness. After examining my bike, and getting the total report on my state of affairs, things went back to normal.

Road asked me to stay at his place, and Pat and Lee teased, "How do *you* rate? He didn't ask *us!*" Road informed them that they weren't cute enough.

The rally organizers predicted 6,000 attendants. Although there are plenty of hotels and motels in town, most of the bikers would be camping. This was not my idea of camping, however. What a horror show. Imagine trying to sleep, while a party is surrounding your little bivouac, and you fit like a sardine in a can? Not I!

Hand in hand, Road and I wandered around and got caught up with each other, while I got acclimated. Everywhere we turned, activities raged on full-force. Lots of familiar faces peppered the crowd, coming from the rally last weekend. News of my mishap had traveled like wildfire, and over and over I had to offer explanations, and reassurances that I was okay. I hadn't realized I'd gained so much recognance, but among the Beemerheads I found that I was fully accepted, and respected.

Eventually, the day 's excitement gave way to fatigue, and I asked Road to lead me to his castle. As soon as we had wiggled our way into traffic, I became antsy, as he zig-zagged in and out amongst a herd of other riders, leaving me to follow suit, or lose him. We broke away from the main part of town quickly enough, (probably in half the time than I would have on my own) and made our way to a trailer park in Bayfield, just east of Durango.

His place was humble, but he had the bare essentials, plus a computer. The shelves, nooks and crannies were lined with books, and files, and research materials. He was indeed a writer.

The bathroom was as big as a closet, and he showed me around the rest of the place. 'Around the place,' meant ten steps down a hall. At the end of the hall, there was a bed, covered with a brightly covered Mexican serape.

Collapse city! I fell back onto the mattress, zonked. One hundred and eighty-nine virginal twisty miles, in this mountainous thin air, merely days after crashing over the side of a cliff into boulders, and all the excitement of my reunion with Road finally caught up with me. I couldn't decide whether I wanted to sleep first, then shower, or shower now then sleep for the rest of the night.

Wanting to freshen up, 'just in case,' I decided to shower first. When I emerged, Road had made his nest extra comfortable for me, and let me fall asleep, while he tapped away at his keyboard.

Later on, he laid down by my side. We shared tender kisses and sweet passion, and then, we slept through the night. Contended. Warm. Uncomplicated.

*   *   *

On Saturday we went back to the rally, and split up for some time of our own. I looked for Nancy, and searched for Cindy. I found Pat.

"You know, last weekend I was so glad to have you with me when that happened," referring to my accident.

"Oh yeah, right," Pat muttered, "if it wasn't for me you wouldn't have even been there, and it wouldn't have happened."

"No!" I cried, "It wasn't your fault. Please don't feel that way."

"Well, it's true."

"No sir! Of all people, you should know. I know better than to overextend my abilities. You didn't force me to go with you. I could have stopped, but—I got carried away" I stammered, sorry I'd brought it up. "Look, I've gone over the whole accident a million times since last Sunday, and came to a conclusion, based on a couple of complexities."

Stopping in my tracks for emphasis, I faced Pat, feeling it necessary to clear the slate. "In one sense, it was my ninety pounds of luggage that sent me over the edge. The extra weight, slightly unbalanced, added to the danger when I began to lose control, until I couldn't handle it. But, that same load of luggage protected my body, and even took a lot of impact under my machine when I actually crashed." I paused, then continued, "So, yes, it was you who suggested we take that road, when I wouldn't have even been in that area. But, don't forget, at the most shocking point in the last six weeks of my life, you were there, right there responding with care, concern and common sense. I am eternally grateful to have had a good friend with me in that moment. Thanks, Pat."

Pat ran his hand over his blond crew cut, and humbly accepted my reassurance that he was not to blame. I hoped I'd convinced him that his presence with me that afternoon was a beacon of light, not a danger signal.

I rode on the back of Road's GS100 for some of the games requiring passengers. He was an excellent player, and his bike seemed exceptionally well-suited for slow speed maneuvers.

The sun was very hot, and baked the dirt. The motorcycles spun tires, and kicked up clouds of dust that choked us. Spectators were scarce, the corral was away from the crowds, and enthusiasm and competitiveness was moderate, and dwindling. As a result, we placed second in the Wienie Bite contest. Another trophy I'll need to ship home.

After games, we replenished our fluids, and split up again for a while. While looking around for a decent bathroom, instead of a porto-potty, I came across Cindy Earle.

We hugged and kissed, and got busy catching up with each other. We did see each other at Paonia, but at the moment, Cindy had one thing on her mind, and I needed to give her some space and time to herself. She had been traveling with a companion on her way to Paonia, then survived a nightmare. He had hit a deer and went down hard, right in front of her. She'd witnessed the whole thing, and had to react, respond and rescue. His motorcycle was totaled, and he was broken. When I saw her, she was holding back tears, and wringing her hands, telling me, "I'm a jinx." I had wrapped my arms around her, soothingly, when she opened her eyes and looking over my shoulder, saw him arrive, in a cast and bandages.

That was when I had to let her go. I hadn't managed to get together with her for the rest of that weekend. Now, here we were at last, able to catch up with each other.

"Everyone was talking about an accident after the rally, and when I heard the rumour, I wondered, anybody I know? Then I was told it was that girl from back East, with the Honda sportbike, and I knew, it had to be you! I've been so worried.

"It's probably a good thing you're in such good shape. It might have been a lot worse," Cindy observed out loud.

"I suppose. Plus, I had on my helmet, which got smashed up quite a bit, and my leathers and raingear. They took a beating."

Cindy noted that I had been hanging around with a couple of guys, revealing that she'd seen me having so much fun she'd left me to myself the two or three times she'd spotted me. I told her of my circumstances with them. "He's very cute," she said of Road, and I heartily agreed.

*   *   *

The rally was wrapped up in the evening by a huge awards ceremony. It was held in an open pavilion skirted with bleachers, lined with chairs, and lawn space up front. I sat with Nancy.

The awards were announced, and Cindy was presented with a very high mileage award, some forty thousand miles ridden the year before. No wonder we're such good friends. She understands me. Her white smile lit up her face, as she sweetly accepted the plaque given to her.

More presentations, lots of raffle drawings, a motorcycle giveaway, and obligatory thank-you speeches went on, all the while Nancy and I talked about the stress and strain of huge crowds, all this fun, and all the testosterone that surrounded us. Her boyfriend was way too busy to pay much attention to her, and she was feeling annoyed at him. But as the night went on, she began to feel better.

Nancy lived in Denver with her nine year old son. She wanted me to take her address with me, so that if I was ever out that way, I would be sure to stay over at her apartment. This was an offer I couldn't refuse. Denver is a perfect distance from Rocky Mountain

National Park, and from the sounds of it, I had an open invitation to show up. Any time. Besides that, I liked Nancy.

The rally was officially over, although most folks wouldn't leave until the next morning. After many warm wishes and hugs were exchanged, Road and I left together.

He was to leave for L.A. on Tuesday, but wanted me to stay with him until then, which was fine with me. We'd have a chance to spend more time together, and maybe even camp-out on horseback.

The evening was warm, and the stars twinkled merrily when I parked my bike near Road's trailer. I stayed outside for a little while by myself listening to the sounds of the night, then joined my charming host, falling asleep before he finished working on his business.

Miles, two days: 221

This is Nancy Cooper of Denver (right) and me on our Honda Interceptor 500s. Hers is a 1985 model which has been lowered and has an aftermarket fairing. Mine is a 1986 model with a custom paint job. This photo was taken when we were at the Top-o-the-Rockies Rally at Paonia, Colorado.

I was once asked if I'd like to meet the president of a certain country. I said, "No, but I'd love to meet some sheep herders." The sheep herders, farmers and taxi drivers are often the most fascinating people.
—James Michener, b. 1907

CHAPTER 16

CRAZY HORSE
July 30   Day 44

*O*ne day, Road led me to someone's house and knocked on the door. His friend, Theresa welcomed us, and offered us a pop. Road introduced us and we began to speak of horses, and immediately I felt at ease.

Theresa was a statuesque woman in her late forties. She had thick, long brown hair, some make-up, very short cutoffs rolled up all the way, revealing long, suntanned thighs, and a denim shirt tied up in the front. She was wearing work gloves, and work boots, and had been involved in some sort of project before we arrived unexpectedly.

She took us outside, and I wandered over to the fence to look at her horses while she and Road talked privately for a few minutes. Then he came to my side and ducked under the fence, inviting me to come and meet the new addition to Theresa's family.

The little golden guy was ten days old, curious, shy and energetic. If we stayed real still, he'd tentatively take one step at a time, and approach, then he'd dash away, erupting into little bucks and twists as he galloped, and then slowed to a magical trot, which made him appear to float.

Road explained to me that the huge ranch across the street was overseen by Theresa, and her younger husband Dan. The horses on this side of the road were their own personal saddle horses, but across the street they were there for numerous reasons, all involving monetary income. Some were retired rodeo horses, some were in training, some were bought and sold, and many were broodmares.

Three ranch hands worked the operation, and lived in the plain house we'd seen earlier. Their duties kept them busy from sunup to sun down, and Road said they were a rough crew but for some reason, they liked him, and granted him special privileges.

Road must have told Theresa that I had some laundry, because she called me in, and showed me to the washer and dryer. The washroom was very clean, and stark. On top of the washing machine there laid a sinister looking knife about thirteen inches long. I set it to the side, curiously, and put my laundry into the washer.

While my clothes washed, Road and I took a walk to the ranch across the street. We sat on the edge of a streem and dangled our feet, and talked about writing, and our hopes and dreams. I asked a lot of questions about living in Colorado, and he assured me that if I were to move, he would help me get my feet on the ground. I told him how glad I was to have had all this time together.

"Yeah. Me too."

We stepped stones for a little while, then put our shoes and socks back on and headed back to Theresa's.

The dark skinned men working at the ranch waved again when we walked by. We went to Theresa's and I tossed my laundry into the dryer.

Theresa was outside polishing a leather saddle, draped over a fence. That big knife was sticking out of her back pocket. She had a fierce expression on her face, and complained to Road about the "F—-ing Arabs over there."

It seemed to me, she was creating a vicious circle. These men come from Arabia and will work for meager earnings, some day to return to their home lands, considerably rich. They come from a culture where women are veiled, and the laws regarding females, marriage, sex, are stringent and severely enforced.

They work here, and are faced with an overseer who is female, and beautiful, and she flaunts it as brazenly as possible. So, today she marched over to the ranch for some detail, with her tied-up shirt and daisy dukes, and her glorious mane spilling down her back. Then when they stopped to stare, she belligerently waved the knife at them, threatening and sneering at them. She thinks they're low-lifes, she treats them with disrespect, and they in turn, act like animals.

I just kept my mouth shut, but my opinion of her went down a few notches.

After my laundry was dry, Road informed me that we were going to go across the street and pick out our mounts. We were going for a ride!

I selected an appaloosa named Crazy Indian, and Road took a bay called Cooter. This was indeed a privilege. This was not the kind of ranch where people rent horses. It is a private business, but we were allowed to take a couple of the horses for our personal pleasure.

After grooming the steeds, we got them saddled up, and I bridled the two of them. The hired hands treated me with respect, and Road kidded with them for a few minutes before we mounted and headed for the hills.

My horse was full of energy and bad manners. I had assured Road that I considered myself an experienced horsewoman, and he did not underestimate my opinion. He warned me that Crazy Indian was quite a handful, and within five minutes in the saddle I readily agreed. The adrenalin coursed through my veins as Crazy danced and sidestepped along the trail, tossing his head and resisting every demand I made. I was not intimidated in the least. This was going to be a terrific ride, and I was definitely going to get my exercise.

Sitting astride this bundle of tension, I was almost glad to have picked him. It was way better than riding a tired bored nag.

We trotted along, holding our horses back. They both seemed to be fighting for the "lead." We were trying to ride side by side, and our mounts would trot faster and faster trying to get ahead of the other. Soon one or the other would break, usually Crazy, and in order to stop him, I would have to spin him around. He needed three or four tight spins in order to "listen up." What I mean by a spin is, as soon as he would break stride and start to gallop, I would pull his head all the way around forcing him to turn in a tight circle, upsetting his balance and making him stop. I had to do this, because he had been so abused in his lifetime, that he only recognized aggressive moves, and so he would resist, resulting in more mistreatment.

"This is the most hard-mouthed cayuse I have ever ridden in my life, Road!" I shouted during one my Indian tornados.

"Do you want to switch?" He gallantly offered.

"No. But maybe if I start getting tired out. My arms are getting a workout, that's for sure." I was enjoying this, but I couldn't get over how beastly this broomtailed appaloosa behaved. He just wouldn't relax.

We trotted along the edge of the same stream, that we had been sitting by earlier. It now seemed more like a river. We came to a place, and Cooter, who was now taking the lead, stopped short, snorting. Crazy Indian prepared for flight. I tightened my grip. Nothing happened. Maybe he's learning.

Road yelled, "We're gonna cross here."

I looked at the rock strewn banks sloping down to the swollen stream, easily seventy feet to the other side, with disbelief. "Here?"

"Yeah. I think this is the place. It's hard to tell for sure, because the water level is so high now," he said, as he directed Cooter alongside the water seeking the best place to cross. The handsome red-brown horse didn't want any part of it, however.

Meanwhile, I was further from the water's edge, looking at the terrain on each side, and the riverbed. It was all rocks. They ranged in size from ping pong balls, to boulders the size of softballs and footballs. The footing looked treacherous. The other bank was nearly choking with trees.

"Road, I don't know about this. Are you sure this is the crossing? There are too many rocks!" I exclaimed.

"Yes. This has to be it. Can you see any place else? They can do it," he said. I watched him urge Cooter to enter the water, but the bay's eyes flashed white and he spun and scrambled back up the bank, on our side. "You go first," he suggested.

"Yeah, right," I muttered, then, to the horse, "C'mon, Crazy, let's go! Hee-yah!" and I clamped my legs 'round his belly as he charged down the bank in three leaps, then spun around and tried to go back to the main trail. I didn't let him complete his mission, and convinced him to try again.

Again, he displayed his power, and refused.

I was still bothered by the uneven and rocky bed. "Road, this is dangerous. I would *never* bring my own horse into these rocks. What if one breaks a leg?"

"Dee, we do it all the time. They're just nervous because the water's so high after the flood we had."

"Okay. If you say so."

I gathered the reins securely in one hand, reached down to stroke Crazy's foamy neck, and firmly directed him straight to the water's edge. I knew he would try to bolt away, but, this time, Cooter came skidding down wildly, and Crazy leapt into the water. It came up past his belly, and we churned up a wake as we made our way to the other side. I could hear the water sloshing behind us, as Road followed closely.

On the other side, there was only one break in the brush and trees that lined the edge of the brook. I aimed my steed's strawberry roan face toward it, and he charged forward.

His front legs came out of the water together, and I felt his muscles gather beneath me. I anticipated he would burst out of the water, possibly at a gallop, and readied myself to stop him before he ran away with me at the top. As soon as his forelegs hit solid ground though, he flung his head to the right and his body followed. He lurched back into the river violently, intent on going back to square one. Instead, we crashed into the other horse and rider.

"No! No! We're going *my way!*" I wrestled him around, and Cooter took it upon himself to get the heck out of Crazy's way, and he bound up between the bushes with Road swiveled around in the saddle trying to make sure I was okay.

Crazy Indian gave up. In a few leaps up the steep bank, he caught up with Cooter, stopped to give his full body a good, water shedding shake, then began his high stepping antics again.

We survived.

After we caught our breath, we simultaneously checked with each other, "Are you alright?"

We were. Thankfully, the collision was between the two horses. When Crazy touched ground, he reared and turned, his forelegs then crashed into the water right in front of Cooter, who was almost exiting the water. Cooter basically ran into Crazy's shoulder. Neither Road nor me were hurt at all, but we did get a little wet.

Now that we made it to the other side of the river, my colorful mounts' acts of defiance seemed like a trifle annoyance. He was aware that I was boss, but still needed to flirt with disaster and keep me on my toes.

The river led us along the base of a tremendous bluff, and eventually the trail took us to an open field. Here was the place to really run. Both horses raced across the field, tails streaming in the wind, necks stretched forward as they tore up the ground beneath their flying hooves. It seems as though weeks of pent up energy was being released, and when we started to run out of field and got closer to the tree line, I hoped that I would have the strength to change my appy's course.

"Which way?" I hollered.

"Go left, towards the bluff," Road yelled back.

My derelict horse wanted to go right. It almost seemed as though this animal really had no clue what was expected of him, he just guessed. Either that or he was incredibly stupid.

"No, Crazy, this way," and one swift kick and a shift of my body, one tug on the reins and he did it! He went the right way!

The shadows had grown long an hour ago, and the sun was sinking, staining the horizon scarlett and orange. We stopped our horses, and while Crazy jogged in place, I implored Road to enjoy the sunset with me.

"This whole situation is like a dream, y'know," I said. "Riding off into the sunset with a great guy, on a wild horse, fireflies and a hot summer night . . . "

"I know. I was sorry that we couldn't go on the camping trip that we'd planned on, but, this was the least I could do."

His facial features, the cleft in his chin, looked more dramatic in the shadows cast by the setting sun. He is so handsome, I thought. "I am so lucky," I said.

"Dee—Diane, I can't think of anything I'd rather be doing, or anyone that I'd rather be doing it with." He said it so seriously, I believed him.

What a romantic date.

Fireflies alighted over the tall grass, and the night stole what was left of the day. The horses had gotten relatively calm, and my arms and inner thighs were feeling weak, but I was still managing Crazy Indian quite well. Road asked if I wanted to trade, but I wouldn't give him up. I'd developed a fondness for his rotten ways, and my heart went out to him.

I shared with Road my guess as to what kind of a life this animal must have endured, to be so spiteful and ornery. He said all he knew was that he was a rodeo bronc in his past.

"You're kidding. A bronc? Do you realize he did not buck even once throughout this whole ride?" Now I was filled with even more emotion for this poor beast, thankful that he didn't practice his profession on me. I crooned to him, and stroked his sweaty neck, and wondered if he noticed. Would he recognize endless kindness?

Suddenly, the prospect of the river occurred to me.

"We've got cross the river again!" I exclaimed apprehensively. "In the dark!"

"Oh no. We're going to be crossing a bridge when we get to the road," Road informed me.

"How are these guys around cars?"

"A little nervous," he said truthfully, then he laughed, "What are you worried about? You're a good rider. Probably better than me."

"You *are* a good rider," I assured him, "for a guy."

"What's that? For a *guy?* I thought you girls hate it when we say stuff like that."

I baited him, and he fell for it.

"I was teasing. You *are* a good rider." I saw him smile, then I added, "But I'm better!"

With that he slapped Crazy's spotted rump and sent him bolting. "Prove it, Missy!"

"Hey! I had him almost cooled down." But, I wasn't upset at all. Miraculously, Crazy obeyed me, or guessed what I wanted right away, because he settled down, and allowed me to guide him towards the other pair.

The ride on the road was short and uneventful. We brought the horses back and as soon as the youngest one of the ranch hands heard the clip clop of their hooves he appeared, and offered to unsaddle the horses and turn them out.

I was about to object, but Road handed the reins over, saying, "Thanks, Dude."

To me he said, "Come on and meet the guys."

He took me into the building they called the bunkhouse. It was really just a small home, furnished inexpensively, with a kitchen, living room, bathroom, and I assume, some bedrooms. It wasn't terribly clean, but it wasn't filthy either. There wasn't enough "stuff" to make it messy. These bachelors appeared to have only the bare necessities, clothes for working, pots and pans to cook with, a table, some chairs, easy chairs and a couch and TV.

They spoke to each other in their language, but when they wanted they used English. The "boss" amongst them was injured that day by a mare he was shoeing. Something startled her and she reared back. He had been working on one of her forelegs, and he caught her knee in his eyesocket, and his brow suffered a good two-inch gash. On her way down, the sharp edge of an unfinished hoof scraped down one shin, shredding his jeans and laying open a raw wound. He was drinking to ease the pain.

The men had prepared supper with the intention of inviting me and Road to dine with them. He excused us, and took me outside to ask me what I would like to do.

"I know they're a bit uncouth, but they have no life. This is their life. But, I could understand if you'd rather not eat here. I'll make something up."

"No. I'd like to eat here. That was nice of them to ask us." I meant it, too.

So, we sat on the couch, and Abdul whimpered and complained about that loco mare, and worried about his job. The three of them seemed to get excited and their voices got louder as they jabbered in their own tongue. Road and I sat uncomfortably for a few minutes, then he spoke up.

"Hey Guys." He jerked his head towards me. "You're frightening the lady. Speaka Englisha, huh? And quit arguing, will ya? Cripe, you want company, then you act like gringos."

After a small uproar, the men apologized, and explained.

"We were not arguing. We just have these troubles." He waved towards his foreman, "Today *this* has to happen, and you know who is going to pay for it . . . And last night we lost a filly. A beauty. We found her caught in the gate this morning. We cannot figure how she did this. Her front leg is stuck in between the rails and all broken." He put his forefinger to his head like a gun, "BANG! We have to shoot her. Big trouble. All this, and the boss is flying in this week. We don't know when. Never does he come, but now, he does, and all hell comes out."

During his litany, the other men interjected a term here, or an expletive there, for emphasis.

"Oh, yes. Big man, rich, powerful. He spit on us. We bust our balls day and night. Last night we hear loud noises, there is thunder and lightening, you know, last night, ya? How did we know the loco filly was getting hurt? We have trouble." He rolled his eyes.

Of the three men, one was a youngster, one was paunchy, and then there was Abdul, neither young, nor old, wiry and pent up. He called out for another beer.

The paunchy one got up, went into the kitchen, checked his pot on the stove, grabbed a beer from the cooler and tossed it to Abdul, who caught it with a curse. Now Paunch was motivated to finish cooking, and in a few minutes he and the youngster began to bring trays of food into the living room, where they placed it on the coffee table.

We had french bread, tossed salad, spaghetti, and a spicy sauce laden with huge chunks of chicken with bones, and onion, pepper and mushrooms. With this, hot green pickled peppers were served. Two men ate from the lids of the pots and pans, in order that Road and I would have dinner plates.

They kept insisting that we eat as much as we could, and everyone simmered down while we feasted. There was a war movie on, and though they seemed to know the outcome, they watched it with great gusto. After dinner, the boy automatically went about gathering the plates, and then cleaned the kitchen and washed the dishes. They would not allow me to help, even when I tried to insist.

These were the f—-ing arabs that Theresa across the street hated so much. Her loss. I had a wonderfully entertaining evening in their humble home, and felt more at ease in their colorful, beer-guzzling, backbreaking environment, than I ever would in the pastel and paneled palace of the plastic person across the street.

When the war movie ended, we got up to go. I simply said "Thank you, for the horseback ride, and for dinner. You have been most gracious, and I think you're all pretty funny."

Abdul had finally dulled his pain, and was asleep in his chair. The other two seemed pleased that I thought they were funny, and they told us to come back again.

I would if I could.

Miles: 75

Though we travel the world over to find the beautiful,
we must carry it with us or we find it not.
—Ralph Waldo Emerson

CHAPTER 17

NEW MEXICO
July 31 through August 4   Days 45–49

*M*onday was spent hiking Red Creek Trail by myself, for a good part of the day, while Road took care of business of his own.

The next morning, I took one last look at Road's tiny trailer, that he called home. In the window, a sign warned that trespassers will be shot. He's quite a character, but very likable. For a couple of weeks, I sort of had a boyfriend. The fact that I was traveling made me "Carp Diem," and I seized the moment and played the role of Gypsy.

The Aztec Ruins were no more than thirty miles south of Durango, just over the border. My motorcycle was once again packed to the max, and I arrived at the New Mexico state sign mid-morning. Hardy grasses, and scratchy bushes came to my knees, and wild sunflowers stood tall, their sunny faces pointed in my direction, as if they were watching me, happily.

I traveled through the Southern Ute Indian Reservation, and parked my motorcycle in the lot at the Aztec Ruins National Monument visitor center. Inside, I thoroughly examined the exhibits of Anasazi pottery, basketry, and blankets of intricate woven designs.

The ruins here were mistakenly named for the Aztec Indians of Mexico, but were actually built by the Chaco people's ancestors, (Anasazi; the Ancient Ones), in the 1100's. Eventually the Chacoan Anasazi's abandoned the site, and around 1225 the Mesa Verde Anasazis moved in, from the north. The original five-hundred room structure was not enough, and later additions and modifications were created, subtle differences in masonry techniques distinguishing them from the oldest construction.

The cost for this educational recreational visit was two dollars. Well worth it, too. The people on staff were kind enough to hold on to my riding gear for me, and I reluctantly went out into dry hot air, and pulled the pants on over my daisy dukes, and slipped my jacket over my leather halter top. At a water faucet I filled my helmet up and dumped it over myself, then got in the wind.

I headed due east on Rte. 64 as it went from a multi-lane stretch, to a two lane that meandered erratically along the top of New Mexico. The temperature soared. Towns bore names with a foreign flair, Blanco, Archuleta, and I encountered places such as Manzanera Mesa, Gobernador Canyon, El Cedro, and Jicarilla (hee-kah-REE-ya) Apache Indian Reservation.

At 4:30 I saw one of those electronic bank signs. The temperature was one hundred and three degrees. At 5:15 it had tempered to an even one hundred. As I got into a mountain range, and the Carson National Forest, it cooled off. I could see rain behind me, but it never caught up to me.

Towards late afternoon I made it to Chama, having fully enjoyed the run along most of 64. There were some twisties, not much, but I discovered that I wasn't scared any more. Since my accident, I had only ridden about four hundred miles, most of it on mountain passes requiring a good deal of skill. I remembered how it had been five days ago riding on the Million Dollar Highway. My adrenaline had been surging every few minutes. By now, I felt more comfortable, even through the extreme heat.

I settled in to the Rio Chama Railroad RV Campground. It costed $12.50, but I allowed the splurge on my ten dollar a day shelter budget, considering the last few nights were free. The campground featured an ancient railroad, a steam train ride, and a nearby museum.

As I set up my tent, I realized it had been ten whole days since I had slept in my traveling home. Ten days since I left the rally in Paonia and crashed.

Time was so different now. Without a usual schedule of work and days off, every day was like a weekend for me. I didn't feel as though time was flying by, in fact, every day was generally so filled with adventure that a week seemed like a month. So much is happening. I am learning so much. Every where I go, there are new things imprinted on my mind, and I want to absorb it all, like a sponge.

Different people have different needs, and although I am a social, gregarious sort, I have a strong need to spend time alone, preferably every day. Lately, I have been in circumstances that didn't allow that, very much. Even though Road gave me plenty of space, and I spent most of the day prior to this, hiking alone, I finally felt as though I was catching up with my Self.

Alone in my thoughts, a loud buzzing sound startled me, and I leapt aside, instinctively. Then I realized, I had just been inspected by a hummingbird. The invisible flurry of wings zoomed up to me again, then the iridescent miniature form of the tiny bird appeared for a second, then disappeared again. Two or three times, the little fairy-like creation zipped up to me, hovered at eye level, then left.

For dinner, I had water and a Power Bar.

Miles: 194

Sometimes during the night the stillness would be broken by the wail of the old train whistle. The track ran along one edge of the campground, and marked the boundary of my tent site, along with tree stumps torn from the ground. In the morning, I woke up and went about my routine. Before I washed up, I spread my sleeping bag over my bike to air it out. After my shower, I used the picnic table for my exercise session, then I fixed breakfast. Tea and oatmeal, oatmeal and tea. Every day I could decide which flavor I felt like having, and thus avoided total boredom with my morning fare.

This morning I had a kiwi to go with my breakfast as well. I used my Swiss Army knife to cut away the fuzzy green peels, and tossed them to the ground for the birds. It was a tiny ground squirrel who snatched up the treat, though.

At the time, I thought he was a chipmunk, of giant proportion. He was reddish brown, and had thin black and white racing stripes down his back. He scampered away a few feet, and with his teeny paws, nibbled the edges until the slip disappeared. He scurried back for the next piece.

I dispensed the peels closer and closer to where I sat. The ground squirrel came close enough that I could see the fluttering of his heart when he sat on his haunches to eat. If I moved, he'd run to the protection of my motorcycle tire, and peek over the rim, waiting for me to give him another morsel. I was delighted.

My water boiled and I finished the kiwi, and began bustling around, so my cute little rodent went somewhere else for a free meal. Campers walked back and forth on the path near my site, and a few greeted me, with a curious glance. I was busy packing up the bike, and didn't invite conversation.

When my Honda was all packed, I walked over to the pay phone near the Office, with my Hostel Book in hand. I was able to make a reservation to spend the night in a tepee! That would be a first in my life.

Getting back to my bike, I slipped my leather pants on over my shorts, put on my boots, and waited before putting on the helmet and jacket until the bike was started. It was already hot out.

My battery was dead.

"Son of a Bee!"

I should have known. There was no warning, but, I guiltily admitted to myself that I had not checked the fluid level since that day in Oregon when I revived it there. I'm all the way to New Mexico, now. What a dummy.

After lashing out at myself under my breath for a few minutes, I looked around at my surroundings. There was my workhorse, smack dab in the middle of the empty, grassy campsite. Why didn't I start the bike *before* loading it up? Well, why should I?

With a huff, and a groan, I started to unfasten the bungees, and set my bags on the ground. With my saddlebags, and everything else spread all around, it was hard to believe I could put it all on this machine of mine, and still drive it the way I do.

I pulled the saddle off, and the side covers, and gently worked the battery free from its snug compartment. All the while my mind was furiously hoping that a solution was available.

Somewhere on the campground I remembered seeing an older style black Gold Wing, and a white-bearded gentleman lounging in a foldaway chair near his pop-up pull-trailer. I walked over to his site, and he was there, still sitting.

"Hi," I said, with extended, gloved hand.

He shook my hand, as I explained my plight. "So, I was wondering, if by some remote chance, if you would have a battery charger."

"Gosh, no. But, can't you push start it?" he advised.

"Not really. I mean, it's too heavy for me to push that fast on this surface, and too tall for me to throw my leg over while running." The thought of it wore me out. "It's not worth dropping it, trying."

This is where a six foot man would come in handy, but this fellow biker was stooped, and had seen his better days. He asked me if I had asked the camp managers.

"No. Not yet. I wanted to check with you first. Thanks anyway." I said.

I entered the Office, and a motherly woman was on duty. I told her how I had been touring solo for six weeks now, and spent a lot of time camping in some pretty remote and rustic areas. Now I was in a commercial campground, and I had reason to be grateful.

She told me to find a guy named Don, on a little tractor. He produced a charger, and I accepted it graciously. He told me to drop it at the Office when I was finished, and offered to help me.

"That won't be necessary," I told him, "but, thanks anyway."

I settled down to read *A Walk Across America,* by Peter Jenkins. Earlier in the pages, I had read his disturbing words about Chama. Now, here I was in the very same area, but instead of fear and dread, I was feeling fortunate and lucky. We were in two different worlds, with some twenty years between our observations, and in vastly different situations.

I got the better deal.

I stopped reading to reflect, and to thank the One who watches out for me each day, testing me, teaching me, and drawing from me the power to make the right choices. Out of all these days, my battery let me down twice, and each of these times, I found myself within reach of a solution.

Rather than curse over a dead battery, I found it far better to be thankful for the circumstances. Had this happened two or three weeks ago, I could have been stranded on the Loneliest Road in America, or camped at one of those BLM camps that I preferred over the commercial places. The fact that I awoke this morning on a site that surpassed my daily shelter budget, turned out to be a blessing in disguise. I wasn't going to let that attitude escape me. I believe it's part of what keeps me protected.

With my battery all charged, I tried to start the bike *before* reloading everything. She started easily, so I put my book away, did what I had to do, returned the charger, and drove away.

For lunch, I stopped at an authentic Mexican restaurant, and ordered a sopapilla. It was filling, and I finished it, even though I was stuffed. Managing a food budget of ten dollars a day, meant every dollar counted, and I tried not to waste food. This meal cost me seven out of my ten dollars. You tell me, where do you go for a dinner that costs three?

*   *   *

I enjoyed the ride on Rte. 64 a great deal. It was pretty, not heavily traveled, and full of sights. While the closest mountains appeared to be covered with pine forest lace, the actual terrain, as I cut through it was sandy, and dry. Scrub grass, dried varieties, small shrubs and sagebrush dominated a good part of the land, but tall pines grew together in stands, creating a lacy look, from my distant viewpoint.

The road itself pleased me, and I found myself looking forward to arriving in Taos, where I thought I would get a good dose of New Mexico's charm.

Along my way, I came upon a ranch out in the middle of nowhere. At it's gate, a startling object caught my attention. There was the figure of a man, hanging from a very thick noose. I skidded to a stop. This can't be!

With relief, I discovered that it was only a dummy, but he had a message to deliver. Overhead, there was a wooden sign, WE DO IT THE OLD WAY.

Suspended from the center of the beam, was a hand made sign, with the words DAD'S DREAM RANCH neatly painted onto sunfaded wood, cut on the sides with the southwestern style notches.

I didn't stay long, because I didn't want to find out what "it" was, nor the "old way" it was done.

Again, I reveled in my insistence on traveling off the beaten path. This is not the sort of thing you come across on any Interstate.

Gradually, the forest thinned, and then quite unexpectedly I found myself approaching a gorge of great depth. A sturdy bridge spanned the gap, and I pulled over on the bridge itself, mindless of the cars that whizzed by now and then. I stared down into the chasm at the ribbon of blue green, and pondered the millions of years it took for this waterway to cut through the striated layers of stone, earth and rock.

I was beholding the Rio Grande River Gorge.

When I was ready, I got back on my Red Pony, and found the station in my head locked on one tune. "I'm an old cowhand, from the Rio Grande, and I learned to ride before I learned to stand . . . yipee-eye-aye, kie-aye." I was doomed.

In the afternoon, I rode into Taos, seeking a place to rest, write postcards, and replenish fluids. I cruised back and forth among the storefronts, and sidewalk displays, noting the southwestern motif everywhere and the molten aura of people on the sidewalks. The heat of the day stamped its mark on the faces of weary, sunbaked shoppers. I parked my bike eventually, and wondered about the indifferent glances which were cast my way, but dismissed them, mindful of the scorching effect that Mr. Sun has upon even the strongest man.

At once the atmosphere changed, when I stepped down two or three steps into a tiny coffee house. Below ground level, it was slightly cooler, and music from the sixties wrapped itself around me while I removed my jacket and gloves. A few flower children hung around talking about a barn dance, and charity events and where to buy the best incense. I asked for a cup of coffee, and claimed a bistro table to sit and write postcards at.

The girls wore flimsy, long printed skirts, and went braless underneath tie-dyed tee shirts. A couple of guys wore cut-offs that came loosely to their knees, and evidently shirts were not required in this shop. Two other males sported very long, stringy hair, love beads, earth toned tee-shirts and skirts! Yes, skirts. The skirts were of a heavy, woolen fabric, also of muted earth tones, and they were wrapped around somehow, and belted with rawhide or rope. Underneath, dirty ankles led to well worn sandles, and the entire effect was not as shocking as you might think. The costume suited the character, so to speak.

So, in between writing sentences to my friends, I sat thinking about the lifestyle these free spirits lead. They did not make me feel welcome, nor unwelcome. They seemed to congregate here, and this was their place. I was merely an outsider, and went unnoticed, like a dog sleeping on a rug by the door.

At last, the hour arrived when I could register into the hostel.

"I want to sleep in a tepee," I stated.

"Yes. When you go in the back gate, you'll see three. You'll sleep in the second one. I think there's another girl you'll be sharing it with, maybe two."

"That's fine," I said. "What about my motorcycle? Is there someplace I can park it, besides right out front here?"

"Yeah, just bring it around the side of the building. We have parking for our guests there."

Just then, the front door opened and in strode a man, fully clad in leather. His thick curly hair was pulled back into a ponytail, and he held the door and stepped aside for me to pass through.

"Hie—anothar baiker." He spoke with a catchy accent.

I smiled at him before exiting the building.

I felt compelled to unload everything off the bike, sensing some undercurrent of mistrust running in my veins, for me, a very unusual event. So, I brought all my stuff into the fenced-in yard, hoping that there would be an unspoken law that hostelers were able to trust each other. It was the outsiders, even the natives of Taos, that might not be trustworthy.

I snooped around in the 'kitchen,' a shelter of sorts, which contained a grimy counter, a dirty refrigerator, a meager assortment of utensils and pans, and an ancient stove. My appetite waned and I looked hopelessly at the flies and bees that made this area their refuge.

The other motorcyclist joined me and after introductions, we decided to take a walk into town to find a decent bite to eat, maybe, and a liquor store, definitely.

I bought some tequila, and a lemon. Anthony bought as much beer as he could carry. We returned to find a few more guests at the hostel, sitting outside, and we sat at our own picnic table, to talk.

As it turned out, Anthony was Australian, and he was spending some time touring the States on a BMW that he bought somewhere in California, specifically for the sojourn. Then he told me of some of the places he'd been.

The funny part began when he said he'd been at the Top-o-the-Rockies BMW Rally in Paonia, Colorado.

"Hey, I was there! I won the Long Distance Female Solo Rider award," I said.

I took a better look at him, and then I remembered crossing his path several times, especially in the evenings while I was at the rally. He was a tall, tanned, good-looking man, with incredible, light colored eyes, muscular arms, and a slightly flabby stomach. His appearance had caught my attention, because of his movie-star face, but I was pre-occupied by another dashing fellow, and I let this Aussie stumble on his way each time I saw him.

"Ah, you were there, too? Maybe you remember where I was . . . I was quite a wreck there, don't remember too much. I got juiced up every day, and tanked at night," he laughed. "So, I had my motorbike set up, with a tarp attached to the fore and aft, making a lean-to. When I wasn't drinking, I was crashed out under there."

I remembered that sight. "I saw your two boots sticking out from under your 'tent,' that's right, over near the building.?"

"Yes! Yes! Oh, that's funny," he said.

I continued, "I remember noticing you, too, but there was no way I wanted to meet you. You have these great eyes, so blue, but, they couldn't even focus. I said to myself, no way. Not my type."

"Ah, well, you know, it's vacation," he shrugged, unconcerned.

His feeling weren't hurt, his ego not tarnished, in fact, he almost spoke of his drunkenness as a badge of honor. I understood. Sometimes, there's a time to overdo it. Sometimes, you can't.

"Some tequila?" I offered him shots, and he accepted. We spoke of the rally some more, and I told him about the day I went riding with the big dogs, but had to go back to the porch.

"That was you?" He slapped his thigh, and hooted. "Ha! Your boyfriend was looking all concerned and worried when he couldn't find you. You should've seen his face when you came pulling in. He was so relieved."

"Oh—so that was *you* he was talking to when I came back. I heard about what you said." All of a sudden it seemed pretty funny, and no longer offensive.

The Aussie asked me, "What did I say?"

"F—-ing woman in a man's world," I reported.

"Oh, did I? You know, I'm not used to this."

I kidded around and told him he was a macho chauvinist, but, that's okay, we could still be friends.

The sun set was gorgeous, as pinks and peach bounced off a thin layer of clouds, and the other hostelers sat at their table laughing and getting to know each other over a few beers, too.

Anthony left for a little walk, and gave me the opportunity to meet some other guests. There was a girl, Anya, from South Africa keeping everyone in stitches as she related tales about her travels in U.S.A.

"Oh yes. I made them give me a discount to go white water rafting. I begged them," she said, then, making her voice all funny she mimicked, "Please, I am a poor, starving, traveling student, *all the way* from South Africa, and this is the *one thing* I have to do in America to be happy. The *one thing*. Please, let me do it for twenty, not thirty dollars, or I cannot do it."

She laughed contagiously. "That is how I got to ride in a helicopter at Grand Canyon, and ride horses at a dude ranch. It is so funny."

I gave her credit for ingeniousness, and her wonderful, infectious personality.

My tequila made the rounds, along with lemon that I sliced with my pocket knife, rather than the rather risky knife from the kitchen. I did, however brave the sticky salt shaker, so when the pint was gone, it was time for me to settle down in my tepee.

The tepee was constructed of white canvas, and was supported by tall, thin tree trunks. Inside, around the edge of the circumference, were five cots, the sixth space was the doorway. I looked for bugs before laying down, then, gazed at the dim interior for a few moments, and listened as the storytelling outside continued. The day caught up with me, as did the multiple shots of tequila, and I slept so soundly that I never heard the other two girls when they came to sleep, near me, in this tepee, in New Mexico.

Miles: 117

Anthony appeared in the morning and invited me to come have breakfast with him down the street. He had met one of the locals and she had asked him to come and have breakfast with her in the morning.

Our hostel was actually outside of Taos, in a town called Arroyo Seco. We were walking in between humble, dilapidated business places. No question that poverty is the norm in this particular area, even though the artsy, touristy Taos is merely minutes away.

Anthony led me to a run-down looking gallery, and as he knocked at the entrance, I peered in through the drabby storefront window. Inside, I could see bolts of materials, wooden boxes full of threads, and skeins of yarn. Remnants were strewn everywhere, and walls were lined with spools of thread, beads, ric-rac, buttons, twine, and what-not.

Just as Anthony began to sound impatient, a blanketed doorway leading to the back room was pulled aside, and the shape of a largess woman appeared. She strode across the floor, and unlocked the front door and allowed us into the gallery, which looked more like a storage attic, and the dusty aroma of all the natural wares assaulted my nostrils, as I looked around in wonder at all the eclectic stuff.

The giant woman looked like she needed more sleep, and her loose, easy dress swung about her generous body proportions as she moved across the room, seeming annoyed that Anthony had actually taken her up on the invitation to breakfast. She excused herself for a moment, asking us to take a seat outside.

When she had wrapped her hair into a coif, and splashed water over her face, she came back outside to greet us properly.

Anthony stood and introduced us, "Dee, this is Lisa—and Lisa, this is my wife, Dee."

If looks could kill . . .

I felt like crawling into a knothole. Here I was, all one hundred and twenty pounds of me, in my shorts and tee shirt, facing off against Lisa, burly, strong, twice my weight, and about a foot taller. Fearing she might snap me in two, I straightened and looked her in the face.

She was glaring at Anthony. He never batted an eye.

In five seconds, she recovered, spun on her heel, and retreated into the store. My foolish friend shrugged his shoulders. "Hie, Aye think she likes mae."

"You didn't have to say I was your wife!" I snapped, but I figured, I could go along with it for the duration of one meal, maybe.

So, supposedly Lisa had been charmed by Anthony when he had taken his walk the evening before. After he'd thanked her and told her he'd come for breakfast, he felt uneasy. What if she put the moves on him? She looked powerful enough to hurt him. So, he returned with me in tow, figuring he would get off, scott free.

Lisa came back on the scene, bearing a tray laden with honeydew, fresh bread, jam, orange juice, black coffee, and brown sugar. She graciously told us she didn't have much, (not even running water!) but we were welcome to share.

She sat on a stool across from me, I tore chunks of bread, and sat and listened to the most lively, debatable, prejudiced, spiteful conversation I'd encountered so far on this journey. Still, it was funny in its own way.

Lisa first spat out her anger at having been broken into the night before. Some things had been stolen, not much, but the cost of the broken window was of major concern, because it had to be replaced, or she could be wiped clean in a night or two. She blamed it on Mexicans. She told how the Spanish hate the Mexicans and the Mexicans hate Native Americans, and the Native Americans hate us all. She spoke of the people around here that are all no good. She had an opinion on everyone, and everything. She commented about the Rainbow groupies, that she called Rain Blows, how they "set up acres of camp, and have their Peace Talks, and Save The Earth campaigns, but s—t and p—s wherever they are, and you can smell 'em a mile away because they don't take showers and they friggin' stink. Rainbows, my a—, friggin' Rain Blows."

Besides her unique hospitality, the thing I liked best about her came after I got her off her "screw the world" rampage, and got her talking about her textile arts supply store and gallery.

"The name *La Vieja Loca* means: The Crazy Woman. I liked that, so appropriate for me, so it becomes my store," she stated, folding her hefty arms across her ample bustline, and sitting back against the grimy storefront window.

Anthony listened as Lisa told him all about the "cold" New Englanders, the "stupid" Midwesterners, how in the south everyone's "in-bred," and so forth and so on. How can one person be so slanted?

I wondered, how do you say *The Narrow Minded Woman?* in Spanish? That would be a more suitable reflection of this woman that weaves.

Finally, our breakfast needs had been met, and having survived this most unusual occasion, I gratefully departed, with "my husband" by my side.

*　　　*　　　*

One hour later, I was on the road, cutting through the heat as I headed north, keeping a mountain range on my right. As I drove through Costilla, I noticed a wizened, old man leading a donkey or mule along the edge of the road. He had tied several of them at intervals along the fence with long ropes, so that they could feed on the grass that grew between the road and the fence. Inside the fence had been overgrazed, and the short stubble was brown and dry.

Then I spied an incredible sight. I was compelled to stop. I had as much time as I wanted.

That is the beauty of traveling alone. No one else that I can think of, would want to spend an hour, dressed in leather, standing in the full sun, in order to watch a poor man's baby donkey come into the world. But, no one in my life will ever be able to take away my memory of the discomfort, the heat that I endured to *live* for this one hour, in New Mexico. I got to see Nature's most fabulous of wonders, the miracle of maternal instinct. I witnessed a newborn's first taste of its mother's milk.

Riding alone, I am able to embrace the things I value.

*　　　*　　　*

At Pinyon Flats Campground, I paid eight dollars, after a two dollar entrance fee into Colorado Great Sand Dunes National Monument. A ranger came by to warn me that I had chosen a site that a brown bear had passed through, just the night before. He asked a neighbor to secure my foodstuffs and toiletries for me. I took a hike to the Dunes Overlook.

The trees were incredible works of art, sculpted by sandblasted winds. They grew asymmetrically, bent over like so many old men and women. Their branches were twisted and gnarled, some bark clung to the trunks like leathery skin, many of the branches had lost their protective covering, and smooth, polished inner wood was exposed. A pair of ravens came along the hike with me, perching in the branches of various trees keeping watch, darting ahead after I passed below them.

When I got to the overlook, I took in the majestic and unusual appearance of enormous sand dunes on display.

Coming from near Cape Cod, I am quite used to the beauty of mountains of fine white sand, ever changing, and mysterious. But here, this monumental example, stretches over one hundred and fifty miles of valley floor, without the ocean surf crashing nearby. It's amazing.

A mule deer raised its head and we gazed at each other from across a ravine, until it bounded off into some ponderosas.

Later, while I was falling asleep I thought about the changes this trip has wrought. Little things have given my excursion more meaning, when necessity drives me to develop the means to cope with every day happenings. How, the need for a daily shower has evolved into a delight to be enjoyed, when circumstances allow. How, my legs have fine blonde hairs growing, and I don't even care. The things we Americans take for granted, have become luxuries in my day to day existence out here, now.

How very satisfied and contented I am.

Miles: 115

The next day, I mulled over a different situation. Just a week ago I was in the arms of 'another man.' In a few days, I would be reunited with my 'sort of' boyfriend, from home. We had spoken on the phone, and made arrangements to meet up with each other during Sturgis Bike Week. I was uncomfortable with the mixed emotions. Instead of being happy to be seeing Russell again, I was dreading it. Russ wasn't the kind of guy that would interrogate. He was so aloof, I almost wished he would. He seemed so unconcerned, and whenever I questioned him about 'things' he would reply with such elusive answers, that I never bothered any more.

For a hundred miles I wracked my brain, searched my soul, scoured my heart, and examined my motives for getting lured by the temptation of this addictive, potent poison known as Russell.

Hope? But, how long have I hoped?

Love? Yes, but not for a long time.

Fun? I doubt it.

Habit? Most likely.

Adrenaline? Strong emotions? Struggles? A chance at winning? What made me want to take a shot of this drug, when I had been clean for more than six weeks now?

Lust. That much I knew. He was my lover. But, I realized, now that I had been with someone else, everything had changed.

Gradually, I wrung out every doubt, anxiety, and worry, and scourged each unrealistic hope or fantasy, then tried to tuck the whole parcel away to a back corner of my mind, where I could retrieve it later on. For now, I had a day to enjoy. I couldn't let my brain ruin any more of it.

The Red Pony climbed the Poncha Pass, elevation 9,488 ft. and sped down through Poncha Springs, then into Salida.

Although only a handful of sites were occupied at Hecla's Junction, a whitewater recreation area, I continued my habit of selecting a site away from other people. After parking the motorcycle, I walked over to the ever present bulletin board with my wallet, to self-register. The fee was $3.

Rafts were beginning to return, and wet and laughing adventurers spilled out, wearing brightly colored life vests. From my vantage point, halfway up a stony mountain behind my tent, they looked like ants, scurrying around, lifting the big, empty rafts over their heads, and carrying them across the lot, to pass them up to other 'workers' on top of the busses.

A family had a well established campsite near mine, and when they returned from their rafting trip, they brought the guide back with them. He had been invited to share their camp, having forgotten to pack his own tent stakes. In the evening, when the parents discovered that I was all by myself, they befriended me, too. Their fire was eventually surrounded by a whole bunch of adventurous men, rowdy from their day on the rapids. Before retiring, the family, a mother, father and teenaged son agreed to hike with me to the top of the stony mountain behind my tent. We'd get up at the crack of dawn.

Miles: 157

One of the most valuable things we can do to heal one another
is to listen to each other's stories.

—Rebecca Falls

CHAPTER 18

NEBRASKA
August 5–9   Days 50–54

*I*t was a rather steep climb, and the thin air had us breathing in exaggerated volumes with each lung full. The older two kept up pretty good, and after a healthy bout of the vigorous exertion, we reached the top, and were rewarded by the extensive view.

The night before, we were so engaged with the four men visiting, that we hadn't gotten to know each other very well.

"What about your folks? Brian's our boy and it would be hard to let him go off on his own, never mind if he was a daughter. Your parents must be worried sick about you every single day. Do you call them often?"

My hiking boot had become untied, I noticed. I always hate it when people start asking about my parents. Tying a double knot in my laces, I straightened and faced Barb.

"First of all, I know I don't look it, but I'm thirty-five years old. I make my own decisions. I've been on my own ever since I was eighteen." I looked away, to the far off horizon. "My mother died when I was twenty one. She must be rolling in her grave now. She detested motorcycles." I looked back at the lady, and sighed. "My father, well, he's gotten used to the idea. He loves me, and knows he can only pray for me. He doesn't really understand why I am doing this, but he seems to be proud of me for . . . " searching for a word, I paused.

The dad finished for me. "He's proud to have raised such a fine, strong, independent woman."

"Yes, I guess so," I fell silent, thinking of my father, wondering, where is he now? How is he? Is he feeling all right? I miss him, more than I thought I would. I hope he knows that I'm having the time of my life.

We started our trek down, much to Brian's relief. This whole conversation was boring him. Someday he would surely understand. Obviously, his was a family of strong bonds. Not everyone is so lucky.

When I was younger, my father was just the man who got up and went to work, building below the ground swimming pools. I didn't ever *really* know him, until a few years ago. But, I did know this, he loved me. He wanted the best for me. He expected a lot out of me. I admire and respect him a great deal.

Lost in my thoughts, I found myself back at the bottom of the mountain, and was reminded to "Come over for breakfast. Joe's cooking."

Indeed he was. There was hot coffee and blueberry pancakes. Joe, the rafting guide, dashed about energetically, preparing our meal. "Served with a smile!" He exclaimed as he flourished a tray laden with the steaming flapjacks.

After filling every nook and cranny in my body, I returned to my own campsite to break camp. The weather looked perfect, and I anticipated an excellent ride to Colorado Springs. With high spirits I thanked Joe, and the family who took me under their wings.

*   *   *

Out of Salida, I took Rte. 285 to Buena Vista, (Spanish for "Beautiful View"), managed the lovely Trout Creek Pass at 9,488 ft. elevation, and feeling on top of the world, approached the Rte. 24 turn-off, which dazzled me with its scenery, and ridability. Up and over Wilkerson Pass, at 9,502 ft. went I, thrilled every minute by the wonder of it all.

All of my senses seemed heightened, as I leaned into one curve after another. All of a sudden, I noticed that every time I was banked over to the left, a horrible scraping sound issued forth, but when I straightened the bike and leaned over to the right, it went away. I became very concerned, and pulled over to investigate.

The source of noise that troubled me became immediately apparent. The lower cowling, my air scoop that broke in my crash, was busted again. It would normally be attached to the Honda's frame, by two screws on each side, but now one side was dangling. Every time I leaned over to the left, the fiberglass cowling contacted the road's surface, and had already been ground down considerably. It was hopeless. The piece had to go.

Sadly, I unfastened the remaining screws, and found that the strain on the fiberglass was beginning to crack it on that side, too. The scoop was too awkward of a shape to carry. There were no trash barrels handy, and I hated the idea of leaving this black object, with its white lettering, *V-FOUR*, just lying on the side of the road like some kind of litter. This thing was not a piece of junk, to me. It was a part of my Red Pony. I needed to lay it to rest.

It seemed appropriate, that I was on a splendid Colorado mountain pass, at this exact moment in my bike's history. I ran my gloved hands over the partly glossy, partly mangled motorcycle part, and gravely set it carefully against a big rock, under a pretty tree, well off from the side of the road, kneeling, and thinking how fortunate I was, that it was this unnecessary item I was leaving behind, and not my beloved motorcycle, altogether.

It was a brief, but special moment. I drove away from that spot imagining that some day, a hiker, or a mountain bike rider might discover the mysterious *V-FOUR* thing, and never know about the forty-eight thousand miles of America that it traveled, suspended merely inches over the roadways where I have been in the last nine years. Most people wouldn't even know what it used to be. But, in my mind, it was *more* then it was meant to be, and today, a piece of the Red Pony is my private little American monument, somewhere near Pike's Peak in Colorado. What a grand place for the memory.

This state is incredibly beautiful. The mountain scenes come from out of my dreams. Again, the wonder of my good fortune surrounded me with awe.

Every person in their lifetime should do something like this. Why is it that only one out of ten-thousand people will escape the societal doldrums and do something spectacular and extraordinary, like this?

How did I get to be so lucky, to believe that I could pull it off?

The answer eludes me. My heart swells.

*   *   *

The Colorado Chapter of Women On Wheels were having a Bike Wash at a Honda shop in Colorado Springs today.

As I rolled into the parking lot, and headed for the hoses and buckets, a tall man stopped and watched me come to a halt. "Hey, is that Dee? From Massachusetts?"

"James!" I yelled, through my flipped up shield. "It's really me! Where's Sally?" I looked around for his wife.

"She couldn't make it," he answered, as he grabbed me for a friendly hug in front of the rest of the Women On Wheels. "She's at the library studying for a big exam. I'm here to represent the Higgins family today."

There were numerous members at the Bike Wash, and I turned my dirty, mud caked on, baked on, tar spattered, scraped and tattered motorcycle over to their greatest efforts to clean her up.

"This is a well-spent five dollars. I don't envy you guys a bit." I laughed as the women tackled the job with gusto. Wet and soapy hugs were wrapped around me, and I slipped out of my leathers, feeling the heat of the day as it beat down into the cement city.

After answering a ton of questions about my travels since the Ride-In, I went into Apex Motorcycle Sports Honda, to price their batteries. The price was steep. It would eat up more than one whole day's budget. But, I had to buy a new one.

There was a department store a few blocks away, where I saved quite a bit of money by buying my battery there. In the relentless heat of the parking lot, while curious onlookers passed by, I filled my new battery with acid, then installed it easily. The sense of relief that washed over me was palpable.

When I returned to the Bike Wash, I pitched in my share for lunch. Two dollars and fifty cents. In the cooler I helped myself to a Diet Pepsi, and then I had my first slice of pizza since I'd left home.

Feeling special that several of the ladies invited me to come and sleep over at their homes, I respectfully explained that Sally was a friend of mine, and I would be going home with James.

James rode a Harley adorned with running wolves. He led me to the city library. We peeked past stacks and around corners playfully until we spotted Sally, her brow furrowed as she concentrated on her studies.

"Hey honey!" He called in a whisper, startling her. "Look what the cat dragged in!"

I popped out from behind a wall, and Sally removed her glasses to see better, then nearly knocked her chair over when she jumped up to greet me warmly. She was so surprised and pleased. James was standing there all proud of himself, like he'd just given her a really neat present.

He asked her if it would be okay if I spent the night at their place. Seemed more like a formality. He already knew her answer. Library patrons were looking our way with disapproving expressions, so we made our exit, laughing quietly to ourselves.

The Higgins brought me home. I met their dogs, two gorgeous huskies. They offered me the use of their washer and dryer, their telephone.

When they asked if I wanted to take a shower, I had to ask, "Why? Can you smell me? It's been a few days."

Naturally, they didn't answer.

"Seriously," I said, "Would you mind if I take a bath instead of a shower? I could really use a good long soak. If you wouldn't mind, I'll just bring my book up there, and read until I turn into a prune."

Sally said, "Of course you can. You won't mind if we go to the grocery store while you bathe? I hope you don't think we're being rude to leave you all alone."

"Heck, no. I don't care. But, please don't go to the store on my account. Here, let me give you some money."

"Don't be ridiculous. Get upstairs right now, before you get a beating! I put out a towel and things. If you need anything, just snoop around and see if you can find it."

Their house was a roomy, fairly new, comfortable, neat and clean home, in a housing development. I poured a hot, bubblebath, and gratefully eased in. Scented femininely, the bubbles felt soft and sensuous, and I languished in this liquid pastime, relaxed and contented.

Although I heard when my host and hostess came home, I stayed up in the bathroom, taking my time, reading my book, and washing slowly. I shaved my legs of their European look, and scrubbed under my fingernails. Ah, the comforts of home. The things we take for granted.

With a thick, fluffy towel wrapped around my head, I emerged from the tub. I slathered some lotion all over my moist skin, and got wrapped up in the cozy robe Sally provided for me while I washed my clothes.

James was tossing a salad, and marinating steaks for our dinner, to go with baked potato, "Is that okay?"

As if beggars can be choosers.

"We thought we'd have steak, to celebrate the occasion. It's so nice to have you with us."

I threw every item of clothing I had with me that wasn't leather into the washing machine, and set it on hot. My things were dirty, sweaty and ripe. I had literally worn every garment since the last time I washed clothes. Undies and socks I had sometimes washed by hand, and many things I'd worn two or three days in a row.

"Do you want to use the phone?" They inquired, again.

"Yes. Thank you." I answered, truthfully.

"There's one upstairs, so you can have your privacy."

My friend Betsy was home when I called collect, and was overjoyed to talk to me in person. Speaking with her made me feel very happy and loved, and re-connected me with the fact that I do have a home, and lots of people love and miss me. I told her about my upcoming tryst with Russell, and she could tell how uncertain I was about it. She advised me to meet up with him, have fun, and then be on my way. Good advice. She told me she'd gone by my apartment a couple of times and played with my cat, and that my roommate seemed very aloof. Finally we'd said all there was to say, and I hung up.

One of the nicest things a person can do for another person who has been on the road for an extended period of time is to allow them to use the phone. Ask them specifically, "Do you need to make any phone calls? Are there any you just want to make, but haven't yet?"

Many people have asked me, can I get you anything? Do you need anything? Help yourself.

But, I'm not likely to spiel out a list of all my heart's desires. I'm afraid to cross the boundaries. So, hearing specifics makes it easy on the traveler. Especially offer use of the telephone, and your washer and dryer if you have one. Even if only three items are dirty, they can be added to a full load. The traveler doesn't have access to easy laundry, and their clothing is most likely quite limited to only a few days. Another thing I found I really missed was rummaging around in a refrigerator. Small things, but real—like eating a pickle from the jar.

James called out from the kitchen, "You want a beer?"

"No thanks." I joined him in the airy kitchen. "I don't drink beer, but I like the hard stuff."

"Margarita?"

"MMMmmm. That would be great."

Sally and I sat in the living room, and talked about our latest motorcycle adventures. (She's had a few of her own.) I inspected all the decorations around the house, mostly wolves, and looked at the many photographs, and books on the shelves.

She told me of her romance and strong marriage with James, and he pretended to be too busy to hear. In and out of the sliding glass doors he passed, checking on the steaks as they sizzled on the grill out on the deck.

On this day I ate a lot. I had to make up for all the days I ignored hunger pains, or camouflaged them with an appetite suppressant. Gosh, blueberry pancakes for breakfast, pizza for lunch, and now this excellent home-cooked meal. It don't get much better than this!

Miles: 167

*   *   *

Sally and James escorted me away from Castle Rock. They had some errands to run, and I was going to look up my friend Nancy, the girl with the Interceptor at the BMW rally. We hit the highway in formation, then they pulled up beside me. We raised our left fists into the air as they veered off to take their exit. So long, friends.

Denver was a confusing network of highways and concrete, signs galore, billboards, pollution, and traffic. In no time at all I felt suffocated and restrained. I found Nancy's apartment in a quiet suburb, without too much trouble.

She welcomed me, clad in a bikini, and grabbed a few of my bags. Nancy reassured me, that I was more than welcome, and she really hoped I'd come, but didn't think I would. My visit wasn't an intrusion.

"To be honest," she said, "sometimes I need an adult around, just to be friends, a woman friend."

The first thing we did was go for a swim in the complex's pool. The cold water engulfed me, offering relief from the heat I had stored up, sitting through all those red lights in my leathers. Nancy and I treaded water for a while, talking, and her mascara smeared darkly beneath her eyes, while her hair was all slicked back. She looked like a sexy shampoo commercial.

Climbing up out of the water, the water streamed down her tanned, well-toned legs. I couldn't help but notice her flat belly and generous cleavage. She's cute as a button, so short and compact. She's got the 'right' hair, usually all gussied up with hair spray, and she wears a lot of eye make-up, but she can pull it off. For all that prissy appearance, she's quite a gal. Here she is, supporting a nine year old boy and doing the best she can, all by herself. My age, too. I couldn't imagine being in her situation, but as we talked, I realized she had things under control.

That night, I slept in Kit's twin sized waterbed. His room had a collage of Daytona Bike Week bandannas from his grandfather, also a biker. When one of the cats settled down at my feet purring loudly, I felt totally at home.

Miles: 42

*   *   *

Nancy had to work. She told me to make myself at home. Kit was staying with his grandmother. I lounged around reading *A Walk West.* Peter Jenkins was also 'in Colorado,' as I sat in Denver reading his prose. I wondered what would happen to him, along the way. I wondered the same about me. The people who came into his life changed a part of him forever. I could relate with his experiences, so different than mine, yet so much the same.

This was a day to reflect, to catch up with myself, to be alone. Yet, I had the creature comforts of running water, a refrigerator, and soft furniture at my disposal. Two cats and a bunny lived here, and loved the extra attention I paid them.

I looked forward to going riding with Nancy. I'd never been out riding with another girl riding an Interceptor, the same as mine. At last, she came home from work.

We rode through some picturesque Colorado towns, ending up on Lookout Mountain, where there was a clear view of the imposing, spectacular high points of the Rocky Mountains. When we came to stop lights, I'd see Nancy's small physique reaching for the ground with one foot, her helmet covering all but her eyes and cheeks. Every time I looked at Nancy on that bike, I thought of my girlfriend Lorrin, who used to ride her Katana with me, back east. I realized I was feeling homesick for my friends. It was a strange and unusual sensation for me, but undeniable. The kinship I was feeling with Nancy was bringing back fond memories of those who I loved and had left behind.

It is imperative for me to explore my feelings, and not try to squelch them. So, I thought of my girlfriends as I rode, and let myself get misty-eyed.

I have a right to be feeling this way. I've been gone for nearly two months. Every attachment I form, I know I have to leave behind. In a way, it gets easier with practice, but still . . . I miss my old friends. I wish I didn't have to leave my new friends behind. Like, Kim in Ohio, and Judy in Washington, Sally, and Nancy most recently, not to mention Road. What's it all about? Why, after all the happiness must I feel so sad, right now, today?

I don't know. It stayed a mystery. In fifty-two days, I'd only felt this lonely sadness a couple of times, maybe three. Yeah, that one day in Badlands, and that other time heading for Yellowstone crying my eyes out, and now today. Thinking along those lines, I suddenly felt better.

Listen to yourself, Girl. Get a grip on. You wanted to see the country. This is the price you pay, and you aint doing too bad, either. Think of all the places you've been, all the things you've seen. All the days you've been essentially on your own. Most every day, loneliness is about as far from your mind as your home town. Embrace your lonesomeness, and move on. You're human, after all.

Okay, so I'm not invincible. I am human. That's good to know. I'm getting hungry, too. Hope we're almost back.

By the time we got home, my heart and mind had had their pep talk, and I was no worse for the wear.

Miles: 55

*   *   *

Nancy sent me off in the morning with a zip-lock bag full of herbal teas, all different varieties. A simple gesture, much appreciated. More importantly, she asked me to come back in my travels. She gave me a spare key and insisted I was to let myself in and make myself at home, even if she wasn't there. After a warm hug, I was off.

Nebraska, here I come.

Having never explored Denver, I spent a torturous, cursed two hours stuck in the commuter maze. The situation was aggravating and somewhat ironic. Here I have traveled the byways and wide open spaces for all this time, no problem. But now, in a well planned asphalt layout, I was considerably lost. The more I back-tracked, missed exits, and changed directions, the more frustrated I got. The more frustrated I was, the more mistakes I made. I was morphing into a leatherized monster.

Where are my open spaces?

Once I managed to get on track, I sped away from the city like a mad woman. So much for my early start.

With Denver behind me, I found a distinctly different side of Colorado, where her face is plain and gentle. The eastern third of the Centennial State is prairie flatlands. My day's mission would take me through a landscape of golden and green patchwork.

I followed I-76 to the smaller State 71. My inner turmoil subsided, I was free. Then another feeling emerged. It manifested itself overhead, as a thin haze gradually thickened into a gray, puffy cover that threatened to pour. My nerves were jangled.

Was I headed for Nebraska? Or was I headed for disaster?

By the same time tomorrow, I would be reunited with Russell. Why was I not excited? A sense of regret swept through me, accompanied by waves of nausea. It was unsettling, and I tried to outride the bad Karma, a useless feat, considering I continued moving forward.

WELCOME TO NEBRASKA

The sign at the border had a covered wagon pulled by a team of mules. It was pocked by fifty bullet holes, the midwest equivalent of "drive-by shootings."

A cute little old man at a gas station told me it was a hundred and two degrees out. "Aren't ya hot with all that leather on?"

"Yes, but I'd rather sweat, than bleed," my standard, effective reply.

I set up camp near Scottsbluff. The hosts were an older couple, and I tapped on their door to ask them about the nearby zoo. "Are you on your way to Bike Week?" they asked.

"No."

"We had lots of Harleys here last weekend, and every year at this time. They get a little rowdy, but they're not a bad lot."

The two of them got an education about my experience with bias among Harley riders, made more intense as the numbers increase. They listened thoughtfully, and made comparisons to another group they called the Gold Eagle riders, which I guessed would be a Gold Wing group, by the description of their plush, giant, silent machines, and their unexpected quiet manners and easy presence.

Two distinctly different stereotypes, sharing the same passion, each in their own way.

Then, there is me.

*   *   *

At Scott's Bluff National Monument, I learned of the hardships faced by pioneers. Scott's Bluff was viewed as a landmark, announcing that one third of the Oregon Trail had been accomplished. It stood 800 feet above the flat, grassy floor, unmistakable. A fur company clerk, Hiram Scott died at the site, and from then on it bore his name. My imagination wandered as my eyes slid across the landscape, imagining the perilous undertaking which so many emigrants did not survive. What a rugged group they must have been.

*   *   *

A few times during the night I was awakened by a noise which began like a chugging sound. *Huff-huff-huff,* about a second apart, then increasing in pace until the train seemed to chug off out of range. I didn't realize I was near a railroad, but a whole bunch of my camps had shared that feature, so far. The weird thing was, after each train departed, a loud roar would fill the air. I wondered about the zoo nearby. Perhaps one of the big cats displayed its displeasure by roaring whenever a train went by.

My dreams were sketchy representations of the uncertainty facing me on the morrow. What kind of mistake am I about to make? My sleep was troubled, my heart unsure. Tomorrow will tell.

Miles: 289

Every table in Bailey's Cafe was occupied. I entered in my usual attire of leather pants, and fringed biker jacket. As I scanned the room looking for a seat, I noticed it was Senior Citizen's day. There was a lot of gray hair in the room.

Two seconds after I appeared, my helmet slipped out of my grasp and fell to the parquet floor with a resounding *CRACK!*

Boy, did that get some attention! I scared quite a few folks, and was mentally reviewing CPR, thinking somebody may have a heart attack. It sounded like a gun went off.

Sheepishly, I grimaced, "Oops!" and squatted down to pick my helmet up off the floor, all the while keeping my eyes on the frightened white-hairs. I stood and grinned, looking around at the startled faces.

"Butter Fingers. Sorry."

I passed between some tables on my way along an aisle, and noticed that the ladies and gentlemen had warmed up to me some. All the tables were being used, but a few people sat alone. I approached the nearest one.

"Excuse me, mind if I join you?" I asked politely, speaking to an older man wearing overalls and a kind expression.

"Why no. Not at all," he replied.

Before a waitress got to the table, I broke the ice and asked the gent his name, what he used to do for a living, and "Tell me about your grandchildren." By the time she'd come by with some coffee, I was already fully accepted by George. He had the same name as my dad's.

The waitress took my order, and left.

"And you rode all the way here?" he stammered.

"All the way. I left home in June, the day before Father's Day. This is one of the best times of my entire life. No—it is the best." How can I explain?

"Aren't you afraid? You could get killed."

"I'm more afraid of some day looking back and wishing I had lived life fuller. We cannot go back and do it over. So what if I die on this journey? Anyone who knows me and loves me will realize, I died doing something I loved. That to me is a lot less scary than growing old, with some disease that traps me in a failing body, surrounded by zombies, and people who are paid to take care of me. No thanks."

"Well, young lady," George countered, "You could end up in a nursing home, just the same."

"But," I shot back, "while there, I'll be able to close my eyes and conjure up the memories that I've created. This girl isn't going down easily. When I die, I will know that I have *lived.*"

The sixty-nine year old man nodded. He was beginning to understand. "You have a lot of courage. You are going to go places. Don't let fuddy-duddies like us old codgers stop you."

"Trust me, ain't nobody stopping this girl when she makes up her mind!" I laughed. "Excuse me, I need to use the ladies room."

After I was done, my waitress stopped me at the counter. She told me she'd overheard some of our conversation, and she was "just so impressed." She wished she had time to sit and chat, but, she was way too busy. Disappointed, she learned that I was just passing through, and would be unable to come back later on.

I returned to my seat, and although George had finished his breakfast shortly after I showed up, he remained. I ate slowly, and talked a lot.

Ethel came by again, "Anything else I can get you?"

"Um, my check, please."

"That's already been taken care of," she said.

Surprised, I looked at George and blurted, "Get out of town! No way. Thank you!"

But, George looked as surprised as I. Touching his fingertips to his chest, he shook his head and said, "It wasn't me."

Ethel informed me, "No, it was Jim and Al, the two that were sitting over there. They already left, but they picked up your tab."

"They're gone? I didn't even get to say thank you."

"They are a couple of 'regulars,' I'll tell them next time they come in," she reassured me.

"Tell them they made my day. Honestly." Aside to George, I added, "I would have gotten steak and eggs, if I knew that was going to happen!"

He chuckled.

*   *   *

Riverside Zoo was next on my agenda.

I love zoos. There is a lot of controversy about zoos, but many people are ignorant about the changes that have been taking place in zoos across America over the last couple of decades. Zoos are now a place of education, and conservation. Animals are more likely to be housed in areas that attempt to portray their natural environment, and many zoos offer mini ecosystems when possible.

There are some zoos that have made me wretch, because of poor standards, and horrible barred cages. The animals although alive, are not *living*. Those should be shut down, but all zoos are not like that. Some are wonderful, learning places. I try to judge, if I were a wild beast, captured, could I tolerate a place like this? Some places are lovely, the animals are well fed and healthy looking. Their homes are spacious and not at all the cement and barred prison cells of yesteryear.

Lions, tigers, and all the big cats are about my favorite zoo animals, so I was saving the best for last. As I moseyed from one section to another, I stopped to inhale the fragrance of the wonderful flowers and grasses that made lovely gardens throughout the property. My plan to camp here at Riverside before meeting Russell had turned out so well. For eight bucks last night, I paid for my sleeping quarters, two showers, and this wonderful time of recreation.

I rounded the building near the lion's den, and scanned the large pen, seeking a flash of tawny hide. There was plenty of greenery so that the cats could lounge in the shade of the trees, or stretch out behind a screen of tall grasses, if they desired.

I followed the fence line, hoping to locate a lioness or two, or maybe the King of the Beasts. When I got to the far corner, I found one of each. The lioness was crouched down on her belly. Her rear quarters were hidden by the thick screen of tall grass. The King stood over her, with one great paw on the ground on each side of her shoulders. He nuzzled the back of her neck, and she tilted her head back dreamily, with her eyes half closed.

A family approached, mom, dad, and three children, and stopped to see what I was looking at. "Look at the lions," they instructed the kids.

The King began nibbling on his Queen's neck, then grabbed a mouthful of her flesh, gently but firmly pinning her. She pretended to try to get away, half-heartedly.

Huff—huff—huff—huff—huff—

What the—? Suddenly I realized, he was mounting her! From my vantage point, I couldn't see their rear ends, but, this pair of lions was about to mate before our very eyes! And, the sound I'd heard last night was *not* a train, but it was this lusty, golden hunk of Beast.

When the mother next to me realized what was going on she cried, "Honey, do you know what they're doing?" she nodded towards the children. "We can't let them watch this." She looked mortified.

Daddy-o looked mesmerized. "Why not? It's a fact of life." He shrugged.

She steered the little girl and one of the boys away, to look at some other animals, but the father stayed, and observed the mating scene, with his elder son.

So did I. The chugging noise I'd heard the evening before, was this lion grunting as he shared pleasures with his tolerant partner. As I watched, fascinated, he hugged her tightly with his massive forearms, as he thrust fervently, his rhythm increasing over the minutes. The pair tuned out their audience, as if we weren't even there. They were at the same time shameless, and modest.

The grunts came faster and faster, then the two beasts shuddered and groaned as the King of the Beasts climaxed. He sunk down on top of her, and she rolled him off to one side, affectionately rubbing her face against his, and licking him. After catching his breath, he pushed himself up onto his forearms, and let out a tremendous roar.

Oh my gosh. That poor lioness. How many times did he want her since last night? At least four times in the night, and now again? Talk about lust.

Who would expect animals as wild and vicious as lions to be so tender, and 'loving'? After his roar, the big guy 'kissed' her all over her face, then yawned and collapsed onto his side. She seemed to gaze over at him, glad that he was satisfied for the moment, before she too stretched out beside him.

All the while, the private parts were discretely screened from our view by the bullrushes. The entire effect was that of a National Geographic TV show, except, I was inhaling the powerful scent of lion scat, sweat, and had the pesky flies bothering me, and the reality of this lion's vocal talents, which I had mistaken for a freight train last night.

*   *   *

At two o'clock I was to meet Russ. I had time to kill, so I rode on over to Scott's Bluff National Monument to hike.

Last night I paid two dollars for my pass to Scott's Bluff National Monument when I came to the museum (aka the visitor's center). That two dollars allowed entry for one whole week—what a deal. So, on this morning, I simply showed my receipt at the gate, and then parked.

Saddle Rock Trail would take me 1.6 miles to the top of the bluff. Long, quick strides took me along the trail which at first led across short and mid-length grasses. Yucca plants and prairie sunflower grew abundantly. In front of me, the promontory rose, several hundred feet higher than the plains surrounding it. During my hike, I stopped to take in the panorama of the grasslands.

Soon, I would be reunited with the man I'd left behind, fifty-four days ago. Emotions played king-of-the-hill inside of me. Excitement. Reservations. Happiness. Dread. Anticipation. Anger. Forgiveness. Desire to get naked with my lover who knows exactly how to meet my lusty needs. Shyness . . .

The unmistakable rumble of a Harley-Davidson tumbled over the landscape towards me. The distance was too far for me to see, but, I was certain it was Russell's Springer.

I went to the Ladies Room and checked my appearance. Flushed, a little sweaty, hair's a mess, shoulders are bare and brown, midriff is bare and taut, my legs have scratches and a good tan. I look just like—*Me!* Ready or not, here I come.

Somewhere between the motorcycles and the bathrooms Russell and I found each other. He looked so big and tall. He stopped walking and turned toward me. I ran into his arms, looking for the smile I'd asked for. That just isn't his style, though.

I checked him out. He seemed bigger than I remembered, but he was always a strapping six-foot-three. His appearance alarmed me. His face was sunburned, with the reverse raccoon look. He had grown a goatee. He looked like a hard core biker.

He growled, "Man, was that ever the most f—-ing boring ride to get here. It felt like four hundred g-d miles. It totally sucked."

Well, dear, I'm happy to see you, too. "I thought it was kind of neat."

"It sucked. It was twice as far as I expected."

With my usual optimism, I tried to appease him, "Well, I rode out yesterday, and it was almost three hundred miles for me, too, but, I thought it was kind of nice, except it was wicked hot out."

He changed the subject, "What do you want to do? Are you ready to leave?"

All revved up, I babbled a little bit about my hike, and the zoo, as we walked to our bikes. Then I fell silent, wondering if he would share stories with me.

"You all set? Hungry? Let's go get a room," he wasn't wasting any time.

At the motel, when we unloaded the bikes, I faced him. "How can you possibly see my motorcycle all scraped up this badly, and not ask about it?" I can't understand this man.

"I figure you didn't tell me about it in the first place, and I didn't want you to gloat."

"Gloat? *Gloat?* Do you know what that word means? Why would I want to brag about such an awful thing?" Already feeling upset, I turned away and mumbled, "It's like you don't even care."

His strong hands took me by the shoulders and turned me around. "Of course I care, Diane. But, you are just so stubborn, and you think you can do it all." His familiar blue eyes gazed at me, and in seconds mine filled with tears.

With a great sigh of aggravation, he admitted, "Look, I don't want to argue. Let's just try and have a good time, okay?"

We decided to eat lunch at the restaurant next door, and during our meal I found that I was reluctant to do much talking. I felt like everything had to be censored, so in a very short time, I stopped saying much of any thing, but instead commented on the taste of my salad dressing, or that the soup was too salty. All shallow topics, shallow and safe.

If I had a story to relate about a rather difficult part of my trip, I got the reaction, "What did you expect?" or that it was my own fault. If I shared a tale of good fortune, and kindness shown by others, it was because somebody wanted a "piece of ass." No wonder I gave up talking to him about it. The best time of my life was being downsized and ridiculed by the man I thought I loved.

I had so much wanted this to be a happy occasion. But, it was just a normal, strained date for us. Just like so many in our past.

We finished lunch, then went back to our motel room. It occurred to me that I had not had a motel room so far, on this entire trip. At the WOW rally I had stayed in a nice hotel for three nights in a row, but that's all. The rest of the time I either camped, stayed at an AYH, or at someone's house. I was proud of that fact, too.

After a shower, I found Russell stretched out on the bed, and I covered his body with mine. His smell unlocked familiar memories, and his firm command over my form began to wash away all the stressful feelings, and replaced them with sensuous, wanton lustiness.

We played Lion.

It felt good to be back 'home.'

The King of the Sheets wanted a nap. I tried, but as soon as the after-glow went away I felt stir-crazy. I felt locked in, confined. I was caged in this stale smelling room, with four walls closing in on me. For some time I looked at my lover, and somehow knew that this would be one of our last times. How can two people be so physically compatible, and yet so emotionally distant?

Lying naked next to him, inhaling his sweet male scent, and listening to his soft breaths as he slept, I marveled over the wonder of it all. For an hour or two, I felt so close to him. Yet, part of me couldn't stand him. Such a miserable, unhappy soul. It was depressing.

Sadly, I accepted the facts. Our love has gone away. Often because I cared so much for him, I confused *Sex* with *Love*. We had good sex. We had lousy love.

The loss of a friend is never easy. I put an arm across his chest, and laid my head against his shoulder, causing him to stir and awaken.

"You've lost weight," he mumbled.

I smiled, "No, I'm probably about the same as always."

"You look anorexic," he commented, and got up.

Feeling terribly insulted, I retorted, "Well, if I lost weight, you certainly found it." Instantly, I felt bad for saying it.

He stood before the bureau mirror brushing his hair. "Hey, most women find me easy to look at."

Irritated, I ignored him and went in to the bathroom. In the mirror I examined my physique, critically. When would he ever stop picking on me for maintaining my figure? I've always had a hard body, slender and strong. My thighs are muscular, and my abdomen has that washboard look. My bosom is small and firm, and I am satisfied with my appearance. Until that thoughtless comment, I had felt pretty sexy in his presence today, but now I felt peeved.

Is it worth a stupid argument? No. He has a right to his opinion. I can't let this bring me down. He's always complained that I'm obsessed with exercise. I covered my unappetizing body with a towel, so I could get some clothes to change into. He was taking me to the best restaurant in the area.

One thing about Russ, he loved good food, and he could afford it. He was a wealthy man, and enjoyed the finer things in life. Towards me, he had always been generous, and I had been spoiled. I knew that someday, expensive meals would be a thing of my past, so I never took them for granted. I savored each mouthful, and sipped my wine, dutifully enjoying its 'body' and 'aftertaste,' like a little rich bitch should.

Later, in our room, we did the wild thing again, considering our limited time together. There was no desire for words, only dirty talk. Again spent, Russ rested, while keeping an eye on the weather channel.

The nineteen inch screen glared it's blue light into our dark room. I felt trapped. Here I am, staring at a nineteen inch square, calling itself 'News' while all I wanted was to be out in the free outdoors, out in the world, making my own news.

I put on my dress and went outside. There was no where to go. I sat at the edge of the parking lot, on a curb. A couple of trees were planted, on the other side. The full moon overhead gazed down as I listened to cars whizzing by, and the sounds of the small city where I was staying.

Resentment leached into my soul.

The same moon that illuminates this asphalt parking lot, is shining down over all of America, and on this warm summer day, I am a prisoner of my own romantic dreams. I wished so bad that I was sitting near a fire, surrounded by trees, and the sounds of insects and birds. Instead, I am sitting in a motel parking lot, like some kind of morose derelict.

The ironic thing was, Russell probably thought that he was doing me some kind of big favor, putting me up in a motel room, with hot showers and a real bed, TV, and ice. But, the truth is, I was miserable. I hated it.

Going outside didn't relax me like I hoped. It wasn't the great outdoors out there. It was civilization, and I was not feeling very civilized. Depressed, I returned to my room, hoping I would fall asleep easily.

"You know what?" I whispered. "I don't want to sound ungrateful, but, I'm hoping you'll spend another night with me, but this time, we'll do it my way. I'll take you to where I was camped last night, it's really close by. I want you to understand what I'm doing, and what is so attractive about it. I swear, almost every night I go to sleep thinking about how lucky I am to be camping someplace so beautiful." I paused. "Right now, when I open my eyes, I could be in Any Motel, Any Place. There's nothing special about it, except you're here. I want you to come camp out with me."

But, I wouldn't get my wish.

Russell said, "I have to meet my friends in Sturgis at five o'clock tomorrow." Just like that.

Miles: 25

One of my favorite activities is hiking. This is a beautiful view along Coyote Valley Trail, at Rocky Mountain National Park. It was specially designed to accommodate wheelchairs. Cameras with self-timers sure come in handy when you're alone. About half of the photographs with me in them, were taken that way, and about half were taken by friends or complete strangers.

I inhale great draughts of space; the east and west are mine, and the north and south are mine. All seems beautiful to me; I can repeat over to men and women, You have done such good to me, I would do the same to you. Whoever you are, come travel with me!
—Walt Whitman

CHAPTER 19

ROCKY MOUNTAIN HIGH
August 10–12   Days 55–57

*E*stes Park acts as the gateway to Rocky Mountain Park, and sits in a valley surrounded by some of the most spectacular scenery in all of America, if you like mountains. But, it is a tourist resort, no doubt. The free feeling of conquering twisties and canyons, gave way to a crushing concern in the grid of too many cars, sets of lights and crosswalks overflowing with pedestrians.

A pick-up stopped beside me at a red light. Standing in the back of the truck, there was a pretty, black Llama looking delicately down at me. While the truck sat at the light, the Llama dropped to its knees, then laid down, still gazing at me curiously with movie star eyes. It behaved as though this were an everyday occurrence, and indeed, it may have been. The light turned green, and for a few sets of lights, I rode along in tandem with this unusual, lovely, shaggy creature.

A man named Lou welcomed me into the H-Bar-G Ranch Hostel, and in a short time had me registered and assigned to a room. "It used to be a bunkhouse for the ranch hands," he informed me. He explained a few rules of the establishment, and made me feel right at home. One night was $8.50.

My bunk house was a humble wooden structure with three rooms plus the bath. The central room was a large living room with a fireplace and a few dusty smelling books lying around. Veering off from the back in a V-shape, were the two bedrooms, each housing a dresser with four drawers, and two bunk beds. Eight women would share the bathroom. Every bit a rustic cabin, there was a broom, and a few cleaning supplies and a note asking people to do their share, with a list of suggested tasks to volunteer for. Although spartan, the place was neat and tidy.

In addition, there was the Mess Hall, a big rectangular room that was monopolized by a long banquet sized table and benches. Three refrigerators and three stoves made certain that plenty of chefs could share the kitchen. An array of utensils pots and pans were situated on open shelves, ready for our use. A few more sat in a dish rack drying. A couple of shelves were marked "free food," where visitors could leave their non-perishable leftovers to share with other travelers. Little paper signs were pasted all over with rules and regulations. "Wash what you use," "All food in frij must be labeled with your name and date," "Help yourselves to free food," "Last one out, turn off lights."

In a nearby room, James Taylor peered down from a poster at the old piano set against the wall. Dart boards, game boards, card tables, couches and chairs made this an inviting Rec. Room reminiscent of childhood summer camp. The old wooden floorboards squeaked as I crossed the room, and the same dusty, warm smell hung in the atmosphere as it did in my bunkhouse.

I sat on my cabin's front porch, daydreaming and watching two horses that roam freely around the Hostel Ranch. A Red-headed woodpecker came to a tree nearby and drummed out a beat, trying to impress me.

Two women came out of the Main Building where I had registered. They spoke to each other in a fast foreign language, walking close together, and giggling. One was very tall, with blond hair pulled back into a bun, and she was pretty. The other girl was extremely cute. Unfairly, disgustingly cute. She wore short cut-offs which showed off her tanned legs, and a tight, lycra bodysuit which shimmered of cranberry, and hugged her perfect, barely ripened figure.

The two girls noticed me by my motorcycle. In broken English they attempted to tell me how much they liked the idea.

"This you?" they asked, all smiles. "Yah?" They held their fists in front of them in a riding motion, twisting the throttle and making revving noises. "Scares—no? No?"

"Tee hee hee."

We couldn't communicate, but, we obviously accepted each other. I managed to learn they were 'Duetch,' and was amused to see every man within our sight unabashedly staring our way. I invited each of the girls to sit on my bike, which resulted in squeals of excitement from their delight. The smaller girl couldn't touch the ground, so she just sat on it with the side stand down, and crouched over in racing position, making up fantasies.

Suppertime rolled around, and I went into the Mess Hall to fix a meal. Several guests came in telling stories of their excursions during the day. Those who rode mountain bikes, and those that fell off of them. Hikers, rappelers, and even a threesome who had tried hang-gliding. Others hobbled in after a day of shopping in Estes Park, forced to rest after overdoing their activities the day before.

Darkness fell over the ranch, and the moon that was so full the night before, was completely hidden by a heavy blanket of clouds. The time came for me to go to bed. In bed I read for a little while, before my sole roommate joined me. She started reading the Bible, after explaining to me that she was on some sort of private retreat.

When she introduced herself to me, the first thing she said was, "Have you been born again?"

I told her, "Every day when I awaken, I am born again. Please don't preach to me."

Where were those two femme fatals? Why didn't I get to sleep in *their* cabin?

Miles: 254

The morning haze hadn't quite lifted, and dew sparkled on the delicate strands of a nearly perfect spider's web, turning it into a jeweled work of art, adorning my humble cabin. A hummingbird, attracted by the citrus I was tearing into, appeared and disappeared, all a-whir and a-blur.

This was my day to play, (as if I haven't been playing every day.) I was going for a joy ride, bound for Colorado Rocky Mountain National Park. Soon I was paying my three dollar entrance fee, and setting forth on Trail Ridge Road.

In 1859 Joel Estes and his son Milton, were among the first white men to see this area, as French fur traders. A conservationist named Enos Mills later began to campaign around 1909, making it his mission to see that this land's pristine nature would be preserved. In

1915, the subalpine valleys, shimmering lakes, and snow ensconced Rockies became a National Park.

Eighty years later, in 1995, Dee Gagnon and the Red Pony traversed the Trail Ridge Road, for the sheer joy of it, as part of their own history in the making.

The fifty mile road would take me higher than twelve thousand feet above sea level, and there I would experience a big difference in the temperature. Three or four hours were recommended to travel the scenic road, in order to use the overlooks and share heart-stopping vistas with other incredulous onlookers.

After a few such stops, I found myself pulling my thick sweater on over my head, before continuing upward, where the wind grew more fierce and cutting. What a good road to ride! I was loving it. All too soon I saw the ranger station at Kawuneeche, so I pulled a quick U-turn, and retraced my glorious path. Trail Ridge Road curved in and out of forested hillsides, rocky slopes, and depressions where snow banks snoozed, even in August. When I got bogged down behind a car traveling too slowly, I would simply pull over into one of the many scenic overlooks, then try again after I feasted my eyes on the glorious vista on display.

In one twisty, wooded region, I rounded a sharp curve just in time to see what I thought at first was a deer, as it bounded out of my lane and up into the edge of the dark forest, behind another of its kind. Large, round, light colored rumps disappeared from view, thankfully, not a close call.

Thus I was reminded to keep a lookout for Bighorn Sheep on the nearby agglomerate highlands, not because of any danger they offered, but because I wanted the pleasure of viewing them. So I passed through one such area, and settled in to cruise easily through a set of wide, loping curves that coursed between gently sloped hillsides.

That's when I saw the Wapiti, a gang of elk. There, mustered together loosely, five or seven of them grazed idly. Nearly as large as moose, they were awesome in their own right, even at a distance. None of them bore antlers, so I wondered if they were all females.

Again, my Red Pony took me higher and higher into elevation greater than two miles above sea level, with not so much as a sputter or falter. My faith in this mechanical beast is fully rewarded, and this road is certainly one of the more stringent tests it needed to pass. On this day alone, I had passed several larger motorcycles, touring varieties, and cruisers, gasping for power, or pulled over, overheated, with disappointed drivers standing by, refusing my offers to help somehow. My 'little 500' continued to prove she's got a lot of heart. I always knew it.

The time passed on relentlessly, barely noticed, until I realized by gradually warmer temperatures that I was nearing the bottom of my trail, and would soon depart this wonderful area, thankfully set aside for America to treasure.

After a quick stop at the grocery store, I returned to the H-Bar-G AYH, weary and relaxed.

The two divas giggled their way into the Grub Room, and I offered them some of my stir-fry, but they indicated that they were full. Still, they sat with me, and we tried to communicate, but mostly laughed. I was still struck by how unbelievably sexy the two of them were, and I'm a woman! The men around here must be going nuts. Just the same, the girls acted like innocent vixens, even while scantily clad for the hot summer climate.

I sat down on a bench to eat, and my foreign friends exited, just as a young man came in. He began to cook his own meal, and congenially made conversation with me.

He was slender and youthful, and I was captured by his talent for story-telling. His name was Paul, and he was thirty-something, just like me. He looked younger, like, fresh out of college.

He countered, "So do you."

He was going through a phase in his life, where he just had to get away from it all, so he'd ended up here. He said that he was an attorney. Esquire, to be exact. He looked very English, was quite cute, and entertained me with his account of the day's events, as he related them to me.

"There we were on this narrow, rocky trail, when all of a sudden, from out of nowhere came a mountain goat, with a tiny baby." His eyes glittered, and he turned away from me for a moment to stir whatever he was cooking, then continued. "That little guy was so cute, he was about this big," he held out his wooden spoon about level with his hip, "and he had the knobbiest knees. He picked his way over the rocks and came right at me. You see, she took him for a hike, to go people-watching. He was looking over his shoulder and saying 'bleaht!,' which means, 'Hey Ma, here's one of those people things right here. Let me see how close I can get to it! See? I'm not afraid, Ma, I'm so big and brave!'

"She leapt down from her boulder, and nervously hopped back and forth, trying to get his attention. 'Son, get away from him! They're not to be trusted, those humans, no matter how curious they seem. They're dangerous!?' " Paul continued his narration.

"But the little guy hadn't learned about us yet, and as I stood ever so still, he came right up to me, and started tugging at my windbreaker with his gums. (I don't think he had teeth yet.) Meanwhile, the mother stamped her feet, and tossed her head, all frustrated.

"I broke all the rules. I had to touch his silky coat. I had to rescue my jacket, too, before he got his drool all over it! Well, then I lost my footing, and scared the baby goat, and he scampered over to where his ma was perched on a big, flat rock.

"He tried to jump onto it, but it was too big, at first. His mother merely watched, all stern, like, she was upset with him for disobeying. He fell and fell, then with practice, placed one tiny hoof, then the next, until he was up there beside his mom."

Mesmerized by this tale, from such an unusual perspective, I listened in rapt attention, unable to hide the smile on my face as I imagined the scene. We talked until the both of us had eaten and washed our dishes.

Having such a bountiful piece of property to call my home for another day, I explored a footpath by myself, amidst an array of wildflowers in bloom, and admired the amazing backdrop that draped itself across the horizon.

Miles: 107

Ah, the Rockies are so lovely in the morning, too.

"I don't want you to go. I am selfish. I want you all to myself," Paul confessed. "Stay here longer, stay here with me," he pleaded. "We can go hiking, and ride horses. I wish you could stay. I do so want to get to know you better. You're so adorable. I don't want you to go. I didn't even know it, until I realized, I can't let this wonderful, fascinating wild spirit just ride off into the wind, and out of my life without at least making an effort. I am selfish, I admit. Please, don't go. Stay with me."

I was utterly tempted.

"I can't. I have to go. The road is calling me." I pulled away reluctantly. I had no desire to start another hit and run romance. "Maybe we'll meet again. You never can tell."

He placed a chunk of rose quartz into my hand, and folded my fingers around it, then pulled my fist to his lips and placed a gentle kiss on each finger.

I nearly melted, but didn't. "I need to go." I charged away, and when I returned I saw that he had run up onto a hillside to watch my departure.

One last time I passed through the ranch gate. As I pulled away from my latest home base, I did not feel like hurrying.

A multicolored string of saddle horses clip-clopped along the side of the long gravel road that took me away from the ranch. My tires crunched over the pebbles, and I idled passed the vacationers on their rented dreams. The cowboy leading the group sat astride a feisty mare, who danced wild-eyed at the front of the line of otherwise bored animals. Its rider maintained a firm, expert hold on the reins, speaking gently to her as I rode by in slow motion. During the time it took me to roll by as quietly as possible, the frightened mare never relaxed a muscle, and neither did I. She didn't trust this contraption, and I didn't trust her. I knew that any moment she could bolt, sending the entire line of follow-the-leaders into a state of chaos, and I wasn't too comfortable with the prospect of trying to escape a string of out of control horses, while I was riding an over-packed motorcycle on a dirt road, lined by fences.

Mission accomplished.

Off to ride the Rocky Mountain Trail Ridge Road again. What a life I lead! This time, I'm just gonna ride it. Not a lot of stops, just one curve after the next, up, up, and over. Keep the eyes open for elk, and mountain goats, and big-horn sheep, and for the little critters that scamper across the road like tiny wind-up toys. I'll feel the temperature drop, maybe hit some sprinkles, then the pressure in my ears will pop, somewhere around two miles above sea level. I've got this place down pat, now. The juniper and pine scent hangs in the air, carrying thoughts of Christmas with it.

Two motorcycles appeared on the road, and we traveled together for the remainder of the Ridge Road. Two red, white and blue matching sportbikes. They cruised along at a good clip, staggered smartly, and allowed position changes when desired. After exiting the park, I followed in their wake, enjoying their style too much to let them go just yet. After all, they were still headed in my direction.

Finally, the two of them pulled into a boatyard. One man pulled his face shield up and called out to me, "Where're ya headed?"

I answered, "I'm going to Denver, but I need to eat lunch soon."

"Follow us. We'll find something and stop together if you want." He flipped his shield down, nodded to the Ninja rider, then twisted the throttle.

We found ourselves in the parking lot of a place promising breakfast all day, sizzling steaks, and southwestern food. After any exhilarating excursion, it is common to cluster by your bikes for a few minutes, removing lids, leather and layers, all the while proclaiming the virtues of the road you were on, the hapless acts of motorists, and sharing the joys of the open road with each other.

On this day, there were no exceptions. So what if I've never met these two before? The smooth, fluid way in which they operated indicated that they were frequent riding companions. I just hitched up with them, and they invited me to meet the men beneath the masks, so to speak.

With great surprise, I discovered that the Ninja rider was a woman. None of her attire gave me a clue, down to her plain, work-type loafers. I had stumbled upon a motorcycle riding married couple, just out for a day's ride. They were Hans and Ursula.

An ordinary looking duo, they were in their forties, and despite their names, did not have light sandy hair. Hans had a Groucho Marx mustache, and glasses that darkened in the sun. Ursula spoke with a European accent, and her tousled, curly hair surrounded a face barely beginning to belie her years.

Inside the restaurant, we found the service slow and forgetful, the food delicious, and the atmosphere rustic. We enjoyed languid conversation, and before we left, Hans and Ursula had determined that they were going to lead me along some fine roads towards Denver, before letting me go. I love it when that happens. Who knows the roads better than your local folks? Especially bikers with exotic names like Hans and Ursula?

The check came, but I was not allowed to contribute so much as the tip. All I could do was thank them.

Outside of the log cabin-styled building, just by slipping into her tan windbeaker, and Shoei full-faced helmet, Ursula transformed into Average Joe Rider.

On the other hand, when I pulled my leathers on, and partially zipped my form fitting custom made leather jacket, braid hanging down from under my helmet, I became Lady Biker.

When Lady Biker gets on the Big Beast of Burden, however, she all but disappears among the pile of baggage.

With tummies full of spicy Mexican food, we traveled through the breathtaking, twisty canyons of Winter Park, crossed the Continental Divide for the second time that day, and coursed through an old ghost town, which had once been a prosperous mining town. The road was carved between rock cliffs, and required constant vigilance. After I passed an unlikely casino situated deep along the road of many switchbacks, I tried to imagine the folks that come here to drink, and try their luck. I imagined some drunk, careering around the next corner, on my side of the road. Thoughts like that keep me alive.

The sky was blanketed by a soft gray cloud, and the potential for rain pressed us onward. We had to go our separate ways eventually, and with warm wishes we waved and disassociated.

I returned to Denver and found Nancy's apartment complex easily. When I pulled around to park by the carport, I saw that her little, red truck was not there. I knew that I was welcome and expected, "sometime, any time." I used the key to let myself in, and made myself at home. My laundry got washed, her dishes got washed, and her pets got attention.

It felt strange to go to bed all by myself in this house when no one was home, but at the same time it felt right. I hoped that one day I could provide my home to a friend, as a refuge in a time of need, with nothing more binding than trust and friendship.

I wrote a note and left it on the table.

> Dear Nancy, you know I'm here, you saw my bike. I got in around eight, washed clothes and dishes. I'm tired and you haven't come home yet. (10:00) I'm sleeping in Kit's waterbed, because that's where you put me before. Thanks, Dee.

Miles: 180

They are able who think they are able.

—Virgil

CHAPTER 20

MILESTONES
August 13–14   Days 58–59

*N*ancy never came home the night before, and I was disappointed that I didn't get to see her. It occurred to me, that after my rendez-vous with Russell, I had simply ridden away, and forgot all about analyzing the visit. Riding my motorcycle in the Rockies had proved to be excellent therapy.

At the kitchen table I stopped to leave a second note.

"Dear Nancy, I missed you. Sorry. It was really nice to know I had a place to come to. I hope I can pass this way again. I'd really like to see you once more before I head east. Thanks again for your hospitality. Your friend, Dee"

The day had already become hot, and I straddled the saddle, and left the city of Denver, this time without getting lost. Experimentally, I headed south on U.S Highway 285 which promised a trek through three National Forests, and over a couple of 10,000 ft. mountain passes. Along the way, it coursed through lush valleys, and offered gallant views.

For lunch, I stopped at Dinky's, a speck of a place along the open road. I stepped into the cramped quarters, where seated at bar stools at the counter, customers sat elbow to elbow.

A poster on the wall beside me was titled "How to spot a redneck in Arkansas," which poked fun at said persona. —Drives a beat-up pick-up truck —wears his jeans real tight —beer cans in back of pick-up —tooth missing —crossed eyes —goes to church on Sundays —gets drunk the rest of the week, etc., etc. Although derogatory, it was pretty funny.

After I studied the poster in a mock effort to prepare myself for the day I might ride through Arkansas, a cowboy appeared in the diner. With him was his adolescent son, dressed in a fancy western shirt, with a rodeo competition number still pinned to his shirt. They were greeted by name, and the chef and waiter engaged them in a loud conversation allowing the boy some bragging rights. Then the proud father turned to me and began drilling me about my motorcycle and the journey I was on.

The cowboy's name was Walker, and I steered the conversation around, to learn about the cattle ranch he owned. He had twenty-four thousand head of cattle, on a 36,000 acre ranch, in nearby Fairplay. Half serious I asked him if he needed any help, which led to a big discussion, and left me with several days fuel for thought.

Interestingly, I found that C & M Outfitters was a business he'd developed out of necessity. Instead of hiring extra hands to help for the fall round-up, or spring drive, and the other major duties of cowboys, he charged people to do the work. A three-day 'adventure' requires reservations and $900 per person. A 'simple' overnight, six hundred dollars. The applicants were screened, because the demands of riding horseback entire days are rigorous, and although this sounds like City Slickers, the work was real. The work was hard. Often, guests' bottoms got blistered.

The ranch also offered big game hunting trips. I wondered, with all this wealth, was this man rich, or was he a poor struggling blue collar worker like the rest of us? He seemed a bit chauvinistic, but I found myself trying to swing a deal.

"Let me clean stalls, or work a day, for room and board one night. I'll even sleep in the horse barn." I thought that would be cool.

At the start of the day, I figured I'd go back to the Arkansas Headwaters Recreation Area. Thinking along those lines, I wondered if that's how that politically incorrect poster about Arkansas Rednecks ended up at Dinky's.

The Arkansas Headwaters Recreation Area was not so much one particular place, but a series of boat launch areas, fishing, picnicking, mountain climbing, etc. A cooperative effort between the U.S. Bureau of Land Management and the Colorado Division of Parks and Outdoor Recreation cares for and develops this property so that the public can enjoy the legendary Arkansas River, and its surrounding natural resources. One hundred and forty-eight miles along the river are managed, offering fourteen separate outdoor facilities, including Hecla's Junction.

The motorcycle was low on gas when I passed through the town of Salida, and I stopped at a store where you could buy a twelve pack of Natural Light for $4.49, and get gasoline at the same stop. (Unheard of where I live.)

When I pulled up to the gas pumps, there were two motorcycles pulled over in the shade of the building. The riders were sitting on the curb, talking, a bearded man and a woman. Their bikes were Harleys.

Matter of factly, I filled up my gas tank, making no eye contact with the pair. Years of experience made me wary of Harley riders. Not that they were bad people, just that usually I was made to feel "insignificant" around them. I repositioned my tankbag, and went into the store to pay for my fuel, really feeling the heat of the day, now that I was no longer in the wind.

As I was putting a bottle of pop into my tankbag, I was surprised to hear, "Hot enough for you?"

I looked up in surprise. "What?" It was the bikers.

"Sure is hot out, today. You should come over here in the shade for a minute and take a break," the man invited, as the woman pushed over a bit, as if to make room for me.

I didn't need a second request. I pushed the heavy motorcycle over to the little bit of shade, and took my Diet Pepsi out, and extended my hand as the pair stood up to meet me.

A little bit stunned, I blurted out, "Thanks for talking to me. When I saw the Harleys, I'm sorry, but I thought you would probably leave if I tried to join you."

"Oh no, not us," the woman said. "Hi. My name is Louise. How do you do?" We shook hands, and she turned to her companion, "and this is my buddy, Jim. He's my riding partner when I'm in these parts."

Louise was dressed like a serious rider, with leather pants, a black, long-sleeved thermal shirt with HD eagle wings adorning it. Her red, white and blue bandanna encircled her neck, and another covered her head. An armored leather jacket was draped over the sheep-skin covered saddle of her bright blue Heritage Softtail. The load strapped on the back of her bike rivaled my own!

Jim's bike was free of luggage. He sat back down on the curb, while Louise and I circled each other's rides appreciatively. Then we even sized each other up. She was few inches shorter than me, and probably weighed about the same. She was well-preserved, in her forties, I guess.

Instantly I felt a kinship. It was like running into a long lost sister, or a kindred spirit. We looked at each other's mammoth packloads, and license plates. She was from British Columbia. (Canada, above Washington State.)

After jabbering together a few minutes, we joined Jim on the curb, and she smacked him playfully on the arm. "See Jim? Here's another woman like me! She's traveling all by herself, and she's young and pretty, too. See? I'm not the only crazy one out there. You don't have to worry so much."

She'd been on the road for some time, like me. But, where I was ultimately working my way to Arizona and Southern California, she was going south-east. Our paths just happened to criss-cross at this lowly convenience store on a hot summer day in Salida, Colorado. But, meeting her gave me a solid feeling. The same one that she expressed to Jim.

See? I'm not the only one!

We exchanged addresses, and she included Jim's number and town, in case I ever needed it. It was doubtful. I already had so many people I could come to if I was in trouble in Colorado, but I took it just the same. Maybe someday it would come in handy. Ya just never know.

Jim said, "Do you want some pizza? We're only going to throw these last couple of pieces out."

I accepted, and the clerk in the store gave me a plastic shopping bag to wrap it in. The three of us spent a good half hour or more in this crummy, hot parking lot, and it was time to be moving on.

Hearing their thunder as they rode away from the rest of my life, I felt enriched. Two Harley riders who truly understand what it's all about. It's not *what* we ride. It's a love for the open road, a passion for motorcycles, and the insatiable need for adventure that should unite our souls.

I proceeded to Hecla's Junction, where I had stayed about ten days before. I cruised around the loop a couple of times, looking for the best place to bivouac. Just as I suspected, there was hardly anybody else camping here, yet. It was still only mid-afternoon. I couldn't get my hopes up too much.

For some reason, I found that I really enjoyed the places where hardly anybody else stayed at. The solitude, the quiet, the sounds of nature . . . the peace had a calming effect on me.

One site looked exactly like what I was looking for, except two guys and a flatbed trailer were situated at the adjacent site, and I wanted my privacy, so I kept on going. The second time around though, I hesitated there for a second, and put one foot to the ground. I really liked this site the best, and it appeared those guys were loading up their gear to leave. They stopped their work and eyed me, questioningly.

"Hey—are you the chick from Massachusetts?" one of them called out, but I doubted that I'd heard him correctly.

I flipped up my shield. "Excuse me?"

He repeated, "Are you from Massachusetts?"

How did he know?

"Well, yes, but-" I stammered, still in the saddle, at the edge of a gorgeous little campsite.

"Joe told us about you. Joe, the rafting guide." That answered my silent question. "We work at Dvorak's Expeditors, where Joe works. He came back a week or two ago and told us about some chick on a cross-country motorcycle trip, all by herself. It had to be you. Who else could it be?"

I thought of Louise, and wondered—right this minute, how many women are out there on motorcycles, on their own mission of self-reliance? There are bound to be at least a couple. But probably not a heck of a lot more than that.

The rafting guides had lots of equipment. Apparently, it's part of the lifestyle of these adventurous types to spend their work week camping, and only going home for their days off. Sounds like fun.

As I got busy unloading my stuff, they finished loading theirs. "Hey, do you want some firewood?"

"Sure. Thanks."

Twenty minutes later, they jumped in the truck and shouted, "Take it easy. We'll tell Joe you said hi."

Behind my camp, there was a narrow, crooked footpath that descended down the steep bank, over rocks that threatened to twist my foot right off at the ankle if I wasn't careful. I carried my pint of orange juice down to the edge of the water, and jammed it in between some rocks in the cold water to keep it chilled.

I set up my tent in a flat spot, underneath a canopy of fragrant juniper trees. Tight reddish-brown pine cones hung at such symmetrical intervals they appeared to represent a woodsy Christmas tree, full of ornaments. Big boulders acted as seats, upon which one could sit and watch the river which never stops running, yet never leaves the canyon. You can listen to the river, as it laughs without ceasing, belying its dangerous and reckless nature.

For old time's sake, I walked over to the other site I had camped at. Three dollars. What a treat. Y'know, when I left home I had faith that I would manage a budget of ten a day for shelter. Blind faith. That's all I've needed so far. I keep my ears and eyes open, therefore, here I am.

I did some paperwork at my picnic table. On the other edge of the river, a red and black train blasted its whistle, and the screech of brakes echoed along the canyon walls, as the train slowed before it arrived at a sharp curve, then it trailed off into the distance with its cargo.

When I began to believe I might truly have the campground to myself, it occurred to me that I had failed to fill up my water bottle. I sort of hoped someone would come, someone with a camper, maybe, so I could beg some water from them. Then, a truck came, and of all places to settle, they picked the site next to mine, which the other guys had just vacated.

Two men in their twenties leapt out, and sprang into action, pronto. They started pulling on those big, rubber boots that fishermen wear.

I saw their rods and guessed, "Fly fishing?"

They stopped, surprised, and answered affirmatively.

Time to make a bargain. "Listen, I'll trade you some fire for some fresh water. When you get back, you're gonna be cold. I'll share my fire with you."

"Well, okay. That's sounds great," they agreed, "but, we're using a water filter. We don't have any bottled water."

"You have a filtering system? How does it work? Do you really trust it?" I revealed my ignorance about the subject.

One of the guys took a minute to show me. "Well, yeah, we trust it. I've never gotten sick, anyway." Conversationally, he squatted down with the manual pump. He had a bottle, which he set on my table. In his hand was a tubular sort of thing, like a plunger, with thin rubber hoses attached. "See, you stick this hose into the water, and this other one you stick into your container, like so." He then grasped the plunger, and slid it in and out demonstrating its use, and explained, "The water gets sucked up into this filter, and is treated, then comes out the other tube into your bottle. Clean and pure." He stood up and smiled. "That's all there is to it."

I thanked him, then wished him luck and he took off with his buddy to hunt the waters of Hecla's Junction.

A ranger came by, and I asked him all kinds of questions about his job, working for the National Forestry Department. Was it a secure job? Enjoyable? I'm sure the pay isn't grand, but job satisfaction must be high. He answered all my inquiries, and told me how to go about getting a job application. I thought with my background in Recreation as a career, my lifelong experiences of camping out, and my insatiable sense of adventure, coupled with a love for Mother Earth, wildlife, and human beings, this could be the job for me.

A quarter of an hour zipped by, and he glanced at his watch and told me he'd be getting off duty soon, and had to take care of a few things before he could go home.

"See ya. Nice talking to you," I said.

It was time for me to refuel my system. Thanks to Louise and Jim, I was going to enjoy some gooey, "room" temperature leftover pizza. Pizza and orange juice, I love that combination, no kidding.

When I got to where I had propped my juice in the rocks, I discovered that the river had stolen it. Darn. That's okay. Now I'll have to try out that water filter.

As I sat at my table eating pizza, another Ranger pulled up in his forestry truck. "Ranger Rick said he came by here earlier and met you," the uniformed man spoke softly. "He asked me to bring this to you." He revealed a big chunk of red watermelon on a paper plate.

Pleased, I expressed my gratitude, and set the gift down on my table.

"He was impressed. He asked me to keep an eye on you, make sure you're okay." He glanced at the Ford parked next door.

"Oh, I'll be okay. I already met those guys. They're out fishing, now. Later on they're invited to share my fire. If they give me any trouble, (which I doubt very much,) I've got a mean, shrill whistle that carries for miles. If you hear it, come running."

Tonight I made out like a bandit. Free firewood, pizza that was given to me, a present of watermelon, even an endless supply of "fresh" water, from the great Arkansas River. All given to me from people I didn't even know. Perfect strangers. Only in America. Well, I know that's not true, but it seems fitting to say it.

Darkness fell over the camp, and as fireflies glittered from three to six feet above ground, I started my fire. It was blazing strong when the two fishermen came back.

They wasted no time coming over to huddle around my fire. They were Steve and Craig. They took their rubber hip boots off, and rubbed their hands together, and exclaimed how glad they were that I had this fire. They had become quite chilled, but the flames were hot, and it wasn't long before they felt warm and toasty.

Steve and Craig told me about their fishing, and I told them about my motorcycle trip. One of us stood to throw another log on the fire, and a million sparks were released to find their way to heaven.

Another train sounded its whistle, and slowed before maneuvering around the dangerous curve across the way.

Craig said, "Three weeks ago, one of those things got derailed, just around the bend, there. Now all the engineers are being really careful. It won't last though. They'll be flying around the turn there in no time. Just wait."

The evening evolved into a comfortable balance between conversation, and quiet reflection. A huge stump was now burning, hot and shimmery. From where I sat, it took on the image of a wild boar, with its mouth all agape, its thick tusks threatening to devour the night.

"You guys, come over here for a minute. Can you see a boar in the fire?"

Immediately, they could see it too. We sat and stared at it for a long while, getting tired. The boar's lower jaw fell off, ruining the mystique, and we were back to gazing at the flickering flames, and coals that looked like lava.

The events of the day finally caught up with me, and I asked the guys to extinguish the fire before they left my site.

*   *   *

This was the end of my eighth week on the road, the beginning of my ninth. I have traveled through Massachusetts, Connecticut, New York, Pennsylvania, Ohio, Michigan, Wisconsin, Minnesota, South Dakota, Wyoming, Idaho, Oregon, Washington, California, Nevada, Utah, Colorado, New Mexico and Nebraska. Nineteen states. I have slept in all but three of them on this journey. Connecticut and New York, because they're so close to home, and because I was driving all night when I traveled through Idaho, I didn't sleep there, either.

My Honda Interceptor 500 has carried me 9,695 alluring miles, since leaving home, and she was still going strong. She looked a little worse for the wear, but considering the flying leap she'd taken, what could be expected?

Two full moons have passed.

Twice I have endured the discomforts of riding day in and day out during menstruation.

Many of the things I wished to accomplish have been met with success. I got to see my Grandma again. For the most part I have taken care of all of my own motorcycle maintenance. The things I packed up for my journey were perfect for the trip. There was not one thing with me that I didn't need, nor was I lacking any one thing that I should have brought, except for the fingernail clipper that I'd picked up along the way.

Yellowstone Park had originally been a top-ranking part of my limited agenda, but, when I lost my wallet, I was forced to forfeit that dream. Instead, I discovered Grand Teton National Park, which left me feeling like, indeed, the latter was probably a better place for me to visit, anyway, on a motorcycle. I wouldn't be making it to Montana this year. In the future, I must, however.

The Pacific Coast Highway was an integral part of my expedition, and I'd managed to ride it from the tip-top of Oregon, all the way to San Francisco. But, as close as I was to the vast Ocean Pacific, I hadn't touched the waters. The road was like a magnet, and I couldn't tear myself away.

On my original mental list of things to do on this hiatus, these things remained.

1. Grand Canyon
2. Yosemite
3. Visit my sister in Tucson
4. Blue Ridge Parkway

On my original mental list, these things I'd done.
1. Visit my Detroit relatives
2. Attend the WOW Ride-In, and the two BMW rallies
3. Pacific Coast Highway

On my original mental list, these things I'd failed.
1. Yellowstone
2. Remain accident free

The river's lullaby was not enough to drown out the thoughts occupying my mind. This journey has given me so much more than I hoped for. Leaving home, I didn't really know what to expect. I only knew I had to go. How could I know? The only way was for me to do it, and find out.

The way I had left my itinerary open, except for my 'original mental list' kept me feeling free, and reduced stress. For now, I was headed in a general south-west direction, so that I could see my sister, Grand Canyon and Yosemite. In between, by now I had learned, I would encounter unsurpassed natural beauty, unexpected human kindness, a variety of character-building challenges, and experience a myriad of new adventures.

Every day was an adventure in itself. I never knew what to expect. Every morning when I awoke, I wondered, what's gonna happen to me today? Who shall I meet? Where will I end up?

Everybody wants to know, "What's your favorite place so far?"

I have to tell them, "Wherever I am, at the moment. That would be my favorite place."

For now, this moment, I am cozy in my humble dome tent, waiting for the sandman to come and work his magic. Will he find me, tucked away where the river bends? Or have the river gods decided tonight it is their privilege to sing me the never ending lullaby, so that tomorrow I can awaken, strong, powerful, and refreshed?

Miles: 233

The scary dirt road taunted me one last time. It wasn't the gravel. It wasn't the curves. It wasn't the hills, nor the poor visablity trying to see around foothills and sand pits. It was the combination of these things. Plus the way the darned rafting company busses would come barreling around the corners in the middle of the road, not expecting to see me there. Not to mention that the road was slanted, and as I moved forward, I'd subtly slide closer to the edges.

But, Motorcycle Safety Foundation had drilled certain things into my cognitive mind. 'Riding a motorcycle is 90% mental, and only 10% physical. —Look where you want to go. —Don't look down. —Keep your eyes level with the horizon.'

Three miles. Fifteen tense minutes.

After that, I coasted along with a series of 14,000 ft. mountains on my right, where they guarded their valleys majestically. This was called the Ivy League Range, where the mountains were named after the high class eastern universities, such as Princeton and Harvard.

Snow capped the peaks, and clung stubbornly to crevices which trailed down the sides, leaving white streaks to contrast against the dark gray appearance near the tops. Overhead, the sky was covered with fluffy clouds, that allowed the sun to filter through, but no patches of indigo offered me hope that it really wouldn't rain.

The odometer on my bike was at 49,968 miles when I left camp, and I glanced at it occasionally, because I wanted to witness its milestone, when it turned to a five and all zeros.

I was riding past Mt. Princeton, and couldn't believe where my Red Pony actually turned over to fifty thousand miles.

We were exactly in front of a pasture containing at least thirty brood mares, many heavy with foal. How appropriate. I pulled over, and parked, taking in the lovely portrait.

The picturesque Mt.Princeton made a dramatic backdrop, where the bays, chestnuts, pintos and palominos grazed contentedly in the foreground. About twenty foals were stretched out on the grass, soaking up whatever warmth they could steal from the stingy orb, that was hiding above the scud.

The farm was more provocative to my fantasies than a mansion would have been. We (as in my Red Pony and me) were near Buena Vista. This is the place where fate would have it that my trusty steed reached the magic number, 50,000. It seemed fitting.

Kodak recorded my odometer, and the scene where it occurred. With a touch of melancholy, I remounted and continued on my trek.

The Interceptor was brand new when I'd bought it. I didn't know how to ride, so I put it on layaway and came by all winter to visit it, and make a monthly payment. I first dropped it at sixty-nine miles. But, as the months and years went by, I got better at riding, and couldn't get enough of it.

This was now my ninth season. Last year I'd broken my wrist in a crash, and couldn't ride from May through September. Now I was making up for lost time. Despite all these miles, and a few accidents, the bike had never needed any engine work. Routine maintenance had become my religion, and that paid off. I adored this motorcycle.

When she turns one hundred thousand, where will we be? Knowing me, we could be anywhere. Maybe Alaska.

Independence Pass had been highly recommended by bikers all over the state, and it was on my agenda for this day. I left the scenic Rte. 24, and picked up the paved, undivided state highway 82 which laid its undulating path from Granite to Glenwood Springs, bringing me over the highest mountain in Colorado.

The pass, like so many others in the Centennial State, was a marriage of beauty and exhilaration. Aspen. Snowmass. I was in a skier's paradise.

When I stopped for lunch, the best I could do was ten dollars and fifty cents, including the tip. Shoot. There goes my food money for the day. This is a pricey area, even though it's summer.

For a couple of hours I took the wide I-70, and still the scenery kept me satisfied. Tonight I was going back to Home Sweet Home, the Grand Junction Hostel, provided they had room.

They did.

My favorite people who worked at the hostel were off duty. I missed them terribly. For some reason, the mix of guests here on this particular day were uninteresting and blase. I shut myself in my room and took care of my daily duties, then went to bed early.

In the same bed that I'd slept in seven different nights before this, the memories of all my aches and pains that I had suffered while I recovered here three weeks ago, came back to me. In some ways it seemed like just yesterday, but in others it seemed like a lifetime.

Miles: 239

Nature is the art of God.

—Dante

CHAPTER 21

UTAH
August 15–16   Days 60–61

*O*n this day, I've endured so many *Eyegasms* that my eyeballs and brain are sore.

When it comes to the most beautiful places I have ever seen, Colorado National Monument is in the top five. I fell in love with the wild vastness and beauty of this series of canyons and mesas, sculpted by ancient earth gods, the wind, the rain, and the ocean of another era.

The road was a serpantine vixen, curving temptingly up and over, daringly draping itself across the sandstone angles and layers, teasing me with her charms, offering me glimpses of exposed bedrock, in warm shades of orange, yellow, rust and red.

I followed Rim Rock Rd., beginning at the East Entrance. Immediately, the road began its memorable discourse, winding upward and onward, one switchback after the next, all the while twisting and writhing, keeping me on my toes. Soon there must be a place to pull over just to gawk!

At Dog's Tooth I pulled over, where a huge rock shaped like its namesake stood, overlooking a spectacular view. Back on the bike I cruised some more, rising into an elevation of sixty six hundred feet. Because I had the time, and the good fortune of traveling alone, I stopped and indulged my hunger for all that is beautiful at nearly every overlook I came upon, Cold Shivers Point, Red Canyon Overlook, Ute Canyon View.

It was at the Upper Ute Canyon Overlook that I came upon the tail end of another pleasure, for on this very day, a club of classic cars from the fifties was taking a stop and go ride along the thirty-five mile Rim Rock Drive. At each stop, for a time, I shared parking with shiny, restored convertibles with tail fins, and chrome, driven by proud owners, their wives dressed in cardigans, and skirts and scarves.

But, because there was only one of me, and groups of them, after a while I left them behind as they spent a lot of time at stops chatting, and comparing details regarding their prized possessions.

Along the stops, I stared off at the distant Colorado River Valley, the purple-gray Book Cliffs, and my nemesis, the flat topped mountain known as Grand Mesa. I followed the snake-like strip over Highland View, Artists Point, past curious phallic Coke Ovens, and on and on, to my favorite place, Grand View, where Independence Monument can be viewed, towering defiantly over a semi-desert, canyon floor.

Alone, I pondered my existence. Our existence. Songs echoed off the canyon walls, wrens, white-throated swifts, pinyon jays. I yearned to hike, but it was too hot, high noon, and I needed to move along.

Continuing, I banked into the turns, checked my speed, and tried to stop smiling. I could be on the Stairway to Heaven.

After my thirty-five miles of elation, I left the place that John Otto had the tenacity to campaign for. He stubbornly convinced citizens to petition Washington D.C. politicians to set aside this piece of land, and in 1911 earned his dream. For this achievement, Otto was given one dollar a month to act as the caretaker of the thirty-two square miles of wild country that he loved so much.

A short burst on I-70 soon brought me to the Utah border. I pulled over to the side of the road, where I set my camera on top of my pack, and ran out in front, to pose for a picture below the state sign. Now that I was crossing the semi arid desert, I sweltered. I removed my jacket the instant I got off the bike.

The sign was a brightly painted sign, showing one of the famous formations of Arches National Park.

WELCOME UTAH STILL THE RIGHT PLACE

1896 CENTENNIAL 1996

Underneath the word "right," in big, red letters, someone had added the word "wing," making it read, "Still the right wing place."

Okay. Whatever.

Going against my usual habits, I strapped my heavy leather jacket onto the back of my bike, choosing to bare some skin through a portion of the desert. The open road was all mine, and there were few traveling over it. Hot wind caressed my arms, and the sun kissed my bare shoulders. Riding my motorcycle, I felt Nature wrap itself around me, as warm and erotic as a lover.

The landscape surrounding me had become barren and stoic, even if I seemed aroused by the atmosphere I was engulfed by. Really, I don't mind wearing my jacket in the hottest of conditions, but it was easy to see what the attraction is, to put yourself in the wind, unprotected.

I took a left onto 128, and traveled through Cisco, and a dumpy neighborhood. Things were in shambles. Such a contrast. One hour ago, I was engaged by some of the most spectacular scenery, and breath-stealing views, and now I drove past places that made me wonder. Did I make some mistake? This is one of the three roads that will take me to Arches National Park? How can such ugliness exist between the wondrous Colorado National Monument and Arches National Park?

The road was outrageously hot and it was boring me. Then, all of a sudden, BAM! I blinked my eyes, and the whole scene changed.

Beside me, the murky-brown Colorado River began its escort service, and tortured me with more incredible scenery. I gorged on the sight of banks, green with lush growth, and canyon walls of etched layers of red-brown rock and sandstone. The road curved along, making me weak with happiness.

At the entrance to the park, I stopped at the Visitor Center, and learned about the geology of this remarkable collection of spires, balanced rocks, natural arches, and monoliths. Regulations were strict, but nothing that would hinder my enjoyment of the place. There was a campground at Devil's Garden within, but all fifty sites were taken. No vacancy. However, I learned of a Bureau of Land Management (BLM) spot that I would check out when I left.

Hot and hungry, I rode through the scorching scenery, and parked at the Windows Section of the park. It was time for lunch. First I stripped down to my shorts then grabbed my wallet, water, and an extremely juicy peach, and headed for the sculptures that are featured on so many calendars all across America. Balanced Rock, Cove Arch, Parade of Elephants, the Windows. All wonderfully carved out of rich red sandstone, by the Great Spirit and Mother Nature.

The extreme heat began to sap my energy, and I did not explore the depths of the park. I returned to the Visitor Center, and studied the wall map, refilled my water battle, brushed my teeth and prepared for a night of rustic camping.

From Arches, I took U.S.Highway 191 south in Moab, and continued for about forty miles, where I began to look for the State Highway 211. This was a modest through road, not heavily traveled, and I settled into the saddle, aware of my freedom, and reveling in the idea that I was living a dream.

Here I was, two months into an extended trip, calling all the shots, cramming more excitement into each day, than any one person ever deserved. I was looking for Newspaper Rock, a smooth stone story board displaying hundreds of petroglyphs, supposed to be put there by Native Americans centuries ago.

Unlike a National Park, this was a mere pull-off, not a big tourist attraction. In fact, I daresay hardly anyone stops to take a look, even though it is visible from the road. Resources I had come across made me aware of eight free campsites across the street from the historic spot.

The camp was there. Hidden, and unobtrusive, I steered my way along a grassy path, and selected a reasonable site. Here I would spend the night, at a bona fide campground that practically nobody even knew about, and it was free! I dropped my gear, and set my tent up on top of a thick growth of tall grass, so soft I didn't unroll my sleeping pad. I had a picnic table, and a grill. Ground fires were forbidden. A short path led me to a shallow tributary. Cliffs surrounded me, scrubby oak, and artemesia sage as tall as I am grew on the edges of my private haven.

During my stay, an old beat up Saab pulled in, with two bicycles on top of it, and a couple had a quiet picnic, and then were on their way. I kept to myself and had a Power Bar and orange for supper.

Newspaper Rock was across the street, and I left my things to go check it out. After reading of its history, a little footpath took me along the base of the sheer rock wall, where a rope kept honest visitors away from the precious etchings, mysterious painted shapes, spirals, and drawings. Skeptically, I wondered how much of this was truly ancient history, and how much was the work of creative teenagers. Who could possibly know, besides the ones who may have defaced the graffiti-like wall?

Little lizards skittered off of the flat rocks along the path before I stepped on them, then they would stand poised, looking at me sharply, before running off on spindly legs to hide amongst their camouflage environment.

The cliffs covered the rays of the afternoon sun, and relief from the desert temperatures was finally offered. A day of particular beauty closed.

By the artificial glow of my flashlight, I got to the business of marking my maps, writing some notes, and keeping track of things. This morning I spent sixteen dollars to have some film developed, but I ate for free all day. When I left the hostel, one of the staff people had heard my days' agenda. He gave me receipts from Rim Rock Rd. and Arches, which were dated to last for seven days. By showing the receipts at the gates, I was allowed admittance. Free food, free recreation, and now free camping. This was a lucky day, and I was feeling mighty good about all of it.

I loved the Southwest, but, despite its beauty, I wouldn't want to live in Utah. Nothing I could put my finger on, just an odd feeling.

When I finished my paperwork, I strolled down to the shallow waterway, and gazed at the moon's reflection in the pool there. After a while, I washed my face, and brushed my teeth, using the water to rinse out my mouth. This time I didn't swallow any. A couple of days after I had drank from the California forest waterfall, I had suffered severe cramps, that I reluctantly had to admit were probably caused by partaking in the untreated water. Lesson learned.

The night sounds of crickets and other noisy bugs erupted like a symphony, easing me into a restful sleep, on a soft mattress of dry grass. Life is good.

Miles: 227

I left the primitive Newspaper Rock campsite, after I'd waded into the pool and bathed, then stretched out upon a flat rock to air dry. The setting allowed my imagination to create scenarios where a line of painted indians appeared on their colorful horses, at the lip of the ridge that edged the cove where I rested, daydreaming.

In Monticello, I stopped to have breakfast at a restaurant. For a time I stood in the doorway, helmet in hand, watching as busy waitresses hustled back and forth, crossing in front of me with a curt

" 'scuse me." Finally, I asked if it would be okay for me to get a table.

The matronly waitress stopped in her tracks, surprised, and stammered, "Two?," eyeing my riding outfit strangely.

Confused, I repeated, "Two?"

"Right this way," the woman ordered, and set me at a table by a window.

I looked at the menu for a few minutes, and when a pot of coffee passed my way, I held up my cup, asking for some. There was a rack of postcards near cash-out, so I went over to pick some out, then began a postcard to my sister in Tucson.

The waitresses bopped all over the place efficiently, except that I was being ignored. Losing patience, I politely complained, "I've been waiting for some time."

"Oh, I'm sorry. I was waiting for your husband," she looked towards the door.

"I have no husband. It's just me."

"All by yourself?," she seemed incredulous. "You're driving a motorcycle? All by yourself?"

"Yes, and I'm starving," I said, placing my order. "More coffee, too, please."

"Right away, miss. I'm so sorry I made you wait. I was wondering what was taking so long. You went outside, and I figured . . . oh, I don't know," she was embarrassed about ignoring me.

I corrected her. "I didn't go outside. I went and bought some postcards by the doorway."

"Let me go put your order in. I want to talk to you in a minute though. I can't believe you're driving a motorcycle! Where are you from, anyway?" she looked like someone who just met a movie star. "Oh, wait a minute, I've got to get to work. I'll be back in a sec." She tore the sheet off her memo pad, and brought it to the cook.

By the end of my breakfast, I felt at ease, and everyone else seemed fascinated. When I stood to leave, all the customers who had looked at me as if I was some kind of outlaw when I first walked in, wished me well, safe travels, and good luck, by the time the door swung shut behind me.

Outside, two young teenaged girls with sandy blond hair lit a cigarette, passing it back and forth between them, as they sat in the shade of the building, on a curb. They carefully checked that no cars were coming before they smoked a drag. I walked beyond them, to my bike, and retrieved my map.

One of the tow-headed young ladies asked, "You ride a motorcycle?"

Duh.

The other one looked up at me, then at her friend. She nodded her head, and announced, "That's what I want to do when I turn eighteen."

So, the strict Mormon faction produces rebels, too. Too much of a good thing can turn bad, that's my belief, regarding organized religion.

I chatted with the girls, explaining that motorcycles are dangerous, and not just a means to "be cool." I pointed out how uncomfortable and hot wearing leathers can be, but as a safe rider, I have certain responsibilities to reduce the risk riding motorcycles presents. But, most of what I said went up in smoke rings. When I got on my bike and started the engine, their admiration was unmistakable. I knew I left a good impression, but wondered what good would it do? I'll bet chances are good, neither one of the little ladies make it to eighteen without a baby or two.

It seemed the norm in this region, that most women have several children, and push a baby stroller, as they waddle down the street, pregnant.

On this day I didn't do any sightseeing, except for riding. My motorcycle has become as comfortable to me as an easy chair. Sitting astride my machine in motion, I feel relaxed, and can now ride three hundred miles before fatigue sets in, and even then, it's my arms and shoulders that are stressed, not my bottom.

I traveled beside the Manti-La Sal National Forest, and Edge of the Cedars. I passed by Valley of the Gods, and bypassed a town called Medicine Hat. Onward through Ute Mountain Indian Reservation, and into Navaho Indian Reservations, I toured, crossing the Arizona border underneath a sky lined by heavy clouds.

This sign displayed a radiant star, on a bright blue background, with shafts of red and orange emanating over a flat horizon.

ARIZONA—THE GRAND CANYON STATE WELCOMES YOU.

The landscape took on the appearance of the Roadrunner and Wile E. Coyote's stomping grounds when I rode towards Monument

Valley. Fantastic shapes, monoliths, buttes, mesas and spires lie scattered across an otherwise flat and vacant land. The images are well documented by western films, and nature portraits, and though familiar with some of the photogenic structures, there was novelty in moving through time and space, watching the changing perspective as my Honda flew over the flat, well-maintained open road.

Native Americans riding horses a bit lean in the loins, supervised as their dogs joyously worked their sheep herds. Dark-skinned, sun-reddened faces peered at me, black eyes squinting against the sun, and cheeks, foreheads furrowed with lines years in the making. With mutual curiosity we sometimes exchanged brief assessments of each other. I am in another land.

In the middle of nowhere, there would be stick shanties set up, mostly open sided, with a roof overhead. The more fancy ones may have a wall where you could see through the cracks as you drove by. These were not homes. They were shops. In the makeshift shade, Navaho women sat, working on their silver and turquoise craft. Tourism was their business.

I yearned to stop, and take a good look at the jewelry, observe the art for an hour or so. Maybe talk to somebody, and learn something about her and her heritage, but I didn't dare. How does one shop, face to face with the maker and merchant of beautiful jewelry and say "I'm just looking?" I could not stop, because I had a budget, and it didn't include turquoise and silver.

When Rte. 160 came to Tuba City, I stopped for gasoline, and a cold drink. Outside the convenience store, I scanned the bulletin board. Ads selling pick-up trucks or horses were fluttering in the breeze, as were postings of local social events and meetings. Four out of five vehicles that stopped at the store were beat-up pick-up trucks driven by black-haired guys, sharing the traits of their ancestors. Many of the trucks carried more passengers in the back of the truck. Most of the individuals I saw were Native Americans, and most were male.

On the bulletin board, I read with interest, a newspaper account, along with a sign written with magic marker expressing indignation over the article. Seems another community had slandered the residents of Tuba City, by complaining about the lack of planning and aesthetics as they began to get sloppy about the appearance of their community. They rebuked their citizens, comparing their haphazardness and slovenly ways to Tuba City, as if they considered this settlement the way we think of the ghetto.

"Do you want our community to end up looking like another Tuba City?" it challenged the townspeople.

A Tuba City resident had responded, saying, "Must we take this discrimination? Succumb to this gross generalization? Let us clean up our properties and stand proud against this sort of slander. Our own people. We cannot stand divided."

I looked around at the village that appeared to present its indigence; a level of poverty which real hardship and deprivation are suffered, and comforts of life are wholly lacking. But, I saw no such thing. Yes, I saw poverty. But, I also saw children laughing and playing. I saw humble shacks, surrounded by fences made from whatever someone could get their hands on, some parts metal, some parts wood, even plywood banged together, at some homes. Chickens scratched dry earth, mutts chased their own tails. Laundry hung in the arid air. Herds of sheep were scattered in distant views, and indians wearing cowboy hats rode scrawny horses, that worked off every mouthful of feed they were fed.

The poverty I observed, was overpowered by a sense of wealth. Richness of spirit, and character. Hard work, and tribal customs, roles of leadership, roles of lesser rank. All these things tore at my heart, as I reread the controversial article, before I mounted up and headed south, satisfied by another taste of America's flavor.

Seventy-five miles later, I entered a totally different kind of city. It was like any other, with street lights, and too much traffic. Dairy Queen, Jack in the Box, neon, and cement. Flagstaff welcomed me, noisily and energetically.

After a bit of a search, I found the Weatherford Hotel, which was the International Hostel I was registered at. Established in 1897, the building was almost one hundred years old, and was registered in the National Register of Historic Places. Theodore Roosevelt and Wyatt Earp were among some of the more illustrious guests who had spent the night there.

After registration, I unpacked everything off the motorcycle and lugged it all into my room. My bike was a mess and I washed it in the parking lot, and met some of the hostelers who came by to say hi. The hostel seemed to be quite the social place, but I wasn't in the mood for festivities.

My day had been spent riding through desert in August, and I didn't feel like wandering around town, although it's supposed to be pretty neat. After all my peace and solitude, I couldn't see past the concrete and artificial lights. At the moment, I wasn't impressed. I was simply tired.

I just felt like drinking tea, and writing some postcards. Grand Canyon was about a hundred mile drive from here, and I would be making the trip, exploring, then riding back, all on the same day tomorrow. I needed a good night's sleep.

Miles: 308

The next time I go to Grand Canyon I want to take a burro ride, but for my first time, I got a bird's eye view. Do you crave excitement? Do you like to try new things? If so, then I highly recommend taking a helicoptor ride. If you're lucky, they might even let you take the controls!

God is making the world, and the show is so grand and beautiful
and exciting, that I never have been able to study any other.

—John Muir

CHAPTER 22

GRAND CANYON
August 17   Day 62

U.S. Federal highway 180 was my chosen path to the
Grand Canyon's South Rim. I traveled through
cool, mountain elevation, and felt as though I owned the road. Not
too many seemed to be using this way. How can this be the road to
Grand Canyon? But, there was no conspiracy. It's not as if some
elves from within the Kaibab National Forest tacked up D.O.T. signs
indicating Grand Canyon ahead so many miles. Nope. A two way
strip of asphalt is somehow less of a road than what I'd expected.
Not to worry. I was loving it.

Hard to believe I was in Arizona, a landscape I believed would
be studded with red canyons, and saguaro cactus, pinyon pines and
scorpions. Instead, I traveled through tall pine forests that if I hadn't
spent just yesterday riding through high desert, I could be fooled
into thinking I was in New Hampshire.

At a point, 180 merged with State 64, and traffic increased as the
distance to the Grand Canyon decreased. About eighty-five miles
after leaving Flagstaff, I was gradually transformed into just another
tourist, on the way to one of the wonders of the world.

Excitement got my heart a-pounding, for I was about to realize a
lifelong dream. Better than that, tucked away in a secret place,
Benjamin Franklin was waiting to fulfill a promise. I had a one
hundred dollar bill that Russell had given to me before I went away.
It struck me as sad, that at the time it was easier for him to give me a
hundred bucks, than for him to express his love for me. But, I chose
all along not to dwell on that. Ever since I placed it in the secret
compartment, I knew I what I was going to do with the money.

Not only was I going to see the Grand Canyon today, I was going to catch my first glimpse of it on a helicopter ride! Two climactic, virginal experiences, together as one, compliments of Russell.

As I neared Grand Canyon Village, I stopped at Papillon Airport, where helicopter flights were offered, and traded in the one hundred dollar bill, the exact piece of paper that Russ had tossed my way "for a treat, or an emergency," for my very first helicopter flight, and my personal introduction to Grand Canyon.

The helicopter was white, with a rainbow slash of color over the rear and tailpeice. A mom, dad and little girl were escorted out to the helicopter that had just unloaded, and I was beckoned by the staff to come along with them. The family got seated in the back, and I was given prime seating beside the handsome pilot!

There was glass all around and beneath my feet. Passengers were given instructions, and then we put soft head phones over our ears, and our sandy-haired pilot, Omar, took the controls.

We rose up, the nose tilted downward a little bit, spun in the air, and we were off!

The flight took us over the striated fissure, while a narrator gave us information, through our headphones, both in French and English. Omar interjected phrases here and there, pointing out certain formations, and landmarks close by. He was only allowed to make shallow dips into the canyon, but as we coursed through the air tipping this way and that, spinning on a dime, and hovering hither and thither, we sat spellbound.

The ride was thrilling, and not at all scary, for me. Riding in a two or four seater airplane was a bit more nerve wracking, even though I'd enjoyed that in the past. Here, the scenery was spectacular from this birds' eye view. The glass bubble where I sat, enhanced the effect, as did the fact that Omar was pretty good-looking, himself. He had that Top Gun look about him, with his aviator shades, preppy haircut, and bronze suntan.

"So you're riding cross country, all by yourself?" he asked me. "How come?"

"I want to see America, in a real and personal way," I told him. "In fact, this is probably the most commercial experience I'll have on my whole trip."

A half hour went by all too quickly, and gently we touched down, and the door opened to let a gust of hot air hit us hard.

I cannot possibly write about the Grand Canyon itself. It is magnificent. What you cannot see, the emptiness between the walls, is as stunning as the colorful patterns, and shadows that display themselves dynamically. Much of the grandeur lies in the wonder of the millions of years of time that took one grain of sand at a time, to carve this monument.

When I was putting my leathers back on, two guys and a girl came over to check out my bike. They found it hard to believe that I had ridden all the way to Arizona from Massachusetts. The lady asked if she could sit on my bike for a picture. She even wanted to put my helmet on. For all the years I've been riding, and the hundreds of female riders that I've associated with, I find it surprising when a dame looks at me and tells me that I'm the first girl she's ever seen in real life, riding a motorcycle.

"Look harder," I advised. "I'll bet you'll see a lot more. Your mind registers 'motorcycle,' and your subconscious assumes, 'man.' " I told her, "Look harder. We're all over the place."

With that, I left the trio, on my way to Grand Canyon Village. The entrance fee for motorcycles was $4.

I spent the day exploring. There was a huge store, full of gifts and souvenirs. There was a food store where I could buy lunch ingredients. There was a visitors center where I watched a documentary covering the history and geology of this national park.

Again, I'll say, the Canyon defies description, but the memory will long be with me. I rode along the East Rim Rd., and parked somewhere, in order to eat my picnic. I stepped over the rope barrier, following the short footpath of thousands of others before me, so that I may sit on a flat outcropping of rock, perched on the edge.

I sat on top of a long sleeved tee-shirt, and had a picnic of smoked turkey slices, a roll, fresh tomato, and an apple. A humble meal, in a supreme setting.

If I could, I would spell out my *feelings* for you. I would heap upon you an aura of Awareness. Insignificance. Wonder. Fascination. Fortune. Timelessness. Timeliness. Spirituality.

You would understand how it feels to *just be*. You would embrace the moments as if they were your last, and hold on to them, and hope that they would serve to remind you that we are all a minute part of some divine plan.

You would come to realize that all of your day to day annoyances, and your greatest worries, they are nothing, in the scope of things. You are your own greatest resource. You are your own worst enemy. All is One. One is All.

Millions of tourists come to visit the Grand Canyon annually. But, I sat alone at the edge, watching as peregrine falcons sailed on the wind currents well below me, and I pondered deep thoughts. Not too many people come to the Grand Canyon alone. Somehow I felt that being alone enhanced this particular occasion.

Ah—but I wasn't alone. The Great Spirit was with me. Perhaps It is a part of me, and I a part if It.

A small family unit stopped where I had parked and came to stand at the overlook. "How can you sit on the edge like that? Aren't you afraid?," a woman asked of me.

I looked around at the stone platform I was centered in. The surface was probably eight feet by twelve. I didn't feel any danger at all.

I answered her truthfully. "No. Why should I be afraid? This rock has been here for millions of years without falling away. Why, in all eternity, would it crack off, today, during my little picnic? I'm not that special really, to be chosen for such a demise."

She looked at me skeptically, and grabbed the arm of one of her teens, before he crossed over the crack, to come onto my precipice. "No way!" she commanded. "You stay here!"

"But Ma—you're so boring," he muttered, sounding very much like a typical teen. After a few minutes, they piled back into their Ford Explorer, and moseyed on along the East Rim.

During the remainder of the day, I hiked some, and took in more information at another visitor center. A commercial tour bus stopped and unloaded its human cargo, made in Japan. A hundred dark-haired people, small in stature spilled out, their smiles curved up in animated chatter. Most of them headed straight to the visitors center, but one couple came my way arm in arm, in order to take some pictures away from the crowd.

I gestured to the gentleman, if he would give me his camera, I would take his picture together with his wife, and the dazzling canyon as their backdrop. His smile widened, and he stepped over to stand beside her.

He understood me, when I handed him my own camera, pointing to myself, with eyebrows raised. He nodded affirmatively, hustled his wife out of the way, and shot me. Before handing my camera back to me, he held up his hand, and haltingly said, "Wait. Me take Wife with beautiful American woman. Okay?" He wanted my picture!

Flattered, I agreed, laughingly. Beautiful American woman? He better get around some more! I'm just a simple girl. She stood beside me, as tall as my shoulder, and seemed so frail. Quickly he snapped the picture, and then they both said, "Bye-bye," and made a bee-line for the jam-packed visitors center.

I hiked off in the other direction, eventually returning to my waiting machine.

My visit had to come to a close. I had eighty-five miles to ride home, and hadn't brought a sweater or sweatshirt. It would probably cool right off once the sun set, and since it was getting close to dusk, I got geared up, and rode away from Grand Canyon National Park.

Ever since childhood, I hoped to one day go there. Of all the Brady Bunch episodes, the two-part special about their vacation and burro ride at Grand Canyon stood out the most. During my departure, I made a new promise to myself. Some day I would return when I could stay a couple of days, at least. I will come back and hike, and camp out, and I will take a guided burro excursion. Some day, when I'm rich and famous, I'll come back.

The temperature dropped a little, as I sped south towards Flagstaff, while the sunset covered the sky with more of Mother Nature's artistry. Before it quite got dark, I took advantage of the empty road, and took the Pony for a gallop.

I crouched down behind the low windshield and cracked the throttle. She thrust forward energetically. The engine took on a certain cadence, and my Supertrapps eminated their special whiny growl. I squeezed my thighs tight, tucked my elbows in and felt the adrenaline surge through me, as my speedo needle crept closer and closer to straight up and down. One hundred and five miles per hour, at that point.

It had been so long since I've been able to ride this baby at top speed. One-oh-five isn't enough. I want more. Need more.

The wind screamed past my helmet, as I sliced through Kaibab National Forest. I loosened my right fist for a split second, enough to arch my wrist over the top of the grip, then cranked it, full wide open. The Pony lunged forward again, akin to my need for speed.

One-ten. Fifteen.

One twenty-five miles per hour! She settled in at that speed. I clung to her back, using full-body contact. My chest covered my tankbag, my thighs and knees hugged the tank, each calf gripped at the sides of my speeding machine. The exhilaration of racing the wind like this erupted like an orgasm, before sanity somehow caught up with me. Only then, did I temper my flight to a loping 90 mph.

Needless to say, it did not take me very long to get back to Flagstaff. I felt terrific.

What a great idea I'd had when I stripped everything off that bike, and left it naked for today's jaunt. Although I'd grown quite used to my cumbersome packload, I did often think about the time when I wouldn't be on a cross country trip, and I wouldn't have to carry my home around with me where ever I go. Let today suffice.

What an awesome day. Mentally, aesthetically, physically. It don't get much better than this. How I love the freedom that this summer has rendered to me.

*   *   *

Back at the hostel, I had my leftover turkey slices, and some rice and vegetables for supper. Most of the hostelers were watching TV together in the common room. I sat at the large heavy wooden dining room table and took care of my notes, maps, etc.

Now that I'd been to Grand Canyon, and I was in Arizona, I could call my sister and let her know exactly what day she could expect to receive me, in Tucson. Phoenix appeared to be a perfect stop for an overnight in between, and I had that invitation from the couple that I'd met at the BMW rally, who sold my gloves to me.

First I called the folks in Phoenix. They readily invited me again, as soon as I said that I was in Flagstaff, and headed for Tucson. Earl gave me directions to their house, and I estimated what time I might arrive.

"We can't wait to see you."

"Thanks. See you tomorrow."

The call to my sister didn't go as smoothly. Why is it that virtual strangers were more enthusiastic about opening their doors to a wayfarer, than my own flesh and blood?

"Well, Diane—you said you would be here in the beginning of August."

She was right. But, that was before I'd even left home. Since then I'd written to her and told her I'd be along, later than that.

"Conny, I am on a motorcycle. I have no agenda. I have no idea from day to day where I'll be. But ever since June, you knew I would be here sometime in August. Now, I am here in Flagstaff. Tomorrow I will be staying in Phoenix, then the following day I'll get to Tucson, to see you and your family."

"I know. I know. Don't get so upset."

Changing the subject, Conny gave me some advice regarding my ride into Tucson.

"What route are you taking? You're gonna take 'Ten' right?"

"Well, no. I usually take the lesser routes," I answered.

"You're gonna be driving through the desert," she informed me, sounding a tad worried. "It's monsoon season, here."

Sounds serious. "What do you mean?" I asked.

"It's monsoon season. That's very dangerous. Listen to me, Diane," she warned. "If you see one coming, get off of the road!"

"What do you mean? Get off of the road?" I asked.

"Get off the road!" she said, emphatically.

"What does it look like? What's a monsoon? Explain. I haven't been here long enough to know what you mean. I don't understand," I pleaded.

"Rainstorms come through the area. There are flash floods. You have no chance on a bike, Dee. Thunder and lightening as bad as a hurricane." (Now *that* I could understand.) "You can see it coming. It's like a whole separate sky coming to take over. You have to get off of the road or you'll get hit by a car. No one can see you. They can't even see the road, and they'll aim right at you if they see headlights, thinking they're on the road." She spoke with authority and concern. "You must get off the road, *especially* on a bike."

"But what do you mean get off the road? I can't just drive into the desert sand on a street bike. Do you mean, get off of my bike and run away from the road? Won't somebody slam into my bike then?

What do I do then? Conny, I still don't understand what you mean when you say get off the road."

"No, if you leave your bike, it will probably get hit. Try to get off the main highway, and shut off the lights. Try to find shelter and let it pass. They don't last real long, but they're furious. Maybe you won't even get hit. I don't know." Her voice trailed off.

"Conny honey. I'll be fine," I fibbed. "Don't worry. But thank you for the warning. I hadn't heard about monsoon season, or maybe I would have made it a point to get here earlier. Anyway," I continued, "I'll see ya soon! Love ya, bye."

"Bye. Love you too."

At the hostel, I still hadn't really met anyone, but had seen some of the guests coming and going. One particular guy had long, straight, thick, black hair, held in place by a leather headband. He wore a breast plate like that which the indians wear on TV westerns. He also wore jeans, a beaded belt, and a suede vest with beadwork on it. He reminded me of a kid all dressed up to play cowboys and indians.

He had made it known that he had just spent several weeks at one of the Hopi reservations, learning of their ways. It appeared that he'd adopted their dress, and he had most assuredly fallen in love with their simple ways.

Here at the hostel, a young girl whose looks reminded me of Molly Ringwald in *Pretty In Pink*, had obviously fallen in love with him. She gazed at him adoringly, and clung to every word he uttered.

My 'chores' for the day were taken care of, and I went out to pick up a couple of wine coolers, then went out to the back courtyard to enjoy the evening with the hostelers that were not stuck in front of the boob tube.

The indian boy and Molly strummed their guitars, and a bunch of us sat around singing songs, and banging knives against our bottles and cans. When a few others joined us, Molly displayed her kooky sense of humor by announcing to everybody, "Does everyone know Adam?" She put her guitar down, and placed her hand on one of the indian's shoulders. "This is Adam," she announced, then added, "He's my brother." Then she kissed him, full on the mouth, tongue and all.

The rest of us didn't quite know what to make of them, but when they finished their deep-throat public display, we applauded. The guitar music resumed.

One boundary of the back courtyard was the brick wall of another building. It had been recently white-washed, and the beginnings of a huge mural were started. Adam was responsible. He had convinced the management that the courtyard was ugly and needed a facelift. He said he had gotten hostelers together, and they petitioned a request to paint the building's wall. At this stage, some line drawings were started, and Adam was asking for ideas.

He wanted to see flags of many nations, and our United States. There would be mountains, trees, streams and other things of nature, and there would be a cityscape. I suggested a huge rainbow, and the idea was accepted readily. One day, I will return, so that I can view the finished project.

Midnight struck, and I decided it was high time that I went to bed. I filled up my new water bottle with a picture of Grand Canyon on it, and put it in the freezer. Then, after using one of the two co-ed bathrooms, I tucked myself into my sleep-sheet.

Miles: 220

The legacy
When I die . . . I want to leave you with something, something
better than words or sounds. Look for me in the people I have
known and loved. And if you cannot live without me, then let me
live on in your eyes, your mind and your acts of kindness . . . Love
does not die. People do. So, when all that is left of me is
love . . . give me away.

—unknown

CHAPTER 23

ARIZONA
August 18–24   Days 63–69

The smell of biscuits hot out of the oven permeated the air. They were served up, one tray after another, to be eaten with jam, peanut butter or honey, as part of the hostel's breakfast. I joined the group clustered around the heavy wooden table, and listened to the conversations going on around me.

One man amazed me with his ability to turn every subject that came up, into an opportunity to preach at us, reciting scriptures, and sharing his testimony.

"Won't you accept Jesus Christ as your personal Saviour?" He looked directly at me. "You remind me of a woman in the ministry, that I really admire. She has been blessed by the Lord, and lifted from a life of sin and hopelessness. The Lord could use you, too, to do His work, if you would only stop and listen for His voice."

I squirmed uncomfortably. He continued.

"He can take your life, and mold you into a vessel of His Spirit . . . " on and on he went, while I said nothing. I tried to ignore him, but he was focused on me, the lost sheep within his reach.

His tee-shirt looked like the kind you pick up at Hard Rock Cafe, but it read, "Solid Rock Christ" instead. He had found his mission in life, but like the addiction he had given up when the Lord saved him, I wondered, how long this one would last.

"You can leave me alone now, you're beginning to irritate me," I cut him off. He was ruining everyone's breakfast.

A "clomp, clomp, clomp" sounded from the hallway, loud, unmistakable foot-falls, that silenced everyone for a second. Who can possibly make that much noise simply walking down the hall? Adam, the indian wanna-be appeared, much to our surprise. Aren't indians supposed walk silently? This guy was quite a creature.

I gave him my chair. Let the preacher try and save *his* soul.

The eclectic group of hostelers continued breakfasting, and I took a shower, then got dressed to go. After a brief interlude on the Old Route 66, I went to Walnut Canyon National Monument.

It was pretty neat, like ruins are. The trail had lots of the plants and trees labeled and described. Along the path, tiny lizards played hide and seek. After a lingering hike into the canyon, and visiting the Visitor Center, and educating myself about the history of these particular ancient dwellings and the 12th century Sinagua tribe, I felt ready to blast on down to Phoenix on the interstate.

Flagstaff sits high, at approximately 7,000 foot elevation. About halfway to Phoenix, the elevation dropped steadily, first to about 4,000 feet, then 3,000. The air got much hotter and dryer. Saguaro cactus suddenly appeared in droves, amongst spiny prickly pear patches. I-17 was patrolled heavily by police cruisers, and in keeping with the flow of traffic, I felt stifled. This wasn't at all like the days of flying without concern, that I had grown used to, in the wide open spaces along secondary roads.

Early in my day's ride, my Interceptor reached fifty-one thousand miles. It's Friday. It was Monday when we hit fifty. When I get to the Alexander's I'll have to lube the chain again.

At around five o'clock I arrived in Phoenix, and entered bumper to bumper traffic, and a million sets of lights. The directions I had were confusing, because I didn't know how the city was laid out, and when my directions said, for example, *Take 7th Ave* and I came upon 7th St., I turned onto it, thinking that Earl probably used the two words interchangeably.

5:15 pm. 103 degrees. Somewhere along the way, I had removed my shorts and top, so that I literally wore only my bikini under my leather pants, and jacket, which I left unzipped, the belt, buckled. Now that I was only creeping along a few feet at a time, and exasperated by directions that didn't seem to work, I was dripping with perspiration. Lost, I finally pulled over at a pay phone and called my hosts.

Patiently, Earl listened to my plight and position, and explained that Avenue and Street are indeed not the same animals, and he redirected me back towards his suburb, and E. Osborn, not a street, nor an avenue, just E.Osborn where he and Jan lived.

When I pulled into their driveway, they were waiting in anticipation. Jan hugged me warmly, and Earl pulled me into the kitchen and told me what he tells everyone else.

"The bathroom is over there, the refrigerator is here. Whatever you want, you just help yourself. Our home is your home."

Jan offered me a tall glass of ice water, and I told her how good the kitchen smelled. She had a pot roast in the oven, and the aroma was sensational. After a cool shower, I was ready to eat.

We sat at the dining room table, where family photographs adorned the walls. The conversation was animated, and talk of travel, and motorcycles, and life's richest experiences kept us seated around the table for a good old fashioned supper hour. I ate like a growing girl. There was pot roast, and browned potatoes in mushroom gravy, with onions slathering all, plus green beans cooked just right. After I'd had three helpings, (ah, but they were small, honest) and we'd cleared the table once, they broke out some photo albums, and set homemade strawberry shortcake before me, with old style baking soda biscuits, and real whipped cream.

Together, we looked at some of their memories, and I saw Montana, and Yellowstone, and other places which I have only dreamed of. Earl had a knack for writing, and I took pleasure in reading some of his prose about his own travel adventures, then Jan and I retired to the porch to enjoy the night air, and get my laundry taken care of.

"How did you decide what to bring with you, what to pack?" Jan inquired.

For the hundredth time since June 17, I found myself explaining. "Months before departure I began working on a list, based on experience, and supposition. Knowing that I would encounter extremes in the climate, and I'd be virtually self-reliant, I packed accordingly."

"Did you plan well?" Jan encouraged me to go on. "What did you bring for clothes?"

I clarified her question. *"Exactly* what?"

"Sure. I'm interested to know how you pack for three and a half months, and fit it all on a motorcycle!"

I began, beginning at my toes and working my way up.

"My hiking boots, which I wear while riding, and otherwise. Also, a pair of flip-flops for camping, they take up hardly any space at all, but are very useful.

"I have five pair of woolen socks, which feel very hot in your desert here, but actually wick sweat away from my skin.

"Since I would be wearing my leathers day in and day out, would I need two pairs of jeans? Space dictated that I only bring one pair. Good call. I've hardly used them at all. When I get to camp, I want to wear shorts. I have two cut-offs, and a pair of running shorts.

Jan left her chair and indicated it was time to toss my things into the washer. We poured another cold lemonade, then she prompted me to finish telling her, what else do I have?

"You're really curious?" I was surprised.

"We're always packed to spend the summer in the motor home, and even that's difficult. I *am* curious."

"Okay, for my legs I also have a pair of sweatpants, great for camping at night, and two pairs of lightweight leggings, which I find extremely versatile." I described their usefulness. "As long johns, or by themselves, dressing up, or camping out, they've been great."

"For tops, I went with a variety of styles, which I could layer. I have a couple of muscle tees, four sportbras, five tee-shirts in various stages of sissor-induced massacre, one flannel shirt, a thermal, one long-sleeved tee, one button down shirt, also very versatile, a sweatshirt and a woolen sweater. Of course, I have a leather halter top, and come to think of it, a denim bustier, and I *think* that's all." I laughed.

"It sounds like so much, but I have found that I have not left anything behind that I might have needed, nor have I brought anything along that I haven't already used, a lot, including a woolen hat, that I failed to mention."

This conversation carried forth, until I had issued a complete listing of the contents of my saddlebags, and everything else.

tent, sleeping bag	and sleeping pad
A socket set	Clymer repair manual
oil filter wrench	clutch and brake levers
spark plugs	multi-purpose flash-light

umbrella	raingear
tarp and rope	small propane stove
nestling pans & flatware	1 med. & 1 lg. towel

This verbal itinerary continued until I had completely exhausted my memory through this game of itemizaton.

Jan and Earl made me feel enormously special, and secured in me the notion that I was indeed doing the right thing, taking this time in my life to achieve the desires of my heart, whatever they may be.

In her wisdom, Jan reassured me that life is short, and love is deep. Happiness is within our reach, we need to open our minds and our hearts.

She shared with me the story of their romance, and I was touched by her openness and strength. She managed to coax me into speaking of Russell and my uncertainty about him. I admitted how I wished I could deal with the situation more effectively, but that I was weak. I saw the partnership she and Earl shared, and the deep friendship and love that bonded them, even in their later years.

"I'm no spring chicken," she declared. "But you're young. You have a whole lot of life ahead of you. There is so much that you have to offer. Don't throw it away for the wrong one."

I struggled with my emotions for a bit, sitting under the Arizona starscape, while the washing machine which was set up out of doors, chug-a chugged nearby. Earl came outside and joined us, and reaffirmed the notion of true love, by telling more stories which made fairy tales seem ordinary.

I went to bed soothed by a loving atmosphere which gave me hope. They were right. I had a lot to offer. Why settle for one who doesn't appreciate me? I want real love.

Miles: 183

Such was the decor of the Alexander guest room, that I awoke feeling like a debutante. Everything was light and airy. Crystal and brass adorned the boudoir. I sat up to stretch in bed and caught my reflection in the dresser mirror. My black tank top and bronzed muscles provided a sharp contrast to the frills and muslin surrounding me.

Breakfast was on. I could smell coffee brewing. All of my laundry was clean again! After I selected my day's outfit, I zipped the rest into zip-lock bags and stuffed them into my bulging duffel bag, and carried it out to the kitchen with me.

Earl and Jan shared a filling breakfast with me, before he spread out an Arizona map and made suggestions regarding area attractions.

"Young lady, we happened to notice your gloves last night. What happened?" Earl held up a damaged glove.

"Oh, do you recognize my gloves?" I asked. "I bought them from you guys at the BMW rally in Paonia, remember? That's how we first met. Look how much they've faded. The back of the hands have turned brown!"

"What's it been? A month? Two? These babies look like they've had *many* seasons," Jan commented.

"We just happen to have another pair of women's small gloves just like these. These are history." He placed a new package into my hands and ignored my protests.

These are worth twenty bucks and they're just replacing them, for nothing? My surprise and confusion showed on my face.

"Thank you so much." I turned to Jan, "They're just like you said, the most comfortable gloves I've had for hot or cool." I inspected them, and tried them on, noting that they were just a tiny bit more snug, as they weren't broken in yet. I picked up my old pair and turned them over. They were indeed faded, and a hole gaped open on the back of my right hand.

"What happened?" Earl repeated.

"Oh, that happened one day when I was checking something out and the back of my hand touched the muffler. It just melted a hole through the material."

"Hmm-m," murmured Earl.

"Better my glove, than me!" I added, and I hesitantly set my old retired pair on the kitchen table. The new ones were too new. The old ones were like riding friends which had shared many bonding experiences with me. Their faded backs perfectly matched the look my leather jacket had achieved.

I laughed. "I hate to leave these behind," I said wistfully, feeling a bit silly. "Oh," I sighed, "It's just a pair of gloves."

Jan squeezed my hand, and sympathized. "In no time at all, you will have bonded with these gloves. At least you know they'll break in well, and that you liked this brand."

Earl added cheerfully, "Just don't be working on your engine with them on, okay?"

Once again, people who used to be mere strangers, stood beside me in a driveway, before grabbing me in a big, long, sincere hug. It happened in Pennsylvania, Ohio, Oregon, and now here in Arizona. Somehow I've acquired people who have claimed me as their own. Family. All over the U.S.

I got settled into my saddle, started the engine, and looked over my shoulder at these two wonderful people who had invited me into their lives. I rode away feeling special, and I pretended they were grandparents, so that's why I could feel so very loved.

*   *   *

Interstate 10 blasted me in no time to Casa Grande. I paid two dollars for entrance to the monument. The *Great House* was constructed in this desert location, using logs of juniper, fir and pine trees which had been floated part-way and carried part-way, from their origin sixty miles away. It was probably a central meeting place for ceremonies among the Hohokam (all used up, all gone) people. A respectable irrigation system was evident when Spanish explorers discovered the site. Once again, as with many of the Native American ancestors, and probably others around the world, their demise, their disappearance remains a mystery.

*   *   *

Ninety minutes later, I was fast approaching Oracle Junction, traveling south on 79, keeping a wary eye on an approaching storm wall. Coming towards me from the left, there was a most imposing sight. From a great distance, across the vast desert horizon, a dark looking sheet hung down from an angry sky, and it crept across the frontier like a sinister army.

Ahead of me, a modest two-way strip of asphalt passively laid itself before me, presenting my only option for escape. Further on, a mountain range created a barrier beyond which Tucson laid in wait. It appeared to be perhaps an hour's ride to the foothills.

The oncoming storm looked menacing, and I realized I was witnessing a monsoon about to happen, unless I could outrun it.

Nervously, I twisted the throttle and moved along at a more urgent pace. The velocity and trajectory of the bad weather seemed to hurdle itself towards me, its only moving target.

Conny's warning came back to me, and echoed in my mind. I could hear her voice, her words, her accent when she'd spoken on the phone to me. *If you see one coming, get off of the road!*

The front was getting closer, and I didn't think I would make it, and started to feel a bit frightened. Spiny cactus and prickly pair cactus dotted the rugged sand on either side of the narrow straightaway. A long time ago I spotted one place where I could have sought shelter, but there didn't seem to be any need for it way back then.

Now the need was eminent. Frantically, I kept on driving, not knowing what else to do. There was no choice, but there was a possibility I could beat the onslaught.

So, this is a monsoon. Am I in danger of a flash flood in these parts? Any place between here and Tucson? Fighting the forces of nature, I felt scared by every gust that slammed into us, actually shifting us sideways when it got really bad. I felt fear. Then determination. Adrenaline surged through my veins. Lightening bolts thrust their crackling fingers down to touch Earth, and leapt away when they made contact with the thorns of the desert.

Get off of the road!

But how? Where can I go? There's no way I'm going to even *try* to drive onto the sand. If I go down, or run over some sort of cactus spine, I'll be in big trouble. Oh—shoot! Why did she say to get off of the road when there is no place to go?

The storm came closer, with a distinct wall of dark gray torrents of rain, and nasty black clouds for the roof. I made a visual interpretation of the word "front," as it pertains to weather. My eyes searched for any kind of pull-off, hoping for a miracle, wondering if I was crossing the fine line from being determined to foolish. But how can that be? When I left Phoenix, and even Casa Grande, the day was picture perfect. This storm chased me. I didn't set out to battle a monsoon.

Nevertheless, thus was the situation.

Suddenly, I came around a slight bend in the road, and an open structure revealed itself to me. In a few minutes, I downshifted and slowed before turning onto a surface covered with loose pebbles. I carefully stopped the bike and planted my two boots, surveying the scene.

It appeared to be a picnic area for travelers, or maybe a Tucson family who jumps in their car for a short ride to the other side of the mountains, for the illusion of "getting away from it all," if only for a lunch brought in a basket. There were a couple of long green picnic tables placed end to end, underneath a shelter of steel supports, open walls, and a roof of rippled metal. Waist high boulders were spaced around the shelter itself, to keep cars out, I guessed, and at the edge of the parking lot a couple of trash barrels were chained down.

The wall of water and wind steadily crept closer, I had only moments to spare. Everything I had, ran the risk of a good soaking if I just let the bike sit out in this deluge. I eased out the clutch partway, and straddle walked the machine in between a suitable space then pulled up close to the table.

Finally, I was able to let out a sigh of relief. We were on one side of the road. Just beyond, as I took my helmet off, I watched the ground surface change colors, first the sand over there, then the highway, and finally the pebbles which began to dance when the monsoon first hit. The wet wall reached my shelter, suddenly filling the air with the sound of the roof being pelted by heavy rains, a sound much like radio static, with the volume turned up a mite too much. With it, came a chill in the air that brought goosebumps to my arms. My jacket, which had so far spent most of the day strapped to my bike, felt just right when I pulled it on.

I didn't know how long I'd have to sit this out, but I was due for a break after all that perceived danger I just survived. I refreshed my take on the Arizona map Earl gave me. Finally, the rain eased up to a light patter and I was ready to make a break for it. It was hard to tell whether I would ride into the tail of that storm, or skirt one of the wings, or did the mountain range cause it to veer off course? The only way to find out, was to get on my Red Pony and ride.

The monsoon hit again as soon as I got into Tucson, but I didn't feel so vulnerable anymore. Anytime I wanted, I could stop. The gusty wind had subsided, and although the rain kept on coming, I kept on going. My leather was beginning to soak through, but I would be at my sister's for several days, plenty of time for it to dry out.

The rain came in torrents then subsided, over and over. One red light after the other forced me to put my feet down in inches of water, and my boots were soaked because I didn't bother to put my booties on. All of this was merely an inconvenience, however, because I was increasingly becoming more excited about seeing my sister and my niece again, for the first time in four years.

It appeared that some roads were intended to be temporary riverways during monsoons. With inadequate drainage, rainwater has no place to go, and it isn't absorbed by the desert sand very quickly, so flooding occurs rapidly in the city streets. Certain streets were flowing with water a couple of feet deep. I couldn't go on.

At a gas station, I stopped and parked the bike to wait. The gas station was at a corner, and the road in front was okay, but the road to the side sort of dipped low, and went under a tunnel or a bridge of sorts. While I sat there, I watched as cars took the corner and the drivers made a choice. Many turned around in the gas station parking lot, while others plunged in, and the water came up over the tops of their tires. One guy who was on foot, stopped on the sidewalk, took his shoes and socks off, rolled his pants up over his knees and then waded across. He needn't have bothered to roll up his pants, because the water came halfway up his thighs, soaking his jeans anyway. I followed him into the gas station store.

"Wow! That's deep! I can't believe that cars are going through it," I exclaimed. "Do the roads flood like this often?"

"Oh yeah, during monsoon season." He and the gas station attendant explained how it is.

"So, how long will it take to go down? I need to get to the other side of that," I pointed to the worst part, "but, it's too deep to ride through."

The shocking answer came, "Oh, it should clear out by tomorrow."

"Tomorrow?" I wilted some, and leaned against a glass refrigerator door. "Oh, man. May I make a local call on your phone?"

"What's the number?" He dialed and handed the receiver over the counter to me.

Conny answered the phone and I told her of my location and predicament. She and her husband and daughter would come in their car to lead me home on "the high roads."

In pulled a big, green Grand Marquis, and out of it spilled my relatives.

At first I didn't know who to look at first. Everybody looked so different! My sister's hair was fabulous. It was longer than I'd ever seen it, cascading in a thick wavy layer of gold and honey and sand colored tresses, all the way to her rear end. She wore a long, filmy dress, and heavy eye make-up, and smiled up at me and hugged me like she meant it, her full, roundness feeling like a favorite, warm memory.

My little niece had shot up like a weed. She was long and lean, nine years old, and so pretty that I just stared at her for a minute, while she demurely looked down, like a bashful, shy doe. While she was fair, and golden like her mother, she was reed thin, and long boned, like her father.

"Can you believe how tall she's gotten?" Conny could see how impressed I was, and she beamed, like a proud mom.

*   *   *

Their big, green boat of a car lumbered through the hatch of avenues, leading me along a roundabout route to my next stopover. At one point, Steve pulled into a parking lot to explain that we might have to cross some water in a few places. I guessed that I could possibly manage that so long as the depth was no higher than my wheel hubs, but I wouldn't know because I'd never passed through water deeper than five or six inches. Steve said we'd get to some intersections where we'd "dip" across, while the rainwater flowed along the road that crossed ours.

"Okay," I mustered up some more bravado. "Let's do it!"

Following them wasn't too bad. Little Elizabeth was sitting spun around in the back seat, to watch me riding my motorcycle behind the car. Every once in a while I'd wave a gloved hand at her, or we'd exchange a thumbs up sign.

The city structure was flatter than others, such as Boston, New York, Los Angeles. Pastel colored shops, adobe apartments, and a strong Mexican influence lined each block. A couple of times I noticed brake lights on Steve's car before it fjorded a flooded area, and nervously I followed suit. After a few successful crossings though, it started to feel kind of fun. I hadn't realized this motorcycle was capable of such a feat. When I got to Conny's, I'd have to remember to lube my chain right away. It was not only getting wet, it was actually *submerged* repeatedly.

We came towards an intersection up ahead, where there was a cafe on the corner. On the walls of the building, a mural of southwestern design was painted, catching my attention. Seated at bistro tables on the sidewalk, a few patrons sipped at their beverages, optimistic that perhaps the storm had passed.

At the junction, I saw Steve's car drive into a waterway deeper than any I had encountered thus far.

"Yee-hah!" I had to pull my feet up off the footpegs, it was so deep. This is crazy. I felt the bike getting bogged by the water, so I gunned it. I can't lose momentum now. What I need is speed, so I can get the heck across this mess.

More throttle! Good! Whew. We're still moving, we're getting out of here. But no! What's happening?

What's going on?!?

As my motorcycle's front tire gained access to good road, I should have been all set, but instead I felt like something had taken a hold of my bike and yanked it from me, like some kind of warped desert sea monster. I tried to steer her, but couldn't escape. My Red Pony lurched out of the floodwaters and then dumped over to the left.

Hard.

Hard and still.

Oh man! Not again!

My leg was caught under the Honda, and I couldn't get up. Just behind me, a man in a pick-up truck managed to stop without running me over. My first reaction was to signal to him that I was stuck. He had to help me.

His front tires were on "dry" road, his rear end was in the "river." He opened his door and jumped out, trying to stay on dry ground. "Okay Guy, we'll getcha up. Are you okay?" He assumed I was a man.

By now, my brother-in-law was aware of my predicament, and he too, was headed my way. I laid on my side, embarrassed, and gritted my teeth against the pain. My leg was twisted at the knee and being crushed. Bystanders on the sidewalks multiplied.

Calmly, I gave instructions on how to go about lifting my bike off of me, while my sister took charge of the crowd. "Somebody call 911! Don't worry. Stay back. I'm a nurse."

When I went down, I stayed with the bike, and didn't tumble or slide at all, but I hit the ground hard and it hurt. As the two men lifted me to my feet, I insisted I was okay, but needed to sit down for a minute. The stranger was totally surprised when he heard my voice and saw that I was actually a woman. I continued to be embarrassed, because when I went into that intersection I felt like showing off, and look what happened. Serves me right.

Steve and the stranger sat me on a bench there on the sidewalk, and I took off my helmet, then started to check myself out. At the moment, my left knee hurt the most, and I pulled my scuffed pantleg up to see how bad it was.

There was a huge egg developing, and a small cut which was bleeding. My sister began asking me typical first aid questions, and I looked past her at the intersection that brought me down.

Steve started in. He knew what happened. He said, "It's those damned trolley tracks."

He was 100% correct. We were traveling along a plain old road, but at this particular intersection, from each side, a set of trolley tracks entered and ran along the portion of road where we were going.

When I rode into the deep water, I could not see the tracks, as they were submerged. Just as I pulled out of the water up the incline, my rear tire sunk into the groove in which the trolley track lies, and not knowing this, I gunned it. Chances are, I might have made it without a mishap, but the fact is, I didn't. I slipped and fell.

Steve said, "You know, they grabbed the car too, when we went through, but at least we have four wheels. One second you were there in my rear view mirror, then I felt the car slip, and the next second I couldn't see you any more."

My elbow hurt a whole lot, and other aches and pains were screaming their presence. I continued my assessment of injury with Conny. Suddenly, I thought of Elizabeth and looked for her. She stood a little off to the side, and when we made eye contact she looked so frightened that my heart went out to her. Tears leapt to her wide, expressive eyes.

"Oh, honey, come here. Come sit on my lap," I beckoned, wincing as I pulled her close to me. Turning the incident into a lesson, I spoke. "I'm okay. Just banged up, see? I skinned my knee, that's all. It's probably no worse than what happens to you at the playground, right?"

Sniff, sniffle, and a tiny nod of the head.

"See? This is why I wear protective clothing, like all of this leather, and my helmet." I thought of how I had crossed the desert that day without wearing my jacket. How fortunate I was that I had put it on when I got to the shelter during the monsoon. "See how they protected me from getting hurt any worse?" All the while my mind was reeling with doubts. I couldn't believe I just had a spill, and right under my niece's nose, too. Son of a Bee!

Meanwhile, there was a heated discussion going on between Steve, the stranger from the truck, and a guy on a bicycle who had arrived on the scene and stopped. They were increasingly agitated about the trolley tracks' construction, and the lack of warning signs posting their presence and danger.

The bicycle rider was livid, because he had once had the same thing happen to him on his bicycle, without the water, but at a much higher speed. He sympathized with me, comparing his six-pound bike, with my four-hundred pound V-Four. Muttering threats to sue the city, he wanted me to testify in court.

"But I live in Massachusetts," I said.

He looked at the bike with all it's luggage. "And you rode it all the way?" He looked skeptical.

"Yeah. I just arrived in Tucson. Just now. This is my sister. I was following them to her place, but decided to make my arrival a tad more dramatic." A sense of humor won't hurt.

Finally, an ambulance arrived. They did their thing, but I refused to go to a hospital on the grounds that my sister was a nurse. Besides, I wasn't sure if I had health insurance any more. Motorcycle insurance doesn't do a thing for the medical bills of a rider, and I didn't want to report this to insurance anyway. There might be some minor damage to my Interceptor, but nothing serious. Not like the Colorado crash.

Conny left my side when the EMTs were flirting with me, and circled my bike. She returned, her eyes as wide as saucers, and the color leaving her face.

"Oh, Diane—your bike . . . I want to prepare you. It really got scraped up badly. One of your horses . . . I'm so sorry to tell you . . . "

She doesn't realize that most of the damage she's seeing happened a month ago. I don't need to tell her that either. Not this minute anyway. What was I supposed to say? "Oh, that? No, that happened *last* month in Colorado when I went over a cliff. That didn't happen today." I couldn't tell her, couldn't admit that the damage came from a different crash. Not today.

The EMTs asked me questions, took my blood pressure and other required duties, then left me under my sister's care. The semi-circle of curious onlookers started to disperse, and I stood up, ready to follow my sister the rest of the way.

This time, I had no desire to get cocky on my machine. Truth is, I ached to get off, because my elbow and knee sent searing, stabbing pains through me as I rode along behind my sister's car.

At last, I noticed that we were on St. Mary's Rd., and we pulled into the complex where Conny lived. She suggested that I unwind in the bath.

It was hot and fragrant, the bathroom spic and span. Beside the tub, a miniature laundry basket held a collection of bath toys, and a little mermaid doll, and her friends. On top of the counter, an array of beauty products and make-up overwhelmed my travel kit, packed with only the bare necessities. I relaxed in the tub, looking at my fresh injuries. Deja vu.

Later on the, four of us climbed into the big, green car, and ended up at Circle K. While there, I bought some shampoo and soap, and a twelve pack of Diet Pepsi, so that any time I wanted a cold drink, I could just grab one, and not feel guilty. I would be here for a few days, and didn't want to impose.

After we got back, I was ready to call it a day.

"Elizabeth, it's time for you to go to bed, too," her mother said.

Nine year old Elizabeth obediently put her things away, kissed her parents good-night and asked if we could stay up in bed to talk, for a little while.

"Okay, but not too late."

I told her we could chat for a half hour, but then had to cool it, because I had to record my day on maps and in my journal.

"Is that like a diary?" she asked.

"Yes. Very much so. Do you want to see it?" I knelt on the twin sized mattress Conny had secured for my visit, and spread out my map on her bed, tracing the route which was highlighted in yellow and pink, all over the face of America. Then I showed her my small journal, and the lists of things I kept in its pages.

She revealed, "I have a diary, too, but you can't see it. It's secret."

I agreed. "That's right. Only you have the right to read it, and only you have the right to share it with others. That's why I just showed you mine just now. Even though I showed it to you now, it would be wrong for you to pick it up and read it some other time. Understand?"

So, we spent our half hour speaking along those lines, and she gained an understanding of what I am doing, and why.

We settled down to write in our diaries. Afterwards, I was granted a most enormous privilege. Elizabeth showed me her day's entry. I was so touched I asked her if I could copy it into my own journal.

Just as she wrote and spelled each word by herself, here is Elizabeth's account of my triumphant arrival into Tucson, and back into her young life.

> Dear Diare-
> Today Anty Dey came to viset use on her
> modersicul. She slipt of and got cote then I
> sheded a lot of teers for her. She was ok thoe
> just a lot of skraces, then we made it safely
> home then we helpt her take in her stafe. Then
> she got to sleep in my room.
> Elizabeth B.

Miles: 141

*   *   *

For five days, I settled into family life, offering my services as a free baby sitter, so that Conny and Steve could enjoy some time off by themselves. For my entire stay in Tucson after that first day, I only rode twenty-eight miles.

On Sunday, the day after my spill over the trolley tracks, I woke up very stiff and sore in my elbow and knee. I had a severe bruise on my left elbow, and another on my left knee, plus cuts and scrapes. The motorcycle had only suffered two broken turn signals. Other than that, not a scratch.

Each day, I spent some time with Elizabeth, some time with Conny, and some time tinkering with my bike in the driveway. They lived in an apartment complex, with a pool in the central courtyard, and I took time to lay by the pool, and cool off with a few dips and some laps. Always, my niece kept me company, and we had fun splashing around together.

Steve spent one afternoon driving me to a couple of used parts stores, where I was able to find the broken turn signals and the 'brackets' or 'stays,' that attach them to the motorcycle. We got the lightbulbs I needed, and stuff for an oil change, spending thirty-eight dollars for that total repair, plus the oil change. Not too bad. Steve helped me replace my broken parts, and I changed my oil. The Pony was good to go.

Days blended into each other, with rum and Diet Pepsi, poolside sun, afternoon showers, shopping in stores, eating out, playing with Elizabeth, getting along with Conny . . . but, I was feeling stagnant in a short time.

It was very important for me to visit my niece, because I hope that some day, when she comes of age, she will decide for herself that she thinks 'Anty Dey' is pretty cool, and she'll want to know me better.

How can she possibly forget an aunt who rides across country on a motorcycle to see her?

*   *   *

One day, a package arrived in the mail for me from my buddy Betsy at home. She wrote:

> Hi Dee, It's always so good to hear from you. Hopefully this time you'll get this letter along with the package. It sounds like you're having a great time and boy, what a book you'll be able to write!
>
> Our State School is on the downside again. They're moving clients out very fast. There was a meeting with the Big Shots about the place closing and where people should go to look for jobs and not to wait because we might be out of a job, etc. People were asking questions but they weren't giving clear cut answers. I got so frustrated that I walked out of the meeting.

Hey! I know! Let's trade places. *You* can cook, clean, do laundry, all the banking, grocery shopping, keep the cats happy, change the bed linen, take out the trash, take care of my son, go to work, and *I'll* learn how to drive your Pony and get the heck out of here! Oh well, it's just a thought.

I hope you have fun at your sister's, seeing her and your niece. Your plants are just thriving! Jonathan helps me water them. He still talks to you on his plastic play phone, then he has me talk to you.

I wonder how your roommate Barbie Doll is doing? Actually, who cares? (Just kidding) It is so hot and humid here. I hope the weather will be good for you in the coming weeks.

Well, until the next phone message . . . Love, Betsy

Another girlfriend of mine, Carol, wrote some cards and letters. She rides, too. Her letters were lengthy and personal, but, here are some parts worth sharing.

Greetings! Hey fox . . . I know I haven't written much but I know you're not bored . . . Guess what? I bought a jade/smoky gray Sportster 1200. It's a beauty, easier to ride than the Ninja, more steering range, I can touch the ground and my wrists don't hurt. Life is great.

Well, where the heck are you? I see you on top of some plateau in the middle of the Grand Canyon with your hiking boots on, tent pitched, Pony grazing, wearing a great tan on your bod. Am I close?

Scoop any hunky cowboys? I hope you don't take it personal if a lot of us lazy, obsessed motorcycle foxes don't write much. We're still thinking of you and our blessings are keeping the sun on your trail. But, if we're not riding, we're watching the rain and thinking of riding, and that's a busy schedule . . . I really like riding the new bike. It felt goofy at first, but it feels good now. It's like riding a thunderstorm. Very loud. Low profile mufflers . . . I've been on a few rides with other Harleys and it was fun.

I'm still working out daily . . . Here is a pretty cool shot of me and my bike, a little blurry, but—I look good. ha ha ha. I hope you're taking lots of photos.

If you hit the Smokies, TN, head for Deal's Gap if you can. Not to be missed. 318 curves in 11 miles. Yes that's a challenge! If you come back along the coast from there you won't be sorry. Kitty Hawk and Nag's Head are gorgeous beaches.

As a loyal supporter to you, I figured I should send at least one long handwritten letter. You must be having a great time. I miss you.

Enjoy yourself. Call me if you get real homesick. I suppose you are visiting some family out there , too. Come home when you're ready. The big, blue marble will always be out there to explore. Come home when you are ready, not just when the calendar says so. Your buddy, love and hugs, Carol

Another note I received which made me feel good:

Dee, Howdy. I just wanted to tell you we had a great time when you stayed at our house. Maybe if you come again we could take the horses to the park and ride. The girls at work told me that we look like sisters. Dan agreed. When you get home and settled, could you send me a better copy of that newspaper article you were in? I'll send you copies of the photos I took while you were here. Take care, Kim Gabriele Shea, Dan, Nicki and Rachel from Ohio

It was absolutely wonderful to get all that mail at the same time. I read, then reread each letter, feeling re-connected with some of those I had left behind.

*   *   *

During my lazy stay at Conny's, I recovered from my latest accident. My bruises were starting to change color, and the scrapes I'd incurred were healing. I finished reading *A Walk West,* caught up on some letter writing, phone calls and general business. I planned to depart on Friday. The details of this week were sketchy and will mostly go unrecorded, due to the nature of my stay. So much of our reunion was of an intense and personal nature, and I want to keep it that way. As my older sister, Geri, used to say, "There's a thin line between love and hate, and you're walking on it." That was the way I sensed Conny now felt towards me, but I will not forsake her. No matter what, she's my kid sister, my flesh and blood, and I will always love her.

miles for 5 days: 28

You gain strength . . . and confidence by every experience
where you really stop to look fear in the face.
—Eleanor Roosevelt

CHAPTER 24

YUMA
August 25–26 Days 70–71

*I*t was good to visit my sister, and it was good to be
going.

Today was a no leathers day. I was headed across the searing
desert, in August. My day of travel would take me into Yuma,
exactly at the California/Arizona border. I would pass beside
Saguaro National Monument and through the Papago Indian
reservation. This trusty water-cooled Honda, would carry me safely
through Covered Walls, and Why, two towns with curious names at
the bottom of your Arizona map. After passing an edge of Organ
Pipe Cactus National Monument, the lesser road then curved north
to intersect with the likes of I-8 and I-10.

The prospect excited me. Stir-craziness was raising havoc inside
my being, and the hot desert roads were calling to me. "Come and
see what beauteous bounty we have for you, Crazy Little Wild
Child." The urge was strong.

Just west of the south side of Tucson, I entered the whimsical
world of the Saguaro (Suh-wah-ro) National Monument, starring
spiny, statuesque, tall, columnar sentries standing poised among the
vast desert flora, like so many cartoon men, with arms akimbo.
Some appeared ready to quick-draw a gun in a moments notice,
others appeared to wave gaily in welcome, as I tooled along, in no
particular hurry to leave this environment. I was a lone rangeress,
riding my sassy pony through a western movie set, with this make
believe backdrop, setting the scene.

The day promised to be a scorcher, and I wore my bikini
underneath my jeans, and jacket. At the end of my day's ride, there
was a man made reservoir, and I planned accordingly.

Each hour was hotter than the last, and I was aware of the danger of dehydration, or heat exhaustion, but didn't seem to notice. I did not heed advice to ride in the cooler hours of evening, because I could not bear to miss out on the sights that this very minute I was engaged with. The heat was a menace, but for me, a miracle. It seemed to transform into energy, rather than sap it. I lavished in it, and like a bit of mercury, slithered along the heat waves, the motorcycle sounding as smooth and untroubled as ever.

Blue-gray mountains shimmered through a haze in the distance, and over the expanse of harsh land, sage lay in wait, dry and brown. Hedge hog, ocotillo, and stag horn cacti grew sporadically, punctuated by the agave, and saguaro, and the cholla specimens. Overhead wispy hints of clouds streaked the pale blue atmospheric ceiling.

As far as I was concerned, this day could go on forever, except, I needed an occasional town, for to gas up, soak down, and replenish my fluids. The stops were far apart, and I easily drank two quarts of water, at each one, but never needed a toilet.

Somewhere, in this forlorn part of our nation, there is an Army proving ground, and smack dab in the middle of this restricted area, is the Squaw Lake Campground and Recreation Area. When I reached Yuma, I'd had just about enough of the heat. It was finally getting to me, around three in the afternoon, at one-hundred and three degrees. I filled up my water bottle, pulled out my directions to camp, and studied them, then wasting no time, followed a strange road through a gate, towards a most unusual evening.

The road took me further from civilization, past what appeared to be barracks or stations, and signs everywhere warned not to leave the main road. At each fork, I would have to refer again to directions which once seemed so clear, but now only confused me. I saw camouflaged vehicles, and a few soldiers marching. I was somewhat spooked. Was I trespassing? How could that be when my CampBook said this is a public rec. area?

Am I mistaken? Will military police arrest me? If so, will I be able to convince them, I'm just Me, I'm no spy?

Signs made it clear there were no firearms permitted, under severe penalty. There was no indication whatsoever that there was such a place as Squaw Lake.

Still, the desire to press on, kept me moving forward, and then Voila!, a blue sign with the little white camper on it pointed the way.

I followed a ramp onto a raised parking lot of tar, and paused for a look around. A blue sparkling gem glistened before me, surrounded by an oasis of lush decorative grasses, which grew thick on the banks. A peninsula jutted into the cool reservoir, in its center was a cement brick bathhouse, and along the edge there were a number of campsites, a few bushy trees, and a boat launch or two.

The ground level was below the level of the ample parking area, and a faint dirt road encircled the campsites down below. I sat atop my machine, directly in front of a sign that had a dirt bike symbol, with a red circle and slash over it. Below the dirt bike was a four-wheeler, and below that . . . I didn't see.

Kind of on purpose.

My vehicle easily slipped beyond the curbing sections, and I flawlessly drove down the embankment, and began my circuitous route around the area, seeking my place for the night, taking notice of only two other occupied sites. As usual, I gravitated to a position away from the others, and then I went to pay my camp fee at the self-pay station.

There was a site with a thick, bushy tree, a narrow entry to the water, and I was satisfied. Carefully I parked my bike strategically, so as to not raise any attention to it. Sort of behind the tree, if someone were looking down from the nearest part of the parking lot. Immediately, I stripped down to my bikini and ran into the water, sinking in up to my shoulders allowing its soothing wet relief.

This is undoubtedly the hottest day of my trip, so far.

I dunked my head under, then as I wiped the water from my face, I realized I was wearing my watch. Oops.

Dripping wet, I quickly set up my tent. Then for a couple of hours I alternated between sitting in shallow water, up to my chin, and watching the sunfish come to check me out and tap at my legs with their guppy lips, or reading *Blue Highways,* by William Least Heat Moon.

Engrossed in the first few pages, I was startled by a shadow which fell over me.

The imposing figure of a uniformed man, clipboard in hand, stared down at me. Self-consciously, I sat up and draped my sarong over my hips, and wished that it was large enough to cover my whole body, such was the way I felt his shaded eyes skimming over my flushed, moist skin.

Sternly he stated, "This is a five hundred dollar fine, right here." He glanced toward my half loaded two-wheeler.

Instantly on my feet, I blurted, "What?"

He crossed his meaty arms, "Can't you read signs? It is posted, no motorcycles allowed. It's pretty easy. We even have pictures on the signs," he said sarcastically.

I hemmed and hawed, pointing out that it couldn't possibly mean street legal motorcycles. "Isn't that discrimination?"

"Look, lady, you can't park your motorcycle down here. There is a five hundred dollar fine which will be enforced." He pulled a pen out.

Half a Grand, for my arrogance. I had purposefully disregarded that sign, for my own convenience. I thought, no one here will see it, except maybe a camper, and why would he care? For all the rules I meticulously obey, whether I think they're right or wrong, I am damned for this one act of rebellion.

Son of a Bee. *That is so much money.*

"But," I tilted my head coyly, and took one tiny step closer, "if I move it now, nobody has to even know about it. You'll give me a moment to put some clothes and boots on, so I can move it, right?"

"Oh. I'm not *authorized* to ticket you. The Park Ranger could come along, and he's the one. He'll write you up in a heartbeat. I'm just coming to *warn* you."

I see, Mister Nice Guy, saviour, hero, chap. Aloud, I muttered, "Gee, thanks." Thanks for the way you went about it.

He hung around as I started to unfasten my baggage, annoyed. Here I'd envisioned barely unpacking at all, and now, not only do I have to unpack everything, but I also have to leave my motorcycle overnight, way too far away for my liking. Then, in the morning, I'm going to need to make a million trips back and forth with my arms full. What an aggravation. Never before have I had to park my motorcycle away from my tent.

I spun to face him, "Would you mind giving me a bit of privacy while I go about my business? It'll take me a while to get dressed so I can ride this thing out of here. I can't do it in a bikini." (Or won't, was more like it.)

Ranger Rod smugly strolled away, whistling sweetly as he went. I resisted the urge to throw something at him.

In ten minutes, I had parked the bike all by itself in the empty parking lot. (Cars were allowed on the campground loop.) There, I discovered that Ranger Rod and the Campground Host are one and the same. He approached me and chewed my ear off, asking me nosy questions, which I answered indirectly. He extended a friendly persona but, one step at a time I backed away. Again and again, I told him I had some writing to catch up on, and wanted to do some reading before it got dark, but he went on and on about I don't know what.

"Okay, I'm gonna let you go, I just want to ask you one more thing," he persisted. "All by yourself . . . don't you get kind of lonesome? You know, a young woman like you, you must get lonely now and then. You shouldn't be by yourself." He was past curious, and now he was prying and pressing me. I had to be careful how I answered.

"No. Everywhere I go, people are curious and befriend me. Look, even you. You came by to enforce a rule, and here we are, an hour later, and I'm still trying to get back to my campsite, so I can be by myself. I enjoy the solitude." I looked at the sun, as it sat low in a sky tinged with soft, glowing colors. "I really need to get back to my site before it gets dark. Thanks for saving me from getting a fine."

Yeah, right.

I scribbled a few notes, marked my maps, and wrote out a post card, as the sunset lingered. Three ducks swam in and out of my private little pool between the reeds. One was a dark colored wild duck, another was a large domestic breed, and the third looked like a mixture of the two. I had nothing to offer them, but they came back periodically, just to make sure.

Before dark, I washed myself under the outside shower, soaping up, and shampooing with my leopard print bikini on. It was still so hot, I didn't want to wear any more than that.

I had noticed tiny hoofprints all over the dirt road, and in the sand at my site. I wondered if a child often came here with her family to ride her pony, but, as I was walking back to my campsite, I heard something hiding in a hedge of bushes. When I investigated, I saw three wild burros, playing hide and seek with me.

The three burros were very small, and had dark brown coats, and eyes ringed with white. The three stuck close together, and when one stopped, the other two would bumble into him, making asses out of each other. They entertained me with their shy curiosity, until, finally they got bored, and went galloping off towards the mainland, and the military testing area.

Back on my cool, damp towel, I combed my hair, and then was captivated by a family of Gambrel quail. There was a mother quail, and as she strutted on her chosen path, her little crown danced with each step. Behind her, a string of five babies followed in single file, much like the Partridge Family.

The quail where I live do not sport fancy Miss America crowns, and I was delighted at seeing this one. She was taking her family for a walk, and teaching them how to hunt for food. She would pause, and peck at the ground, then the little chicks would mimic her. She knew that at each little pile of burro droppings, which resembled walnuts, there would be a feast of bugs, and this she demonstrated several times, always moving along after the first three joined her. They would then run along after her, the last two would take a swipe or two as they passed the pile-o-poop, and then they'd cheep-cheep-cheep and run helter-skelter after the leaders.

As I watched, Number 1 and 2 seemed to catch on as to where to find a batch of bugs, and they veered away from their mother, making a beeline for a fresh pile that they'd spied. Number 3, 4 and 5 followed them. Number 1 and 2 saw that Mommy was not too close by, and they skeedaddled after her, but the last three became engrossed by their banquet.

Suddenly Mommy noticed that her entourage had shrunk, and she began to run about, back and forth, piping out a frantic call, hysterically. I was caught up in this simple drama, as she called and searched for her stupid little babies, who I could still see, but she could not. They were running towards her cries, then one or another would turn back for just one more bug to chomp. Once one turned back, they all would. Their instinct to stick together was strong.

Helpless, I could only watch, until the little guys tumbled over a ridge, and spotted their frenzied mother. They peeped and she continued screaming until they all came together, and then, matter-of-factly, they fell into formation, in the same ranking order as before, or so I imagined.

Charmed, I watched them file out of sight.

Night fell. Still, it was way too hot. Wicked hot.

Much as I would have liked to sleep under the stars, I felt nervous so close to all the marsh grass. There would be snakes, and other creepy crawly things. Plus, it was so hot, I wanted nothing more than my bikini on, and felt too vulnerable to everything in general and nothing in particular to lay down and sleep outdoors, in that state of near nakedness. My snoopy sheet acted as my mattress inside my tent, muggy and breezeless. I doused myself with bug spray, and lay down to sleep, finding that my damp towel draped over me served to keep me a bit cooler.

So hot, I had trouble falling asleep. Instead, I practiced mental relaxation. The animals that had entertained me since my arrival, had me filled with peace. Friendly sunfish, three ducks, three wild burros, and the quail family. Here, the desert teamed with life.

Finally, I slipped into the realm of dreams and mental restoration.

*   *   *

In my dreams, I heard a man's voice, vaguely.

"Motorcycle Girl," repeated a bit louder.

I stirred. I think I'm dreaming.

"Motorcycle Girl!" A bit clearer this time, coming closer. My tent doorway comes into focus. I am not dreaming. I cannot see him, but I know he is out there.

I sit up, peering into the darkness. "Huh?"

I can't see anyone. "Yeah? What?"

My eyes adjust to the night darkness, and against the night sky I can make out a silhouette, way over by the bathhouse. The night air was so still that his spoken voice seemed to come from much closer.

"You awake?" he asked.

"No—I'm sleeping," I blurted. I *was* sleeping.

Silence.

In a quiet gentle tone, I heard words that concerned me, "You want some company?"

"NO!" I shot back. "Who is that, anyway? Who are you?"

"Someone you were talking to today," came the vaporous reply.

Some one I spoke with today? The family camping closest to me didn't even speak English, and I never met the other people camped on the other side of the peninsula. I knew it was the Campground Host, I just wanted him to say it. Does he think I don't know that it's him?

My heart began pounding. The nearest people are within shouting distance, but they don't even understand English.

He must be crazy. Do I want some company? It's the middle of the night! Way to go, Buster.

But the problem was, I felt threatened. For the first (and only) time during this entire journey, I reached for my weapon. For real.

Above the thumping of my heart, I listened for footsteps, but heard nothing. I laid down, with pepper mace securely gripped against my sweating sternum.

Here's my predicament. This man is the Campground Host. This is the person that is supposed to protect me. I am camped in the middle of a military place, where they drop bombs, and test battle tanks. I suspect that the only people who even know about this place and use it, are the soldiers and their families. That idiot standing out there made it a point to leer at me appreciatively, thinking it was a compliment or something. He also can turn in my license plate number, because he had found me violating the "law" when I had parked my motorcycle at my campsite.

If he decides he wants me, he could easily overpower me. He could rape me, and maybe no amount of screaming would help me, because people "don't want to get involved." Then, when I make a claim, it's his word against mine.

My mind was racing. I felt the edge of paranoia. A minute or two passed.

"Nice night out." The comment came from the same place.

My reaction was instant.

"GO AWAY!" I commanded.

"Oh," he says. "Okay."

I stayed on my back, with my head near the open tent door, my hands still clutched around my weapon. One step at a time, I listened as his feet crunched over the terrain, and faded away.

Fear lie in my throat like a bitter lump. This girl, usually so sure of herself, was afraid.

What if he comes back later? What if I fall asleep like this, and blast myself in the face with my own weapon because I hear a noise and it startles me. What if I just let the big, fat, sweaty guy maul me, instead of fighting him off and getting beaten? Could it be that bad? The thought frightened and repulsed me.

This is the sort of thing that all my well meaning friends and associates worry about. I understand the truth in their concern. This is not a good scene, even if it seems to be over.

My brain continued on its horrific course of imaginings, and I felt terribly vulnerable.

Since I could not possibly sleep, I made an effort to change my thought patterns. The man had walked away, after I firmly ordered him to do so. I hadn't lost my cool. I am not a helpless waif. I am strong, and trained in self-defense. I have pepper mace, and I will use it. Tomorrow will come, and I will leave this whole memory behind, as is.

Maybe I'll even realize that I was overeacting.

NOT.

It's the middle of the night for crying out loud! What time is it anyway, I wondered. I groped for my watch, and reached into the tent side pocket for my trusty mini mag light, and discovered my watch had stopped. It read 10:45, so it had to be even later than that now. Maybe even hours later. I set my watch down, hoping that it would dry out after its little swim.

Such a day. I need to get rested, for tomorrow I must conquer the desert, again. With false security, I gradually slipped into never-never land.

Miles: 347

My tent door was open. There were demons in the dark night, skulking around, relishing the scorching and hellish night temperature. A scratchy finger slithered into the depths of my tent, and traced a path across the tops of my toes.

My foot flinched with such a violent lurch that I awoke with a start, sucking in a breath of hot desert air. There was silence and a stillness all around me as the night suffered, and I went back to sleep. My arms rested overhead, near the tent doorway.

Deep in dreamland, I was yanked back to this purgatory because I felt a scratchy weight creep across my fingers and palm of one hand. Instinctively, my wrist flicked and my elbow jerked forward, and I flung something across the tent before I could stop myself.

This time, I snapped awake enough to realize that there was a substantial sized bug inside my tent, and that is what had crawled over my foot, then into my hand just now. It could have been a scorpion, I didn't know.

Suddenly, I was wide awake, and on my knees, horrified. Whatever it was, I wanted it out of my tent! I shivered at the thought of how it had crawled on my skin, and scared me. I was mortified that I had flung it all the way into my tent, instead of outside. I had settled in to my tent upside down on this night, with my head near the opening to catch the slightest stirring of stifling breeze. I'd lost my sense of direction and tossed the perpetrator against the back wall of my tent, instead of outdoors.

I could hear the thing as it scuttled across a clear space on the floor of my tent. My eyes tried to focus, but it was too dark. Heart a-pounding, I reached into my tent pocket for the flashlight that I always kept there. Son of a Bee! It wasn't there. I didn't put it away after I looked at my watch earlier.

It would be on the floor, or on top of my baggage, or nestled into my pile of leathers. I would have to feel around for it. Gingerly, I touched here and there, searching for it. The monster clattered across the top of my tankbag, announcing its path over my plastic mapcase, then disappeared into the crevices and mountains where my flashlight could be hiding, too.

My hands were afraid to look. I needed my flashlight, but in feeling around for it, I might encounter whatever it was that had me in a fright. I froze, to listen for the sound of its movement again. My ears would do the looking, now.

I pulled a map book out of my tankbag, and waited, willing my eye pupils to dilate even more. My heart beat echoed through me, and I continued to tremble, amazed at my fear.

Bugs are okay. They're pretty fascinating. I enjoy observing them, marveling at their ugliness, or colors, mini armours, the oddness of their creation. But, I like to be the one in charge. I *do not* like them crawling on me unexpectedly. I would not be able to relax until that thing was gone. I would never, *ever* leave my tent door completely open again, either.

Finally, whatever it was, crept off of materials that softened its hook-like foot-beats, and I was able to zone in to its location. A faint dark blur appeared against the grayness of my tent bottom, near the door opening, and I desperately scooped at it, and threw the map and the critter out the door, yanking at the doorway zipper in a near panic.

I sat back on my heels, sweat running in cool riverlets over my bikini clad body. My heart beat quieted and slowed, the pressure in my chest and head cleared, then I laughed out loud for the sheer absurdity of it all.

Twice in the same night, I was filled with fear. Two kinds of fear, one that stemmed from threatened security, the other from distaste. After seventy days of practically no fear, I learned that I am not immune.

Also, that I am as strong and level headed as I would like to be.

My breath and my body heat seemed unable to escape through the screen mesh of my tent door, but, there was no way I was going to relive that creepy experience. Since I knew that the bug or scorpion was outside, I felt around and retrieved my flashlight, thinking it so ironic that the one time I didn't put it away, I needed it most.

Exhausted, I stretched out once again, pulling my towel across my bare skin, wishing I could untie my bikini strings and sleep completely naked, but knowing that I couldn't. This desert oasis proved to be a testing ground for more than those in the military service. I congratulated myself for passing.

*   *   *

In the morning I got all packed and ready to go. I trotted over to the outside shower with my helmet and doused myself thoroughly, filling my helmet up and dumping it over myself just before pulling on my jacket, ready to depart.

As I rode across the ample, but empty parking lot, I saw the Campground Host's door swing open, and his rotund figure tumbled out.

I feigned bright friendliness, and waved gaily in his direction. Stupid fool, I thought. Do you sincerely think that I didn't realize that was you during the night?

He held up his hand, in a signal for me to halt.

I did no such thing.

I sped west on I-8, towards Calexico, a town just north of a city called Mexicali. The Mexican/California border separated the two. Rather than stop, I banged a right, and headed north on a lesser road, Rte. 86, which ran me between the Salton Sea on my right, and the Anza-Borrego Desert. My destination was the Joshua Tree Monument where I hoped to find an available campsite, but I had to take a zig-zag course to get there.

Somewhere along the line, I stopped to get gas and make a phone call. There was an air conditioned convenience store, and a ruddy faced police officer with a protuding gut stood before the counter flirting with the young girl working there. His attention turned towards me when I walked in, though. I had to wash my helmet shield, and had elected to change into shorts and ride for an hour or so like that, so I could catch some sun.

The cop puffed out his chest and boomed, "Whattaya riding?"

Not caring for his macho attitude, I answered, "A motorcycle."

He rolled his eyes, and replied, "I know that. What kind?"

"See for yourself," I quipped, then changed my mind, lest he follow me out and bother me through-out my breakfast. "No wait!" I stopped. "It's a Honda Interceptor."

"You should be riding a Harley," he stated.

"Why is that?" I spun around at the door.

"Well, they're the best. You should be on a Harley. You look like a Harley girl."

"Oh, brother," I sneered. "Who are you to say what I should be riding? You don't even know me."

I walked out of the store, and left him to brag about the virtues of Harley-Davidson to his virgin admirer, while I sat on the sidewalk and looked over at the machine which had successfully taken me some twelve thousand miles in the last ten weeks, with nary a complaint.

People like that bug me. He doesn't even know what he's talking about, or who he's talking to, but he's certain that he's right.

I found myself cruising along some agricultural farms. Great croplands of neat and uniform trees, lush with green growth plaited the earth in a pattern which seemed to move as I drove by. In the distance, a disturbing haze muted the colors of the mountain range.

A line of palm trees, date trees actually, formed a decorative border along the farthest edge of the crops. I wished I knew exactly what it was being raised here. Feeling so much a foreigner, I drank in the fragrance, and captured the visual scape for my mind's eye to keep.

Suddenly, my right thigh felt as though a searing pipe had been thrust into it. I had driven into a bee, and it got stuck in between my bike and me. It had bitten me with such a vengeance, that there was a chunk of skin torn from that delicate area, the size of a pencil eraser. Pain coursed through me causing a waves of nausea which I stifled. I hoped I hadn't suddenly become allergic to bee stings.

Because I am normally covered by a layer of leather, I am usually protected from the assault of bees that I've driven into. I don't even notice them. I feel a thump, and wonder, what was that? But today, my choice to go ride in shorts served as a simple lesson.

My nausea passed, and with relief I knew I was not in danger of anaphalactic shock. I would live. I'd be making it to see the Joshua Trees.

Through that valley of fruit trees, I hit a lot more bees, and had sticky yellow pollen smeared all over my helmet. After a couple of hundred miles I was weary. I stopped to refuel again, and washed my helmet, drank a lot of water and doused myself with a hose that I found around the back.

* * *

Within the Joshua Tree Monument are almost ten different campgrounds to choose from. My resources indicated that none of them had showers or drinking water. The camping fee? Free.

I selected White Tank, because it only had fifteen sites, which meant I had a better chance of enjoying my solitude.

After paying a three dollar entrance fee to the monument, I collected my map and other informational pamphlets, and excitedly drove into the Colorado Desert in California. Although there are some Joshua Trees in Arizona, there are very few. This is the place where they will flourish and survive, protected by the monument and existing in the harsh environment.

Slowly, I cruised through the desert region, aware of the drastic change in scenery from just two hours earlier. The life force here is rugged, tolerant and patient. In the lower desert portion of the park, the creosote bush rules, and spidery ocotillo stands add an interesting effect, and the suspicious jumping cholla cactus are also predominant vegetative species.

Besides the cactus, stunning displays of geological displays decorated the vast, textured surface. Granite monoliths, faces exposed to passing visitors and the brutal sun, lay scattered in random piles, as big as apartment complexes. Twisted rock, and caves, rocks that looked like pebbles, but were as big as cars created a scene like a giant child's sandbox, with stone structures started, half tumbled, then deserted.

The desert changed and the unruly Joshua Tree dominated the land. I would do further exploring after I got settled.

When I came to White Tank, a small red car was parked, and a girl in the driver's seat dangled some crackers out the window. She and her passengers gestured wildly for me to get out of the way. I looked in the direction of their gaze, and saw the tail of a mangy dog disappearing in between some rocks.

In faltering English, she rudely exclaimed, "You stupid—you scared him away! Coyote."

Oh! That's what it was. I didn't even think!

"Coyote! You're not supposed to feed them anyway," I replied, just as sharply. I held up my official map and guide, rapping at it emphatically with my other hand. "You don't feed *wild animals*. It's against the law!" Just in case they didn't understand, I added, "Bad. Bad."

She shot an expression, the guys and girl with her laughed, and they backed out and left me there.

Having seen the coyote, I turned and looked at the immediate area. Across the road, there was a porta-potty, and I was near the site that the coyote had crossed through, before he disappeared from sight.

That was my omen. I was to set up camp right here.

I had to ride eleven miles to the city called Twentynine Palms. There I gassed up again, and purchased a mango, two "foot long" sausage dogs in buns, and two strawberry wine coolers for dinner. I was buying supper from a gas station, again. The meal was four dollars. It's hard to keep it under ten dollars a day for food, but, with sacrifices, it was possible. I raced back to my campsite, mouth watering for my spicy dogs.

My campsite was a work of art. There were fantastic boulders as big as buildings in a particular arrangement which looked like a group of five whales arising from the surface, nose first. In between my imagined herd of whales, I found a delightful little clearing which provided shade, and a cooler temperature.

Ceremoniously, I settled down with my back against one of the giants, and arranged a single wine cooler, and my mango within reach, while I prepared my dogs with extra condiments and onions. I bit into the first dog, and caught a glimpse of tawny fur, as it flitted past an opening in between two 'whales.'

My camera's in my tankbag. I've got to go get it in case he comes back. Maybe I can get a picture! I scrambled between two boulders, and trotted to my bike, with hot dog in hand. Ten seconds is the most I took, and my remaining dog and paper plate was all *he* took.

That mangy coyote *stole my supper!* I couldn't believe it! In ten seconds, that mutt grabbed my spicy dog with onions and mustard and relish, and took off with it, paper plate and all. In my hand, I held half of my first dog. Thank goodness I had bought two. I took a bite, then went out of my rock garden the back way, like the coyote must have done. I wasn't going to leave my paper plate lying around, but, I think he ate that too, because it was nowhere in the vicinity.

He was a delicate thief, and didn't knock my wine cooler over, nor did he steal my mango. I sat down amused, and enjoyed the remainder of my supper. The coyote returned, and I peered at him from between the rocks, knowing full well that he knew exactly where I was. Slowly I raised my camera for a photo of my unsolicited companion.

In my travels, I had noticed four dead coyotes on the roadsides. I've wanted to see some in real life. What a comedy it was, that the *first* live coyote in the wild that I ever encountered *stole my supper* within ten seconds! Little creep. I loved it.

Miles: 260

. . . Life no longer shuffles past me, the pine needles of each
moment still blow from tree to tree, but now I call their names,
gathering only those I desire to my breast . . .

—Laura Stamps

CHAPTER 25

BAKERSFIELD
August 27–29   Days 72–74

*I*n the morning, I sat at the picnic table as the morning sun yawned and stretched its rays over the Joshua Tree Monument. Shadows angled sharply over the landscape, and the day dawned, still and stark.

I rode through the Mojave (say, mo-hahvee) Desert, during the first part of the day, and then got onto Rte. 58, which ran me fast and furiously towards the major city of Bakersfield, California.

Annis Cassells had written directions to her house for me, when we were at the Ride-In. I knew it would be okay for me to simply arrive and knock on the door, but so many weeks had passed.

Expectantly, I parked in her driveway, dismounted, and rang the doorbell.

The door swung open, and a young teenaged girl appraised me from the inside. She was pale, gangly, and wore wire rimmed glasses. "Can I help you?" she asked.

Confused to see a young white girl answering the door, where I expected to see an older black woman, I stammered, "Is Annis here?"

"Annis?" the girl repeated. "She doesn't live here any more."

I visibly drooped, and turned away, discouraged. What could have happened since the Ride-In, that she's moved away already?

"Wait a minute!" the girl called. "Let me get my foster mother. She's out back by the pool. She's Annis' friend, maybe she can tell you what to do."

I paced back and forth between my motorcycle and the front steps. What kind of reception can I expect to get here? Here I am, a stranger from clear across the country, and I'm riding a motorcycle!

Within the house, I heard voices and footsteps coming my way. The door was thrown open wide, and there I was, face to face with Annis' friend, Sharon, who had been at the Ride-In, in Washington. I had met her briefly when I had breakfast in her room before a small group of WOW gals went off riding to Mt. St. Helens.

Sharon flung her arms around me, and cried, "What a pleasant surprise! What are you doing here? Are you staying?"

I stepped back, still confused. "How? What? Wait a minute. Annis gave me the directions to get here. Where is she? What are you doing here? Of course, I'm glad it's you, I thought I just showed up on some stranger's doorstep."

"Annis had to move out since the Ride-In, but this is my home, and I hope you can stay." Her smile was genuine, and light brown curls bobbed around her face as she peeked over my shoulder at my machine. "Come on. Let me open the gate, and you can bring your bike around."

Two mini-schnauzers yapped away from behind her heels. "Sh-sh-sh. Margaret! Edward! Be quiet, will you? . . . I hope you don't mind the dogs."

"No. I love animals."

Sharon's best friend, Linda, was visiting at the moment, and had been at the Ride-In, too, so it was fun catching up. They called Annis to tell her I was in town, and she planned to come over to see me the next day.

"So, how's it going? Are you having a good time?" they asked.

"This is undoubtedly the best time of my life," I told them.

"Have you had any trouble? Has your bike been running good? What do you do about maintenance? Do you take care of it yourself?"

I described my accidents, the dependability of my Honda, and how I do most of the maintenance, but have brought it into a shop periodically for professional service.

"How far have you gone?"

"Hm-m, about twelve-thousand miles, in a little over two months."

I answered one question after the next, enjoying all the motorcycle talk, and talk of roads and places I've been, they've been, we both have been. Finally, I tired of all the talk.

The hospitality I received was what I had come to expect from Women On Wheels, although this time I had my own room, and a private swimming pool in the back yard. The girls were planning to watch a rented movie that night, and after my shower and laundry were all taken care of, I actually looked forward to an evening curled up in an easy chair, watching a good movie.

Somebody made popcorn, and before long we were four women, engrossed in *A River Wild,* cheering Merle Streep on, during her strong performance as a courageous river guide on a raft, through a harrowing and suspenseful drama.

As soon as the movie was over, I brushed my teeth and went to bed. How lucky I am to be alive, and to have such good friends. How fortunate I am to have somehow dredged up the means to follow my dream. Where did I find the determination, the strength and courage, the stamina that have made all of this possible? Where did my faith come from? What sets me apart? Is there something wrong with me, that I should enjoy hardships and freedom more than comfort and security?

I bow my head and pray. Thank you, oh Great Spirit within me . . .

Miles: 261

My situation at this Women On Wheels home found me so comfortable and welcomed, that I didn't want to leave first thing in

the morning. I wanted to tarry, and enjoy small luxuries, such as playing with the dogs, using a telephone without standing attached to it by a short metal cord, getting a pickle out of a jar in the frij. I wanted to enjoy large luxuries, such as lounging in the built-in swimming pool, or reading my book out on the deck with a glass full of iced tea. Sharon went

Annis Cassells, Sharon Dormire and Linda Mapes, Women On Wheels members, pose with a friend's dog and Edward and Margaret, in Sharon's pool area, Bakersfield, California. Annis was my roommate at the WOW Ride-In. and Sharon later took me in, more than once.

to work for the day, giving me instructions to make myself at home.

At Sharon's dining room table, I thought of my father, and wrote him a letter. I told him how much I missed him, and that I was sorry if I caused him to worry. I was having an incredible experience, and America has me enchanted, her people amaze and welcome me with open arms. I described how much I had traveled, and how thankful I was that I was doing this, no matter what anyone had said to discourage me. I let him know how he could check up on me if he would only dial my telephone number at home, and he could leave me messages. Most of all, I told him how much I loved him, and gave him credit for raising me to be the person I've become. I then added the most important letter I'd sent all summer to my pile of postcards to go out later that day.

While looking at my map, I discovered how close to Las Vegas I was, and that's where my old friend, Thomas, lived. I picked up the phone, but reached his answering machine.

"Hey, Thomas! This is Dee—Diane. Sounds good to hear your voice. Listen, I'm at my friend's house in Bakersfield until tomorrow. Oh, today's Monday. So, anyway, try and call me if you get this message so we can set something up. Are you ready for a vacation? I'm here, waiting for you to keep your promise. OK, before we get cut off, here's the number . . . "

Outdoors, there was a private deck, and sparkling swimming pool. I poured my iced tea, changed into my leopard bikini, grabbed a towel from the linen closet and headed out to the pool with my sunscreen and book. After slicing through the water for fifteen minutes, I slipped onto a raft and floated around the pool for a few hours while reading, or napping.

I used Sharon's toiletries to fill all of my little containers of lotion and shampoo, etc. She had told me to help myself. Another small gesture, greatly appreciated.

Finally, she got home from work, and in a half hour Annis showed up on her Gold Wing. We squeezed each other happily, and then I was hustled out. Sharon came around front with her flashy cruiser, and Kelly pulled on a leather jacket which fit her as if she were a scarecrow. We were off for a ride to Lake Isabella.

Sharon moved right out, once we left the confines of the city. I followed her, and Annis rode tail, with Kelly as her passenger. As I boogied after Sharon, I wondered why she was driving so fast. Then

I wondered, how come she doesn't get pulled over? I used to like to drive fast, but, I constantly worry about getting pulled over by the police. We sped along until we entered yellow mountains, and began our curvaceous trek along a road loaded with switchbacks. I slowed to my own pace, slightly embarrassed, but relieved that Annis was no longer right behind me, for she had dropped back, as well. Ironically, I am not *experienced* at driving fast, despite the motorcycle I ride.

Much like automobiles, certain models get more attention from police. Like, Corvettes or Camaros, sportbikes get clocked just for driving by, it seems. Because they are so capable of great speeds, the cops seem to pick on them more than the other kinds of bikes, like Sharon's cruiser, or Annis's Gold Wing. They can be going fifty in a forty mile zone, no one notices, but I can go forty-five in the same zone, and get pulled over and written up for speeding. As a result, I tend to adhere to posted speeds in urban areas, and whenever I drive "too fast," I feel stressed. But, sandwiched between their two unobtrusive mounts, I skimmed along, enjoying the challenging ride, while the late day sun turned the sky outrageous shades of red, orange, yellow and pink, before washing over a purple velvet empyrean, which darkened into night.

We stopped at a Mexican restaurant and trooped in with full leathers, causing lots of people to stare. Having a few other women with me dressed in such a manner, made me feel different than at other times when I am alone, and a stranger.

After a fiery dinner, when the bill came, I took my wallet out, with full intentions of paying the tab, with the money I'd saved by sleeping and eating at Sharon's.

"By the way, Annis," I said. "Thank you very much for inviting me to stay over Sharon's. I've been having a great time."

Annis and Sharon laughed, and Annis assured me, "Oh sure, anytime you want, you just come on down. Sharon's door will always be open. Just tell her it's fine with me!"

We all laughed about the way things worked out. I was thrilled that Sharon had accepted me into her home, even though it was Annis who had invited me. These gals were tops.

Even after arguing, they would not let me pay so much as the tip. Graciously, I thanked them.

"If you are ever in New England . . . you'll have to let me take care of you guys the same way. No argument!" I stated, then added, "For all that has been given to me by Women On Wheels all over the country, my only hope is that someday I have the privilege of returning these favors. I sometimes imagine that it will all happen at once—I'll come home from work and find Kim Shea, and Judy, and Maggie and Sally and James . . . all of you waiting in my driveway, looking for a place to lay your heads. Wouldn't that be a riot?"

Later on, I realized I hadn't had to spend a cent all day, making me feel like the richest girl on Earth.

Miles: 112

"Here, take our Golden Eagle pass. It lets you into National Parks and Memorials for free, just show it at the gate, get it punched, and you're all set," Sharon said.

"How did you get this?" I wondered, as I turned it over in my hands at the breakfast table. "You're not old enough, and I certainly can't pass for a senior citizen."

Sharon and Linda laughed and said, "I hope not!" Then Sharon jumped in to explain. "Anyone can get one. You don't have to be a senior citizen, and it costs, I don't know, thirty or forty dollars for a year. Because King's Canyon is about my favorite place in the whole, wide world, I get my money's worth, easily."

Linda, who had come over to have breakfast with us before work added, "I'm surprised you aren't using your own, Dee."

"I didn't know about it," I admitted. "Actually, I've seen it posted on the entrance signs, but never inquired about it. I just assumed it was something for senior citizens."

"Why?"

I shrugged. "Golden Eagles? Y'know, like golden ages? I just never asked, that's all. Gosh, I wish I'd learned of this about two months ago. Think of all the money I would've saved." I set the card down by my dish of cereal. After some consideration, I asked Sharon to take her pass back. "Why don't I just buy my own? Thanks, anyway."

Sharon wouldn't hear of it. "I'm serious, Dee. You take this with you now. You said you would come back here after you see your friend from Vegas. Just bring it back to me then, or if you change your mind, I trust you'll mail it to me." She put it back into my hand, and folded my fingers over it, with finality.

"Okay! I'll take it." I shook my head. "You guys are just too good to me. Thank you."

*   *   *

After breakfast, I set forth to ride the hundred or so miles to Sequoia National Park and King's Canyon. The Ash Mountain Entrance engaged me almost immediately with a winding road, with steep, sharp curves, and signs warning vehicles longer than twenty-two feet that they would be unable to make the tight turns along a major stretch of this road. That was an understatement. The drive led me through a series of hairpin turns, and climbed upwards at an impressive grade. The going was slow, slower still because I had to ride behind small cars that were laboriously creeping upwards, ever mindful of the drop on one side or the other, as we wound our way up to an elevation of over six thousand feet.

Sequoia is America's second oldest National Park, with the year 1990 considered to be its centennial year. Its most remarkable feature is the giant trees for which the park is named. I recalled my three days of riding amongst the Redwood groves along the Pacific Coast, and made comparisons between these staggering big trees.

My emotional state was now more settled than it had been then, considering my drive along the west coast had been only the second leg of my journey. By now, I was well traveled, and felt comfortable with the role of gypsy.

The General Sherman Tree is said to be the World's Largest Living Thing. It stands proud, ruler of the Giant Forest, within a cathedral like setting. Where the trunk meets the ground, its circumference is almost one hundred three feet around, and the cinnamon-colored bark encases a trunk that stands two hundred seventy feet tall, and weighs an estimated fourteen hundred tons! But, as magnificent as these facts are, more-so is the realization that the General is the mightiest of a forest *full* of trees, with statistics almost as astounding.

A short walk on a beaten path brought me to the toes of this Earthly god, believed to be around two and a half thousand years old, give or take a century.

Thankfully, John Muir, a man I have grown to admire increasingly with each passing week of my western travels, and residents of the San Joaquin Valley, had enough foresight and scruples to preserve this place. How do we ever get back the things we have destroyed? The Giant Forest is irreplaceable. I walked back to my little V-Four feeling humbled and awed.

The road from there was much less tenuous than it had been on the way in. Shucks. There is something about riding over the tightest of turns, while ascending or descending a steep mountainside. I followed the way through forest, and turned off to have a picnic at a designated area.

Picnic tables edged a busy parking lot, and I pulled in and stopped in a sunny area. Getting comfortable, I removed my leathers, and then set up my picnic lunch of fresh fruit and vegetables that Sharon had provided.

Nearby, a man in running shorts was stretching his hamstrings, looking as though he had just returned from a run. He came over to chat.

"Are you a dancer?" he asked. "You have great legs."

The guy was middle aged, I would guess, and long and lean as a runner should be.

I laughed, "No, I'm no dancer, but thanks. It's nice to hear a compliment like that now and then."

"I hope you don't take it the wrong way," he said, and I assured him that his comment had been welcomed. He continued to stretch, and drink water from a bottle, while I asked about his training.

"Isn't this awfully rugged terrain to be jogging on? It's steeply graded. You must be training for something."

He agreed, but told me he often runs in places such as this, because the beauty surrounding him elevates him above the pain.

I finished my orange, grapes, celery and carrot sticks, and several crackers, before washing my hands at the bubbler and refilling my water bottle. When I returned to my motorcycle and got into my protective gear, he noticed my license plate, and reacted.

"You're kidding! Did you ride this thing all the way?"

"And then some," I answered.

"You've got guts, that's all I can say," he remarked. "Have you ever been frightened? I mean, there are a lot of weirdos out there."

I retorted, "Listen Mister, you're out running around in National Parks all by yourself. Do you feel vulnerable? Or do you wonder why more people don't do it, too? I mean, what if a wild animal gets you?" I mocked, "and you've already tired yourself out? You could get killed."

"That's not likely to happen," he answered. "Okay, okay, I get it. You probably hear that all the time, don't you? I bet you've got things all under control, though."

"Well, I try."

"Good, keep it up. Be safe. I guess I've got to let you go now." He watched as I positioned myself between my tankbag and the load of luggage piled up behind me. "So, where can I get me a girl like you? Strong, nice looking, brave, self-assured . . . "

I laughed again. "Catch me if you can!"

*   *   *

As soon as I emerged out of the forest, the landscape changed dramatically. All that had been spectacular, receded in my rear view mirror, and became memory. I can't get over the haze. Air pollution. A dirty sort of mist hovered over the surface of Earth, like a forgotten, dismal cloud. It occurred to me that scenes I'd seen on TV, included this smog, but I'd always thought that it was the kind of mountain mist that appears around mountains in the distance. Here, the backdrop was way too close. The TV cameras capture this, but our personal experiences filter the truth.

California is suffucating in it's own vapor.

Once I hit Fresno, I headed northeast on state 41, for another hundred miles. I got into Yosemite, for free, thanks to Sharon's Golden Eagle Pass, and then I got a camspsite as the daylight slipped away. There was a self-pay registration station, and I paid ten dollars to set up camp for the night.

Miles: 285

When I first open my eyes upon the morning meadows and look out upon the beautiful world, I thank God I'm alive.
—Ralph Waldo Emerson

CHAPTER 26

YOSEMITE
August 30 through September 1   Days 75–77

*Y*osemite. The very word evokes a memory of such awe and grandiosity, that I should fail to describe it. Yosemite. The Incomparable Valley.

Everything is huge, larger than life. The trees stab at the sky like venerable stilettos. Granite rocks lie in wait, more solid and unyielding than any fortress. The lakes are pristine. At any moment, one could expect to come across a squirrel as large as a cocker spaniel, and not be surprised. I felt like I had somehow managed to find my way into Gulliver's Travels.

I wasn't so happy with the campground, except for its convenience. Too many feet had trampled the earth into a dusty, dirty surface. The place was overused, beaten. I would rate it quite low on the scale of all the places I had camped over the course of the summer, ah—but this was Yosemite. I was within minutes of majestic scenery and bliss. So, although my campsite was not the private, lush kind of setting I've come to adore, I was willing to pay the ten bucks a night, and to stay here for three nights, in order to stop and smell the roses at this famous vacation destination.

After breakfast, I left Wawona for a day of exploring. In mere seconds, I was cruising along a curvaceous drive, which jetted through deep forest. Just as I began to get into the ride, I came upon an orange traffic sign, warning that there was road work ahead, and to watch for the flagger.

Dutifully, I stopped behind a line of station wagons, suburban vehicles, camper trailers, and cars. At the front of the line, I saw the flagger, with her neon vest and stop sign in hand.

The woman pointed down the row of cars and signaled, with a wave of her arm. I unzipped my jacket. The woman motioned again, and I looked at her, up there in the distance. She waved her arm, hand-signaling to the front of the line of traffic.

Supposing that there must be a contractor coming forward from behind, I turned my head, but only saw that the line behind me now equaled the line in front of me. I looked forward again, and the slender lady seemed to point directly at me.

I sat back, and pointed at myself. "Me?"

She nodded her head up and down, beckoning me to "come."

She can't mean me, I thought. I looked around once more. Again, she repeated her motions when I looked forward. What does she want?

Questioningly, I slipped away from the line of traffic, and idled up to where she stood with her stop sign. She clearly directed me to the first position in the line of detained vehicles.

Incredulous, I beamed beneath my full-faced helmet.

The lady, a very beautiful black woman, came to my side and told me that she knows that "the bikers hate getting caught behind all the others." She was giving me an open road, once we got the go ahead.

"Thank-you!" I cried, still not believing this simple, yet eloquent act of kindness. "You just made my day! I wish that happened more often."

There was a huge tract of road receiving an entire facelift, and the wait was unusually long. All the motorists had turned off their engines after a time, and many were standing around in the road. The traffic controller and I had a conversation.

Her name was Tina, and she asked me lots of questions about my motorcycle, and seemed enthralled that I had ridden from Massachusetts to California, but then when I filled her in on the scope of my journey, she simply sparkled with excitement. During our chat, she was interrupted by her hand radio, and I heard her reply to the transmission, and then add, "and there's a *girl* riding one of those kinda bikes that you like, over here."

Our movement was pending, and she repositioned herself to the proper place, and twirled her sign around, to say, SLOW. With a meep-meep, and a wave, I left her behind. Politely, I traversed the distance past all the sweaty, dirt-streaked workers, as they leaned on their tools awaiting my passage expectantly. They'd heard the word. There's a chick on that bike out front. WOW.

As soon as the coast was clear, I had the road to myself. There was no one ahead of me for the next several miles. I tooled on by Inspiration Point, revved the engine within a deep tunnel, and entered Yosemite Valley, where the views were so majestic, I had to pull over just to ponder the beauty.

Two weeks ago I was at the Grand Canyon. There, I had *expected* to be filled with some kind of inexplicable raw emotion, but not here. Frankly, I didn't know what to expect. I needed to pick a few "fabulous" destinations for my limited itinerary before I went away, so, "Eeney-meeny-miny-mo, Yosemite's one place I'll go." Now, I sat astounded by unexpected richness.

Eventually, I made it to the Visitor Center, where I parked the motorcycle next to a few others, and did the tourist thing. Y'know, watched the films, studied the displays, looked around in the department store sized souvenir shop where you could also buy groceries . . . then I hopped on the free shuttle bus, and let it bring me hither and thither all over the place.

On one of my bus rides, I shared my seat with a man and his massive backpack. He told me a story. He and his son, (just a boy) were out hiking together and they witnessed the fall of a rock climber. The father and two other hikers found the victim, and performed CPR, while the son ran for help. The climber had suffered a severe head injury. He never recovered.

After this sobering tale, the shuttle halted, and the man hoisted his backpack to his shoulder. "This is where we get off, son," he said to the lad, and to me, "enjoy your visit."

I got off the bus at a trail head which led me through groves of pines, where squirrels, and bird life thrived. The gentle path took me to Mirror Lake. There, visitors cooled off at the edge, or sunbathed on large rocks left behind by glaciers maybe four hundred thousand years before. Snow capped mountains, proud and handsome pines towered, and thick, rounded shade trees crowded around the smooth waters. "Mirror, Mirror, heed our call. Who's the fairest of us all?" The matchless beauty of Mother Earth's countenance reflects forever upon the silent surface of Mirror Lake.

During my return trip, I left the beaten path, and delved into a thicker portion of forest, and sat on a fallen tree near a narrow footpath. Forest critters soon ignored me, and boldly played in the branches of the very tree upon which I sat.

After a time, I finished my hike and hitched another ride with the shuttle bus for a lift back to the commercial hub of the park. I dallied in the store, mostly captured by the myriad of professional photographs on souvenirs of all sorts. Everything from place mats, to highly varnished clock faces, to writing paper, or tins of candy became hosts to the images of Yosemite's famous scapes. I realized that in my two or three days here, I would barely explore a fraction of this National Park in California.

Later, in a magazine, I came across a tidbit of information. In Yosemite's fledgling year, 1864, one hundred forty seven outdoor enthusiasts visited it. In 1995, I was one of 4,101,928 outdoor enthusiasts to clamber within its boundaries.

After eating a picnic lunch, I rode around the village, hopped on the crowded bus again, checked out the Nature Center, and climbed to a spectacular view of the whole valley. The Sierra range, Merced River, and El Capitan, Cathedral Rocks, Half Dome, and other famous formations, formed the "Incomparable Valley," and time stood still, while I stood and stared in awe.

Around me, travelers shared their wonder, and passed field glasses to total strangers, so that each of us could gaze at the sights "up close."

There were waterfalls spilling over the sheer rock faces, and I learned that they were mere trickles at this time of year, compared to spring time, when the mountain snows melt.

Eventually, I'd had my fill, and headed for 'home,' riding back along the winding road that cut through the rugged scenery, and offered glimpses of the magnificent structures that made up the heart and soul of Yosemite.

A dead forest had captured my attention during my early morning ride, and as I passed through it again, I pulled over. The pines, stood defiant, like rapiers puncturing the deep velvet sky. Their bones were bleached, and the branches were no longer clothed in greenery. At their feet, a lush green layer of young broadleaf trees created a carpet that would someday become forest, along this stretch of road.

I could only wonder about the death of these pines. Was it fire or disease that claimed the entire stand? Finally, I moved on. The traffic worried me, as I sat on my steed, unprotected, at the non-existent edge of the road.

The road crew had made some progress, a queue had formed, and I waited my turn. Insightful Tina was gone. My timing was good, however. As I had sat up on the ridge pondering the fate of all those ponderosas, everyone in their cars waited impatiently at the road construction site. But, a minute after I got there, the flagger sent us on our way.

Back at my dingy, dusty Wawona campsite, I settled down to relax and read.

Before dark, a slim, tanned young man was walking by my site. He stopped to look at my Pony.

"This your bike?" he asked.

"Yes."

He eyed it, then said, "Can you do a wheelie?"

"No."

Another pause, circling the machine. "How fast can you go?"

"A buck twenty-five," I replied.

"Oh," said he. Not yet ready to go, he continued with the questions. "So, how come you don't do wheelies?"

For once, the barrage of questions was completely different than the usual, "Aren't you afraid? etc." I invited the guy to sit down for a spell, and I told him how and why I ride motorcycles.

He revealed that he was one of the road crew workers, and pointed to a section of the camp that seemed well established. "That's where the road crew gets to stay while we're here. Come on over for the campfire later on if ya want, and get a few beers."

"Well, thanks. I might, but, I don't know," I answered without a commitment either way.

He stood up to go. "Name's Phil," he said.

"Phil," I repeated. "Lover of horses."

Surprised, he stammered, "How did you know that?"

"Simple. I love horses, and anything that has something to do with horses, I remember, and your name means lover of horses."

He walked away, and I went back to my book.

*   *   *

The next morning, I went out on the bike, deciding on Glacier Point as my destination. Again, I came upon a line of tourists, held up for a half-hour, while the road crew strove to improve the road, laying down a perfect, seamless surface for our travelling enjoyment. Still, drivers and passengers behaved impatiently, forgetting to be thankful for the hot labor these men and women do all day, toiling and sweating, while we're all here to play.

As I maintained my position behind the scores of oversized campers, Phil happened to notice me, and came over to talk for a minute. I explained that I'd turned down his invitation, because I didn't want to party with all the guys. I asked him to come over to my camp after he finished work. He said he'd be there at 4:30.

I spent the day, gazing, wandering, and taking in more of what Yosemite had to offer. As I tooled along, I came to a place where the pine cones stunned me, for their size. Never had I seen anything like it. At home, when I tell people I saw pine cones that were as large as my entire lower legs, who will believe me?

Park laws make it illegal to take anything from the grounds. Flowers aren't to be plucked, stones can't be kept, and these steroid cones must stay here. With four million visitors a year, the protection is mandatory for the future of the park. I understand, but I *can* take a photograph.

The next time I came upon a patch of such seed-carriers, I parked precariously halfway between two easy curves, then tried to set my camera up for a timed-release picture. I needed to hold the pines, to show scale. My camera wouldn't sit on my empty saddle, and I tried to move the bike around to work it to my advantage.

That's just when a park ranger came on the scene. When he found out I wasn't broken down, he admonished me for parking so foolishly where there isn't a pull-off.

"It was only supposed to take a second," I appealed. "I can't take these amazing things with me, and I was trying to get a picture. Will you just snap a photo for me real quick, and I'll be on my way?"

The man agreed, then waited while I happily tossed the giant cones back to the ground. "Those are the cones of the Sugar Pine," he volunteered, and stooped to pick up a small, pitchy, tightly clustered pine cone. "This is the unlikely seed of the Redwood Tree. Surprised, huh? But, it's true. Now, get on out of here, before you get us both run over."

Later on, I returned to my campsite, where Phil joined me. He had me hop into his pick-up truck so that he could show me a place where I could sneak a shower. We spent a couple of hours together looking around the Pioneer Yosemite History Center. Nobody seemed to be around. There were antique wagons, and carts, farming implements, and together we tried to figure out how they all worked. Under a shelter, we saw a series of old carriages, and some of the first horseless carriages, a fine collection of stages.

Phil was a wealth of information about cars, and how their engines work, so it was pretty fun having this private tour.

We found a corral of horses, ponies and mules. Trying to be an instigator, Phil suggested I hop the fence and try riding one. I looked around, and didn't see anybody. This part of "town" was closed, but I couldn't take the risk of getting into trouble. To climb aboard a tired nag within a crowded paddock just wasn't worth it.

Back at Wawona, Phil dropped me off, and tossed a heap of logs over to my fire ring. He then parked his truck over where all the workers were settled, a couple of hundred yards away. Across the span, I could hear them teasing him good-naturedly, calling out, "Phil's got a biker chick!" They were already sounding a bit rowdy, but Phil just ignored them, and walked away.

"Here, I brought you some ice for your wine coolers. They must be warm by now," he said. "I have some Dinty Moore stew, too, and some other canned goods. Whatever we don't eat tonight, take it with you."

He set the cans on the table, and I started to build a fire. Phil left and came back with a couple of folding chairs. We opened a couple of cans of stew, and put them into the coals after the fire was established, and ate right out of the cans after they bubbled.

The night seemed to arrive early. It had to be this casual company that I was graced with. Phil was young, didn't really know what direction he was taking. We stayed and talked about life, and growing up. I told him a little about my summer. The evening was relaxed and easy, until the coals died down and we decided to call it a night.

Suddenly, all seemed awkward. He stood up, and backed away, dragging a chair with him. I folded my chair and brought it over to him.

"Thanks for your company. I had a really nice time," I said.

"Yeah. You're pretty cool." He shuffled in place, shyly. "Well, I've got to be up real early," he started to turn away.

"Hold on, don't go yet," I blurted out, impulsively. "Let me at least give you a hug."

He held onto the two chairs as I hugged him, quickly. Realizing that I was embarrassing him, I released him before he could react. "Good night."

The brook that ran through the camp could be heard in the stillness of the night. As I fell to sleep, I thought of the XXL presence of all the things of nature that dwelt in this Yosemite National Park.

Miles for two days: 155

Sometime this morning, I don't know what hour it was, I heard a truck spin its tires on gravel. Phil must have left to go fishing with his friends, as planned.

After some more sleep time, I got up, and took a long time breaking camp. I was in no hurry to leave the lovely, large, lofty Yosemite. Besides, I was heading back to Sharon's for the night, and knew I'd have it real easy. No setting up of camp, no worries or cares. I'd have a chance to get squeaky clean again, visit with my friends, eat something interesting, and sleep in a comfortable bed.

I returned to Bakersfield on a multi-lane highway 99, for once choosing a faster way, rather than the one less traveled. Living dangerously, I had my jacket strapped to the back of my bike for an hour or so, to get some sun on my arms. Twice in the same minute I was stung by bees. Once on my waist, which felt like a sword stabbed me in the side, and then on my throat. You would think I'd learn, after the other day. I pulled over, applied cortizone, and put my jacket on again. Protective gear works even in the event of *not* crashing.

No one was home when I got to Sharon's, so I let myself in, as instructed. Sharon was expecting me, and had even left a note on the table welcoming me "home."

Feeling comfortable, I made myself at home. Apparently, Sharon felt the same way, as though she knew she didn't need to cater to me, and that the guest in her home could be trusted. She got home later than expected, made sure that I was all set, and excused herself to go to bed early. She said Kelly was sleeping over her friends' house, so I could use her room.

What a life. When I go home, I'm going to invite friends to sleep over just for the fun of it. I'm going to call up others and see if I can come visit them, once in a while. What's a couple or three hundred miles between friends? I'm doing that day in and day out, this summer. Why not several times each summer in my own region? Why miss out?

I'm having the time of my life, and it's not getting old. Every single day has been full of surprises, lessons, adventures. But, it wasn't luck that got me here. It was an irrepressible desire, an urge, a calling.

I feel special. I am.

Miles: 196

There is something about dead trees that really captures my attention. They have such an artistic quality. I have to resist the urge to stop and take a lot of pictures, but sometimes I've just got to do it. I limit myself to using only one or two frames, and usually get good results. I took this solitary shot at Yosemite National Park in California.

flex-i-bil-i-ty   Freedom. The ability to adapt to any
situation with ease.

CHAPTER 27

LAS VEGAS

Labor Day Weekend 1995   Days 78–80

*L*inda and Annis came over for breakfast. After big
hugs, photos and promises to keep in touch I was off,
with Annis riding with me for a short distance.

Before long, I was cruising through the desert. The ride from
Bakersfield to Barstow was a hot one, and it took an hour longer
than anticipated.

Thomas was supposed to be waiting for me at the McDonald's
Train Station, but after I circled the jam-packed parking lot a few
times, dodging over-heated tourists spilling out of their air
conditioned vehicles and gasping for air, I came to the conclusion
that he, nor any other motorcyclists were there.

My bike sat melting in the hot sun. I was beginning to get
worried about Thomas, so I called his sister's house. She was not
surprised to hear from me. Thomas had broken down in the desert
on his way. He was still coming, but he was going to be late. I had
instructions to wait for him where I was.

Not too long after that, a blue Eclipse aimed right for me, and just
before I jumped out of the way, I saw the tinted window glide down,
revealing Thomas' grinning face.

"Hey woman! Been here long?" He stopped the car and jumped
out. We grabbed each other tightly, "You look great."

"So do you."

"Let's get out of here. Follow me to my sister's. We'll figure out
what we're gonna do, there."

When we got to her house, on the edge of town, he suggested I
leave my bike in his sister's garage and ride to the California
beaches with him in his new car. What could I say? His motorcycle
just seized up, and he had left it on the side of the road in the desert,
thumbed a ride back to Vegas, and hopped in his car.

I was disappointed, but under the circumstances I felt worse for him. I tossed the bags I needed for the weekend into the car trunk, put my bike in the garage, and took off.

Riding in the cushiony comfort of the sleek, sporty cage, I soon forgot about my disappointment that we weren't on motorcycles. We had a long ride ahead of us, and we were able to catch up with each other and talk.

It was so good to see him. He seemed like a friend from home, because that's how I knew him.

In '93 Thomas was riding through my town on a motorcycle so laden with luggage that it looked like a cartoon. We met, and became friends over the five weeks he stayed nearby at another sister's home, painting houses to raise up money to fund more travel. I took him on some rides, we went hiking, he met some of my friends and we'd kept in touch ever since. When I told him of my plan to take off on my own trek, he was the most encouraging person of experience that I knew. I had looked forward to riding with him on the west coast so much. Now I felt really glad to have this familiar companion from my past, with or without his bike.

He drove me to Huntington Beach. We strolled out on a long pier that jutted out into the water. He took off his shirt, revealing his Bruce Lee bod to me for the first time ever. Back east, he wore only baggy clothes, and said he was terribly underweight. I had been curious, because I liked him, but now as we strolled, I noticed the smooth, golden brown skin, the sinewy way his arms and shoulders looked. His perfectly hairless torso, that angled down to a flat, washboard waist and a trace of hair leading from his navel, to someplace under the waistband of his pleated trousers.

My open appraisal seemed to please him, and we launched into a discussion about working out, lifting weights, changing your body shape, etc. He told me how hard he had to work to gain size. This I could guess. He had the potential to be a skinny, tall, runt. Instead, I was alarmed at how fine he looked, compared to what I'd imagined two years before.

We walked on the beach and watched the sun go down, then went to Powerhouse Gym on Santa Monica Blvd. I had a great workout. It was the only gym I visited during my whole journey. I went easy on the weights, the stairmaster felt great, and I left the place showered, pumped up and hungry.

Thomas settled me into a chair at "Studios," an expensive restaurant, ordered a bottle of wine, and urged me to get whatever I wanted. I ordered giant shrimp, covered in cajun spices, skewered and barbequed, served on a bed of rice. He got a big, fat steak. We talked, and learned more about each other, knowing that we are two distinctly different types of persons, but the combination was pleasing.

We walked down the Boulevard, taking in the L.A. sights and nightlife. We kept bumping into each other, then apologizing. When I took his hand, it was a simple solution to an awkward problem. His fingers felt long and bony, compared to others I had known, but strong and charged, like electricity.

Thomas had advised me to visit L.A. During numerous telephone calls during my planning stage he insisted that if I was going all the way to the west coast, that I couldn't miss it.

"I don't care about the cities. I'm not a city girl. I want to see the parks, and nature, and small town America. The big cities mean nothing to me, besides a place to avoid unless I have a particular reason to go there." I resisted.

He pressed on. "There is so much activity, so much to see and do."

I countered, "Not for me. I don't know where to go, I'd have to leave my motorcycle all packed up wherever I go . . . " I had a million excuses.

"It's not that bad. I didn't have any trouble."

Finally, exasperated, I told him point blank. "You're a guy, and you have street smarts. Who would mess with you? I'm not going into the big cities. I don't care."

Still, he refused to give up. "Tell you what. I can use a vacation. When you get out this way, you give me a call and talk to me. I will take time off from work, jump on my bike and escort you there."

That was an offer I would consider. There would be two of us. He knew all the hot spots, and I would arrive with him. It wouldn't appear as if I'm looking for a good time, or I'm a naive runaway, and even though I'd rather not make the big famous cities my destinations, it would be nice to see my pal. If I had a smidgen of homesickness, seeing him might help, so here we were.

Much to my surprise, the hustle and bustle of the City of Stars wasn't as distasteful as I anticipated. Having Thomas as my guide made a big difference, than had I come by myself. As we blended in with the youthful crowd, I softened enough to really enjoy myself, in the midst of all the commercialism, the concrete, asphalt, plastic, neon, glitz and glamour.

We had plans to stay at the Huntington Youth Hostel, so we wound up there eventually. Rather than sleeping in separate quarters with others of the same sex, we opted to share a room together.

Shyly, we took turns undressing in the room, while the other used the bathroom down the hall. There were several hostelers, but they were all strung out from too much sun, sand, surf and whatever else they overdid that day.

Thomas was stretched beneath a sheet when I came back into our room. Our room was stifling. We took a good look around and found much to laugh about. We were enclosed in a perfectly cubicle room, with pasty blue-gray walls of cracked plaster. From the center of the ceiling dangled a singular bulb. A piece of cardboard was somehow attached in a manner that prevented the glare from shining down directly on the bed. We pretended that at any minute some Goon would come, and exchange our bed for a table and chairs, and interrogate us relentlessly.

I needed to unwind. I was not relaxed enough to sleep. Among my personal effects I had a small bottle of massage oil. Gently I told Thomas that I couldn't sleep, and if he would lie on his stomach, I would give him a massage. It would relax both of us, I promised.

Miles:142

*　　　*　　　*

On Sunday we went to Venice Beach. What an eclectic arrangement of shops, visitors and entertainment. In typical Hollywood fashion, girls in bikinis roller-bladed along the boardwalk. The shops were held up primarily by young men who took their jobs seriously, as they leaned nonchalantly against them, smoking cigarettes. Running along the shop fronts, ran the boardwalk, crowded with tourists, beach combers, fashion horrors and trend setters. On one side of the boardwalk, lined the shops where punk seemed to be the main theme. On the other, an assortment of performers claimed their territory, and solicited donations for their talent.

Thomas and I strolled along, popping into shops, sniffing incense, checking out duds for me of leather and lace, looking at hemp jewelry, beads and sunglasses. Tie dye abounded, as did gauzy dresses, and swimwear. Surfboard shops and rollerblade rentals tempted active visitors, and sidewalk cafe's selling icy cold beverages supported the curious onlookers.

We paused to watch a pair of chiseled, leather skinned men display acts of swordsmanship, and feats of daredevils. They walked across broken glass, one man laid on the broken glass with melons on his chest, and as sweat streaked down the brow of his partner, the second man slashed the fruit into slices and distributed them to the onlookers. Then they juggled with fire, swallowed flaming swords, and did other macho tricks, unabashedly asking for handouts.

A few yards beyond, a small boy swayed to the music that his big brother played on a record player. Bringing a microphone top his mouth, he lip-synced a tune or two, capturing the adoration of little kids who wished they could show off like that. His moment of glory was stolen however, when an even smaller tyke, about two years old, dressed in a red military jacket and shiny shoes, stepped into the center of attention. As Michael Jackson music blared on the radio, the toddler rocked and rolled, putting on the moves, twirling, moonwalking and grabbing his crotch. Again, a hat was passed, by the small little Michael wanna-be.

Then, there was a Greek statue, set up on a pedestal, surrounded by transfixed faces. As I got closer, I realized that this was a man, dressed in a toga, and entirely covered in silver paint. Only his eyeballs, and the interior of his mouth showed his true grit. From underneath his pedestal, classical music flowed, and he posed, silent and dignified for minutes at a time, and then, gracefully and gradually he changed position, before freezing in that form for another lasting duration. One hesitant woman was nudged by her boyfriend to stand beside the statue for a photograph. Magically, he profluently transformed into a genteel man, with hand extended towards her, palm up.

One after the next, there was entertainment, ranging from freak shows, to soapbox preachers, to propaganda pushing extremists, to genuine talent. Back and forth between the shops, and the artists who caught our attention, we spent much of the morning.

We bought a huge slice of gourmet pizza, and a Coke, then sat on the beach to eat it and share it with a mutt. Kites sailed overhead, girls in thong bikinis giggled and flirted with surfer boys. Stoic old folks inched by on flimsy legs, with looks that showed distaste, or disbeleief, making us wonder, whatever are they here for? Certainly they knew what to expect.

Thomas gave me a choice; continue traipsing the strip, or sunbathe on the beach?

I picked a spot, and laid down on the hot, soft, white sand. The sound of the surf enveloped me with its relaxing rhythm. Thomas and I did not speak. We simply enjoyed the hot sun and salt air.

Thomas had encouraged me to "live dangerously," so I was wearing my leopard print thong bikini, with matching sarong. I dropped the sarong self-consciously, and turned to lie on my stomach. For years I knew of the triangular patch of pale skin above my buns, but the tan was acquired in the privacy of my back yard, or my apartment balcony. This was something new, to be exposed like this. Not only in public, but so nearby a friend of the opposite sex.

Hey. We're just friends, I told myself. Still, I couldn't bring myself to ask him to spread sunscreen on my backside. I rested, tense and expectant, trying to relax. Fifty feet away a man displayed his browned buttocks, as he read a book, his manhood squeezed into the tiny thong he wore. I tried to remember; I'm in California. Anything goes! My being in a thong is no big deal. Look around, they're all over the place. Besides, my butt is okay, I think.

After a while, I stopped worrying, and simply enjoyed the warmth of the sun as I basked in it. I was thoroughly relaxed, when I felt a warm sensation, like silk, caressing my right upper arm, elbow and forearm.

"Does that feel good?" Thomas' voice broke the silence.

I felt it again. "MMmm-m-m-m," I murmured.

I cracked an eyelid and saw Thomas holding a fist over my arm, and funneling a trickle of sand, spilling it onto my skin, where it cascaded over each side of my arm, softly falling down.

After five or so handfuls, the stream of sand moved to my shoulder, then along my waist. Slowly. Sensuously.

Huskily, he asked, "What does it feel like?"

I didn't answer immediately. I felt the warmth flow along the edge of my other arm. "It feels like silk, or like a feather duster," I finally answered.

"Does it feel good?" the voice said, questioningly.

"Yes. Very." I kept my eyes shut.

Ever so slowly and gently, the sand coursed over my skin, tickling me near my waist and lower back, and the bottoms of my feet, but I didn't flinch. I was aware of Thomas' movements, as he shifted his position around me, to outline my body, one handful of hourglass sand at a time.

The sand stroked an outer thigh, and ran along one cheek, then the other. My sensuality was blooming. I became aware of my breathing, and tried to keep it low and steady so that Thomas wouldn't know my secret. He was turning me on, and how.

"Do you like this? Do you want me to stop?" he teased.

"Yes, I like it. It feels good. I don't want you to stop—only if you want to."

He grunted as he moved around me. I felt something nudge my leg, announcing his mutual arousal, but I pretended to ignore the contact. He pulled away, pretending to be oblivious to his own erection, as well.

Time stood still, and slowly Thomas circled my form, continuing to pour a silver stream of beach sand along the edge of my figure.

I heard footsteps as people walked by, keeping their distance, but once, a group of three of four guys stopped and gawked. I could not see them without moving my head, but they sounded like adolescents.

"Oh dudes—dudes. Check this out," and to Thomas, "Man, can we take a picture?"

He said, "Sure."

I felt them scuffling into position around me, and was shocked when I heard one of the guys squeak, "I can touch it?" a second before he had cupped his hands over each of my sandy buns. Thomas was in my sights, and he sheepishly shrugged his shoulders.

The silly young men ran off, all excited about their exploits on the beach, obviously tourists, just like me.

Sternly, I reprimanded Thomas. "Since when do *you* tell someone it's okay to touch *my* butt? Huh?"

"You're just so irresistible. I didn't even stop to think." He flattered me as he apologized, but we both knew the whole thing was theatrics.

The intrusion tore me from my fantasies. It's probably the only time I'd ever be on a public beach in a T-back. Before letting me get up, Thomas spelled my name in the sand beside my physique and took some pictures. A couple of mounted policemen rode by.

Thomas proudly commented, "She looks naked, don't she?"

They glanced our way and grinned, and steered their horses onward. Thomas explained that he covered every stitch of fabric with sand.

I was getting stiff from being still for over two hours of languid attention, so I lifted myself out of the sand and worked out the kink in my neck. I ran into the surf and washed the sand off, then feeling renewed, headed down the beach wrapped in my sarong, with Thomas by my side.

We couldn't stay serious, and ran and splashed and played like lovers. But, we knew better. We're just friends. Right?

After spending the entire day, we jumped in the car and headed away from Los Angeles. We drove for a few hours and grabbed a motel to spend the night.

During the course of the day we had covered a number of topics, had enjoyed people watching and had fun simply playing. We talked about ourselves and about our friendship.

Mostly, Thomas impressed upon me that he knew about the feelings that were confusing me, regarding sexual attraction, restraint, and seemingly endless temptation. He had traveled for long durations at different times in his thirty years, and he understood. He wanted me to know that he was here for me. He didn't want to complicate anything. He knew that I was lonely.

I didn't. Until I started to think about what he meant.

"Diane, it's important for you to understand. From the time that I met you in Massachusetts, I respected you, as a motorcyclist. Since then, I've also regarded you as a friend. Now that you're here with me, I need you to know that I'm not going to hurt you. If you want me, I understand. It doesn't have to be love, but I am here if you need me. No matter what, you will always be respected by me, as a motorcyclist first. That's how you came into my life, and that is how you will always remain in my mind."

His words provoked some deep thinking, because I perceived a message. I could love him an' leave him. He liked me enough, but wasn't going to let himself get tied up with expectations. I was under no circumstances allowed to toy with thoughts of love. He could, however, comfort me.

During the long car ride I pondered over these things. Funny, I never expected to be in this position. It would be so easy.

We got in to a motel and had a meal at a Denny's nearby. By the time we'd had hot showers, it was late. We were wiped. Thomas fell to sleep moments after he told me good night.

Hours later, when I awoke, Thomas was holding me, his face buried in my long, fragrant tresses. Contented, I snuggled closer. Sweet dreams.

* * *

He was up and out of bed before I realized it was morning. We had spent the night not too far from his sister's house, so we got there at an early hour. I changed my mind about going to Las Vegas. Originally, I had no desire nor intention to enter the City of Glitz. Now I realized that I could extend my visit with Thomas by a couple more days if I accepted his offer to stay with him.

He had a dentist appointment late that morning. We had a two hundred mile trip ahead of us. We figured that would take close to four hours, depending. I didn't want to fly through the desert on his tail, or vice versa. He didn't see any need for that either.

After quite the discussion, we arrived at the conclusion for me to take my time, and drive directly to his apartment. He would leave the door unlocked for me.

"I'm just gonna leave my stuff in your trunk then, and drive the Pony with only what's already still packed up."

The bike now carried the large soft-sided saddlebags, my tent, sleeping bag, and sleeping roll. Thomas had my clothes and personal effects. After a quick hug, I got on my bike and set out to find some coffee, after seeing him off.

For breakfast, I sat on a gas station curb, drinking a huge coffee and nibbling a banana nut muffin. I was at the edge of Barstow, and it was already getting uncomfortably hot, sitting there in my leathers.

A pick-up truck drove in, and a hard looking character with tattoos covering every inch of skin from his wrists to his short sleeves leaped out, looking curiously my way. Surprisingly, he spoke to me when he came out of the store. He started to describe a long motorcycle trip he'd taken on his Harley Knucklehead, but stopped with a shrill whistle when he'd circled around to the back of my bike and saw the license plate.

By the time he'd left, I was nearly done with my coffee, and downed the rest of it. I bought a bottle of water, to arm me for my desert crossing.

My ride was uneventful. Hot, fast, long, hard riding. The divider lines smeared into one blurry streak when I focused on the road before me. The desert inched past my peripheral vision.

It felt grand to be back in the saddle, but it seemed that my main objective was just to arrive at Thomas' and take a nap before he got home from the dentist. I was overtired from all the night life I was experiencing, and now Las Vegas! Isn't that a City that Never Sleeps?

When I got closer, I saw the mountains form a circular fortress around a desert floor. Spread across the middle, was Las Vegas in the daytime. I aimed towards it, and glad to get off of I-15, followed Thomas' precise directions, until I was pulling into his apartment complex.

The longer I had ridden, the thirstier I had become, but I kept pressing on, not wanting to stop. I was roasting in my leathers the second I hit the city and merged into traffic. Every set of lights was like Hades. With great relief, I pulled into my friend's courtyard.

The door to his apartment was locked.

No way!

But, yes, the door was locked. I looked at my watch and groaned. It was 11:30, exactly when Thomas' appointment began. I had no idea where his appointment was, but it had to be in Las Vegas.

The sun beat on my backside as I looked in the window. I was melting.

I took off my jacket and shirt, having a sportbra on underneath. I wandered aimlessly around the block of apartments seeking shade, but there was absolutely none. Minutes ticked by. I began to wither. I sat on my AGV helmet, on the concrete, leaning against his brick wall. I could hear a phone ringing. I could hear the answering machine after it picked up. I heard my name.

"Diane. Pick up the phone. Diane. Diane—are you there? Pick up the phone. Di—Diane—I thought you'd be there by now. Never mind."

On the other side of the wall I tried the door knob for the hundredth time. It was no use. I was stranded. I applied more sunblock, drank the last sip of water and wished I had worn shorts underneath my leathers. I thought of the Burger King I saw nearby on my way in. It's always freezing in those places. I thought of the zillions of air conditioned buildings just moments down the street and around the block, but I was too hot to dredge up the energy to move.

I sat back down on my AGV stool, and tried to think cold thoughts, like the time I was riding over the mountain pass in Wyoming, running out of gas.

A man turned to lock the door as he left his apartment next door to Thomas'. He nodded my way, "Hello." Then he left in his sportscar.

The sun raged, casting its rays straight down at me, as I drooped in the concrete and brick enclosure. I cursed myself, for just on the other side of the entrance, I knew that my clothes lay in a heap. I cursed Thomas, but knew that this stupid error was exactly like something I would do.

In his haste, Thomas automatically locked the door, without thinking. He probably didn't even realize I was locked out.

The man who lived next door returned. Listlessly, I watched as he unlocked his door and dropped two bags of groceries inside. He turned to look at me. "Are you waiting for someone?" he asked, with a slight edge to his voice.

"Yes. My friend Thomas lives here. He was supposed to leave the door unlocked for me, but I guess he forgot."

Instantly, the man's expression softened. "Please, come out of the hot sun and wait inside." He held his door open for me.

The heat had gotten to me, and there was no disguising the whooziness that had washed over me. I sort of reeled into the living room and lurched toward the couch there.

"Let me get you some water," he said as he disappeared into the kitchen and returned with an icy glassful. "My name is Nick."

"I'm Diane, thank you," I said before downing it, and then, "May I just lay down on your couch for a little while? I think I've gotten too much sun."

"Of course, how long have you been out there?"

"Well, first I rode out from Barstow," I began, "I got here at 11:30. What is it, one o'clock now? I was dying."

Nick brought me a pen and paper and I wrote a note for Thomas, telling him where to find me.

After about twenty minutes, I felt a little better, and opened my eyes to look at this kind person.

His thick, curly head of hair was black, and his skin was a reddish brown. He was rugged, muscular, and hairless, right down to his shaved legs. He looked Hawaiian. He sat hulked over some books at his dining room table, just minding his own business. Once, he looked up and seeing that I was no longer practically delirious he smiled, then went back to his studies.

Later, taking a break, he started a conversation. I steered it around, to find out that he was a dancer for one of the shows that does a Hawaiian theme. His apartment was spartan, classic, immaculate, and his living room contained little more than a couch, chair, low table, TV and weight bench. We exchanged stories. He asked me a few questions about Thomas, explaining that everyone keeps to themselves.

I was grateful that he had come to my aide. Soon, he turned back to his studies, and I rested some more, falling to sleep.

Thomas arrived and sheepishly collected me. After an exuberant description of my torture session, and hearing his side of the story (now that all was well,) we laughed about it. Just as I'd suspected, he went off meaning to leave the door unlocked, but . . . those things happen.

After we'd gotten ourselves settled in, Thomas continued to spoil me rotten. He took me to nearby Henderson to gamble with the locals.

"The locals stay away from the Strip. Instead, we'll go to a less glamorous casino, where everybody knows each other, and we play as a team against the house."

So, I went with him into Henderson, and he tried to teach me the basics of Black Jack. Just as he said, everyone seemed to know each other, and many were curious to find out who I was.

At first, I didn't have a clue as to what was going on in the game, but after a little bit of coaching I started to think I was getting the hang of it. Just as I would make a decision about my next move, Thomas would tell me what to do. I found that to be quite annoying. "I know. I know. Let me do it on my own," I snapped, then I'd make a move that I thought was safe, and the whole table would get flustered at me. The strain of their forced politeness was about to burst blood vessels.

Thomas would correct me, and tell me how I screwed up, then he'd place another bet for me. I seemed to be winning more often than not, but I guess that wasn't good enough.

"You play. I don't want to play any more. I'm not having fun. I'd rather just watch you," I whined.

After he ran out of his spending money, we left. I had about thirty dollars that I had somehow managed to win, and with it I insisted on taking him out for dinner, my treat.

At first he disagreed, but when I reasoned that it was free money that I won, using *his* money to begin with, he relented. We went to an out of the way little hole in the wall Oriental restaurant, where you go in and select the foods you want stir-fried to order, and the style, Szechuan, sweet and sour, or garlic and sesame.

After dinner, I was escorted into the bright lights, and blaring extravaganza of Las Vegas itself. We strolled up and down the Strip, seeing the wondrous gimmicks all the different hotels and casinos use to attract customers.

I saw a volcano of molten lava, witnessed a battle of pirates, and wondered about the logic of a city that can enforce a water ban amongst its residents, and yet justify a moat of water deep enough to sink a ship, for one of its shows. I used the marble ladies room in some hotel, and marveled at the gaudiness everywhere.

Once again, it was very late when we called it a day. Thomas pushed a pile of clothes off his bed to make room for me. I undressed in the bathroom and took a shower, and when I was done I quietly snuck into bed beside my buddy Thomas, as he slept soundly.

As I reflected on the last few days I felt surprised at how much fun I had, even though I had been in big, bad cities. I was glad that I had followed through, and actually accepted Thomas' offer to have his vacation with me. I knew for a fact that had I ventured into Los

Angeles or Las Vegas on my own, the experience would have been dull and boring, compared to the memories I had amassed in my old friend Thomas' company.

Miles:160

Thomas Grant, a friend from my past hosted me for three days and showed me a really good time. Here we are at Venice Beach, California, living a little on the wild side, where anything goes. Notice my name spelled in the sand.

Today I will delight in the fact that my life may grow in a way
that is different and special and wild, a way that may cause
others to bristle and grind their teeth . . . Only when I honor
my own desires am I able to honor the paths of others.
I am a woman with enough power to do anything I choose.
Today I shall practice this truth . . .

—Laura Stamps

CHAPTER 28

ZION

September 5–7   Days 81–83

*T*he time had come to replace my rear tire, again. I
didn't even get six thousand miles out of it! In less
than two months I had worn it down, much of the time riding
through the desert during the heat of the day.

Thomas called a recommended shop and made an appointment
for me. My tire preference is Metzeler, but they didn't have my size
in stock. You would expect the Motorcycle Tire Center USA would
have every tire imaginable, but, you would be wrong. In Colorado, I
had to accept a Dunlop, and now in Las Vegas, I had to take a
Battlax. Certainly, one disadvantage of long-term touring is having
to take what you can get, rather than exactly what you want.

The tire would be slippery, I was warned, and should be scuffed
in cautiously for the first hundred miles. Piece of cake. Before I'm
settled in for the night, I'll have that doubled.

I cruised through Vegas, not along the Strip, but in ordinary
business zones. A woman stood at a set of lights wearing a
signboard. PREGNANT 6 MONTHS. NO HOME. NO JOB. PLEASE HELP.
I thought of a careless person who gambled away every last cent,
and every ounce of dignity. Caught up in a fantasy of getting rich
quickly, she ended up poor, and living on the streets begging for
people's mercy.

All over the place, people begged. I couldn't get it. How can
intelligent human beings throw away everything they have worked
for, with reckless gambling? How can you reach into your pocket

and spend your very last twenty dollars, thinking it will bring you millions? How do you let yourself lose it all?

Thomas was home when I got there, and helped me lug all my bags outside. Ruefully, he watched me pack. I could understand his feelings of sadness and envy. He knew the freedom I experienced. He had been there before. Today he would watch me ride away towards more of the unknown. Tonight he would pull his welding mask down over his face while sparks fly, and he'd wonder how far I have made it. Day after day, the monotony would get to him, but I wouldn't know what's coming around the next curve. Literally.

"Time to go," I stated, heeding the call of the open road, somewhere yonder.

We squeezed each other tightly, then stepped apart. "I wish I could go with you. Seeing you leaving like this makes me remember what it was like. You are so free. I'm jealous. Be careful, Di."

"I will. Thanks for everything."

Fifteen minutes later, I was cruising northeast. I clipped through a section of Arizona before entering Utah. In a town called Hurricane, I stopped for gas.

There were two men with motorcycles gassing up. One had a Harley, the other had a sportbike. When I came out of the store, they said "hello."

One was a tall, lanky, sandy-haired man. He commented on the enormous load I was carrying, and asked where I was headed.

I had developed many ways to answer that question vaguely, but I had a good feeling about these guys. It happens, but not often, that a Harley rider shares the road with "rice." I trusted my intuition.

"I'm going to Zion National Park."

"Hey! So are we! We're almost there." He walked to the rear of my machine, then gasped. "Massachusetts? You've got to be kidding! Jeez Girl, how long did that take?"

Now comes another shocker, I thought. "This is Day 81 since I left home."

"No way. Ken, don't you feel about this big right now?" He held out a thumb and forefinger. "Where have you been?"

"All over."

"By yourself?"

"Yup."

"You've got guts!"

"So they say."

The other guy, quiet until now, spoke up. "How is it, riding that bike long distance like that?" He wore a one piece leather suit of blue and white which matched his CBR.

"You should know. You're here from California." I could see his license tag. "That's quite a hike, too." I ended up asking them for their company. "You want to share a campsite? It'll be cheaper."

"You sure you want to do that?"

I felt like I could trust them. "Listen, most of the time I am alone. I'd like to hang out with you. I trust you will watch out for me."

They agreed, and we headed off, a trio of excited characters bound for the spectacular mystery of Zion National Park. We rode in staggered formation, with me sandwiched in the middle. I felt secure and happy at my simple twist of fate in having met them.

At Zion, I paid twenty-five dollars for my own Golden Eagles Pass. Our camp fee was eight dollars a night, which we split three ways. We were allowed to set up all three tents on one site at Watchman Campground, within a gorgeous canyon. Formal introductions were made at last.

Ken, who rode the blue and white rice burner, was from Southern California. Scott, from New Mexico, rode a black FXR Super Glide. They were about my age.

"So, did you guys meet on the road and become friends?"

Ken answered, "No, we've been friends for what—twenty five years now?"

Scott affirmed with a nod, as he pounded in another tent stake.

Ken continued, "I got married and moved, but every year Scott and I get together for a motorcycle trip."

Scott stood up and stretched. "His wife's really cool. Not too many married guys get to take off like this."

"Yeah, she's awesome. She's my best friend. I miss her already. She's not into taking long trips on the bike, especially this one." He jerked a thumb towards his CBR 900 with the uncomfortable looking passenger pad. "So, she does her thing and I do mine. We trust each other. I love my wife."

I was impressed. There is hope. There *are* good men out there.

After we had set up camp, we went to a Mexican restaurant and sat on the porch overlooking the cliffs that personalize Zion, as the sun tainted the sky a brilliant, fiery orange.

Much later in the night, a thunderclap startled us with its force, and was followed by flashes of lightening practically on top of us. The rain came, warm and wild. The electric storm was incredible. Probably the most fantastic and enjoyable weather I'd seen. Every time the lightening flashed, it created drama. It glittered and flashed like a strobe. The cliffs would be silhouetted, a black mass surrounding our campground, then moments later another series of bolts would light up those same cliffs into ornate walls of orange sculpted rock showing its face all aglow. I was mesmerized. Enraptured.

"Can you believe how *beautiful* it is?" I exclaimed, gleefully. "This has to be the most powerful thunderstorm I have ever seen! Look at all the lightening! Do you see the beauty? The changing face of the canyon walls around us? Can you see it?" I cried.

I ran into the middle of the field and twirled in the rain, feeling it drench my clothes, my bare arms and legs. I tilted my head back and drank in what I could, and danced and twirled while the thunder crashed and the strobe lights of heaven made havoc.

"Dee, come back her under cover. You're crazy!"

I laughed and twirled. "No! This is a gift for me. After braving monsoons while riding, after so many days scorching in the desert sun at high noon, this rainstorm is mine! I need the moisture. I want to get wet! I've been through worse, nothing can stop me now! Come on!" I was a wild woman. "Come out here with me."

"You're wild! Totally loco."

"And I don't care."

The storm ran its course, and we were the only ones outside. Tired, soaked and thrilled, I sat down at the wet picnic table and listened as the thunder crossed the sky from mountain time, into the pacific time zone. That same kind of storm had devastated me in other times and other places. Tonight I was elated. There was no way to explain. It just happened that way.

After that climax, there was nothing left to say, no way to improve on the day or night. We bade each other good night and retired to our three separate tents.

Miles: 197

"Sir, pull into this parking lot!" the ranger signaled with his palm outstretched, facing me.

Shoot! Now I'm in trouble.

I parked sedately while the bespectacled ranger stood near the tunnel opening, blabbing into a hand held radio. He left his station with a stern expression, his hands on his hips.

My raingear and helmet kept my identity from him.

"Sir, did you cross the double yellow line?"

I nodded my head up and down.

"Were you riding with the other two fellows, and did they violate the law as well?"

Oh please. I rolled my eyes.

"Don't turn your back on me, young man. Turn around and face me," the voice of authority spoke.

Restraining a smirk, I pulled my helmet off and faced him.

"Excuse me—young lady, I mean. Where did the other two go? Did they cross the double yellow line inside the tunnel, too?" he repeated.

I was annoyed. "Why are you asking me? You know the answer. You've already been on your radio with the woman at the other end of the tunnel."

"Don't get smart with me! You sit here. You're going to be detained. We have a policeman coming to talk to you."

"You mean, to give me a ticket," I guessed.

"Whatever."

At last, a park police cruiser swung in, and the driver strode over to me, pen and pad in hand. He asked if I had passed traffic within the tunnel.

"You know that I did," I looked him in the eye. "Normally, I wouldn't, but because I knew it was one way traffic, I took the chance. I'm sorry." I tried to appeal to his sense of good will.

"Who are the other guys? Are they friends of yours?"

"Yes."

"What are their names and where are they from?"

Gosh. What's with the third degree? "Scott and Ken from New Mexico and California."

"Scott and Ken who?"

"I don't know their last names. We just met yesterday."

The uniform scratched some notes.

"License and registration."

I groaned. "Um, they're in my tankbag, back in my tent, at Watchman."

"You're supposed to drive with your license on you. That's the law." He wrote another note.

"I have twenty-four hours to produce them. That's the law, too."

"Do you know your license number?"

I recited it.

"Where'd your friends go?"

"That's what I'd like to know."

"Nice friends," he remarked, snidely.

The whole situation was beginning to bug me. "Look, I'm sorry I passed inside the tunnel. I thought it was safe, and I went for it. Have mercy. I'm admitting I was wrong. I learned my lesson. Next time I'm tempted to screw up, I won't do it."

The square-jawed policeman ordered, "Wait here." He went to his cruiser for several minutes.

When he returned, he gave me a ticket. "I'm fining you fifty dollars for crossing the double yellow line and passing cars inside the tunnel. It's payable in seven days, or you can appeal and get a court date."

Sighing, I took the ticket. "I can't believe you actually ticketed me. I was compliant. How come other people do whatever they want, all the time, speeding, passing and everything else and never get caught, and good folks like me get penalized for one mistake?"

"That's just the way it goes," he said. "Hey, I gave you a break. I could have added fines for not having your license and registration on you."

Glumly, I muttered, "Thanks a lot."

He climbed into his car, leaving me to continue my ride, after the one hour delay. I would never find the guys. I continued following the Mt. Carmel Highway.

The road curved and swooned over a fantastic landscape, while my mind replayed the events which led to my latest episode with the police.

*   *   *

The boys and I set forth to ride and hike in the park. There was a tunnel over a mile long which we looked forward to riding through. We saw that the tunnel opening was guarded by a lady park ranger.

Remembering the beautiful, black girl, Tina at Yosemite, I rode ahead to ask this traffic guard for special privileges.

"Get back in your place! What makes you so special?" she snapped.

I returned to my place. "What a witch!"

Traffic was held up, and let through only one direction at a time. Finally, our section of waiting motorists got the go ahead. As we passed Wonder-Witch, she issued something into her walkie talkie, and then we were swallowed by the tunnel.

We were having a roar of a time in there, revving our engines, downshifting and upshifting, making lots of noise. The three bikes' individual voices combined, the rumble of Scott's Harley, the whine of Ken's CBR, and the growl of my Supertrapps. We beeped, hollered, laughed and whooped, making pandemonium which reverbated down the length of the shaft. You can imagine.

Suddenly, Scott shot out to the left lane and sped forward, with Ken in hot pursuit. The tunnel curved gently and I lost sight of them. Son of a Bee. Last night I complained to them about crazy drivers who do stuff like that. Knowing that there would be no oncoming traffic, I went after the men. I overtook the head of the procession, and just as I swerved back into the right lane, the tunnel opening appeared, and so did a stern little ranger.

All that aggravation because I wanted to play with the boys. Where *were* they anyway?

*   *   *

After a few miles, I relaxed. Navaho sandstone, layers of varying shades of orange, pink, tan, red, tan and white were exposed by erosion over thousands of years. The effect was dreamy and artistic, a photographers ideal. Being alone, I pulled over frequently to "Just Be." I ran my hands over the smooth, slickrock and touched different layers, noting how the texture from one shade to the next was different. I crushed a tuft of sage against my skin.

There were beautiful scenes to enjoy, imaginary faces and goblins to gawk at, found in dollops of rock formations which geologists call hoodoos. I marveled at the testimony of Utah's beauty.

At the East Entrance, I turned around for the return trip. I meandered back, and found that Wonder-Witch was waiting at the tunnel exit. She glared at me as I went by.

When I pulled into Watchman Campground, my friends hadn't come home yet. Off with the raingear, and time for a sponge bath.

It wasn't until sunset, that I heard the motorcycles arriving. Before he had even parked the Harley, Scott raised his voice, "Hey Girl! What happened to you?"

"You don't want to know. *I* got a ticket for passing in the tunnel." I told my tale of woe, and showed them my bona fide ticket.

"We pulled over to wait for you, but then another ranger harrassed us. If we went back for you, we would have been nabbed, too."

Scott added, "Heck, you've come cross country by yourself, traveling alone for nearly three months. One little day at Zion without us wasn't gonna hurt you. You're an independent lady. We knew you'd make do, and we'd catch up with you later."

These guys were aces. First they got me into cahoots, then they insisted on helping to bail me out. Each of them gave me fifteen dollars towards my fifty dollar ticket. I slipped the money into the ticket envelope gratefully, and thanked them sincerely.

"Good night, Lady Di. Maybe you can think about going to Bryce Canyon with us."

"We'll talk about it in the morning."

After I was zipped into my roomy tent, I listened to the murmur of my friends' low voices, and contrasted it to last night's background noise, the thunderstorm. Every day brings something new.

Miles: 47

In the morning we went riding in the park, and then hiked to the Emerald Pools. There, we were treated with cool air, in what seemed like a rain forest. Moss, ferns and broadleaf trees abounded. Vines climbed the walls and flowers became hanging gardens. A waterfall cascaded over a cliff, and we stopped talking to listen to the myriad voices of Mother Earth. We continued on the trail to see the Upper Pool, and having been satisfied by our one hour hike, began our descent, a little slower. We knew our time together would soon be over.

They tried to convince me to visit Bryce Canyon with them, but, much as I wanted to, I had to be moving on, in a different direction.

Back at camp, as we got packed to go, Ken asked Scott for some tools, to fix something on his Honda.

"Sorry, I left them at home."

"I have some tools and a socket set with me," I volunteered.

"Figures," Scott said good-naturedly, "Here we are on a two week road trip without any tools, but it's a girl who comes prepared."

I reminded them, "I'm on my own out here, for three and a half months. I *need* my own tools with me, just in case."

"Yeah, just in case some macho guys forget their own!" Ken laughed. "So can I use your socket set?" It was a minor procedure, and soon we were all squared away, packed up and ready to roll.

Leaving Zion, we rode in each other's company for a few miles. When it was time, we pulled over and bade each other farewell. One more time, I had to say, "So long. Remember me, as I will remember you."

Interesting geology is a main attraction at Zion National Park in Utah. In this particular area, the rock striations look like cake batter. Other places within the park feature fast rivers, hanging gardens, waterfalls, and dramatic canyons.

I have accepted fear as part of life . . . I have gone ahead
despite the pounding in the heart that says: turn back . . .

—Erica Jong

CHAPTER 29

RENEGADE

September 7–9   Days 83–85

*A*ll by myself again, I felt anything but sorry. The way things changed from day to day was a good thing, a welcomed thing. In the company of others, I felt fortunate and social. In solitude, I delved inward, examining myself, my soul, and my response to this way of life. In solitude, I focused on the sound of my machine, and the color of the dirt in a new region. When I was by myself, I paid attention more, to the temperature, the passing scenery, the flight of a falcon.

Rte. 89 unfurled into another land, one less dramatic than Zion, but still beautiful. Cliffs of rust, brown and orange gradually muted to shades of pink, tan, and yellow, as the miles wore on. Desert landscape lie spilled across the land now, and I crossed the Utah/Arizona border again. Pastel stripes layered decorative arrangements over buttes, mesas and plateaus. This was the land of the Navaho.

At a crossroads, I recognized Tuba City, where I had passed through on my way to Flagstaff. Gosh, only three weeks ago? Seems like a year's worth of experiences since then . . . Grand Canyon, my sister in Tucson, Joshua Tree Monument, Bakersfield, Yosemite, Vegas . . . and through it all, I've had time to stop and smell the roses, feel the prick of a cactus spine.

In Tuba City I gassed up, looked beyond the hogans into the outlying pastures of sheep and sheep-herders on horseback, remembering the richness that I discovered through their poverty.

From there, I had to alter my course dramatically, having ridden way off a direct route, for the sheer joy of seeing the western open spaces, and to be in the saddle a few hours longer than I had to be.

Camping at Navaho National Monument was free, and admission called for a stamp on my new Eagle Pass. As soon as I had selected my campsite, a man walked over and introduced himself. "My name's Joseph. I am a guide for Tag-A-Long Tours, and this week have only one client. I think she's pretty sick of me by now." He laughed, his eyes crinkling under a mop of curly dark hair. "Anyway, do you like Szechuan? I'm making a stir-fry, and will have more than enough. Come on over when you get settled."

"Okay. I had crackers and V-8 planned for my supper."

"Nah, that's no good. I'll feed you like a queen." He turned, and I watched his husky, athletic form depart.

As I set up my tent, I wondered why the majority of people think that a woman wouldn't be safe, traveling alone. It seems to me that just because I am by myself, I'm offered more opportunities for strangers to show me how kind, helpful and generous people are. I love America, and I love how I wasn't afraid to follow my dream.

Joseph called out, "Dinner will be ready in five minutes."

Nothing like fresh vegetables and chicken in a spicy sauce over rice, when all you were expecting was crackers and V-8 juice. I put away a generous portion, then cooled my palate with a slice of watermelon.

Joseph's client, Carmen, kept to herself. Perhaps he was right. Maybe she had grown bored with her vacation.

After dinner, I went back to my humble abode and took care of things I did daily. In between chores, I gazed out over the expanse of red-rock canyons that etched their way over miles of undeveloped land.

This particular campsite had the grandest view of any place I bivouacked at, ever. My site sat on the edge of a smooth, rock drop-off, sloped steeply to lose itself under a carpet of sturdy trees. The landscape stretched before me, in a fissure laden property of red-rock glory.

I took a walk, and by the time I returned to my campsite, the sky was a vivid palette of midnight blue, orange, scarlet, fuchsia, violet and gold, enhanced by the clouds that floated near the horizon. Five or six people stood staring at the spectacle as it unveiled its miracle, the birth of an evening.

"Welcome to my campsite, Strangers," I exclaimed.

The onlookers turned to me, noticing my tent for the first time, so mesmerized by the sunset, were they. "Oh, sorry. Forgive us. We're going now."

"No. Welcome. I'm happy to share the view." The sun set at last, and one by one the other campers returned to their own campsites.

I had been invited to tea, so before too long, I went across the way and met Mr. William Hiney and Buzz, from Atlanta, Georgia, who had also been invited by Joseph to spend the evening. The older gents regaled me with stories from the early 1900's, and drilled me about my adventures.

"Sure glad you ain't my daughter. I'd be worried sick."

The sky was spattered with stars when I walked home to my tent in the moonlight. As I undressed in my tent, I looked out one last time. A coyote peered at me from the edge of my site. I held its gaze, until he silently padded off. I felt touched, as if he had some kind of message for me.

Miles: 263

Enjoyed a righteous breakfast with Joseph and Carmen, except for the yellow jackets which came from all directions. Breakfast was a bowl of strawberry yogurt, with granola mixed into it, but I had to look at each spoonful before depositing it, to make sure there were no bees sitting on my next mouthful.

Joseph kept imploring me to "Eat it up. I'm not taking any of it away." After he'd washed the dishes, and began packing the Tag-A-Long truck, he insisted that I take the remaining granola cereal, a large zip-lock bag full.

Carmen seemed less reserved than the day before, as if she was happy that this was the last day of her guided tour.

I returned to my lovely, free campsite, and got to work. After a trip to the john, I donned my leathers and mounted up. Joe was standing on top of his vehicle, securing his supplies. We shouted to each other, and Carmen raised her eyes from the pages of her book to watch me go.

*   *   *

People who have traveled all over America were eager to share information, and would often ask me if I had been through Monument Valley. There were two highways that could take me by the red sandstone formations, and I chose the way that would take me along the easterly border, then north into Utah. The road was in terrific condition, and I sailed along effortlessly, engulfed by the ultra-western looking display of spires, buttes and wind sculptures. One of the most attractive features about Monument Valley, is its lack of any additions. No buildings, bill boards, no signs or concessions stood in the way of the natural view.

At a town called Mexican Water, I met with US191, and crossed into Utah. Monument Valley was behind me, and the depth of the orange and reds in the dirt faded to tans and pinks. Gradually, I came to accept the inevitable; I'm leaving the red rocks that I love so much. In another day or two, everything will be different.

So long, Southwest.

Then, a familiar sight came into view, the mountains of Colorado!

A strange feeling overcame me, as if I was coming home. Maybe it was because I was going to Road's castle. Thinking of it made me miss him. I didn't know if he'd be home, but I sure hoped so. Either way, he had shown me how to let myself in, and insisted that I make myself at home if he happened to be away.

The sky overhead had changed as I took my erratic course over two hundred miles of varied terrain. My need to get to my destination became more urgent as I tried to beat a storm building over the Sleeping Ute Mountain, but I lost the race when I got to Cortez.

When you're riding two or three hundred miles practically every day, fifty miles is nothing, so when I got caught in the downpour in Cortez, hungry and anxious to see my handsome Colorado gunslinger again, I didn't stop to put on my raingear. Durango is only about fifty miles away, and it's warm out, I figured.

That was a stupid move which resulted in a 125 pound female, sopping wet, doggedly refusing to stop until reaching her final destination. No matter that the teeth are chattering, and the body is shivering, and the belly aches for a meal. The next stop will be in Durango, unless the beast needs gasoline first.

I made it to Durango without gassing up, and went directly to Road's place, chilled to the bone. As soon as he heard my bike, he stepped outside the screen door to greet me with a big smile and open arms. He made me feel wanted and very welcomed.

Together we unloaded my bike, and brought my stuff in out of the rain. Once I was safely off of the bike, my body began shaking violently, in an effort to warm up. Road saw this immediately, and turned the shower on, instructing me to take my wet things off and, "Get in. Now."

He laid out some sweats for me, then left me alone while he ran errands. When he returned he found me asleep, curled up in a blanket on his bed. When I awoke, the unmistakable warm scent of home baked bread filled the air.

"Hey, you waking up now?" Road asked sweetly. He came to sit near me and hugged me, wrapped in his blanket of Mexican origin. "So, how ya been since I last saw you? What's it been, five weeks?"

"Yeah, I think. Maybe more. I've covered a lot of territory. After New Mexico, I came back into Colorado and visited a couple of different friends. Then I went to Nebraska."

"Nebraska—what's in Nebraska?" Road asked.

"You don't want to know," I evaded, "but, I came back to Colorado, went all over the place, then hit Utah, and Arizona. I went down, when my tire got caught in a trolley track during a monsoon, in Tucson."

"What happened? Did you get hurt? How about the bike?" Road asked, concerned.

I told him about it. "Luckily, I was planning to stay at my sister's for a few days, anyway. By the time I left, I was all set, and the bike was good to go."

I tore at some hot bread that Road placed before me, and asked him to open a bottle of wine for me. "Sure," he said after a tiny hesitation. "I was saving it for a special occasion, but you are it. You are a special occasion, to me." He had such a winning smile. Gosh, what a cutie.

"Thanks."

"So," he poured two goblets of cabernet, "how'd it go with your sister?"

I told him all about my visit there, and "then after that I went to Yosemite, and Los Angeles, Las Vegas, and Zion National Park, which I loved. I just left there yesterday morning."

"All right. I guess you got around some," he lifted his glass for a toast. "This one's for you. Thanks for coming back to see me."

"Thanks for having me."

I was still exhausted, so Road tucked me in and left me for the time being. I slept like a log through the night, not a very romantic specimen, I'm sure, but I was comfortable. I was with the man called Road.

Miles: 263

My map of Colorado was spread out before me, crisscrossed with pink and yellow highlighter marks. None of the other states could compare with Colorado, the way I kept coming back. How many roads I had traveled. How many mountain passes I'd traversed.

Road looked over my shoulder, and helped me settle on the best way to get to Denver. There was no direct route, so I picked one of several different options for a zig-zig course.

He asked about the different colors.

Excitedly, I explained, "At the end of each day's ride, I mark my route in an alternate color. Where the two colors meet, I know that's where I spent the night. This turned out to be a really smart idea. I can look at my big map of all the states, and see that this is the distance I prefer to travel in a day." I held up my thumb and forefinger, with about three inches between. "So, then I figure out where I'm going, and see if there are any hostels, state parks, campgrounds or Women On Wheels in the vicinity."

Road nodded, comprehending it all. "Sounds like a good plan."

I showed him the large U.S. map I had, two feet by three feet. He was a lover of maps, and took some time to appreciate the record of my journey.

"Hate to say it, but it's time for me to wrap things up," I said, as I folded the map, and put it away. A half hour later, my motorcycle was packed and I was ready to have breakfast in a Durango restaurant, with Road as my companion.

We ate our generous portions, laughed and talked, and made promises that would be almost impossible to keep.

"Remember, I say things now, but years from now, everything could be different. Like, if I got married, or something, not that I ever expect to get married . . . " I rambled. I had to be going, but, this time I knew I wouldn't be traipsing back into Road's back yard any more. This time, it was good bye.

"You know that I have people, Dee. If you should decide to move to Colorado, don't forget what I've told you. You will always be welcomed here. I will help you get your feet on the ground. No strings attached."

"Thanks, Road. I know it." We stood out by my motorcycle, facing each other, holding hands. Road kissed each of mine, and we embraced on the sidewalk.

I climbed onto my motorcycle, feeling much like *The Renegade*, going through life, riding into somebody else's heart, and then leaving it behind, taking with me only memories, my bike, and my sleeping roll. Oh yeah, and ninety pounds of luggage.

Road squeezed my shoulder, and because you can't kiss with a helmet on, he touched my nose and winked at me, for the last time.

I started my bike, looked over my shoulder and pulled away. I was going to miss him. Two thousand miles is a long way, even for a rebellious guy and a wild woman.

*   *   *

For a moment, I let myself feel sad, but then, the road took me to the bottom of the Million Dollar Highway. This was the road that had taken me to the BMW rally in Durango, a week after my big crash off the cliff. It was a twisty, writhing, stretch of road encompassing mountain passes over ten thousand feet in elevation. Sunlight Peak. Coal Bank Pass. Molas Divide. The extra beautiful Red Mountain Pass. This should have been an awesome day to ride.

The moment I got onto the first few curves at the foothills of the Million Dollar Highway, it began to rain. Not a light drizzle, but a steady, heavy drizzle, which forced me to stop right there, while I could. On with the raingear, at the start of my day's ride.

The ride was challenging after the first ten minutes or so. Instead of glancing at scenery, I had to pay attention to wet and slippery roads. The sky was dark, and stayed that way. I stayed dry, but my Gore-Tex gloves were leaking. After a while, it was chill city, for me. The temperature dropped, as I climbed and descended each mountain, with determination.

At Montrose, I banged a right onto highway 50, through more beautiful scenery which I had to ignore, while I concentrated on the rigors of hundreds of twisties in the rain.

I crossed the Continental Divide for the final time in this year's trek. Shortly afterwards, I turned left, and drove north on highway 285.

By this time, I have ridden about two hundred miles, and have been miserable from the get-go. When I pulled over in an open stretch of valley, and dug under the rain cover for my map, I groaned with the discovery that I still had another hundred to go, at least.

When the going gets tough, the tough get going.

The stretch through the valley allowed me some freedom to ride fast, but then I was up into the mountains again, and had to slow way down. I had been riding all day, and now it was getting dark. Besides that, my helmet had developed a serious problem.

The face shield on my AGV helmet, had two little vents at the top, which could be slid open, or closed, but when I crashed at Grand Mesa, one of the vent covers had broken off. I had never noticed any detriment, however, during this particular rain storm, the rain hit me at such an angle, that single raindrops would smack me right on my open eyeball. Each time stung for a few seconds, then caused my right eye to water.

When the night fell, my speed decreased accordingly. I couldn't see. It was terrifying.

Not only did that tiny hole assault my right eyeball, it allowed rainwater to get on the inside of my shield. During daylight, it hadn't been a problem, but after sundown, it crippled me. Because I had slowed down, cars would ride up on my butt, and they couldn't pass me. Their headlights would reflect in a kaleidoscopic array inside my face shield, blinding me. There was no shoulder to pull over onto, to let them pass. I rode agonizing miles.

I tried wiping the helmet, but my gloves were saturated and only made it worse. I was doomed.

By God's grace, I survived. At one point, I came upon a refuge, a service station, at last. I went in and made a bowl of steaming hot chicken noodle soup, and laced it with jalapeno pepper rings. That ought to warm me up.

As I wrapped my hands around it thankfully, I wondered how I could ever go on. I was planning to go to Nancy's apartment. She said it was to be my home away from home.

This was Saturday. She had told me that there was one weekend that might not be so good. Somebody was getting married, and she might have a lot of relatives crashing over at her place. Gosh, I bet it's this weekend, but I can't remember.

A girl about twelve, and a man about fifty arrived. My bike sat out in the pouring rain.

"Doesn't look like a very nice day for a ride," the man commented, sympathetically.

Totally bedraggled, I looked his way. "It isn't."

After he purchased a couple of cokes and snacks, they sat at the table near mine. "Where're you headed?"

"I have a friend in Denver. This morning I left someone in Durango. He said Denver was only two hundred miles, but I've already ridden three."

"Today?" the man's jaw slacked open. "You've ridden that thing three hundred miles in one day? Have you had rain all day, too?"

"Yep. From the moment I got on the Million Dollar Highway," I muttered.

"You have guts. You must be a lot tougher than you look," he said, while his daughter stared at me, her head tilted a little to one side.

"I'm having a really rough time. Now that it's dark, I can't see, because my shield is leaking. Cars get behind me, so close I'm afraid they'll hit me. They are impatient, but I am so vulnerable. Don't car drivers realize how they make it worse for us bikers, when they get on our tails? If they'd give me room, I could have enough time to safely pull over and let them get off my butt, but instead they crowd me, and make it impossible. I'm not ready to die."

"Thank you. I've never thought of it that way before. In the future, I'll try to remember, that biker could be you!" He rubbed his chin thoughtfully. "By the way, my name is Jack, and this is my daughter, Lauren."

"Pleased to meet you," I replied. "I'm Diane."

"Where are you going in Denver? Why don't you just stay at my place? I have an extra room. You're more than welcome," Jack invited.

"I can't. My friend is expecting me," I lied.

"Are you sure? My place is just outside of Denver. You can see your friend tomorrow," he pressured.

"No thank you, really." Something made me feel uneasy. "I should go to her house."

"Here, let me give you my phone number, and if you need anything, you holler."

"Maybe you can help me, now," I implored. "My friend lives in Lakewood, and I've been there before, but never from this direction. Can you give me directions to Lakewood?"

"Oh, sure. Where's she live?" he asked.

"I told you, Lakewood," I answered.

"Yes but, what's the address?" he pressed.

"It doesn't matter, does it?" I felt Nancy's privacy was at stake. "If you can get me to Wadsworth Blvd. I'll be able to find my way from there."

"Oh, Wadsworth? We'll be going right by there. Tell you what!" he exclaimed, "Why don't you follow us, and we'll lead the way. You won't have to watch the road. Let me be your eyes. We still have Kenosha Pass, then you won't have much farther. I'll lead you directly to Wadsworth Blvd. I don't want anything happening to you."

He had seemed a little pushy, but now I felt enormous relief. I had a guardian angle to lead me through the danger ahead.

"Thank you," I said to him. "Thank you," I whispered toward the starless heavens.

I was warmed up, and ready to do it.

As I followed the car, I felt better. He kept ahead of me, slowing whenever I dropped back. The hour was after ten. I was tired, and my hands started to get cold again, inside the wet gloves.

I worried that Nancy's apartment would be a full house. I felt desperate enough that I would beg her to let me unroll my sleeping bag, and sleep in her pick-up truck bed. It was parked underneath a carport. I would arrive in Denver, and beg her guests to feel sorry for me.

City lights appeared at last. I followed Jack and Lauren into the grid of streets and signs. In a little while, Lauren hung out of the car window and pointed to my exit.

As soon as I got there, I knew where I was, and found my way to Nancy's. Having doubts, and feeling self conscious to arrive in such a ragged manner, I worked my way into the apartment complex and over to Nancy's carport. It was empty! She wasn't home.

This time, as I unlocked her house and let myself in, I felt at home. I surveyed the scene, and did not see anything to indicate that the place was being used for a cheap motel by twenty relatives. Great! I wouldn't have to sleep under the carport!

At this point, after the incredulous weather I'd splashed my way through, I wouldn't care if I had to sleep in the bathtub. I was dead.

I had to bring everything inside to dry out. After a hot cup of tea, I settled into Kit's bed. I shivered at the thought of how tenuous today's excursion had been. The circumstances had made for one, very trying day.

It's amazing what extraordinary feats one can accomplish, when one has no choice. You do it, because you have to. Tomorrow has got to be a better day, but not a more worthy one.

Miles: 384

One of the best things about taking secondary roads is the unexpected little surprises you come across. This is an example that I found along Route 36, which runs along the northern border of Kansas. This marker indicates that I was virtually standing in the Geographic Center of the United States.

Oh the worst of all tragedies is not to die young, but to live until I
am seventy-five and yet not ever truly to have lived.
—Martin Luther King, Jr.

CHAPTER 30

THE COUNTDOWN BEGINS
September 10–13   Days 86–89

Snuggled into Kit's twin-sized waterbed, with Jingles the cat curled up near my waist, I had fallen fast asleep. But, when I heard voices, I awoke and realized Nancy had come home.

She came up the stairs and peeked her head into my room. I sat up on one elbow and announced, "I'm back!"

"Hi! I see! Are you comfortable? Don't get up—go back to sleep. I'll see you in the morning." She stepped away and closed the door, leaving me to snuggle back down, with a smile on my face.

After a good night's sleep, I got up when I smelled coffee brewing. Nancy greeted me happily, and poured a cup for me. "I put your clothes into the dryer."

"Oh thanks. I hope you don't mind. I helped myself," spoken out of courtesy. I knew it was okay.

"Don't mention it, Dee. Of course, I want you to make yourself at home," she reassured me, as she fed the cats. By the time we were on our second cup of java, her boyfriend, Jim showed up.

After telling them about my harrowing ride the day before, I explained how it felt to come in to Denver and drive straight to my home away from home. Jim left, and then I was able to fill Nancy in on all the good stuff that had happened since I had seen her in the beginning of August.

"Let me get my log book. So much happens every day, it's hard to keep it straight." I pulled the little brown notebook out of my tankbag, and opened it to the diary section. "Gee, exactly one month ago I was here. It seems like an eternity."

"Hey, you were going to see your old boyfriend, when you left my house. How did that go? I remember how worried you were," Nancy reminded me.

"I dunno. It was strained. I'm glad to have seen him, but . . . I don't know what's going to happen with us." I paused. "Being out here on my own, I've met some other guys. You remember Road—from the BMW rallies?"

Nancy flashed her dimples and answered, "Oh, yes. He was a hunk, and it was obvious he liked you."

"Right. I've gotten to spend quite a bit of time with him, and we had so much fun. Of course, a few visits isn't the same as being in a relationship, but, being with him made me think. For several years, I haven't really given anyone else a chance, but now that I have, I've discovered how nice it is to be admired and enjoyed, genuinely. No hard feelings, or smoothing things over. No biting my own tongue. Everything was so comfortable. With Russell, I don't think it's worth the struggle."

After plenty of girl talk, the laundry I had thrown in the wash the night before was done, signalling me to begin packing. "I'm glad you came home last night. I would have been disappointed if I didn't see you this time. Remember that other time, when I spent the night and you never even saw me? I felt like Goldilocks."

"Yes. We'd gone camping with Jim. Kit will be disappointed that he didn't get to see you one last time, but he spent the night at his grandmother's."

"Tell him thanks for giving me his waterbed."

It took some time to get the bike packed, because I kept stalling. "I can't believe what a good friend you turned out to be. You've been better than a sister." I felt a lump in my throat. "Thank you. It means a lot to me."

"Me, too, Dee. I think you're pretty special, yourself. I'm glad we met, and that I have had a place to offer. It's worked out well for both of us. Trust me. You have given to me, too—more than you know."

"Well, this is it. Today when I hit the road, I am essentially homeward bound, for the first time."

"Okay. Be prepared. The eastern part of Colorado is nothing like the parts you've enjoyed so much." She tilted her head toward the sky. "I hope you don't get rain."

"Me too." It looked awfully gray.

I pulled my bike backwards out of the carport, then got my gear on, while Nancy watched. We hugged and said good bye, and then it was really time to go.

One hour later I had broken free of the tangled interstate traffic, and was sailing along on an open road which stretched in between golden fields of grain, while purple mountain majesties faded in my rear view mirror.

No! Stop! Turn around! *That* is where I *belong*.

I cruised through a town called Last Chance, and then Cope. I couldn't help thinking, "This is how I cope. I ride my motorcycle. I ride it far."

The land was flat, and the Colorado Rockies that I had loved so well, had fallen from view.

I struggled with emotions, as I hurdled eastward. Three months have passed, and I always felt like I was moving forward. Right now, I felt sad, as though I was leaving something behind.

Another leg of my journey began, when I departed the Mile High City this morning.

The Kansas state line came into view, and I pulled over for my photograph.

WELCOME TO KANSAS

The plains unfurled below a heavy cloud cover, and the day offered a comfortable temperature to ride in. Prairie Dog State Park appeared to be about a hundred miles further, and I whined along at a pretty fast clip.

Every now and then, a car or truck would be traveling west on the same road. Each time, the driver would raise a hand off the steering wheel to wave, or lift his arm from the edge of the open window, as a greeting for me.

At first I thought, there must be somebody around here, that they have me confused with, but after several incidents, I tried to beat them at their own game. It seemed like everyone was so happy to see someone else on this long, empty stretch of highway, that they simply had to wave. The next time someone came along, I threw my gloved hand up first.

That seemed to be the big entertainment of my ride. Plus, the speed which I could drive along this straight, flat road. The speed limit seemed irrelevant. I went whatever speed I felt like, and today

I felt fast. The wind made me feel better, even as I sped along in a direction, opposite of where I would like to be.

Oh boy! I see some excitement ahead! *There is a bend in the road!!!* I tilted the bike, an umpth of a degree and executed the curve. Wow. That was exciting, I jest, but that's how it was. The road was so straight, that a minor bend in the road, was a tiny relief from the monotony.

But, even though the drive could have been more fun, I enjoyed the pretty farmlands, the flatness of it all. What a contrast to the scenery just a few hundred miles back. There were beautiful weather beaten barns, and new structures, acres and acres of agriculture, and I felt as though I was miles from no-where.

But, I wasn't.

I entered Norton, Kansas, and spent the night at Prairie Dog State Park, right on the main drag.

Miles: 316

During the twilight hour, all creatures great and small began their daily routine. Frogs, turtles and fish swam below the water's surface, searching for insects to feed on. Storks and egrets waded in the water, shrouded by silver mist. Coyotes flickered in and out among the cottonwoods, keeping an eye on the feathered creatures, while another band of coyotes sent a hundred prairie dogs running for cover. Overhead, a hawk circled and cried out. Each group was the hunter, and yet, it was also the prey.

The coyotes announced their whereabouts, vocalizing their antics in a high pitched chorus. Their daily jaunt through the prairie dog village is comparable to a sweepstakes shopping spree. Total chaos, greed, sloppiness and sheer joy charges the atmosphere. The pack is out for a romp, rather than to actually hunt. They are well fed. But, for all the fun the coyotes are having, their targets are terrorized. The prairie dogs lie low until the danger seems to have passed.

A flock of geese came in for a landing on the lake, and I tried to sleep some more. Later on in the morning, I got up and looked around. All was quiet and still. Eight egrets decorated the edge near my domain. Because I was the only camper on this entire loop within the park, I considered it mine. My kingdom delighted me.

After my shower, I broke camp, and headed east on US-36. Desirous of a large breakfast, I found myself seated in the Town and

Country Kitchen. In a moment, my waitress came to take my order, in her little gingham dress and apron.

Sounding unoriginal, I asked her, "Has anyone ever told you that you look like the actress Geena Davis?"

Blushing, she giggled and said, "You think I look like an actress? I don't know who she is."

"Oh, come on. Thelma and Louise? She was one of them, in that movie," I said.

"What movie?"

"Thelma and Louise! I can't believe you don't know of that movie. These two gals take off in a car and . . . oh, never mind. Some day if ya get a chance to see it, you ought to," I suggested.

By now, all attention was focused our way. Before we knew it, everyone had the girl turning this way and that, as they checked her out and agreed that she did look like Geena Davis.

Throughout my breakfast I had company, as Geena came by in every spare minute to ask me questions about my travels. All the usual topics were covered. Why? How? Aren't you afraid?

"So what do you do for a living that you can just take off this way and travel all summer?" asked Geena.

"I *was* a recreational therapist, but I quit my job in June so that I could do this."

"But why?" she seemed puzzled.

"Why not?" That wasn't the proper answer. It was too cliche. "A few things steered me towards that decision. Mostly, because I wanted to. We all think we have to work, day in and day out. We can't do anything without taking our daily job into consideration. Ever since kindergarten, we have our months, weeks, days and hours scheduled."

"You're lucky you could do it."

How many times will I hear that? "Luck? It wasn't luck. I took a chance. I quit my job of sixteen years. I had to pay four months rent in advance, so that I will have a roof over my head when I return. I left my home, my friends and family. I have no idea what I'm going to do for work when I return. No, it's not luck. It was a decision."

I continued, "At this time in my life, I have no mortgage, no husband, no kids. This is the time in my life I had to do it. Either do it, or spend the rest of my life wishing I had."

She shook her head, and stood up when Mickey arrived with my breakfast. "This girl is interesting. You should hear what she's been up to all summer."

Very briefly, I summarized my trip, but wanting to change the subject, I asked about life in Kansas, the heartland of America.

Mickey went to the cashier's counter, and returned with a postcard. On it, a teenaged girl stood in an endless wheat field, wearing a dress that billowed around her knees. Over one shoulder, a dangerous looking sky poured itself into a funnel which touched down on the horizon, artfully decorated by a red barn and a windmill.

"This is my sister." Mickey went on to tell me how her mother won a prize in a photography contest with this picture. "Actually, they were just going outside so that my mom could take some practice shots, and my sister went out to model for her, when all of a sudden, this tornado appeared. My mother's as nuts as my sister, and they stayed out long enough to get this photograph."

Interested, I studied the photo, looking at the use of light, texture, color, drama, all that creates art, insomuch that Mickey came to me with four more. "Here, you can have some. They're a gift from me. You need to save your money."

"Why, thank you," I exclaimed.

At the next table, three older folks finished their breakfast, having told me about their excursion to Florida in their huge home on wheels. When Mickey brought them their check, the younger gent asked for the pleasure of paying for my breakfast as well.

The woman with them lingered behind when they went to pay at the register on their way out. She placed her hand on my shoulder and leaned closer. "You seem like a wonderful young lady, so full of life and courage. Choose your paths well. One day you will have many memories to last you, when your body betrays you and you cannot do the things you wanted to." She straightened. "I do not wish to envy you. I say this to encourage you. All of my life I put things off until 'after.' Now, 'after' has gotten here, and I am too old for my younger dreams to make any sense any more."

She smiled at me and her eyes became watery. Outside, a car horn tooted, and my elderly advisor joined her companions.

I left Norton, Kansas with five postcards and a full tummy, compliments of small town American folks.

Back in the saddle, I fairly flew across Kansas. US-36 continued in between farmlands of hay, corn, sunflowers and what else? Not much. I kept thinking of Dorothy and the Wizard of Oz. The wind blew across the plain in a steady current, which kept the motorcycle at a slant, but I didn't have to fight for my right to ride. The road lent itself to a cruise of 70–75 mph, with nary a bend or grade to contend with. When the occasional vehicle came my way, I looked forward to "the wave." It was about the most exciting thing since breakfast.

While touring, the first one hundred miles goes by without a thought of distance, and the second hundred starts to remind you that you're locked into a limited position for an extended amount of time. During that time, my thoughts will typically flow from my latest escapades, to the environment I am passing through, to imagining what my destination will be like. On this day, I was troubled by something new.

The countdown.

This being my eighty-seventh day, means I have two weeks of travel left. Only two more weeks. For some reason, two weeks seemed altogether too short. My usual tactic of rearranging my thoughts to look at the bright side didn't seem to help. The countdown has begun.

I analyzed my love life. I thought of Road, and Thomas, and Russell. What am I leaving behind? I worried about falling into the same rut I had been in before. How can I go back into a relationship that doesn't enhance my life? After all the changes and growth, after all that I have accomplished, and the dream that I am still living in . . . how can I settle for one who will not hold me close and treasure me, like a precious gem?

I worried about work, or lack of it, when I get back. What will I do if I can't get a job? What if I end up only working five or ten hours a week at the gym? What kind of full-time job will I seek? What will make me happy? Can I settle for a job, any job, because it pays the bills?

How much have I sacrificed, really, for this wild act of selfishness and discovery? I've always gotten paid to have fun. Can I accept a mundane job, because I have to have one? I honestly don't think I can.

Feeling twinges of despair, I finally got a hold of myself, and decided firmly that some things I can do nothing about, right now, out here, so leave them alone. Why ruin the moment, worrying about the future?

Right this minute, I am tooling through Kansas on a motorcycle! For crying out loud, ten years ago I had no idea that one day I would even own my own bike, and I'd never been further west than Michigan.

Kansas! Any second a tornado could form, just like at Mickey's house, and really perk things up. Just imagine.

This twister picks its way across the acres of wheat, touching down at intervals, and since I have no idea what else to do, I just keep riding, hoping to outrun it. That's how I solve a lot of problems, after all. I ride, and ride, and ride. So, there we were, my Red Pony and I, until suddenly we were plucked from our path, and I hung on desperately, with my eyes squeezed tightly shut, and after spinning dizzily inside a thunderous whirlwind, I find that we have been deposited atop a nice soft haystack, one hundred miles away. Well . . . that was the happy ending.

The setting here, along with the monotony of the road and unchanging scenery reinforced my imagination, and I was able to dream up about ten scenarios in which I suffered a tornado, got separated from my means of transportation, or left it alone in search for safety, only to discover its destruction when I emerged.

I scanned the horizon, and searched the fields to my left and right. Only a narrow ribbon of highway lie stretched before me, seemingly my only means of escape. I wondered how much I would be hurt, getting flung back down to earth after a violent flight. After every place I have been, all the things I have seen, would I live or die in this simple, golden state we call Kansas?

When things get dull, I rely on my imagination to liven things up.

Quite unexpectedly, I came upon two points of interest.

US-36 is named Pony Express Highway, due to its history as a main overland route for the young men (and orphans) who craved danger and adventure, as mail carriers, riding horses at breakneck speed, in a relay that called for great courage, stamina and fast horses. I found this quite fitting. After all, my motorcycle is my Pony Express, and I am the fearless rider.

The second was a sign constructed by the side of the road. It showed the contour of our country, and Kansas is depicted, a rectangle in the middle of the US. The sign reads, THE GEOGRAPHIC CENTER, and explains that this location is the exact point where a plane map of the 48 states would balance if it were of uniform thickness.

There I was, in the center of things, as usual.

Ever since I took to long distance riding, I've listened to people whine about Kansas. I don't need to agree with everybody. I loved Kansas. Crossing paths with people who wave because I happen to be traveling on the same road as they are . . . Having an inkling of trepidation, knowing I was in tornado country caused my imagination to soar, and kept me entertained. Seeing beautiful barns, aged to a pewter appearance, sagging into the next century, the sunflowers bobbing their cheery heads in the breeze . . . all of these things pleased me, making up for the lack of curves and hills.

Even my lunch stop amused me, as the man in overalls who clung to a ladder painting the building outside, washed his hands at the sink behind the counter, before he fixed me a sandwich.

By the end of the day, I ended up at a WOW house as planned, after a full day of riding which I rated easy and fast. Joan was surprised to greet me at her door. I had called her during breakfast, but she'd never gotten my message.

Her husband was away on business. She set me up with my own room, and went out for a jog while I did my laundry. Her house was immaculate and spacious, set among other immaculate, spacious houses. Joan treated me to dinner at a pub, and we enjoyed meaningful conversation. Later on, I sat on her screen porch and watched hummingbirds come to the feeder.

Miles: 368

In the morning, Joan put on her business suit, and left me in her home, while she went to work. Leisurely, I packed up and left. Until I came here, I didn't even know this woman, yet I was treated like a guest of honor.

I cut through Kansas City, crossed the Missouri border, then continued in a more or less southeast direction, on secondary roads. The terrain was hilly, the roads straight, and lots of deciduous trees offered shade from the sun. It was a perfect day to ride.

When I rode through a town called Peculiar, Missouri, I thought of some of the rather unusual names I encountered over the summer. Ten Sleep, Wyoming. Cope, Colorado. Why, Arizona. Now, I crossed the Arkansas border, and found myself on Looney Tavern Highway.

After dark, I finally arrived at Old Davidsonville State Park, just outside of Pocahontas. I paid $6.50 for site 15 and wearily set up camp using my headlight.

Miles: 382

By 10:30 AM the sun had burned off any drizzle and fog. I rode into Pocahontas for breakfast, but couldn't locate a restaurant. After a few loops through the quiet town, I pulled over by an autobody shop.

There were two men working on a nondescript heap of metal. One guy was ducked under the hood, another's legs stuck out from beneath it.

I flipped up my shield to shout, "Where do you get breakfast around here?"

The tow-headed man extricated himself from under the hood, and turned my way. He smiled at me, clearly displaying a missing tooth, right in the front. "What you say?" he drawled.

I repeated, "Where do you get breakfast?"

"You wanna go over the bridge-" He offered unclear directions. The other guy rolled out from under the jalopy, and I almost fell off my bike. He had all his front teeth, but he looked at me with proverbial crossed eyes.

Arkansas! I thought of the silly, politically incorrect poster back in Colorado. Here was living proof. Amazing.

Eventually, I found the breakfast place. When I parked, I noticed a miniature dachshund peeking out of a car window. After breakfast, I saw that same little hotdog running around the parking lot. I returned to the diner and told a waitress.

A teenaged girl came outside to collect her dog. She came over, eyeing my motorcycle appreciatively. "Is that a Harley?" she asked.

Considering my bike is the extreme opposite of a Harley, I couldn't resist humoring her.

"Why, yes. It is," I said.

She nodded seriously. "If I ever rode a motorcycle, it would have to be a Harley, too. I love them."

Okay, so I'm in the deep south, almost. Not where I planned to be when I first left home, but that's okay. What little contact I've had with folks around here has been interesting and amusing.

I continued in a southeast direction, got bogged down in Memphis, Tennessee, then was released and hurried on into Mississippi. Holly Springs National Forest gave me a break from the heavy traffic I endured.

These past four or five days I have felt an urgency to push on, and not waste any time. My time was running out, but I still had something to look forward to.

The Blue Ridge Parkway, which stretches 469 miles from Cherokee, Tennessee, all the way to Waynesboro, Virginia is one of my all time favorite motorcycle roads. Even after all the traveling I did this summer, I felt the same way.

For now, I was heading southeast, hoping to sleep at a WOW's house in Atlanta. There were no more mountains or hills for my ride today, and for the first time in months, I was east of the Mississippi River. Amazing.

I settled at the spacious and lush Tombigbee State Park. The campground was clean, green and nearly empty. After studying my maps for a while, I went to a pay phone and called Joyce Warren, of Atlanta.

Joyce had been one of the WOWs who originally wrote me a letter of invitation. She answered the phone.

"Hello, Joyce? This is Dee Gagnon, the WOW member that is traveling all summer. I am in Mississippi now, and can make it to Atlanta tomorrow. Will it still be okay for me to sleep over?"

Joyce sadly replied that this wouldn't be a very good time. She explained she'd just had a car accident and broke her collarbone.

I interrupted, "But, don't you see? This is perfect timing. I have been sent to help you. Please let me come. I've had that injury, and know how hard it can be. Just getting dressed is a struggle."

After hearing my point, Joyce agreed. She would allow me to help her out, in exchange for a place to sleep. "Great, I'll see you tomorrow evening." I hung up, took a little walk, and thought about *Chicken Soup for the Soul.*

Another day comes to a close.

Miles: 258

That best portion of a good man's life, his little nameless,
unremembered acts of kindness and of love.

—William Wadsworth

CHAPTER 31

ATLANTA
September 14–17   Days 90–93

I spent most of the day in Alabama, riding in between cotton fields. Great white puffs of fluff were evident on the low lying plants, and my imagination took me back to another century. Rte. 278 carried me among the cotton fields, lots of forest and farmlands. It was hot and sticky out.

The effects of long, hard riding for many days in a row, are wearing on me. I am fatigued, and fighting an ounce of depression.

WELCOME—WE'RE GLAD GEORGIA'S ON YOUR MIND

Atlanta was crazy with construction, frantically preparing for the Olympics, but just after sunset, Joyce Warren welcomed me into her tiny house in the suburbs. She didn't have much, but she had a heart of gold. There was corn on the cob in a pot on the stove, and grapes in the refrigerator. That was the extent of our dinner, simple and delicious.

Her little house had a guest room, and I was ready to collapse earlier than usual. Joyce asked me to stay an extra day, so that I could meet up with the rest of the Atlanta Chapter of WOW. They had an Annual Fall Campout, which would be taking place that weekend. Excitedly, I agreed to this unexpected surprise. They were going to a good place, and it was on my way. I could really use a day of rest, and wanted to wash my dirty, rained upon motorcycle, too, while I was here.

Miles: 386

Last night, I couldn't sleep. It's the same thing that happens whenever I'm over-excited or stressed. My next ride will actually have me pointed homeward, northeast. I'm so sad.

At 2 AM, I finally took some Sominex, which did its job. I slept late, too. In the last few days, I have crossed two time zones, losing two hours. At night, I'm not tired yet, then morning comes too soon. I was able to catch up a bit this morning, in the empty house, after I got up to help Joyce get dressed, with her broken collarbone and cast. In addition to that complication, Joyce lived with a permanent disability, which resulted from a stroke, even though she was young. The left side of her body was crippled. She had very little use of her arm, and her gait was awkward, but she was thankful that she could walk on her own. Now, she had to deal with an injury,too. She never complained, and accepted my assistance graciously.

Joyce only worked half a day, so that she could enjoy my company. She took me to McDonald's for lunch, and we both ordered salads, after I told her how I hadn't eaten at any fast food burger joints all summer. Before we'd finished eating, the reason she brought me there was evident. The Altanta WOW Chapter Director showed up and gave Joyce a package, which she turned over to me. Inside, was a red tee shirt bearing their club's logo. I accepted the gift, humbly.

Joyce and I spent the afternoon at Zoo Atlanta, a wonderful place of education and ecology. We had a nice time getting to know each other, and then we got into her rented car to go to a favorite restaurant of hers. I stuffed myself with a barbecue sandwich and unlimited salad bar. After dinner, I washed my bike in the driveway, and she told me of her involvement with Women On Wheels. She loved the motorcycling lifestyle. She joined WOW, and offered her talents as secretary.

"I wish there was such a thing as automatic motorcycles. Maybe I could ride my own, since I wouldn't have to 'clutch' it," she said.

"There *are* automatic bikes. I don't know much about it, but, I know that there have been some made. You've got to look into it! That would be great if you could get your own bike," I encouraged.

*　　　*　　　*

The next morning, Joyce took me to another fast food joint, where I had breakfast with the Atlanta gang. Joyce claimed she didn't want to go on the camping trip, on account of her car accident. She had pre-registered for a ten-dollar meal ticket, which she gave to me, refusing to let me pay her back.

Across America, all the WOW people have been so kind and generous towards me, and I have appreciated every single action. But, Joyce was the epitome of them all, for it might be easy for someone who 'has it all,' to share a little, but when a person has almost nothing, and they give it *all* away, their gifts are a real treasure. Her rewards in heaven will be great. She will certainly wear a crown, and will dance with joy.

Fourteen motorcyclists, mostly women, decided whether or not to put on raingear, before leaving the city. We rode to T.W.O. (Two Wheels Only) Campground, in Suches, Georgia, on a twisty, wet, mountain road. There we set up camp, in between rain spells. Our required meal tickets bought us a fabulous steak dinner, cooked on the grill. We had a blast. I was happy to be with a group who weren't fair weather riders. This was my last weekend on the road, and it was an unexpected pleasure to have so many comrades camping out with me.

The men hung a tarp overhead, and we partied under it, as the night continued to get wetter and wetter. Cathy Davies, one of Women On Wheels National Big Wigs, got out a needle and thread and mended the torn lining inside my leather pants. I tried 'Boiled Peanuts,' but didn't quite develop a taste for them. The night waned, and I fell to sleep with the sound of rain gently falling.

Miles: 85

Sunday morning arrived, damp and drizzly. We were the only ones staying at T.W.O. that weekend, and we took advantage of the lodge, where we could order breakfast and hot coffee. By the time I'd finished my bacon and eggs, it stopped spitting out. Everyone was in good spirits, as they planned the remainder of their day.

For the first time that I could recall, my tent was wet when I put it away. Considering that I'd been camping out for three months now, that was a pretty good record. Even though many nights I had slept with the patter of rain overhead, it had always dried by the time I got up.

The gang from Atlanta wished me well, and then I hit the road, alone. It wasn't raining, but it didn't look very promising. I wore my raingear, right from the start.

The famous 'Deal's Gap,' with 318 curves in 11 miles, is a special right of passage amongst sportbikers. 'The Dragon,' as it is referred to, waited for me, writhing in the mist of the Great Smoky

Mountains of Tennessee. I charged forth on my mighty steed, ready to do battle.

Under lousy circumstances, I made my way to US 129, and with my overpacked bike, and a front tire starting to show show signs of wear, I tackled the treacherous roadway, in fog and rain. Visibility was poor, and I was unable to hang and bang the way I wished to. Instead, I moved along carefully, vowing to return on a better day, sometime in my life. Riding 'The Gap,' in the fog and rain wasn't scary, but rather, it was disappointing.

Riders who obviously knew the road intimately, streaked by in tight packs of lime green, florescent orange and sinister black, out for their usual Sunday ride. I was the amateur.

I somehow missed the 'Crossroads of Time Campground and Motel,' where I would have stopped to buy the prestigious tee-shirt, *I slew the Deal's Gap Dragon,* and on the back, the dragon lounges against a tree, munching on a muffler, and it says, *But, sometimes The Dragon wins.* I mailed some money to Cathy Davies and asked her to pick one up for me. It would be one of my few souvenirs.

I took the Foothills Parkway, but most of the beautiful mountain views were still shrouded in clouds. Touches of autumn began to appear, along the sides of the road. It didn't quite clear up, but it didn't rain very long, while I was riding. I got settled at Elkmont Campground in Smoky Mountain National Park, for eleven dollars. After a hike, I went to bed early.

One week from today, I would fall asleep in my own bedroom. I felt sad about it.

Miles: 158

I can learn from anyone, but I do not stop at that.
I go on trying to learn from myself.

—Zane Grey

CHAPTER 32

BLUE RIDGE PARKWAY
September 18–20   Days 94–96

*I*t was still raining when I awoke. I had to pack my tent away, all wet again. In my raingear, I left the invisible Smoky Mountains.

The Blue Ridge Parkway stretches 469 miles from Cherokee, Tennessee to Waynesboro, Virginia. It is an ultimate favorite road of mine. When I made plans for this trip, I intentionally 'saved the best for last.' It was supposed to be a soothing balm, to counteract any sense of sadness as my journey approached its end.

The Parkway has a lot to offer, in the way of nature, fantastic scenery, geography and history. Numerous pull-offs allow a traveler to stop and stretch their legs, read about the view there, and take their time. It is not a road to hurry on. There are no bill boards, no street lights, and the road is in an immaculate state of repair at all times. As I rode along the crest of the Southern Appalachians, I drank in the cool, moist air, and stopped at numerous overlooks. In between, I cruised along, slightly over the maximum speed limit of 45 mph, occasionally getting bogged down behind slow moving vehicles. No problem, I'd pull over at an overlook, gawk at the scenery, then take off and close the gap I'd created.

There are only a few places to stop for gasoline, refreshments, rest rooms or souvenirs. At one such stop, I met a trio of Harley riders, two guys and a girl. High on the virtues of the Parkway, they immediately struck up a conversation with me at the gas pumps. Soon we were joined by a man riding a white Gold Wing.

Someone noticed the shallow tread depth on my front tire, and recommended replacement. I had been keeping an eye on it, myself, for the last week.

"I'm only a thousand miles from home. I 'm going to get a new tire as soon as I get there," I assured them. Soon, all three men were giving me their two cents, while the woman sat on her bike, waiting patiently.

I wasn't too worried about the tire. A thousand miles seemed like such a short distance to me, now. Why spend the money?

The Gold Wing rider opened his back trunk, and took out a thick reference book from Honda. Quietly, he came over and showed me that there was a Honda shop just off the Parkway, in Boone, North Carolina, about a hundred miles north of us. I appeased them all and took the address and telephone number. Satisfied, the Harley riders mounted up, and roared off, southbound.

The Gold Wing rider wore a white cowboy hat, and chain smoked during his rest stop. We told about our 'vacations,' and I learned he was from Canada, and his name was Lawrie. He was easy to look at. Without the pressure of the others there, he urged me again to do something about that tire.

"It's not bald. It's still got quite a bit of tread left," I argued.

"Yeah but, you're on the Parkway, and it's all curves. That will eat up a lot more of your tires." He looked overhead, "And the weather doesn't look like it will be too good, either. You're probably looking at a couple of days of rain, and that's slippery. You really should get a tire. You're close enough to a shop, it's not even out of your way."

Stubbornly, I wouldn't be swayed. "I'll think about it."

September is an excellent time to be on the Parkway. It is much less traveled. Lawrie and I left together. He rode faster than my customary speed and he wasn't stopping at frequent overlooks, as I had been. For a time, I stayed with him, but then I pulled into a scenic overlook and let him go. Later on, I passed one of the pull-offs in time to see him stamping out a cigarette. In a few minutes he caught up with me. For a time he rode at my dallying pace, then he moved away with a wave. Throughout the day, we rode in this manner, at times together, at times apart, but sooner or later I would come upon him, pulled over and waiting for my company.

I had told him that I would be camping at Linville Falls. When I got there, there he was, lounging on his Wing waiting for me at the entrance.

"This is where I stop for the night," I said.

Lawrie asked me if I wouldn't like to continue with him. He was going a couple of hours longer. It was still early, only five o'clock. He said he was getting a room, and it would be nice if I would come along.

I would have loved to have continued with him, but needed to bide my time. I had to stretch about a thousand miles over a week. I was tempted to go on with him, but did the right thing. "I'm sorry. I'm going to stay here. Thanks anyway. Have a great vacation. It was fun riding with you today."

Lawrie took off his cowboy hat, put on his helmet, and waved good-bye. I paid nine dollars for my campsite, and went hiking.

Miles: 200

It rained during the night, but not when I got up. As I packed, my conscience got the best of me, regarding my front tire. I decided it would be stupid of me if something happened, since I was riding on an almost bald tire. Boone was only seven miles off the parkway, at an exit about thirty miles north. I'd go in to Boone, leave my bike off, eat breakfast someplace, then be good to go.

I placed a call, the shop was open and they said, "Drop in." Suddenly, I felt much better. Responsible.

I got to Boone, stripped the bike, then left it, while I located a joint where I ate a big breakfast. Afterwards, I returned to the Honda shop, to wait a little bit longer.

The door opened, and I smiled when I saw a white cowboy hat. "Lawrie! You came back to ride with me!" But then I saw more. His face was strained, and I noticed bandages, and a pant leg cut off at the knee. "What happened?" I cried.

"I hit a deer this morning and totaled my Wing," he replied, miserably. He told me exactly how it happened, and my heart filled with sympathy. Amazingly, he was barely hurt. He broke a finger, and scraped up one leg pretty badly, but that's about it. He came to the Honda shop to see if they had any Gold Wings. "In white," he specified.

My bike was done, and I paid a hundred and nine dollars for the job. There was nothing I could do for my unfortunate friend, so we said good-bye, again, and I left him with best wishes.

How lucky I didn't go with Lawrie the night before. I would have been riding with him this morning, and would have seen him crash, and had to avoid, not one, but two deer, plus a sliding nine-hundred pound motorcycle and a tumbling man. All on wet roads, with a bald front tire.

I was very lucky.

*   *   *

After my new tire, I only rode for about four hours. I settled in to a huge campground at Rocky Knob, along the Parkway. I cruised around a few big loops, and settled in to one, where I was the only camper. There was one loop hosting about fifteen touring rigs, complete with trailers, but that group was having way too much fun. They were obviously well marinated, but I felt more like having peace and quiet.

I scouted my loop, and gathered enough wood for a gentle fire, suitable for thinking deep thoughts. It sure is beginning to look like autumn. I've been gone so long.

Miles: 162

When I woke up, the skies were gray, but it wasn't raining. I finished riding Blue Ridge Parkway, but only pulled into a few overlooks, due to poor visibility. There were some turkey buzzards close to the roadway, and I stopped to observe them for a while. They look wicked and ugly when they're not in flight.

I had lunch at the rather fancy Peaks of Otter Restaurant along the Parkway. I had been there with Russ once. I wanted to replace the memories. Mission accomplished. Now I remember animated conversation with a clutch of senior citizens from Florida.

Skyline Drive is attached to the Parkway, and so I continued my northward trek, on this scenic, curvaceous road. Touches of autumn are even more obvious, the further north I get.

I stopped to camp at Loft Mountain, along Skyline Drive, in Virginia. As soon as I got onto the road leading to the campground, I spied more than a dozen deer. One deer stood in the center of a site on the D-loop. She stamped her foot, and I stopped my bike. She turned tail, and bounded away. She was my omen. Stay here.

Miles: 202

Into each life some rain must fall,
some days must be dark and dreary.
—Henry Wadsworth Longfellow

CHAPTER 33

RAINY DAY BLUES
September 21–22   Days 97–98

*W*hen I got up, I searched the sky for some kind of promise for sunshine, but only saw a thick white firmament overhead. After a shower, I began breaking camp.

The majority of camp sites were empty, but an older couple was camped with a small truck and trailer a few sites away. As I hitched my saddlebags onto the motorcycle, and proceeded strapping the rest of my nomadic possessions onto it, the gentleman from across the way strolled by and asked me a number of questions about the Honda.

"Please, come on over for breakfast. My wife and I have more than enough," he invited.

I accepted, gladly.

After my work was done, I went over and officially met Vernon and Vivian from Pennsylvania. Vivian's blue gingham apron covered her front side, protecting her from bacon splatters as she stood before a gas grill, delegating small tasks to her husband. "Bring out that canned fruit, too, honey, in case Diane wants some." She added that the potatoes wouldn't be ready for another fifteen minutes.

That allowed me a perfect opportunity to take a walk. I started along my way, and came upon a young deer grazing. It raised its head and watched fearlessly as I came a bit closer. I froze, and the deer tore another mouthful of tender leaves from a bush and chewed, all the while keeping an eye on me.

The deer at this park were numerous, and spoiled, almost to the point of being tame. Step by step, I closed the gap between the deer and myself, until I backed away, not wanting to violate the code in which wild animals should be treated as such, no matter how cute or docile they may seem.

My walk revealed eight more deer, in the ten minutes I took. Each time, I gazed at their graceful beauty, their slender match-stick legs, their large, liquid eyes. Such a seemingly delicate creature, and yet such a menace, if I was to zoom along woodland roads without actively searching for their presence. What happened to Lawrie yesterday reinforced that feeling.

Back at Vern and Viv's, I ate a bit of fruit, then helped myself to bacon, eggs, and home fried potatoes with onions and peppers.

We shared stories of how much we enjoyed camping in the great outdoors, and I answered the typical questions I had gotten used to. Viv and Vern couldn't imagine how they would feel if I was their daughter, but I tried to put their minds to ease.

"Campers are good people, right? Here I am, a total stranger, stuffed on your food and hospitality, because you invited me. How do *you* know you can trust *me?*" I challenged them gently.

"Some things you just know—you have a feeling. Your spirit, and your friendliness just shined through, and we thought we'd like to meet you and make sure you don't leave hungry," Viv said.

After a pleasant breakfast, I said good-bye. I pulled away slowly, leaving Loft Mountain Campground behind.

The rest of my ride on Skyline Drive went much like yesterday. The road was full of curves, but it was wet, and the overlooks offered me repeated views of fog filled valleys, despite the fact that I'd hit the road as late as noon. The drive was an effort, rather than a joy.

After Skyline Drive, I continued north, crossing through a corner of West Virginia, then into Maryland on Rte. 11, which amazingly, was a lousy alternative to the Interstate. Stop and go traffic, one city after the next, too many cars, trucks and red lights interfered with everyone's forward progress and their moods. By now, sunshine was a memory of mine, and I wondered if I would ever drive out from under this bleak, damp weather canopy.

*   *   *

The biggest thrill of my day occurred when I came upon a Dunkin' Donuts coffee shop. I hadn't seen the trademark pink and orange sign for ages. In my home state, there are coffee shops on nearly every corner, and Dunkin' Donuts is the king of them all. My motorcycle seemed to pull in and park on her own accord.

When I burst through the door, it was with genuine excitement and glee. There were no other customers at the moment, and I exclaimed, "You don't know how *happy* I am to see you!" The aroma was sensational.

The two girls behind the counter looked at me dully. I blubbered on excitedly for a moment, about how I have traveled for months and this was the first Dunkin' Donuts I'd seen for ages, and I've been dying for a real cup of coffee. Two tepid faces peered through me, and my tirade fizzled out. Talk about needing personality makeovers—these gals were zombies.

Inside, I spread a map before me, and figured out where I would camp that night. While I sat with my large cup of hot, delicious coffee, a guy came in with Wall Street Journal under his arm, and after getting his cup of joe, sat at a small table near mine, striking up a conversation about the weather.

"Not a very nice day to be riding," he noted.

"I know it. I don't think I've seen blue sky for a week. Last time I remember seeing sunshine, I was in Atlanta, and I've been riding ever since," I replied.

"And where're you headed?"

I told him of my journey. He stared in disbelief.

"Did you have any bad luck?" he wanted to know.

"Why does everybody always want to know about the bad stuff?" I implored. "Tell me something, in the last three months of *your* life have you encountered any bad luck, yourself?"

I lightened up and explained that for the most part, my experience was incredible and that people were wonderful to me. "Right now, I've had just about enough rain, drizzle and clouds to get me down. I'm having trouble keeping warm, and then I'm setting up camp at night, which doesn't help to warm me up. No fires, the wood is wet, and I can't afford to buy it." I stopped complaining.

After the man's curiosity was satisfied, he left me with some kind words, got into his Yuppie mobile, and returned to his world of cubicles and spreadsheets.

The break warmed me up for a little while, and I worked my way along the busy metro streets of Hagerstown. Progress was slow. The motorcycle odometer turned over to fifty-seven thousand miles. I figured I was about six hundred miles from home. It was hard to believe that my expedition was coming to an end.

Off and on I encountered mild drizzle, the kind that covers your face shield with a fine mist, then evaporates, leaving a thin film of grime on it. All day, the traffic got in my way. The point of my day seemed to be lost in my desire to reach my destination, so I could just get off of my bike and maybe have a good cry. Emotionally, I was feeling strained. Was it time for me to be getting my period? No. Then what is wrong?

A car cut me off, and I stifled a rising urge to dismount, pound on the window and scream at the driver. Road rage? Me? That's not like me.

Hating the negative feelings, I needed to focus on something other than the external environment. The traffic, the ugly sidewalks, the dingy, wet look of everything . . . the way I had to keep putting my feet down, because there were too many lights to keep rolling, how many more hours of this? Part of the problem that was eating me, I knew. This is only the beginning. I have come closer to the over-populated, super-congested Northeastern United States.

This is the way it is.

While still in Hagerstown area, I decided to stop and stay at Cunningham Falls State Park. The camp fee was twelve dollars. Prices going up, value going down. It comes with the territory.

After I set up camp, it began to sprinkle. Lacking any motivation whatsoever, I did nothing physical to improve my mood. There was a waterfall, but I was chilled, damp, and despite knowing that a walk to a beautiful natural sight would warm my body and my spirit, I sat at my picnic table watching droplets as they formed little riverlets which eventually spilled over the edge to the spongy earth below.

At last I began to relax. My thoughts shifted. So many things I have learned. The reasons I took this trip never had sharp edges. Mostly, it was a little voice inside my head that said, *What do you mean I can't? Watch me!*

Sure, I had a decent job, but I was no longer happy with changes that were taking place, so I just quit! Just like that, after sixteen years. People don't do that! But, I did.

Yet, before going out and getting another job, and locking myself in for another sixteen years, I figured, heck, I'm not taking two weeks off in between jobs. I'm gonna do it in style and take the whole summer off! When in my life will I ever be able to do something like this again?

Now what? What will I do for work? What do I want to do? What can I do? What if it takes me a long time to get hired? As great as this summer was—did I make a huge mistake?

Somehow, I thought that maybe during my travels, somebody out there would meet me, and tell me that I am exactly what they are looking for. Strong. Adventurous. Intelligent. A risk-taker. Outdoorsy. Physical. Somehow, I hoped that an outfit Out West would make me an offer that I couldn't refuse. I imagined my life turning around as I led a string of horses on spectacular mountain trails by day, and rode my motorcycle across the desert at night. But, I did not seek work out there, only pleasure.

These things I considered, but didn't dwell on. As close as I was to coming home, I decided, now is not the time, nor the place to be worrying about a job. Right here, there's nothing I can do, so why waste energy worrying? Forget about that for now. Think about something else.

So many unexpected observations were made on the road. Things I didn't plan on. Lessons learned. The courage that I had to draw upon sometimes. Little things that I never knew before. Details never noticed, large things overlooked.

How in the course of a day's ride, when I was riding due north or south, I would see my shadow sliding alongside of me, and in it, I could see myself. My shape, my flying fringe, my helmet, the great bundle strapped on behind me, gradually shrinking, then hiding under my machine at noontime. Then, later on, the darkened image would emerge on the opposite side, and lengthen as the day wore on. Day after day I watched, and learned to judge the hour, by looking at the shadow that my Red Pony and I cast upon the ground that we covered.

Then, across the weeks, coming across road kill, specific to its region. In New England, we see mostly squirrels, then opossums, raccoons, and an occasional rabbit. But, this summer, I have seen armadillos, coyotes, elk, and other strange (to me) critters, common enough to lie rotting on the roadsides by the dozens.

Did you ever notice how often you will see two of a kind, dead, within mere feet of each other? Not just that, but, have you ever seen a raccoon cry? I have.

Squirrels—they come in gray where I live. But in some parts they are reddish brown. In some parts, almost black, and as big as cats, practically.

There were places I rode, where at perfect five second intervals red-winged black birds stood watch at the sides of the road, each effectively guarding his section of the bug buffet. Territorial, each claimed a parcel of road shoulder, and when insects were knocked down by moving vehicles, the opportunistic birds would snatch them up, if it should happen to be his own territory. Sometimes, I noticed this practice for hour long stretches of road.

Landscapes of such variety create this land, America. I used to refuse to *think* of traveling in other countries. I always said that I wanted to see my *own* country first. Well, I have done that. Today I can say, I have seen my country. I have woven my life in and out of these United States, taken the back roads, and tasted the flavor of small town America.

Would I do it again?

In a heartbeat.

This year I saturated myself in the red rocks, canyons, deserts, and sagebrush of the west. For several days, I had literally lived on the topographical edge of our continent, skimming along the great Pacific Coast highway.

Still, the one state I always imagined would be my dream land, I didn't step foot in. Montana. I'd been so close, but then I lost my wallet, and then realized how far Washington was, and that I would have to miss the Ride-In, or else miss Montana. I thought I might go back, but I got caught up in the Rockies further south, and fell in love with Colorado.

The future will bring me back to Montana. This is a promise I have to myself.

My objectives for this trip, did I meet them all?

Montana and Yellowstone Park—No
Grand Canyon—Yes
Yosemite—Yes
Visit my Grandmother in Michigan—Yes
Visit my sister in Arizona—Yes

Attend WOW Ride-In in Washington—Yes
Attend two BMW Rallies in Colorado—Yes
Stick to my budget of $30 day—Yes, on average

The sky had gone from dull gray, to dark, and I shivered to think of the frantic moments I would spend in my tent, stripping out of my layers, so that I could go to bed. But, in a minute I would be cozy in sweats, and I'd run to the ladies room, clean up, and end this day with a prayer for sunshine and warmth.

As down and out as I felt today about the weather, I recalled the days on end, filled with warmth and sunshine. So much, that I would invite riders to stick with me, because the sun followed me everywhere I went.

Just three more days, and I would be home. I wished I could just go home, see all of my friends and my cat and stay for about two weeks, and then pack up a different set of clothes to live with, and leave all over again.

I don't think I'm ready for a routine. How boring it will be to filter back into a schedule, after all this freedom and serendipity. What about my roommate situation? Somewhere deep inside, I know I have the strength to confront that issue, and resolve it.

Thoughts of magnitude shifted in and around my mind. Images of maps, and calendars, help-wanted ads flickered like reminders of things to come. Blue eyes focused on me adoringly through a mist . . . I lay dreaming of my Siamese cat.

Another pair of blue eyes gazed at me, troubled. I squirmed and tried to look away, but was attracted and bound to them. Russell? What is *he* doing here in my dreams? He doesn't belong! Please stop torturing me. You will never understand the things I do, the way I am, or the Spirit that guides me. Strong enough to become a gypsy, I am. Before those magnetic blue eyes, I weaken. The relationship should be over. We've had our time apart. But, I cannot be sure if I will stay away.

In my dreams, I coaxed a silver stallion to my side, and he allowed me to spring onto his moonlit back. My legs wrapped around him tightly, and we bounded off across misty meadows, and up a blue-green mountainside. I felt as though I was flying, and with each galloping stride I heard the steed's effort. We became enclosed by mist, and broke out above it. Below, appeared a thin layer of clouds, and I saw the nation spread out below, like a patchwork quilt.

The phantom horse spoke to me, "All of this is yours. What your eyes have seen, your heart has believed in. From deep inside you have found the courage to fly, even when all others denied it. Continue to love yourself, Child, and continue to love your world. There are many treasures, but only the faithful ever discover them."

The mystical beast came to the Eastern side of the country, and I saw how there were no more open spaces as we got closer to the coast where I lived. He slowed and began spiraling down, to let me off.

"Please don't set me down here! Take me back to the mountains, and the desert. Take me back to where I was."

The gentle beast touched Earth, and I slid off his back and dared to place my cheek along his sweaty neck and inhale the horsey fragrance that always serves to calm my soul.

With his silver mane tumbling over his arched neck, he turned to look at me with the deepest eyes I'd ever seen. "I'm sorry, Diane. It is you who must take *where you were,* with you. Hold it in your heart. Share as much as you can with anyone who will listen. From now on, *where you were* will always be a part of *where you are.*"

My eyes began to water, and I pressed my body close to the stallions warm, solid shoulder.

"It is time for me to go now. You are a blessed Woman-Child." Softly he nickered, and faded away into the starry velvet sky in my dream.

Miles: 183

There was drizzle and a very heavy cloud cover when I crawled out of my tent and looked around, shivering. I made a beeline for the bath-house and pressed the hand dryers repeatedly as I washed up, in an attempt to heat the room a little bit. I changed into the same clothes that I had been wearing the day before, because I didn't have much choice.

My spirits were low. I was not enthused about this day's ride, at all. The sky promised rain. Again, my tent was wet. I had to pack it away, just the same. I boiled water for tea, and my last package of oatmeal.

I felt depressed. I was depressed.

The pine grove wept upon me as I worked, great droplets of accumulated mist, falling ker-plop, ker-plunk. Surely, Mother Nature must be sad, for She has been gloomy and gray, and crying off and on all week. Perhaps She shares my emotion, and empathizes with me, as I reach the last days of my journey.

Maybe, She is helping me. The fun and freedom, the escape from one sort of reality, and the birth into another type of reality, has done me good. How can I possibly want to return to the old ways? Perhaps, Mother Nature is creating in me a need, and desire to go home.

For so much of the summer, I was blessed with the very best weather. If it was to continue, it would be that much harder to return. But now, I am forced to ride another day in dampness, cool temperatures, and negative feelings are developing. They manifest themselves in my gut, like a cancer.

Painstakingly, I packed my damp gear into place. The campsite was empty, except for my beast of burden, and my riding garments on the table. I made one last visit to the ladies room, which doubled as a refuge where daddy-long-legs thrived.

A sad-eyed girl peered back at me as I washed my hands before the mirror. I smiled, but although her expression changed, the vacant look stayed in her eyes. There was nothing I could do for her. I walked away.

In the next five minutes I dejectedly covered my body with a layer of damp leather. Thankfully, my boots were dry, and I struggled to pull Totes on, in order to keep them that way.

Totally lacking excitement, feeling heavy, awkward and clumsy, and fighting a feeling of despair, I mounted my Pony.

The stillness of the dank forest was disturbed when I started the engine, and then I departed.

I was The Lone Ranger, but I was not looking for new episodes. I was experiencing a sense of loss. I was leaving behind all the grand adventures.

The gloomy, heavy atmosphere was oppressive, and even as I continued down the road, I couldn't shake the morose emotions that welled up inside me, and spilled out over my eyelashes. I couldn't fight it. I merely accepted the inevitable, and eased on down the most difficult road I had to travel, the road that would take me away from the life I had been living.

Route 15 took me out of Maryland, into Pennsylvania. I figured I'd make Harrisburg in under one hundred miles. If I forced myself to get beyond that city, I would stop and have lunch somewhere around the halfway point. Hopefully, the weather would hold out, and I could conquer the second half of the day with some muster.

Gettysburg was along my route, but hardly caught my attention. I cut through the traffic, glancing at patriotic statues of soldiers on valiant chargers. Monuments, and stone pillars stood firm, silhouetted against the morbid looking sky. I thought, I must come back here some day and learn something.

But now, my main concern was to keep on keeping on. I wanted to outrun the rain, yet up ahead looked just as sinister. The riding was somewhat slippery, and my shield was grimy from fog and road dirt. The motorcycle was as smooth and reliable as ever, and when that thought crossed my mind I tried to think of some more pleasant thoughts.

On the top of the list was my cat. My warm, soft, cuddly kitty. She was one positive factor about my going home. I wondered how she would react. Would she remember me? A dog, you can be sure about, but cats are so darn independent. I was her human, but I ran away. Would she punish me in feline fashion, or would she take me back unconditionally? The cat has been with me for ten years, and never before did it shun me when I took off on my motorcycle jaunts. Yeah, but I never split for three months before. Still, I knew I would be very happy to hold her again.

After ample time dwelling on Shadowfax, hunger and deep chills nagged at me. I had left the multilane highway, opting for route 11, which runs along the Susquehanna River for some time, before veering northeast. Most of it, I found disappointing. The going was slow. The surroundings, not my cup of tea. I concentrated on my driving, and felt impatient at the many sets of lights. Now and then the road opened up, and I could ride fifty-five.

Finally, I picked out a place to eat. I stopped at an establishment, and thinking ahead, grabbed my raingear. Inside, the lights were dim, and there was a small clientele scattered about. As I chose a booth, a couple of guys at the bar looked my way and offered some comments regarding the weather. It didn't look good, they said.

I ordered a bowl of hearty soup, pasta salad and a sandwich. The soup was good, the sandwich was okay, the pasta was not. Suddenly, a few people barged in from out of doors, drenched. I looked out the window and it was coming down in buckets. Shoot.

My luggage and tankbag were encased in their raincovers. Now it was my turn. Using the ladies room to change, I gave myself a fright when I saw how disheveled I appeared. I didn't care. Physically, I felt much better, now that my tummy was full, and I had warmed up.

Back at my seat, I prepared my mapcase directions, and psyched myself up for the rotten ride ahead of me. I get to go sit on my wet saddle, and ride through at least a hundred more miles, so that I can set up camp in a wet forest. Oh, boy, I can't wait.

Nobody likes to ride in the rain. Some hate it more than others. I don't hate it. I'll ride to work in the rain, just so that I can take a ride on my lunch break later. If I have plans to attend a charity event, then it rains, I go anyway. Of course, it isn't my favorite of conditions, but I love to ride, period.

However, there comes a time when enough is enough. For six days in a row I have worn raingear. I haven't seen the sun, nor felt the warmth of its rays in a week. Blue sky? Where? Not anywhere near me.

As I followed the roadway along the river, the rain came in torrents. I might as well just ride through the river.

This is most definitely the most dreadful day of my entire journey, I thought. Worse even, than the day I went off the cliff in Colorado. Worse than the day I nearly ran out of gas in Wyoming. Even worse than the scary, wet day that I rode to Denver. At least each of those days contained hours of pleasure, and provided spectacular scenery. People that I encountered were friendlier, helpful and curious. Today, nobody seemed to see beyond their noses, let alone care about anything, namely me, except for the two guys at the bar who warned me of the weather. Gotta give them credit, I suppose.

Miles dragged by eternally. My 'waterproof' gloves were sopping wet. At stoplights I could wring my hands together, and squeeze out half a cup of rainwater. If I had to take them off, I knew that I would have to struggle to reinsert my wrinkled, red, numbed fingers.

My motto came back to taunt me. How many times had I quipped, "Ride with me and the sun will shine?"

Just the same, I remembered, many times people asked me about the rain. "What do you do when it rains?" "You don't ride in the rain, do you?" "Have you had much rain?"

The answer that developed after weeks of responding, was this— "I have had such good weather, almost every single day, that I wouldn't care if it rained for my last ten days. I would deserve it. I've been disgustingly fortunate, so far."

The time has come, and I realize my error. I *do* care that it's been raining all week. I *don't* like it. I want it to stop!

Shivering has set in. My hands are numb. Although the gloves are wet, I believe that they are still keeping me warmer than if I went without. My nose is like a leaky faucet, and I wonder if I'll ever make it to Scranton.

Any mountain that is climbed, is taken one step at a time, and mile by mile I forged ahead, searching the horizon for brighter skies.

Scranton wrapped itself around me, and without undo fuss released me on the other side. I continued on Route 11 through Clark's Summit, keeping a lookout for a package store. For hours, I had a blistering desire to bring some brandy to my next camp. I passed out of town, empty handed. Under no circumstance was I going off the main road to find three mouthfuls of fire.

Maybe the next town. Nope. However, this game kept my mind occupied and alert.

At last, I reached Lackawanna State Park, in Pennsylvania. I paid twelve dollars. By the cost of camping these days, I know I'm back east.

As I slowly circled the campground loop, I tried to imagine how I was going to possibly make the best of this day. How was I *ever* going to warm up? This depressing mood is sure taking a lot out of me. What is wrong with me? Normally, I can lighten up.

I parked my bike on a tar parking spot, and took my blue tarp over to the picnic table. Keeping my warm and dry helmet on, I hitched the tarp over the picnic table, using bungee cords and a length of twine I had carried with me throughout the trip, but had never touched, yet. As for the tarp, I rarely used it either, but tonight these items were better than gold.

The whole job took at least an hour. Stringing up tarps is something I have no experience with, and it proved to be quite a challenge. The work got my blood moving, and I didn't feel like a shivering wreck, anymore.

All of my bags got transferred from my bike to the table, where they would be protected from the rain. I went to the ladies room, to get out of some clothes. My entire upper left quadrant was soaked. There was a tear in my rain jacket, at the front of my shoulder, after the Colorado cliff incident. Today's downpour had trickled in, and gradually I had been getting wetter and wetter, on the inside. No wonder I was so cold.

There must be something warm that I can put on, in my bag. I slopped back to my site, and rummaged through my duffel, feeling grateful that I still kept all of my clothes in zip lock bags. The baggies were wet, but their contents were dry. I found some clean sweats, my thermal jersey, and camp shirt. My red wool stockings would make a difference, too. I knew from experience.

My leather pants were wet, despite my raingear. With the rain coming down as hard as it did, for as long as I was in it, the seams of my Gore-Tex garment eventually betrayed me. When I was astride the motorcycle, rain would spill down the front of my helmet, along the front of my jacket, then accumulate in a puddle in between my thighs. The puddle had saturated my gray long johns, from the waistband, to my knees.

I stood by the hot air blower and took off all the wet clothes. After I was dressed in dry things, I felt warmth return. I collected the wet things and wondered what to do with them. There seemed to be nobody camped here, besides me, so I draped them over the wooden stall dividers. I knew they wouldn't dry out, but, outside they would probably get even wetter.

Reluctantly, I crawled into my raingear. I was tempted to stay in the bath-house until dark, but changed my mind. I haven't sunk that low, have I? Instead, I went to my camp shelter, and got to work.

There was a thick layer of pine needles to set my tent upon. I found a spot a little higher than the surrounding ground, where I would assemble my humble home. My Coleman dome had a roomie 5'7" square floor surface. It stood five feet high, held up by two supports that cross over each other at the top, and attach to all four corners. A separate rain fly completes the package, which I tended to use only when necessary. I had gotten very adept at setting up camp, and as I went through the motions I reminded myself, 'Tonight and tomorrow night—then I'll be home!'

I passed the first set of shock-cords through the sleeves, and began popping the next into one long pole. The elastic cord inside *broke* and as it recoiled into its shortened length, the long pole disintegrated into several two-foot lengths which fell to the ground!

Now it breaks? I slumped to the ground. I *had* to get the tent set up. I collected the sticks, and tried to string the cord through them, one at a time, but, because it was elastic I could only go so far.

A mean voice mocked, inside my head. 'Ha! What are you gonna do now, smarty pants? You think you're so tough, but so far, it's been way too easy. Now, how will you handle this? Is it time to give up yet? Huh? Huh? Ha ha ha!'

Out loud, "I'm *not* giving up. I'm going to make it work," I continued trying to piece it together. Sometimes, I almost sobbed from frustration. Why is this happening now? This day has truly been a test of strength, will and stamina. I sincerely believe most people would have given up, *hours* ago. Even men.

I got situated at one corner of the tent, and fed the corded portion of tent pole through it, and tied a skinny knot at the end of the cord. One by one, I carefully attached the other lengths trying to keep enough pressure on the whole assembly to keep it together. My theory was that if I could manage to get that far, and if I could raise the tent, whatever forces were available would keep it together. The only hard part was keeping the sticks together while manipulating them at the same time.

I worked at it, desperately wishing, for once, that I had a partner. Then, it would fall apart again, and I'd be glad I didn't, because by now they would have cussed me out, for refusing to give up.

Then, I did it! I raised the tent, jammed the end of my stick into the tent's grommet, and hurried to reinsert the final two corners. My tent was up, broken or not! The interior of the tent was as wet as the outside, because I'd been at it for an hour. I took my towel and dried the tent interior, after attaching the rain fly. Whew.

After I tossed my bags inside the tent, my work was done. I settled down at the picnic table to read *Blue Highways*. Although I was still quite chilled, I didn't want to settle in to my tent so early. It would make me stir crazy. I would wait for darkness, before turning in.

While I read my book, occasionally a camper would come rumbling through the campground. Each time they slowly crawled past my spot, I wished them onward. "Keep on going, keep on going. You've got the whole place to settle. Don't stop near me." I just didn't want to be situated so close to comfort, after all the ordeals I'd battled on this day.

Using a pair of bungee cords on one corner of my overhead tarp turned out to be a clever happenstance. When the rain filled up the tarp to a certain point, the weight of it would stretch that one corner, and then it would all spill out.

So, in the steady rain, I sat huddled under my blue tarp, wearing my white raingear, reading a book about a man who struggled to find himself, by driving his van on America's blue highways.

A small, piggy-back trailer rolled into Lackawanna, and selectively cruised the loop, three or four times. With a twinge of selfish anger, I begrudged the driver, when he parked in the site right beside mine! Son of a Bee!

The pages of my book distracted me, and I pulled my woolen hat down a little further and got back into the story. Before darkness fell, I looked up when I heard soggy footsteps walking by.

"You know, you're welcome to come inside with us where it's warm and dry," he said, pointing next door to the piggy-back camper. "I've been where you're at, and it's no fun, so, come on over if you want."

I didn't say anything, and he didn't wait for a reply. I got back into my reading, and he walked on. Then, I couldn't concentrate. *Come inside—warm and dry—with us.* Who's "us," I wondered. Him and his wife? Or is it two guys? Why didn't I ask who "us" is? I stole a glance their way. The windows glowed with yellow light. *You're welcome—I've been there, it's no fun.* He's right. Maybe I'll take him up on the offer. First, I'll just finish this chapter.

After I had made my decision, I read William Least Heat Moon's words about the interesting characters he'd been befriended by, with interest. In due time, I reached the end of the chapter, and put the book away.

I dodged raindrops, and rapped on the door of the camper. The door swung open, and a burly arm reached down for me to grab. There were no steps, so I placed a boot on the door jam, at waist height, and was hoisted in.

"Hi! Welcome. I am Rob, and this here is Bob," he greeted me, with a sparkle in his eye.

I shook hands with the two of them, but my eyes were on the central feature of the room. I was standing in a tiny, cramped trailer, where every inch was utilized. To my left there was a tiny stove and sink, and counters and cabinets. Ahead there was a bunk, and a bed, below. To my right was a padded bench, and cabinets overhead, but, as I said before, the central feature of the room had my full attention.

It was a table. It's tabletop probably measured 18" x 24", and it was completely obscured by the variety of liquor bottles set upon it. They glistened like jewels, and I couldn't disguise my happiness.

"All right! Do you know how badly I wanted just a shot of brandy to warm me up? This is great! I'm so glad I decided to take your invitation," I blurted unashamedly.

"Well, you've come to the right place, what would you like? We drank all the brandy the other night."

I picked up each bottle, and settled on Peach Tree Schnapps. Rob did most of the talking, and asking of questions. He's the one who had invited me in the first place.

"You know what?" he declared, "When I saw you out there, I didn't really see *you*. I thought you were a man. Mind you, I didn't really look, but you have all that crap on, y'know, your rain suit, and that hat . . . I thought you were reading the Bible." He laughed. "Now, that would have been something, if you were a holy roller, and then came in here with Bob and me."

Then I had to explain what I was doing all by myself, and the book I was reading was a book about a guy like us. I learned that these two were a couple of Canadians on their way home from a trip to Florida. Rob was a story teller, and I couldn't be sure how much of what he said could be believed, but I was amused.

"Drink up, eh? We can't bring any booze over the border, so we've got to finish it off. We've only got a couple of days to go."

The little interior was so warm, with our body heat, and a lantern, that we actually opened windows. I remembered my clothes hanging in the bath house, and when I mentioned it, the men told me to bring them in.

Soon, I was warm enough to shed the rain suit, and felt quite at home with Rob and Bob. We toasted to our travels, we toasted to our meeting. We toasted for hope of sunshine on the morrow, and we toasted for the fun of it.

Rob, chubby and ruddy faced, had a constant smile, and brown curly hair. He prodded his buddy Bob for verification regarding some of his stories. He told me of his many get-rich-quick schemes, and showed me a collection of shark teeth that the two of them collected on the beach. They were going to make them into jewelry, claiming special powers. They gave me two fine specimens.

We killed off several bottles, none of which were full to begin with, before I finally decided I must go to sleep. "We have room in here, if you want. You don't have to sleep outside." Rob offered, clearing one of the cushioned "beds."

"It's true. I will sleep in the cab, and you can stay here," Bob assured me. "It's no trouble. I usually sleep in the cab anyway."

I told them, "You know what? If I hadn't already gone through the trouble of setting up my tent, I would take you up on it, but, I'm all set up. My tent stays dry inside, and my sleeping bag is warm. But, thank you anyway."

"Take this blanket. You can put it under your sleeping bag, as a buffer from the cold." They placed a heavy blanket in my arms. "Leave your things in here. We won't be going anywhere."

Before I got out the door, we laid plans to have breakfast together. These guys were sent by a Goddess. When I settled in to my sleeping bag, I was in a much better mood, than had they never arrived on the scene. What a day.

Miles: 227

It is a strange thing to come home. While yet on the journey,
you cannot realize how strange it will be.
—Selma Lagerlof, b. 1858

CHAPTER 34

GETTING HOME
September 23–24, 1995 Days 99–100

*M*orning arrived, still wet and cool. The heavy cloud cover hadn't budged. Within my tent, I reached for my riding pants, but changed my mind. The leather had gotten soaked through, and they were still wet. I opted to wear jeans, crossed my fingers and hoped for no more rain.

Rob and Bob's breakfast gave me an excellent start on the day. I sat in the humid, stuffiness within their trailer as potatoes fried in bacon grease, and absorbed as much warmth as I could. Then, I returned to my campsite to pack up my wet stuff, then had one last cup of coffee with my Canadian friends, and said good-bye.

The day's ride was a trial. My Gore-Tex gloves were soaked. The temperature outside was cool. I took I-84 out of Scranton towards New York, and forced myself to travel fifty miles before stopping. Each mile seemed like ten. At last, I passed my fifty mile mark, and took the next exit. There was a McDonald's, and I made my way straight to the ladies room.

I peeled my bulky, wet gloves off, and stood with my red, stiff hands under warm, running water. Then I took over a hot-air hand dryer, placing one glove at a time over the nozzle, trying to dry them out somewhat. Lots of women and girls came and went about their business, casting strange glances my way. To them, I must have looked a little bit nuts.

Back on the highway, the wind cut right through my still-wet gloves, and soon I was cold. Wearing blue jeans on the bike when I am used to leather, I felt the wind pass right through the fabric, but I thought wearing wet leather might be worse. At least I had a warm, woolen sweater beneath my leather jacket, to buffer its dampness.

For another agonizing fifty miles, I suffered. In order to avoid hypothermia, I knew I had to stop every hour. If only the sun would shine, but the sky overhead was covered with clouds as far as I could see, in any direction.

At the thirty-five mile point, I fought to keep from shivering. I rode with one hand at a time, while I held the other against my hot engine, finding some relief. Having a throttle lock, I was able to warm up my right hand that way, too. Every mile began to feel more like twenty.

Finally, I had ridden a hundred miles since leaving Lackawanna Campground, so I took the next exit and found a fast food joint and used the bathroom in the same manner as before. People walked in and complained about the heat, as I stood before the blow dryer, shivering. I didn't care.

Without having anything to eat or drink, I got back out on the highway. In mere minutes, I was cold again. I was in New York, and had wanted to make it to Connecticut, but I didn't think I could do it. Already, I had decided my next stop would be after only twenty-five miles. I didn't think I could safely ride fifty more.

It started to sprinkle. I started to cry.

At the Middleton/Maybrook exit in New York, my Red Pony slowed, and disobediently left the highway. I didn't fight her, and she took me into the parking lot of a Super 8 Motel. Thankfully, I dismounted.

My cold and clumsy feet plodded across the parking lot, and my wet and wrinkled hands pulled open the heavy door. My body shivered, and I heard my voice stuttering the words, "How much for a room for one?"

It was an out-of-body experience.

I heard the reply, "Eighty-seven dollars, Miss."

Suddenly, I felt my Soul reuniting with my Body, and I gasped. Eighty-seven dollars? That's a super rate? "Whoa, I'm sorry, I can't afford that." I hung my head and turned to go.

"Miss? Wait a minute. We do have one room for only $32.25, including tax."

I spun around. That was a fifty dollar difference! Still, it was a little more than one entire day's budget. But, it was sinking in, I was nearly home, and I still had plenty of money.

"How come one room is eighty-seven and another is thirty?" I asked.

"That one doesn't have air conditioning."

I couldn't believe it! How lucky and funny of a situation is that?

"Air conditioning? I'm *freezing!* What I want to know is, does it have *heat?* And can I control the heat from inside my room?"

She said, "Yes. There's a thermostat in there."

"Where do I sign?"

*   *   *

In my room, I filled the tub, loving the bubblebath I still had sample packets of. I used two. I cranked the temperature up as high as it would go. I spread my stuff everywhere, to dry, on my extra bed, over lamps, the curtain roads, chair backs. What a mess. I was ecstatic.

I sank into the tub and smiled.

Thinking back to the earlier part of the day, I thought of how cold I was. I had ridden along, thinking I should get a room, after all, my tent was broken, and everything I owned was wet. It would make my next day a lot smoother, if I could start out in dry clothes and my leather pants.

Having never stayed in a motel of my own accord, or on my own, throughout this entire journey, I realized that I've been on the road for *ninety-nine days.* This is *the last night* of my trek. Staying in a motel under these dire circumstances would not mean I am a wimp. I have proven myself already, over and again.

I had wanted to drive all the way to Connecticut, which wasn't far, really, but in my condition, it was an unnecessary goal. By stopping sooner, I could end my misery, and have further to ride the following day, but in acceptable attire.

Stubbornly, I had headed out after my second warm-up break, but thankfully, something snapped, and now, here I was, in a steamy haven, safe and sound.

I ordered a large calzone from a nearby pizza place, and carried it back to my room. Heat blast through the door when I opened it. I cracked a window a little, to let some steaminess out, but kept the heat cranking. Already, some of my things had dried. Having stopped so early in the day, I was surprised at how tired I was, but having nothing better to do, I settled into bed, and fell asleep.

I tried not to think about the next day.

Miles: 109

During the night, I got up to turn the heat down, a little. By morning, most of my belongings were bone dry. My motorcycle was filthy. I packed slowly. This was it, the tail end of my journey. I didn't plan for anything special, just a trek on the Interstates, then I would be home.

My feelings couldn't be determined.

Autumn has clearly arrived. On either side of the highway, here and there, loud colors splashed over the ends of branches. It would look so much better if the sun would come out, and the sky would turn blue.

My ride was infinitely better, now that I had dry gloves and clothing again. Staying at the Super 8 was a real treat, after having roughed it for so long. I went into Connecticut, and eventually saw signs for Boston. Traffic and congestion increased. I was getting closer to the overpopulated extreme east coast.

As the hours passed, the territory became more familiar. It seemed strange, because it was suddenly autumn in New England. I had bypassed summer, in a way. It all started to seem like a dream, as if I had never been away at all. None of my summer traditions had been experienced. Instead, strange and lovely happenings had fallen into my path.

I hadn't played in the surf at Horseneck Beach, but I had sun-bathed at Venice Beach, California. I hadn't ridden with my South Shore Women On Wheels chapter in Mass., but I had spent time with Women On Wheels members all across America. Smoky, the Appaloosa I usually rode, stayed out to pasture, but I had ridden horses in Ohio, Washington and Colorado. For months, I didn't have a job, but every day I had a lot of work to do.

When I started out in June, I saw newly planted crops, and the corn was knee high. Baby cows and horses were still nursing their mothers' milk. Now the corn was taller than me, and the calves and foals were half grown. I, myself had grown a lot, too.

This trip was a turning point in my life. From the day I had the idea to do it, to this very minute, as I traveled seventy miles per hour, back to where I started, a certain amount of growth and empowerment has enriched me.

I might be poor in pockets, but I will *always* be rich in spirit.

*   *   *

MASSACHUSETTS WECOMES YOU

After getting lost in the confusing, construction torn apart city of Providence, Rhode Island for an hour, I finally found the Massachusetts state line. How ironic that I could travel thousands of miles in unknown territories, but get lost thirty miles from home. Back on an old, familiar highway, I traveled, feeling curiously strange. What is my life going to be like from now on?

When I saw motorcyclists, I waved as usual, but felt like pulling them over and sharing my tale. How could they know how far I had come? My trip was nearly over, but I didn't want it to end.

I got closer to Brockton, the city where I lived, and exited the highway. I did not feel excited. It was more a sense of wonder, at how things actually looked, compared to how I remembered them. I felt a sense of loss. I felt like I was dreaming. Had it been a dream?

I had less than a mile to go, and then, I was home. I scanned the parking lot at Belmont West Apartments, and didn't see my roommate's car. Good. I needed time for the transition.

I bumped up over the curb to park in the yard, like always. For a moment, I just sat there, looking up at my balcony on the second floor. I took a deep breath, then another. I reached down and kind of hugged my motorcycle, "Pony, we're back. Thank you for carrying me safely for so far and for so long."

Miles: 234

*   *   *

I took as much as I could in an armful, to the doorstep. For the first time in fourteen weeks, I took two keys out of their hiding place in part of my luggage, relieved that they were still there, and I let myself in. The hallway was bright and airy, wide and inviting.

Up the two stair landings I climbed, with my heavy armful of gear. I stopped at Apt. 23–10. My key slid into the slot, and I stumbled in, dumping everything on the floor.

Hungrily, I drank in my surroundings. It looked brighter than I remembered. Larger. Nicer. All in a second this registered, then I thought of my cat.

"Shadow, I'm home." I called, and waited expectantly. I heard a little squeak, and then a mew. From out of a cubbyhole hiding place, her dark, little face emerged, and she sleepily looked at me with her blue eyes.

"Meep," she squeaked again, blinking, and stepping around the edges of the room, towards me. She seemed to be uncertain, almost as if she was thinking, 'It *sounds* like my human. It *looks* like her-, hmm, leather-, it even *smells* like her. Leather! And that big round hat she's got! It *must* be her! It just *has* to be!'

Suddenly, with a full volume "Meow!" she trusted her instincts, as I fell to the floor and scooped her up, hugging and rocking, as tears streamed down my face.

"Oh Shadowfax. My Shadow. Leaving you was the hardest part of this whole summer. I missed you so much."

Shadowfax purred loudly, and rolled around, rubbing her face all over me, as if she couldn't get enough. Neither could I. I was so glad Barbie wasn't home, because she wouldn't understand, and I wouldn't have had my privacy as I was reunited with my beloved pet siamese cat. I didn't think that I'd cry, but now I was sobbing.

Finally, we disengaged, and I unloaded the rest of my well-worn luggage. I recorded the final odometer reading and did the math. From the time I left one hundred days ago, until now, I had traveled *seventeen thousand, three hundred and eighty one incredible miles.*

Total Miles: 17,381

I had traveled through thirty-eight states, having slept on the ground and eaten with the locals in each of them. (Not the other way around!) I had tasted the flavor of America. I did what others said I couldn't do, and I did it by myself. I had lived a dream, achieved a major ambition, and I was ready for another.

So, how do I go about writing a book?

> *Here I am, safely returned over those peaks from a journey far more beautiful and strange than anything I had hoped for or imagined—how is it that this safe return brings such regret?*
> —Peter Matthiessen, b. 1927

AFTERWORD

*A*bout work. It was Sunday, September 24, 1995 when I got home. On Monday I called the YMCA to report my return. The response? "How soon can you start?" I said, "Tomorrow." Fantastic. I knew that I shouldn't waste time worrying.

In a few months, Las Vegas Thomas came to visit his sister in Massachusetts. He invited me to go on a ski trip to Vermont with them. She had two small boys. By the time I returned, I had a steady job providing child care for her family. For three years, I watched Thomas' nephews until they were both in school.

During the next two summers, I also earned income working for the Motorcycle Safety Foundation, Massachusetts Rider's Education Program.

In between juggling these three jobs, I worked on writing this book. I know the meaning of poor, struggling writer, but I love each of my jobs, and I am happy.

*A*bout characters you met in DeeTours. Pennsylvania JoAnne has since traveled out of state on her motorcycle, sometimes with her husband John, and sometimes on her own. We see each other on occasion, at bike rallies.

Ohio Kim and I have seen each other annually, write letters and e-mail, call each other and love each other like sisters should. We will have a life-long friendship, and it all started at the beginning of my journey.

My Grandmother in Detroit has since died of breast cancer.

Michigan Maggie and I have frequently met up at bike rallies.

Kathy Heller, former National Director of WOW was diagnosed with breast cancer in early 2000. She was to be my editor, but she needs to concentrate on getting well. She has been very supportive.

Road and I never saw each other again.

Pat and I were happily reunited at a BMW-MOA Rally in New York, quite unexpectedly. I never thought I would see him again, and didn't know how to find him. We now stay in touch.

Denver Nancy took me in again during a subsequent cross-country trip. It was as if we never parted.

I see California Annis, Sharon and Linda at the Women On Wheels Ride-In, annually.

Las Vegas Thomas is a guy friend who I love very much. He calls me regularly and we talk on the phone for hours. I see him when he visits his sister in Massachusetts.

Atlanta Joyce ended up owning a Honda automatic and has since died of complications from her stroke.

*A*bout others. My father died six months after my journey ended. I spent two weeks beside his death bed. One of his friends said to me, "So, *you're* the adventurous one." My dad told his friends about me! I was proud of the title he gave me. Out of seven children, I was the adventurous one.

What happened with Russell? Well, I used to love him, still do, but it's all over now. We agreed to break up, shortly after my return, and I never saw him again. Often, he shows up in my dreams.

Barbie Doll and I decided against sharing our apartment after I returned. People should live with people they like.

Interestingly enough, it took me three weeks before I picked up my car out of storage. Driving it for the first time frightened me.

My cat Shadowfax is alive and well five years later, as this book goes to press. She has given me unconditional love for sixteen years, so far.

*W*hat about my Red Pony? At this very moment, she is parked in the garage at Whitehorse Press, in North Conway, New Hampshire, as I wrap up the final details of this publication. Exactly *today,* the odometer turned over 100,000 miles. I own another motorcycle now, too, but my Red Pony will always be my favorite.

WOMEN ON WHEELS
THEN AND NOW

*W*omen On Wheels was founded in California by an avid woman motorcyclist in 1982. Its purpose was, and still is, to unite all women motorcycle enthusiasts, whether they ride their own machine, are motorcycle passengers, or future motorcyclists. WOW has riders in their teens, in their eighties, and every age in between! They ride every make and model of motorcycle imaginable; the focus of WOW is on the member, not the machine. WOW members are located throughout the United States, Canada, and several foreign countries.

In 1983, in an effort to keep in touch with members around the world, a quarterly newsletter called The Wheeler was published and distributed. Today, the WOW publication; entitled Women On Wheels, is a bi-monthly magazine consisting of stories and articles written by the membership, as well as information about new products of interest to women riders, and happenings throughout the motorcycle industry.

WOW members experience the fun and excitement of riding together, supporting each other, socializing, sharing adventures, and helping special charities- all the while projecting a brighter image of motorcycling. In fact, promoting a positive image of motorcyclists to the non-motorcycling public is a top priority. Women On Wheels was awarded the Hazel Kolb Brighter Image Award in 1993 by the American Motorcyclist Association- an honor we're all especially proud of.

Local chapters are formed by WOW members throughout the country for support, camaraderie and fellowship. Currently, there are over 65 chapters in at least 28 states.

Each year, WOW sponsors the Women On Wheels International Ride-In at various locations throughout the country. Attending this rally provides not only a great ride, but also the opportunity to renew old friendships, make new ones, and share the unique experiences of the area. Women On Wheels now has over 2000 members and is still growing!

Full Membership includes: Subscription to WOW Magazine, Membership card, directory, pin, patch, helmet decal, bumper sticker, windshield stickers, courtesy cards and other benefits as they become available.

To become a member:

Call toll-free 1-800-322-1969

or visit www.womenonwheels.org

Tell them you heard about WOW from *DeeTours!*

HOSTELLING INTERNATIONAL AMERICAN YOUTH HOSTELS

*T*he 225 hostels in Canada and the United States offer more than a place to stay, for $9 to $25 a night. North American hostels are comfortable, environmentally sensitive places for budget-minded travelers like you, to lodge for the night. Hostels are friendly, people-oriented places filled with others who are looking for the same things as you are, adventure, excitement and an opportunity to discover this marvelous world.

For more information visit
http://www.hiayh.org

or write HI-AYH National Office
733 15th Street NW, Suite 840
Washington, DC 20005

tel. (202)783-6161

Kim Gabriele Shea took this photograph of me posing with my Red Pony and her Shetland Pony, Lightning, at their place, Pine Rock Ranch, in Toledo, Ohio. Lightning was twenty-seven years old, and 'raised' Kim and then her two daughters, Nicki and Rachel. Lightning now gallops with the Spirits in the Sky.

How to Contact the Author

I would love to hear from you.
It is my hope that *DeeTours* will encourage you
to live life to the fullest and to follow your dream.

To order more copies, or just to say hi:

Ms. Dee Gagnon
DeeTours
PO Box 2141
Taunton,MA 02780-0974

(508)583-0299

RedPony09@aol.com

www.deegagnon.com

Make check or money order payable to *DeeTours*
in the amount of $24 per copy
plus applicable tax and $4 shipping per book.